ARCTIC   OCEAN

Reykjavik

ICELAND

FAEROE IS.

Scapa Flow

NORTH
SEA

LL

ÁNTIC OCEAN

Dieppe

Lorient
St. Nazaire

AZORES

Lisbon

MEDITERRANEAN
SEA

Toulon

Oran   Algiers   Bone   Tunis

Gibraltar
Tangier

MADIERA

Rabat
Casablanca

CANARY IS.

# LEARNING RESOURCES CENTER

MONTGOMERY COUNTY COMMUNITY COLLEGE

Cognitio Ad Futurum

1964

## BLUE BELL, PENNSYLVANIA

*Also by* HENRY H. ADAMS

THE UNITED STATES AND WORLD SEA POWER
(Contributing author)

SEA POWER: A NAVAL HISTORY
(Contributing author and co-editor)

THE GREAT SEA WAR
(Contributing author)

TRIUMPH IN THE PACIFIC
(Contributing author)

TRIUMPH IN THE ATLANTIC
(Editor and contributing author)

YEARS OF DEADLY PERIL: THE COMING
OF THE WAR 1939–1941

1942: THE YEAR THAT DOOMED THE AXIS

YEARS OF EXPECTATION: GUADALCANAL TO NORMANDY

# YEARS TO VICTORY

by

HENRY H. ADAMS

DAVID McKAY COMPANY, INC.

New York

YEARS TO VICTORY

Copyright © 1973 by Henry H. Adams

LIBRARY OF CONGRESS CATALOG CARD NUMBER: 72–95154

MANUFACTURED IN THE UNITED STATES OF AMERICA

ISBN: 0–679–14007–7

TO THOSE WHO SERVED

# Preface

*Years to Victory* tells of the last years of World War II from the Allied landings in Normandy on June 6, 1944, to the utter defeat and unconditional surrender of Germany and Japan. As the dignitaries assembled on the deck of the United States battleship *Missouri* in Tokyo Bay on the morning of September 2, 1945, the Axis had been totally destroyed. At the moment of the Japanese surrender, the sun broke through the clouds, giving a celestial display of Japan's national emblem, the Rising Sun, an ironic symbol of Japan's deepest humiliation.

As in the other books in this series, the story is told to emphasize the home front and the little man and woman as well as the leaders and the battles. I have attempted to re-create what it was like to be alive during the war years whether you were in service or at home, working in the factory or on the farm, whether you drove a truck or a tank, whether you tended your Victory Garden or flew a plane over Germany or Japan. No book or series of books can tell the entire story of World War II; at best they can only be representative of the people, the actions, and the times.

The first book in this series, *Years of Deadly Peril*, tells of the opening of the war on September 1, 1939, when Nazi troops smashed into helpless Poland, and covers the period until the Japanese attack on Pearl Harbor on the morning of December 7, 1941. The second, *1942: The Year That Doomed the Axis*, describes America's darkest hours and the long way from defeat everywhere to the decisive battles of Midway, Guadalcanal, El Alamein, Stalingrad, and the invasion of North Africa that began the road to victory. The third volume, *Years of Expectation,* continues the story from the German and Italian defeat in North Africa through the defeat of Italy, the neutralization of Rabaul, and the opening of the Central Pacific drive against Japan, with the bloody lessons of Tarawa well learned to pave the way for the rapid advances told in this volume.

Everyone who was alive during the war years is a part of these four volumes, because what he did and what he thought affected those years. Even with the hardships and tragedies, national unity was never greater than it was then in the United States. The aim was victory, and the goal was to get back home to a way of life that was good—not perfect, but good. This was not a war to "make the world safe for democracy." It was fought to destroy the evil apparent in Nazism and in the Bushido code of Japan. But most G.I.s were not even that abstract in their thinking. They simply wanted "to get the damned thing over and get back home." *

This, then, is the story of "the damned thing," and it is a story of everyday trifles, everyday slogging, everyday amusements as well as a story of uncommon valor and uncommon dedication. It was a time of team loyalty and team spirit to the ship, the plane, the "outfit." Everywhere Americans went, they took America with them. There was a Times Square at most overseas bases. Sign posts gave the distance and direction to Brooklyn, San Francisco, Dallas, Miami, and Hollywood. Everywhere were pinups of sweater girls, glamour girls, and Petty girls. Everywhere were signs proclaiming that the mythical "Kilroy was here." Baseball diamonds, football fields, volley ball courts sprang up wherever land and leisure could be found.

The war ended and the men came back home. They had left a part of themselves overseas and had lived an experience which would forever set them apart in some way from those who had remained at home. Yet they took up once again the ways of America at peace. But when they met other men who served, they still cast back to the time when . . .

This project would have been impossible without the encour-

---

* The author heard this remark innumerable times during the war.

agement of friends and participants, many of them now unfortunately dead. To Vice Admiral Friedrich Ruge, Federal German Navy, Retired, who was Rommel's naval aide at Normandy, I am indebted for insights into the German attitudes in the weeks before D-Day. Admiral Harry W. Hill, USN, Retired, told of his part in the capture of Eniwetok, including the fortunate discovery of a Japanese secret chart disclosing the minefields. Rear Admiral Charles E. Coney, USN, Retired, who commanded MacArthur's flagship *Nashville* at the Battle for Leyte Gulf, kindly loaned me his scrapbook and told of MacArthur's determination not to leave a combatant ship on the eve of battle.

Other friends, too numerous to mention, have given great assistance and have been my guides through archives in London, Paris, and Rome. My especial thanks go to my wife, Catherine, who has never lost faith in this long project. Now that it is completed, it is hers as well as mine.

Henry H. Adams

Annapolis, Maryland
June 1973

# Contents

# Maps

# YEARS TO VICTORY

CHAPTER ONE

# Normandy to Notre Dame

*. . . the huge bottoms through the furrow'd sea,*
*Breasting the lofty surge: O, do but think*
*You stand upon the rivage and behold*
*A city on the inconstant billows dancing;*
*For so appears this fleet majestical,*
*Holding due course . . .*

Shakespeare, Henry V

*Do? Make peace, you fools! What else can you do?*

*Feldmarschal Gerd von Rundstedt*
Oberbefehlshaber West

T HE loneliest man in the world sat at the head of a long table
in Southwick House near Portsmouth, England. He was
General Dwight David Eisenhower, U.S. Army, Supreme
Commander, Allied Expeditionary Force.

He had to decide whether to go ahead with Operation
Overlord, whether to land at Normandy on D-Day, June 6,
1944.

Surrounding him were twelve senior staff officers, but they
could not help him now. They had all had their say, but now
Eisenhower had to make the decision. The twelve included his
Chief of Staff, Major General Walter Bedell Smith; the Deputy
Supreme Commander, Air Chief Marshal Sir Arthur William
Tedder; the Air Commander, Air Chief Marshal Sir Trafford
Leigh-Mallory; the Naval Commander, Admiral Sir Bertram
Ramsey; and the Army Commander, the jaunty turkey-cock,
Field Marshal Sir Bernard Law Montgomery, who flouted the

I

military dress of the others by wearing baggy corduroy slacks and a turtleneck sweater.

Just twenty-four hours earlier, as the rain pelted down outside and the protesting trees bent before the unseasonable westerly winds that sent clouds scudding across the leaden skies, Eisenhower had postponed D-Day from June 5 to June 6. An unforeseen low had been born over Greenland and had grown and grown until it merged with another one which had sprung to life near the Azores. The two low-pressure systems joined forces to form a major storm advancing on the English Channel. Not in years had such a storm afflicted England in early June. While its 25- to 30-knot winds were no menace to the big ships of the two navies which would shepherd the crossing and help with their guns as the troops went ashore, the seas those winds would build up would swamp the smaller craft laden with seasick men too miserable to worry about the Germans waiting for them to land. If they could land. Those winds could build up the surf on the beaches so that nothing could land.

Ships had been underway for days, coming from ports all along Britain's west coast as far north as Oban, Scotland, and from Northern Ireland as well. Other, smaller craft, had to come back to refuel and start again. One convoy could not be contacted by radio and had to be rounded up and headed back by an ancient Walrus pusher plane belonging to the Royal Navy.

Admiral Ramsey warned Eisenhower that if there was another postponement, they could not go on June 7. Too many ships and landing craft would need refueling.

Then there was the problem of security. The troops had all been fully briefed, and if they were returned to shore in southern England, a leak was as certain as it was that the sun would rise on the morrow. Although all southern England had been sealed off from the world, no one allowed in or out without a special pass, no mail allowed to leave the British Isles, including even diplomatic mail of friendly and neutral nations, strange things had happened. The Top Secret Operation Plan for Overlord had turned up in a Chicago post office. A harried sergeant had misaddressed it to his sister. Vital code names appeared in crossword puzzles, names such as Omaha and Utah, two of the landing beaches; Mulberry, the Naval Plan; and Overlord, the main plan itself.

Already, thanks to "Cicero," a German spy working as valet in the British Embassy in Turkey, the Germans knew the code name Overlord and its meaning. They still didn't know the time and the place. They were trying to find out.

All these things and more went through Eisenhower's mind at 0400, June 5, 1944, as he sat at the table, his hands clasped in front of him. But there was one other factor that he was considering. There might be a break in the weather.

Earlier that night, Group Captain J. M. Stagg, RAF, had come into that room with two other officers. They were the top meteorologists available, and they had predicted the storm that still raged outside.

After describing the weather picture for the past four hours, Stagg went on. "Gentlemen," he said, "there have been some rapid and unexpected developments in the situation . . ." A new weather front had developed in the Atlantic. He could promise that the weather would begin to clear in a few hours and that for two days at least there would be fair skies at the landing sites, or if not fair skies, at least no more than a moderate overcast. It was literally a heaven-sent opportunity.

Everyone had his say, but only one man could make the decision. Eisenhower sat quietly, looking at his hands clasped on the table before him. As much as five minutes of utter silence went by. Then he spoke.

"I am quite positive we must give the order . . . I don't like it, but there it is . . . I don't see how we can do anything else."

He thought a moment longer. Then a look of decision appeared on his face.

"O.K. We'll go."

There was no time to applaud the decision. Everyone hurried from the room to set in motion the invasion that Hitler was confident of hurling back into the sea.

Across the Channel, work to repel the invasion of France had been going on for months, leisurely for a time, and then

3

energetically ever since the dynamic Field Marshal Erwin Rommel had arrived to inspect the defenses and later take command of Army Group B.

Ever since the raid on Dieppe in August 1942, Hitler had been concerned about a possible full-scale assault along the French coast against his *Festung Europa*. As Commander in Chief West (*Oberbefehlshaber West*) he assigned sixty-seven-year-old Field Marshal Gerd von Rundstedt, a capable, highly intelligent officer of the old Prussian school. He ordered von Rundstedt to build an Atlantic Wall so strong that no invader could penetrate its bristling defenses. The 15,000 concrete strongpoints would have taken 300,000 men to man and ten years to build, as Rundstedt later testified.

Nevertheless the work went forward. Concrete blockhouses and strongpoints were built up and guns were sited to provide enfilading and direct fire on all likely landing sites. The work might have gone faster had it not been for the fact that French forced labor was employed. Somehow the work was often sloppy. Too much sand was put in the concrete so that it crumbled under strain. Sand also found its way into the moving parts of machinery and in the lubricating oil the Germans used.

Where they could not sabotage, the French were able to get the word out on what was going on in their areas. Pierre would tell Jacques that at Pointe du Hoc the Boche had installed a new gun. Jacques would tell Madame Dupont, who told Georges, who got the word to Gaston who had an illegal radio transmitter or René who had equally illegal carrier pigeons. Presently a note would be made on a document in a room in London, and another tiny bit would be added to the mosaic that made up the Allied picture of Hitler's west wall.

There were tens of thousands of Jacques and Pierres and Madame Duponts. And their names were not all French. From Norway to the Pyrenees and from the Pyrenees down to Rome and below, these men and women risked capture, torture, and death to contribute what little they could to the ill of the occupiers of their homelands.

Their results were amazingly successful. Never has such an accurate picture of defenses been built up of enemy-held territory. Never have so many thousands of individual bits of information come in by so many routes to add up to a vast picture of a sham.

The Atlantic Wall was a myth, at least as it was depicted by German propaganda broadcasts, as directed by club-footed, mind-twisted Joseph Goebbels. The British traitor William Joyce, known as "Lord Haw-Haw," seemed to know all the details. So did "Axis Sally," better known as "The Berlin Bitch." She was particularly effective. After opening with the haunting strains of "Lili Marlene," which had become as much a British song as a German one, she would go on to tell of white crosses already marked with your name, and would promise that your personal effects would be forwarded to your next of kin once the invasion had been smashed. As far as it succeeding, it was a laughing matter. On cue, sounds of raucous laughter came over the radio before being replaced by "Lili Marlene" again.

On November 6, Rommel arrived in the west and examined the Atlantic Wall with a highly critical eye. A master of the war of movement, as he had proven himself in the African desert, he showed himself to be no less a master of fortifications. The Atlantic Wall was, as he described it, a "figment of Hitler's *Wolkenkuckucksheim* (Cloud Cuckoo Land). It was all show and no substance.

Rommel set about correcting the situation.

After his trip of inspection, which covered the entire western wall along the sea, Rommel, on January 15, 1944, was given command of Army Group B, which included the Seventh and Fifteenth Armies, and which was responsible for the defense along the entire coast from Holland, past Calais, Le Havre, Cherbourg, around the Brest Peninsula, and down to the city of St. Nazaire at the mouth of the River Loire.

Since even an Army Group was spread thin in covering this long front, Rommel began to build defenses that would immobilize the invaders. He would not begin his defenses at the water's edge. He would begin them under water, well out, so that the assault troops would be cut to pieces before they ever set foot on shore. Underwater obstacles were rigged to jab through the bottoms of landing craft. To make doubly sure, mines were tied to the points of these obstacles. At high tide, which as everyone knew was the moment an invasion had to come, these traps would be concealed by the water.

Other ingenious obstacles were set up and wired together so that a boat or a man passing between them would set off the mines. "Rommel asparagus," tetrahedrons made of old railroad rails, were scattered about in and out of the water, mined and sharpened on the ends. No matter which way they were rolled, at least one sharp point was always up. Inland, old artillery shells, set on stakes and the fuses wired together, lay in wait for paratroopers.

Guns were shifted to command all the beaches. Caves were used for gun sites, and where they were not available, casemates and blockhouses were constructed. Incessantly he argued with his superior, von Rundstedt, for more men. It was in vain. Von Rundstedt had a different idea of the strategy of defense.

To Rommel it was perfectly clear that the defense had to be static in the *bocage* country of Normandy where high dirt and stone walls cut farming areas up into tiny plots that restricted movement to roads that could be blocked easily. There was no point in talking of rushing reserves to the point of attack. With Allied aircraft supreme in the skies over France, any movement of reserves would be stopped before it ever got started. In Rommel's mind, the defense in depth had to start below high tide and extend as far inland as possible. If the defenses were breached, there was no way of stopping a huge Allied build-up in France.

Rommel's views, however, did not prevail. Von Rundstedt, in his headquarters in Paris, decided to keep the reserves well back, under his control, and release them only when the Allied main attack was revealed. In addition, he kept the German Panzer divisions out of Rommel's direct control as well. They were formed into a Panzer Group commanded by General Freiherr Geyr von Schweppenburg, who had little experience in handling armor in battle. Yet he opposed Rommel's views, wanting to keep his Panzers well back in fear of airborne attack.

You have no idea [Rommel told his Chief of Staff Fritz Bayerlein] how difficult it is to convince these people [von

6

Rundstedt and Schweppenburg]. At one time they looked on mobile warfare as something to keep clear of at all costs, but now that our freedom of maneuver in the West is gone, they're all crazy after it. Whereas, in fact, it's obvious that if the enemy once gets his foot in, he'll put every antitank gun and tank into the bridgehead and let us beat our heads against it, as he did at Médenine. To break through such a front you have to attack slowly and methodically, under cover of massed artillery, but we, of course, thanks to the Allied air forces, will have nothing there in time. The day of the dashing cut-and-thrust tank attack of the early war years is past and gone—and that goes for the East too, a fact, which may, perhaps, by this time, have gradually sunk in.

The question had not been resolved by June 6, and then it became academic, because the initiative after that belonged to the Allies.

It was by no means certain that the Allies would be able to make a successful landing on the continent of Europe and maintain it and build it up until massive armies could proceed eastward across France and the Low Countries into Germany itself. It was going to be a very risky proposition indeed.

In conference after conference the British had dragged their feet on a cross-Channel invasion, preferring to soften Germany up by hitting around the edges before undertaking the riskiest of all operations. In conference after conference, the Americans had urged that the cross-Channel operation would take precedence over everything else. In entry after entry in his diary, General Alan Brooke complains of the American lack of strategic vision in failing to understand his peripheral strategy. The Americans were inflexible, he wrote on repeated occasions.

To the Americans the British were opportunistic, especially the mercurial Mr. Churchill, whose fertile mind came up with ideas he wanted executed immediately, regardless of whether the means were at hand and regardless of how his schemes upset previously agreed upon plans. To the Americans the British "flexibility" was irresponsible. Since America had to produce most of the tanks and ships and planes and guns and food and equipment, the American leaders had to have definite goals. Factories could not be retooled overnight to take

7

advantage of opportunism. There was need for a long-range plan and there had to be reasonable certainty that it would be carried out.

Also the British tended to look on the war in the Pacific as a kind of side show, to be fought when it was convenient, but it must make no demands on ships and planes and men that might be needed in Europe. As the American Joint Chiefs of Staff saw it, a victory over Germany would not mean much if Japan were permitted to run wild in the Pacific.

Given these differences in viewpoint, it is remarkable that the British and Americans ever did agree on a strategy and carry it through to a successful conclusion. Much of the credit for the success must go to a relatively unknown British officer, Lieutenant General Frederick E. Morgan, who, on March 13, 1943, was appointed "Chief of Staff to the Supreme Allied Commander (designate)." General Morgan quickly shortened this title to COSSAC, and with the aid of nearly 500 officers and 600 enlisted men—nearly half of them Americans—set to work planning the invasion of Europe.

His headquarters were at Norfolk House, St. James's Square, in London, conveniently near the War Office and the Admiralty. There was plenty to keep COSSAC busy. In addition to the main landing, they had to plan minor amphibious operations to keep the Germans off balance and prepare a plan for the occupation of Europe in the event of an unexpected German collapse. But the main job was the preparation for the cross-Channel attack, soon to be code-named Overlord.

Examining every possible landing site from Norway to Portugal, Morgan and his planners settled on the two most likely areas: (1) the Pas de Calais and coastal areas of Picardy from Gravelines to the Somme, and (2) the Normandy coast between Caen and the base of the Cotentin Peninsula.

The more obvious of these, the Pas de Calais area, was soon rejected by COSSAC. To be sure, it offered many advantages. It gave the shortest sea passage for invasion and follow-up forces, it was hundreds of miles nearer to Germany, and it gave prospect of early seizure of a major port, either Antwerp or Le Havre. But there were too many disadvantages. It was the obvious point of attack from the German point of view and the defenses would be heaviest there. It would take a large follow-up force to seize either Antwerp or Le Havre quickly, too large to be landed rapidly with the available shipping. The operation was likely to bog down, and that could be fatal.

The Normandy area was more lightly defended, but it lacked a major port. Cherbourg might be seized within two weeks after the landing, but would the Germans leave any facilities in shape to be used by the conquerors? The Normandy area offered more room for maneuver by large forces once the *bocage* area was passed.

Eventually COSSAC came up with a preliminary plan calling for invasion with three divisions between Caen and the base of the Cotentin Peninsula, with eight divisions as a follow-up. An invasion of southern France in the Toulon area would be mounted at the same time.

At the Trident Conference in Washington in May 1943, the tentative date for Overlord was set as May 1, 1944, and the date was confirmed at Quebec a few months later. Now COSSAC had the time and the place, but they could not do much more in the way of precise planning until they had a commander. It was President Roosevelt's fault that they did not have one sooner. It was his choice to make, and he stalled, wanting to give the job to General Marshall, but unable to face the loss of his services on the Joint and Combined Chiefs of Staff. It was not until December 3, 1944, in the second Cairo Conference, that Mr. Roosevelt announced the appointment of Eisenhower to the conferees, and it was not until Christmas Eve that the story was given to the press.

Following a brief visit to the United States, Eisenhower arrived in London on January 14 and absorbed COSSAC into his own staff—Supreme Headquarters Allied Expeditionary Force—soon to be known as SHAEF. Ike kept his old friend Major General Walter Bedell Smith as Chief of Staff and offered General Morgan command of a corps. Morgan, however, unselfishly decided to remain with SHAEF as Deputy Chief of Staff in order to provide continuity in high-level planning.

9

Even before his arrival in London, Eisenhower had seen the COSSAC plan and had seen that the front was too narrow and the three-division strength too weak. General Morgan agreed completely, but there was nothing more he could do with the resources allocated to him. In order to get the 6 more transports, 47 more LSTs, 71 more LCIs, and 144 more LCTs that would be necessary for an expansion of the beachhead to five-division strength, the Combined Chiefs of Staff approved postponement of Overlord for a month and the invasion of southern France until August 15, so that the shipping planned for that operation could first be used at Normandy.

The most pressing of all problems was that of a major port. No one believed that Cherbourg could be taken swiftly or that it could be used for some time after it had been taken. What the Germans had done to the port installations of Naples was proof enough of that. In fact, it was highly questionable whether enough strength could be landed across the Normandy beaches to take Cherbourg in the first place. The Army insisted that unless a major port was taken and in service in a matter of days, Overlord could not be launched. At a meeting on a hot day in July 1943, this problem was being discussed for the hundredth time or more. No solution appeared. Then British Commodore John Hughes-Hallett cracked a joke.

"Well," he remarked, "all I can say is, if we can't capture a port, we must take one with us."

Everyone had a hearty laugh and the meeting broke up.

But Commodore Hughes-Hallett got to thinking. Was it a joke? Would it be possible to take a harbor across the Channel and set it up on the far shore? He had once thought up an idea for a "quite improbable four-footed pierhead that could climb up and down its own legs and could be connected to the shore by an articulated pontoon pier that would carry traffic." Churchill had seized upon the idea and had told the engineers to get to work on it.

Commodore Hughes-Hallett set to work and the next morning presented a preliminary plan to COSSAC.

Of course, his plan took a good deal of revising, as ingenious minds began to deal with it, but in the end two huge artificial harbors were constructed in the landing areas—Mulberry A off the American beaches, and Mulberry B off the British and Canadian ones. Outside of each Mulberry was a ring of floating steel breakwaters, constructed of floats barely awash, but deep enough to break up the wave pattern. They were called "bombardons." Next was an inner breakwater, 2,200 feet long consisting of concrete caissons called "Phoenixes," as tall as a five-story building. These were towed across the Channel at a rate of about 3 knots and sunk in place to keep them stable. Then there were the "whales," pontoon causeways, anchored on the seaward end on the Lobnitz pierheads, the same "improbable" devices Commodore Hughes-Hallett had thought up many months earlier. For further shelter, especially for the small craft at the beaches, was a line of sunken ships, each of which had come across the Channel under her own power to be sacrificed for the cause. The line was called "gooseberry," and each scuttled ship was a "corncob."

The Mulberries were enormously costly in money and materials, but it is quite certain that there could have been no Operation Overlord without them. For when Cherbourg was finally taken, the destruction of the harbor and the port facilities was much more extensive than it had been at Naples. It was weeks before Cherbourg was able to handle much cargo, and by the time it was, it was scarcely needed. The Mulberries were operating far beyond their planned capacity, and they continued to do so until Cherbourg was fully rehabilitated.

While German intelligence agents worked to find out the place and date of the landings, Allied counterintelligence agents were working even harder to keep the secret from them. Everyone cleared for top-level planning of Overlord was given a special security clearance known as "Bigot." In the spring of 1944 in London, if you were not "bigoted," you were a nobody. The trouble was that a few persons, all too frequently of high rank, let their positions go to their heads. One day Eisenhower received a report that an American major general at a cocktail party was taking bets on the date of D-Day and was talking too freely. Since he was "bigoted," he was reduced to his permanent grade of lieutenant colonel and sent home to a lowly and insignificant station. The Navy had its way of dealing with loose talkers. They tended to be sent to the most miserable tropical backwater station available. A common saying in the Navy when an officer fouled up was, "Here's where Funafuti gets a new laundry officer."

Since something was bound to leak to the inquisitive Germans, the Allied counterintelligence men tried to make sure that what it was would be misleading. Just as "Major Martin" had pointed away from Sicily a year earlier,* a phantom Army Group pointed away from Normandy, toward the Pas de Calais area.

Dummy headquarters for this "First U.S. Army Group" were set up close to Dover, and all of southeast England, throughout Kent and in the Thames and the Medway, teemed with phoney vehicles, landing craft, and other deceptive structures. In East Anglia and Kent were dummy encampments of tents and building shells, with enough life in them to deceive Luftwaffe reconnaissance aircraft. German pilots wondered at the weakness of the antiaircraft fire over southeast England as they photographed and photographed the massive build-up of the "First Army Group" practically undisturbed. The gunners were very careful not to hit the German planes if they could avoid them. It was quite a different story over southern England!

In reluctant command of this army group was the only American general the Germans really respected, George S. Patton. In the doghouse ever since the slapping incident on Sicily, Patton had spent a period of exile in the Mediterranean with nothing to do during the fall of 1943. When he arrived in London, no one seemed to know just what to do with him; Eisenhower was very sure he would need him later, so he put him on the shelf with instructions to keep his mouth shut. If he must speak, he was to count to ten first!

In spite of Eisenhower's instructions, Patton was soon in trouble again. Asked to speak in a local British ceremony,

* "Major Martin" was a dead body placed in the water off Spain. In a pouch with him were documents indicating that Sardinia and Greece, not Sicily, would be invaded in July 1943. See the author's *Years of Expectation* (New York: David McKay Company, Inc., 1973), pp. 123–24.

Patton refused until he was assured that his remarks would not be reported to the press. Then he made a nice little speech about Anglo-American cooperation and friendship, but made the unfortunate statement that after the war Britain and the United States would rule the world between them.

Despite promises, Patton's speech was given to the press, and the howl was almost as loud as that occasioned by the slapping story. American and British journalists and American congressmen interpreted his remarks as an insult "to our gallant Russian allies," and yelled for Patton's removal because of his unwarranted meddling in political affairs. Once again, Eisenhower stood by Patton. After a thorough tongue-lashing, Eisenhower told Patton that he would retain command of the Third Army as planned, and went on, "You owe us some victories; pay off and the world will deem me a wise man."

Meanwhile Patton continued to command the fictitious First Army Group.

Air attacks also played their part in the deception. Although bombers gave the Normandy area a good working over, they paid even more attention to the Pas de Calais. Tons and tons of bombs rained down from Ostende to Calais to Abbeville, and the Germans were convinced. They readied themselves for the assault, and nineteen divisions remained anchored there until it was too late.

The employment of air power was one of the most vexing problems facing Eisenhower. It had been so in the Mediterranean and it threatened to be equally bad in northern Europe. Eisenhower as Supreme Commander never enjoyed the scope of authority that Nimitz and MacArthur had in the Pacific. Those two officers had unquestioned command of everything in their respective areas, whether it flew, floated, rolled, or walked. In Europe, Britain's Bomber Command and the U.S. Eighth Air Force reported to the Combined Chiefs of Staff, and Eisenhower's initial directive gave him no command of these vital air units. This was a situation he simply would not accept. "I stated unequivocally that so long as I was in command I would accept no other solution" than direct control of strategic as well as tactical bombing. The Combined Chiefs yielded and a compromise was worked out which gave Eisenhower general but not specific command of air operations. As late as May, senior airmen were insisting that "fighter protection in the assault area must be organized on the principle of unity of the entire operation; individual protection could not be permitted in any part of the area."

As it developed, air power in Europe was never integrated with the ground fighting as it was in the Pacific, but it was a lot better than it had been in the Mediterranean.

Almost as soon as Eisenhower gained his limited control of strategic bombing, he had to make a decision not to the liking of the "strategic" airmen. In preparation for the invasion, the plan called for German reinforcements and reserves to be immobilized to the maximum extent possible by means of air attacks. The "strategics" generally favored bombing of oil supplies in order to immobilize the Luftwaffe and leave the German tanks and trucks useless behind the battlefield. Air Chief Marshal Leigh-Mallory, however, who was responsible for air operations in connection with Overlord, favored the "transportation plan," which was to attack rail centers and marshaling yards in France, Belgium, and Germany. Eisenhower ruled in favor of Leigh-Mallory's plan, and the "strategics" were gradually converted, but the British Ministry of Home Security objected on the grounds that too many innocent civilians would be killed. These casualties might even jeopardize the undergrounds in France and Belgium which we were counting on to sabotage the Germans as the assault troops came ashore. These objections reached the British Cabinet, and Churchill called upon Eisenhower to change his mind. Eisenhower refused on the ground that in his opinion and in that of his leading airmen, the success of the invasion might be at stake. Grumpily, Mr. Churchill subsided.

The day and hour of D-Day were set by nature. A lot of things had to be just right if D-Day was to come off at all. Experience in the Mediterranean had finally convinced the Army that night landings seldom achieved surprise and merely added to the confusion as gunners could not see their targets, coxswains could not see landmarks, and troops could not see terrain features and so take adequate cover. For these reasons, planners wanted to land on the various beaches after sunrise, after there had been time in the early morning for visual shore bombardment and visual bombing of the German defenses.

Since the plan called for two airborne divisions to be dropped during the night before the landings, the planners wanted a night in which the moon rose late so that the transport planes could come across the Channel in darkness but so the paratroops would have moonlight for their dirty work behind the German lines.

Then there was the question of the tides. In the Channel off Normandy the tidal range is between 19 and 21 feet. Since the beach gradient there is in the neighborhood of 1 to 100, this meant that there was a lot of beach exposed at low tide that would be covered when the waters were at the flood. The Army, naturally enough, wanted to land at high tide so that the troops would be exposed to fire from the beach defenses the minimum time. Furthermore, they wanted a second high tide before dark so the landing ships and craft could get supplies as far forward as possible.

Naval advisers pointed out the weakness of the high tide plan. With the number of underwater obstacles Rommel had placed in position, there was no way to guarantee that they could land any troops at all on the desired beaches. At high tide these obstacles would be submerged and deadly. Coxswains could not see them and the sharp points and the mines would blow holes in the bottoms of the landing craft before the troops got anywhere near dry land. Instead, said the Navy, let's land near low tide so the obstacles will be exposed. Then demolition experts can clear them out before the waters rise again, leaving marked boat lanes to the beaches. Each succeeding wave can land higher up until near midday the maximum effort can be made against the defenders.

After much discussion, a compromise was worked out. H-Hour would be one to three hours after extreme low water, with the tide beginning to rise, but affording time for demolitioneers to do their job. It meant exposing troops to gunfire with little cover for a good long time as they walked through the wet sand, but it was the only idea that gave any prospect of success.

Only three days each lunar month fitted these requirements: the time of assault, the condition and time of rise of the moon, and the condition of the tide. In June 1944, those dates were the 5th, 6th, and 7th. A fortnight later, on June 19, a three-day period would begin giving the proper time and tide but no moon. After that it would be a case of waiting until early July.

There was to be no more waiting. "O.K. We'll go."

And so began the greatest amphibious operation in history. And so men began to die who might have lived a little longer if those words had not been spoken. But they had to be spoken if the war was to be won and if decency and freedom were to be given a chance to work.

As the ships turned their prows to the courses that would lead them to Normandy, a warning was silently passing overhead, unknown to them and unknown to the Germans—almost.

In France, in Norway, in Denmark, in Holland, in Belgium, in Italy, in every country conquered and occupied by the Nazis, groups of men and women huddled around illegal radio receivers, listening to regular broadcasts of the British Broadcasting Corporation. To be caught listening to these broadcasts meant imprisonment or slave labor at best and death at worst, but the men and women still listened. Not only did they receive the truth of the war news, but a regular feature of these BBC broadcasts were coded messages which spoke of loved ones safe in Britain. Sometimes the coded messages were signals to resistance groups of alerts to a weapons drop or an operation to be undertaken.

"It is hot in Suez," said one message. "Napoleon's hat is in the ring," said another. Were they signals or personal messages? German intelligence listeners could not tell.

On the night of June 1, however, German monitors did hear a message that spoke volumes: *"Les sanglots longs des violons de l'automne."* ("The long sobs of the violins of autumn.") The German intelligence genius, Admiral Wilhelm Canaris, had learned that the invasion would be signalled to the French

16

underground by broadcasting two lines of the poem *"Chanson d'Automne"* by the nineteenth-century French poet Paul Verlaine. The first line was a general alert. The second line would mean that the invasion would take place within forty-eight hours.

The German monitors reported the information, and the German Fifteenth Army in the Pas de Calais area was placed on the alert. When the word was reported to Berlin, no action was taken because it was assumed that von Rundstedt had ordered an alert. Von Rundstedt assumed Rommel had done so, and Rommel apparently distrusted the whole thing. The result was that only the Fifteenth Army was prepared to meet the invasion. The Seventh Army at Normandy heard nothing about it.

A little after 2215, June 5, Lieutenant Colonel Hellmuth Meyer, counterintelligence chief for the German Fifteenth Army, was listening to the BBC broadcasts. Suddenly there it was: *"Blessent mon coeur d'une langueur monotone."* ("Wound my heart with a monotonous languor.") It was the second line of the Verlaine poem. Rushing into the dining room of the quarters of Hans von Salmuth, Commanding General the Fifteenth Army, Meyer reported excitedly, "The message, the second part—it's here!"

Salmuth put down his bridge hand and ordered an alert. Then he picked his cards up again and began to play. "I'm too old a bunny," he remarked, "to get too excited about this."

For some reason von Rundstedt failed to order a general alert along the entire front, and for some reason Seventh Army was not notified. Whether Rommel was notified is not clear, but if he was he could do nothing about it. He had left that morning for a trip to Germany to see his wife and get a few days' rest before going on to Berlin to thrash out with the Führer the command relationship between himself and von Schweppenburg.

Rommel was not the only officer to be absent from his headquarters that night. No one expected anything to happen. The weather was too bad. Von Rundstedt was on an inspection trip. Other senior commanders were on their way to Rennes

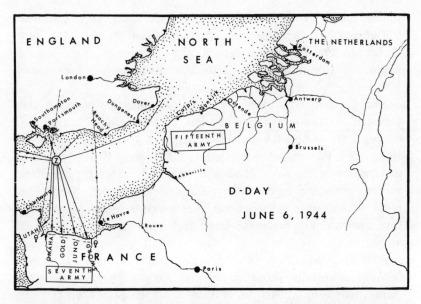

where a war game exercise was to take place on how to repel the invasion—if it came at all.

It was coming. The 5,000 ships that were standing in for the Normandy beachheads were on the move, routed to pass through a circle ten miles in diameter south of the Isle of Wight and then on through their proper lanes to the selected beaches ahead of them. The official name of the circle was Area Zebra, but everyone referred to it as "Piccadilly Circus," and the traffic problems were not very much different.

The assault areas were divided into five beaches: Utah and Omaha in the American Sector, and Gold, Juno, and Sword in the British Sector. On paper they extended from the mouth of the Orne River in the east to Quineville, halfway up the east coast of the Cotentin Peninsula as the western boundary. Actually the beaches were not contiguous, as reefs and other obstacles separated them. It would be an early objective of the landing troops to join up and have a continuous front.

On they came, while the Germans relaxed. In such weather nothing could happen. Soldiers who had to be outside took what shelter they could find, and those inside prepared for another monotonous night.

Back at his camp, Eisenhower had little to do other than wait for reports. His subordinates had to carry out the plan now, and he had to leave them to it.

Overall ground commander was, of course, the opinionated Montgomery, in charge of the First British Army Group. He had the First U.S. Army under Lieutenant General Omar Bradley, and the Second British Army under Lieutenant General Sir Miles C. Dempsey. Bradley's two divisions would take on Utah and Omaha Beaches, while Dempsey's three would attend to Gold, Juno, and Sword. The Eastern Task Force, commanded by Rear Admiral Sir Philip Vian, was responsible for getting the troops to the British beaches and for giving them support with their big guns as necessary. The Western Task Force, Rear Admiral Alan G. Kirk, USN, had similar responsibilities at Utah and Omaha.

While the ships were making their way, each in its assigned lane and assigned station, hundreds of aircraft were passing overhead. Three airborne divisions were crossing the Channel in C-47s, in the biggest airborne operation ever undertaken. On the east of the assault area, the British Sixth Airborne Division was to land and seize bridgeheads over the Orne River to prevent any German counterattack from turning the flank of the invasion. On the western end of the line, two American airborne divisions would be used, one to protect the right flank and the other to seize the important bridges which would permit the troops on Utah Beach to break out into the interior.

Behind Utah the neck of the Cotentin Peninsula is almost severed from the rest of France by a series of swamps, rivers, inlets, and drainage ditches reminiscent of the bayou country faced by Grant in the siege of Vicksburg. If the Germans held the exits from the beaches, the Utah landing could be pinned down, at the mercy of German artillery.

To prevent such a catastrophe, the U.S. 101st Airborne Division, under Major General Maxwell D. Taylor, was to drop southeast of Sainte-Mère-Église, seize the concrete causeways across the swampy ground, and block enemy reinforcements coming from the south through Carentan. At the same time the 82nd Airborne Division, Major General Matthew B. Ridgway, would land west of Sainte-Mère-Église to seize the crossroad there and prevent counterattack from the direction of Cherbourg.

The weather that was protecting the advancing ships from detection made the air drops a special kind of hell. Even though Pathfinder aircraft preceded the transport planes, they had a hard time finding their markers, and the drops were widely scattered in all three areas. This dispersion did have the advantage of confusing the Germans, who thought the drops were larger than they were. Reports began to reach German Seventh Army headquarters shortly after 0200, and a full alert was ordered against airborne assault. But the Germans were so convinced that the full assault would be made in the Pas de Calais area that they considered these drops mere diversions and ordered only a routine watch over the beachhead areas.

Even though the drops were widely dispersed, sometimes by as much as twenty-five miles, gradually groups of men found each other and began to operate as teams. They did this despite equipment losses as high as 60 percent in some cases and in imminent danger of stumbling over the land mines Rommel had emplaced. Attempts to build up their strength the day following the landings by glider operations were generally disastrous. Most of the gliders crashed in the short fields of the *bocage*. Still the airborne troops held on and made life miserable for the Germans behind the lines.

Now the time approached for the main event. Through the darkness of the short summer night the ships and craft were approaching their assigned areas for landing. The Germans still suspected nothing.

To greet these callers from the sea, the Germans on June 6 had fifty-eight divisions in France, thirty-three of them "static," that is, provided with no transport and intended to man fixed defenses. The static divisions had a large portion of partially trained troops and a goodly number of misfits, too old or too young or too crippled to fight. But twenty-four of the remaining twenty-five divisions were first-line outfits, and many of them had seen service in Russia. They had experience, they had high

morale, and they had guns. What they lacked was reinforcement.

Air operations against German transportation lines had
succeeded beyond the highest expectations of the Allies. Every
railroad bridge west of the Seine as far as the beachhead had
been knocked out. At least 1,600 trains, a large number of them
carrying supplies for the Normandy area, were backed up east
of Paris, unable to proceed because of blown bridges and
torn-up track. German efforts to move supplies by truck
generally failed because the trucks had been hard hit and the
motor roads were in not much better shape than the railroads.
Later many of the reinforcement troops advanced to the front
on bicycles.

Generally speaking, Allied intelligence officers had done a
good job in reading the German Order of Battle, that is,
identifying which units were stationed where, and in what
strength. But they had missed one important shift that made a
lot of difference.

The troops going into Omaha Beach had been briefed that
they would be opposed by only one regiment, and a second-rate
one at that, belonging to the 716th Division. What they did not
know was that that division had been relieved by the 352nd and
that one of its regiments together with the best one from the
former division were manning the beach defenses. The rest of
the 352nd was in reserve at Bayeux, only a few miles behind the
beach. The carrier pigeon that would have brought this
information to London was shot down by German antiaircraft
fire!

At Omaha, H-Hour was set for 0630, and as it approached
the ships began to move into position. First came the minesweepers, which had the job of buoying the approach channels
and the transport areas as well as sweeping mines. A tardy
group of sweepers nearly threw everything into confusion,
because the bombardment group had to slow to keep from
running them down. This in turn slowed the transports and
landing ships and craft, and some of them milled around in the
water scaring everyone to death. Luckily there were no
collisions, but there were plenty of close scrapes.

The fire support ships formed up to begin the thirty minutes of pre-invasion bombardment that had been planned. It was not enough time, but the Army would allow no more, wishing the maximum amount of daylight for the troops on the beaches.

By 0430, most of the assault troops were in the landing craft and on the way to holding areas or to the beach. It was a long, long way they had to go, for the transports were anchored eleven miles out in a line parallel to the beach, out of respect for the big guns supposed to be mounted at Pointe du Hoc. This turned out to be a mistake, but no one knew it at the time. As it was, the troops were subjected to a wet, miserable ride ashore, and most of them were seasick despite the issue of dramamine before they left the transports.

The ride ashore was but the beginning of their miseries.

At 0530, a small-caliber battery near Port-en-Bessin opened up on *Arkansas*, the oldest battleship in the Navy. *Arkansas* and accompanying destroyers promptly replied, and the offending battery was temporarily silenced in a few minutes.

At 0550 the scheduled pre-invasion bombardment began. In addition to *Arkansas*, there were battleship *Texas*, H.M. cruiser *Glasgow*, French cruisers *Montcalm* and *Georges Leygues*, the latter known to American signalmen as "George's Legs," and eight American and three British destroyers.

The bombardment was as successful as it could be in the time allowed. It is estimated that 50 to 75 percent of the German defenses were knocked out.

The rest were supposed to be finished off by aerial bombardment, and the troops in the landing craft approaching the shore listened for the *crump-crump* from the 1,285 tons of bombs that were supposed to smash all the strongpoints at Omaha. They listened in vain. Forecasting cloud cover at Normandy on the morning of June 6, Eighth Air Force headquarters ordered blind bombing through the overcast. They also ordered a thirty-second delay in the drop, with the result that every bomb fell one to three miles inland. Not one of the beach defenses was destroyed.

Assault troops who had been briefed that aircraft would utterly demolish German strength at the beach looked on in disbelief. Where were the planes? No one heard any bomb explosions, and the German guns kept right on firing at them. As far as they knew, the bombers might as well have stayed in England.

Even the Japanese defenses at Tarawa, Iwo Jima, and Peleliu could not compare with what the Germans had at Omaha Beach. First, the beach gradient was the gentlest of all, rising one foot in every 190 until near the high-water mark. Thus the landing craft would ground far out, and a vast stretch of beach was exposed at low water. In this area there was no cover at all, and the Germans had placed their obstacles most thickly there. The demolition teams were supposed to cut lanes through these mortal barriers before they were covered over by the rising tide which that morning would rise 22 feet.

Behind the high-water mark, there was a sea wall made of concrete and protected on the seaward side by heaps of big, smooth pebbles called "shingle." These offered no footing for men and no traction for vehicles, even tanks. Behind that was coiled barbed wire called "concertina," which would entangle man and machine alike.

Once those obstacles were passed there was only open beach, with a few abandoned villas which the Germans had converted to strongpoints. There was no cover for about 200 yards until one reached a bluff too steep to be climbed by vehicles. There were four natural exits through the bluff, ravines carved out by centuries of erosion. Seizure of these ravines was the key to success at Omaha, and the Germans had set their defenses well to command those ravines.

One of the most fearsome obstacles turned out to be not one at all. A conspicuous cape known as Pointe du Hoc* rises about 3½ miles west of Omaha Beach, and on it the Germans had erected a 155-mm. battery in a position to enfilade the beach and also to take transports under fire. It could also turn on Utah Beach to the west. Because of its estimated range, 25,000 yards, the transports had anchored far out, condemning the assault troops to an eleven-mile ride in the landing craft. No

* Consistently misspelled in records and in many histories as Pointe du Hoe.

23

one believed that either Utah or Omaha beaches could be taken unless the battery on Pointe du Hoc was eliminated.

The elimination job was given to 200 men of the Second Ranger Battalion under command of Lieutenant Colonel James E. Rudder. American Rangers were the counterpart of the famed British Commandos, and they yielded nothing in toughness and fighting spirit to their British opposite numbers.

Here is what they had to do at Pointe du Hoc:

They had to land on a rough beach, covered with shingle, under fire from several well-placed machine gun positions and then scale a nearly perpendicular cliff, 117 feet high—the height of a 10-story building—and then capture the battery from determined defenders on top. They then had to hold on until troops could work their way through the defenses at Omaha and relieve them.

"No soldier in my command has ever been wished a more difficult task," wrote General Bradley, "than that which befell the thirty-four-year-old commander of this . . . Ranger Force."

"First time you mentioned it," Rudder remembered, "I thought you were trying to scare me."

On the way to the beach, the British skipper of the leading escort vessel mistook Pointe de la Percée for Pointe du Hoc, and the Rangers were nearly there before the error was discovered. The error made little difference in the end, but it did cause useless casualties as the landing craft had to buck both wind and tide on the three-mile voyage parallel to the coast and under German guns. Arriving at Pointe du Hoc forty minutes late, Rudder and his men went to work.

Germans along the top of the bluff had seen them coming and were set to "repel boarders." But as Rudder and his men came to the cliff, well-aimed naval gunfire drove the defenders back so they could not interfere.

In rehearsals for their task, Rudder and his men had devised several plans to get them up the cliff quickly and with as little loss as possible. Their LCA landing craft had been equipped with rocket launchers, which had grapnels and lines or rope ladders attached. The grapnels were supposed to dig in at the top of the cliffs and then the Rangers would swarm up. In addition, the Rangers had light sectional ladders which could be put together into a 112-foot length. As a final device, they had borrowed 100-foot extension ladders from the London Fire Department.

The Fire Department ladders didn't work, but everything else did, and within thirty minutes after the landing, 150 of the Rangers were either on top of the cliff or on the way up. The defenders had been kept at a respectable distance by naval gunfire. Only 15 Rangers were wounded, these from hand grenades dropped before the Germans had been driven off.

When they reached the top and overran the battery, they could hardly believe their eyes. The much-feared guns were only dummies, made out of telephone poles. The Germans had removed the real guns in order to strengthen the emplacements, and the work had not been completed.

While part of his men kept the German gunners from getting out of the battery, the rest pushed on to the road between Grandcamp and Vierville, where they set up a perimeter defense. They were astonished to discover four of the six missing guns and blew their breaches off with thermite. That evening, Rudder had to abandon the perimeter defense and fall back on the battery, where, ammunition running low and half his men casualties, he managed to hold out until he was relieved on June 8.

While Rudder's attack on Pointe du Hoc was successful, Omaha Beach was turning into a disaster.

Nearly everything that could go wrong did go wrong.

The plan looked beautiful on paper, but it didn't work out that way.

We have already seen that the naval bombardment was too short to knock out all the beach defenses, and that the air bombing that was supposed to take care of the rest never came anywhere near the beach. To take care of any German installations that might escape these first two attacks, the British had designed an amphibious tank (called DD for dual drive) which was supposed to swim in from LCTs supported by "bloomers," accordion-pleated canvas screens. Once ashore, the bloomers were to be discarded. In tests the DD tanks had stayed afloat, but their buoyancy was critical. As it turned out both at Omaha and Utah, in rough water it was nonexistent.

In the eastern section of Omaha Beach, twenty-seven DD tanks were launched from about 5,000 yards out. The bloomers began to collapse almost at once, and the tanks went down like the useless hunks of steel they were. A few managed to swim to the line of departure, but only two made it ashore. Three more were put on the beach by the skipper of an LCT who closed the ramp after he saw the first one go down and made for the beach himself. He landed them, as it were, dry-tracked.

All twenty-eight that landed in the western sector of Omaha were set ashore by the LCTs that were carrying them. Conventional tanks were landed as well with the first wave, and they all became targets for German guns and were either destroyed or pinned down for a long time.

The swiftly rising tide had not given the demolitioneers enough time to cut the planned eight lanes through the German obstacles and booby traps. Only five were cut on that tide, and they could not be called "clean." This failure, combined with poor visibility, the inability of coxswains to distinguish landmarks and their unfamiliarity with the currents, resulted in one of the biggest foul-ups in any landing operation. Only two battalions landed anywhere near the right place, and most of the rest were set eastward by the current so that one battalion landed clear outside the limits of Omaha Beach itself. In some places outfits were intermingled and no one knew what to do or where to go.

There was no shelter on the beach itself. The G.I.s had to somehow make their way across the exposed sand and take what shelter they could at the foot of the seawall where the guns could not reach. This refuge, however, proved more illusory than real, for many guns could fire along the seawall, and men were being hit and were dying with horrible frequency.

As reports came in from Omaha Beachhead, Eisenhower's thoughts must have turned to a scrap of paper he had stuffed in his pocket the night before. On it he had scribbled a communiqué to be released if the invasion failed:

26

Our landings in the Cherbourg–Havre area have failed to gain a satisfactory foothold, and I have withdrawn the troops. My decision to attack at this time and place was based on the best information available. The troops, the air and the navy did all that bravery and devotion to duty could do. If any blame or fault attaches to the attempt, it is mine alone.

Just about the time a picture of disaster at Omaha was piling up at SHAEF Headquarters, things began to improve on the beach.

Nearly everyone who was there credits the Navy with saving the day at Omaha. Rear Admiral Carleton F. Bryant, commanding the gunfire support ships, called by voice radio, "Get on them, men! Get on them! They are raising hell with the men on the beach, and we can't have any more of that! We must stop it."

While the big ships, *Texas*, *Arkansas*, *Glasgow*, *Montcalm*, and *Georges Leygues*, stood off in deep water and lobbed shells on assigned targets or in response to plane spotters, the destroyers moved in so close to the beach that several of them touched bottom. Badly hampered by the lack of shore fire-control parties, who had either been killed or whose radios had been drowned during the landing, they fired on the targets they could see, taking extreme care to avoid hitting their own troops. Destroyer *McCook* took on some batteries that had been casemated into the cliffs and whose fire was enfilading the beach. Her skipper, Lieutenant Commander Ralph L. Ramey, observing that the guns were too well sheltered for direct fire, started shooting at the cliffs themselves. In a few minutes an entire battery fell onto the beach as the cliff supporting it gave way. A few minutes later, another blew up.

That took care of that particular emplacement.

That afternoon, *McCook* received the surrender of another battery on the bluff behind the beach. A white flag appeared, and an hour was consumed trying to establish communication. Finally Ramey signalled that the ship would resume firing immediately. A hasty blinker message from shore answered: "Ceize fire!" Ramey ordered the Germans to give themselves up to the nearest Americans and kept his guns trained on them until they did.

Destroyer *Carmick* helped out when her C.O., Commander Robert O. Beer, observed a group of soldiers firing rifles at a particular spot on the bluff. *Carmick* obliged with a few 5-inch shells on the same target, and then Commander Beer had the satisfaction of seeing the soldiers move out and advance past the former strongpoint.

These actions are only typical of the support of the destroyers on D-Day, and many more tales could be told. Literally the only artillery support the men on Omaha Beach received that day was from the 5-inch guns of the destroyers. Gradually this support had its effect.

Just before noon, units at the extreme ends of Omaha Beach were able to breach the German defense barriers and advance up the bluff to take position on the high ground and get at the Germans from the rear. As the tide receded, demolitioneers were able to clear more passages through the underwater obstacles, and streams of supplies and many vehicles began to land with the supporting troops. German defenders of the ravine exits had been accounted for, and soon a steady flow of troops, tanks, and vehicles was moving inland to form up with other units. The momentum of the assault was regained and was not lost again.

On the other beaches things were much easier. This is not to say that they were a pushover. Far from it. But there was never any doubt that they would succeed.

At Utah Beach, mines were the most telling weapon. In fact, they caused more casualties than anything else. They were of a delayed-action type which went off only after a certain number of sweeps had been made, and they were successful in sinking destroyer *Corry*, a PC, three LCTs and two LCIs.

From seaward the terrain of Utah Beach is featureless, with no marked capes or church steeples or prominent chimneys to guide seamen. The bombardment succeeded in obliterating what few markers there were, and the result was that the main landing was made 2,000 yards south of where it was supposed to be. At precisely 0630, twenty landing craft of the first wave touched down and the troops waded ashore, pleasantly surprised to find no surf, no obstacles, and no enemy gunfire. The only question was, where were they? It was clear that they had not reached the right place, but were they north or south? Brigadier General Theodore Roosevelt finally figured it out and reported what had happened to flagship *Bayfield.*

The error, as it turned out, was very fortunate. If the landing had taken place as planned, one battalion would have come under enfilading fire from two casemated batteries, and the scene would have resembled that at Omaha. As it was, the beaches where they did land were lightly defended, and there were few obstacles to contend with.

Everything went so well at Utah Beach that Admiral Moon was able to report, "there is little to write about the assault" except that it was "essentially according to plan."

The next problem was to keep the momentum.

In the British Sector to the east, things went generally according to plan so far as the landings themselves were concerned. It was a larger operation than that in the American Sector, comprising three full divisions—two British and one Canadian. Gold Beach, which joined the eastern end of Omaha, extended from Port-en-Bessin to La Rivière, although the initial landings were to be made only in the eastern third of Gold, which was the objective of the British Fiftieth [Northumbrian] Division.

Next to the eastward was Juno Beach, which extended to the Calvados Reefs north of Caen. It was the target of the Third Canadian Division, while Sword Beach extended eastward through Ouistreham and the mouth of the Orne River, and was to be taken by the British Third Division. These three divisions and their follow-up elements comprised the British Second Army under Lieutenant General Sir Miles C. Dempsey.

At all three British beaches, the resistance was light compared with that at Omaha, and the lodgements were made with fewer casualties than expected. It was after the landings that the trouble developed.

By early morning of D-Day, it was apparent to the German commanders on the Western Front that a major invasion was in the works. Rommel was recalled by telephone and immediately gave up his trip to Berchtesgaden. He arrived back at Army Group B Headquarters about midafternoon.

Already the Twenty-First Panzer Division had mounted a counterattack from its position south of Caen on the British Sword Beach, but Hitler refused to release the Panzer Corps which would give enough strength for the operation to succeed.

Hitler, by this time, had taken over what amounted to tactical command in the Normandy area.

My functions in Normandy [Rommel told his son later] were so restricted by Hitler that any sergeant-major could have carried them out. He interfered in everything and turned down every proposal we made. The British and Americans had only two bridgeheads to begin with, a weak one on the Cotentin Peninsula and a somewhat stronger one near Bayeux. Naturally, we wanted to attack the weak one first. But no; Hitler thought otherwise. The half-hearted dispersed attack which resulted was simply nipped in the bud. If we pulled a division out, Hitler ordered us to send it straight back. Where we ordered "Resistance to the last round," it was changed from above to "Resistance to the last drop of blood." When Cherbourg finally surrendered, they sent us a court-martial adviser. That was the kind of help we got.

As Rommel noted, he wanted to make the key point of his defense the town of Carentan on the southeast side of the Cotentin Peninsula, just behind the Utah beaches. Here he believed the flanks of both American beaches could be turned before they had a chance to build up and the danger to Cherbourg would be averted.

Hitler, however, decreed that the main resistance would come in the Caen area in order to keep Montgomery from driving directly on Paris. He knew Montgomery's reputation, and he had more respect for seasoned British troops than he had for the untried Americans led by the untested Bradley, whose last combat command had been of II Corps in Sicily.

Then there was Patton. So far as Hitler knew, and he believed it wholeheartedly, Patton's imaginary U.S. First Army Group was still pointed at the Pas de Calais area. Patton he knew, and

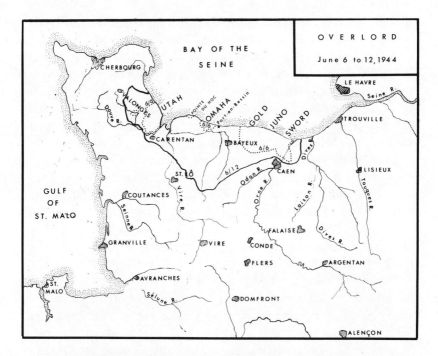

Patton he respected. There would be no letting down of the German guard east and north of the Seine.

Although von Rundstedt asked that elements of the Fifteenth Army guarding the Pas de Calais area be released to him to assist the Seventh Army and act as general reserve, Colonel General Alfred Jodl refused even to put the matter up to the Führer. He even refused until late in the day to release Panzer reserves. By the time he did, it was too late. The lodgement was secure.

By the end of D-Day, the Allies occupied three beachheads, two of them, Utah and the British areas, well established, and Omaha still a tenuous foothold. Fortune favored the Americans at Omaha, however, for the Germans, acting on the erroneous report that the Twenty-Ninth Division had been repulsed there, did not mount a counterattack.

The three British beaches were soon joined after the thrust of the Twenty-First Panzer Division was parried, and Dempsey moved to reach his D-Day objectives. But it was too late. Here

31

it was that the Germans made their principal stand, and Caen was not taken until D-plus-42-Day, July 18.

Although the delay in exploiting the British beaches was irritating, it did not disrupt the main plan, for the British were to pin down the German reserves while the Americans made a drive on Cherbourg, the major port considered essential to the success of the entire invasion. Until it could be captured and cleared, the Mulberries would have to work.

The Mulberries were literally set up under fire. Blockships began to arrive on the afternoon of June 7, and were enthusiastically shelled by Germans who mistook them for troop ships. They congratulated each other and gave loud cheers as the blockship crews opened the scuttles and sank their own ships in place to form the breakwater. The rejoicing Germans credited their own gunnery.

When the Phoenixes began to arrive the next day, they too were sunk in place, much to the bewilderment of the Germans who could not imagine what on earth they were. Then the other bits and pieces began to arrive, and in ten days the two "Gooseberries"—subdivisions of Mulberry A, one for Omaha and one for Utah—were doing the work of a major port. Mulberry B in the British Sector was performing equally well.

It had to do more than that, for no sooner was Mulberry A finished than it was partially wrecked by the worst June storm in forty years in that part of the Channel. During the daylight hours of June 19 the sea built up so that unloading had to stop and so it continued for the next two days, while the Phoenixes, bombardons, and Lobnitz piers were pounded by the heavy seas while salvage crews worked until they dropped in the shrieking wind and torrential rain. Positioned under the lee of protecting capes, Mulberry B was scarcely affected.

In a few days, Mulberry A was back in full operation, though it never regained the picturebook neatness it had before the great storm. The supplies kept coming.

The American beachheads were soon linked up as more troops were landed. By this time Bradley's First Army comprised four corps, which were growing in strength as every day passed. While V, XIX, and VIII Corps held an aggressive

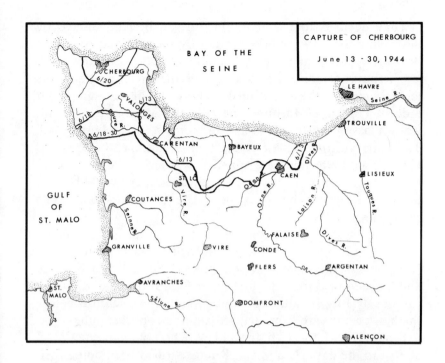

BAY OF THE
SEINE

CHERBOURG
6/20

VALOGNES 6/13

6/18

Douve R.

6/18 - 30

LE HAVRE

Seine R.

TROUVILLE

CARENTAN

BAYEUX

6/13

ST LÔ

Vire R.

Orne R.

CAEN

Dives R.

6/15

LISIEUX

Touques R.

GULF
OF
ST. MALO

COUTANCES

Seine R.

Orne R.

Laison R.

GRANVILLE

VIRE

FALAISE

CONDE

Dives R.

ST.
MALO

AVRANCHES

Sélune R.

FLERS

DOMFRONT

ARGENTAN

ALENÇON

defense posture from Caumont to Carentan, Major General J. Lawton Collins, a veteran of Guadalcanal, took his VII Corps westward across the Cotentin Peninsula, reaching the sea at Barneville on June 18. He then turned north, and by June 20 was attacking the outer defenses of Cherbourg.

Hitler, as usual, ordered Cherbourg defended to the last drop of blood. The defenders had been cut off from any hope of relief, for the Germans had neither the Army strength to retake the Cotentin Peninsula nor the naval strength to evacuate Cherbourg by sea. The American and British navies were lording it over the Channel, and not even E-boats (the German equivalent of PT boats) dared stick their prows out of harbor. The two senior commanders in Cherbourg, Lieutenant General Karl Wilhelm von Schlieben and Rear Admiral Walter Hennecke, knew that the fall of the city was only a matter of time, beset as it was by a modern mechanized army and by the strength of naval gunfire.

It was only a matter of time.

33

They decided to use that time to the best advantage by destroying the port facilities so that by the time the Allies got the port operational again, it would be too late to do any good.

Cherbourg fell on June 25, and when the American liberators looked down on the demolished port it was a discouraging sight indeed. The Gare Maritime, the railway station at the harbor, was a mass of twisted steel, and the ruins were booby-trapped. The same was true for the Darse Transatlantique, the principal harbor. Scuttled ships were mined as was most of the wreckage both ashore and in the water. Any salvage expert would have to be very expert if he was not to be blown to bits while performing his work.

Salvage work was the responsibility of Commodore William A. Sullivan, USN, who worked with Rear Admiral John Wilkes, Commander U.S. Naval Bases, France. So well did Sullivan and his men work that the first Liberty ships began discharging cargoes by July 16, although it was another two months before the harbor was safe from delayed-action acoustical mines.

Rommel had foreseen the fall of Cherbourg, predicting it almost to the day. He and von Rundstedt had been doing their best to make Hitler and OKW headquarters realize the seriousness of the situation in the west and how Hitler's orders, made without any knowledge of the situation, were wasting German manpower all to no purpose.

From his aerie at Berchtesgaden, Hitler was wont to survey the world battle scenes and issue his orders based on his intuition when the professional judgment of his staff was not to his liking. Stung by the charges that he knew nothing about the Western Front, he agreed to meet Rommel and von Rundstedt at Margival on June 17.

Margival was a symbol of both success and failure to the Führer. Here had been erected an elaborate underground command post to use during the invasion of England. It represented success that he was able to set up such a thing on French soil; it represented failure in that he had never been able to invade England.

Ever since late summer, 1940, Margival had been shut up,

manned only by caretakers, while Hitler's attention was centered on the east and the south. Located a few miles northeast of Soissons, it provided all facilities needed for such a conference. A nearby railway tunnel protected the Führer's special train.

Promptly at 0900 the conference began. Both Field Marshals, Rommel and von Rundstedt, looked militarily smart, despite having had to drive more than a hundred miles on short notice and with very little sleep. Hitler, in contrast, looked tired, worn, nervous. He held a handful of colored pencils which he toyed with ceaselessly. He sat hunched in a chair while the Field Marshals stood in his presence.

In frosty tones, Hitler displayed his displeasure at the feebleness of German resistance to the invasion and demanded that not a foot of additional ground be given up. Cherbourg must be held at all costs. It was a speech which lacked the old fire Hitler had once been able to command. And it bore not the slightest relationship to the actual circumstances.

Rommel tried to set the record straight. The Germans had fought magnificently, but they could do no more against Allied superiority on land, at sea, and in the air. The only hope was to pull back to some defensible line.

Hitler rejected all this. He listed a whole series of fortresses, none of which must be given up: IJmuiden, Walcheren Island, Dunkirk, Calais, Cap Gris Nez, Boulogne, Dieppe, Le Havre, Cherbourg, St. Malo, Brest, Lorient, St. Nazaire, La Pallice, Royan. It was the fortress concept that had led to the loss of von Paulus's Sixth Army at Stalingrad and von Arnim's Army Group Africa at Tunis. But Hitler had learned nothing. Some fortresses were taken, some, like Lorient, held out until the end of the war simply because it was not worth the Allies' effort to take them.

Hitler talked instead of the great secret weapon that was going to save them all, the V-1, a pilotless rocket that was faster than any airplane and had only the day before been launched against London. Rommel and von Rundstedt demanded that it be directed against the Allied beachheads.

35

No, said the rocket expert who had accompanied Hitler. The weapon was too erratic. Its target error of nine to twelve miles would endanger German troops.

Then turn it on the ports in southern England which were supplying men and materials at the rate of two to three divisions a week.

No, said Hitler. He proposed to terrorize Londoners into suing for peace. In vain was he reminded that the entire resources of the Luftwaffe had not been able to achieve that goal in 1940. He argued that soon hundreds of jet fighters would join the V-1s in finishing off England.

At lunch Hitler was furious with both Field Marshals. He glared at them as he bolted a plate of rice and vegetables, which a faithful attendant had first tasted lest the food be poisoned. He took pills and medicines from various packets and liqueur glasses, two SS guards standing behind him all the while.

Before the conference ended at 1600, Hitler had agreed to come closer to the front to see for himself what was going on. Yet when a staff officer the next day phoned to confirm the arrangements, he was thunderstruck to learn that the Führer had returned to Berchtesgaden. It seemed that an errant V-1 had strayed off course by some 90° and had landed squarely on top of the headquarters at Margival. Although the explosion caused comparatively little physical damage, it frightened Hitler back to Germany for good. Never again did he visit the west.

Promises he had made for reinforcements in the west were never kept. On June 20, the Russians opened their promised offensive and quickly smashed the German position on both sides of the Smolensk–Minsk highway. Hitler put the Western Front out of his mind and turned his full attention to the Russian threat.

Even as von Rundstedt and Rommel were meeting with Hitler, the last German hope of containing the Allied bridgehead was collapsing. A Panzer offensive against Montgomery from Caen to drive him to the coast failed because Allied air opposition cut its mobility to nil. The divisions had to be committed piecemeal and were defeated one by one.

36

On June 29, Rommel and von Rundstedt flew to Berchtesgaden to argue with Hitler again. Rommel asked point blank how he expected the war could still be won. Von Rundstedt was even more outspoken. Both Field Marshals expected to be relieved of their commands, but conceived it their duty to tell the situation as they saw it.

Only von Rundstedt was relieved. A few days earlier he had said something to the Führer's lackey, General Keitel, and Keitel could not forgive it. Keitel had inquired what was to be done in face of the developing bad news in the west. Von Rundstedt's reply had been short and to the point.

"Do? Make peace, you fools! What else can you do?"

Keitel told Hitler that von Rundstedt was a defeatist. He was replaced by Field Marshal Günther von Kluge.

Von Kluge was not pessimistic. He had been fighting in the real war in the east and was impatient with the jumped-up commanders who saw only defeat in a relatively minor engagement in France. He regarded Rommel as a creation of the Führer and of Goebbels's propaganda machine who did well when everything was going his way, but who crumbled when the going got tough. He went to the west determined to set everything right.

Hardly had von Kluge arrived in Normandy than he changed his mind. He, too, learned that Allied superiority was too great, particularly Allied air power. No solid plans could be made by the Germans because they could never tell when, if ever, a body of troops would arrive at a given place.

But there was room for concern on the Allied side as well. On July 1, only a fifth of the area had been seized that Overlord planners had expected. In the east, German defenders held on stubbornly at Caen, and in the west the marshes around Carentan and the hedgerows—six to twenty-seven feet in height—hampered movement.

A general drive along the western part of the line began on July 1, but it met unexpectedly stiff resistance. Bradley thereupon proposed that the general advance be halted and that troops be massed for a breakout in the St. Lô region. Eisenhower and Montgomery went along with the plan, for it seemed to offer the only prospect of success. Besides, Eisenhower had another shot in his locker—Patton.

Before Operation Cobra, as the breakout was called, could come off, two events of great significance took place.

On July 17, Rommel was returning to his headquarters at La Roche-Guyon after a visit to the front. Near Vimoutiers three British fighter-bombers appeared flying low and strafed the car in which the Field Marshal was riding. The driver was killed, and Rommel seriously injured. His left eye was partially crushed and his skull was fractured. His days of command were over. He had less than three months to live.

He did not die of his injuries, although Hitler tried to tell the world that it was so. He was murdered on the direct orders of the Führer.

For months, several generals in Berlin, on the Eastern Front, and in the west, Rommel among them, had known that the war was lost. They saw a higher patriotism in their loyalty to Germany than to the man they had come to view as a fanatic madman. For the previous week Rommel, von Kluge, and General Heinrich von Stülpnagel, Military Commander of Occupied France, had been meeting to discuss a surrender to the Western Allies, to prevent useless loss of life, and to spare Germany the agony of invasion of her homeland.

The military situation was hopeless. Everyone agreed on that. The only question was whether the collapse would come in two weeks or two months. Hitler's orders only made matters worse.

On July 15, Rommel had sent Hitler his last report, virtually an ultimatum. No one was going to be able to say that he had not given full warning as was his duty as a soldier. If Hitler ignored the warning, then steps would have to be taken.

> The situation on the Normandy front [he wrote] is growing worse every day and is now approaching a grave crisis. . . .
> Due to the destruction of the railway system and the threat of the enemy air force to roads and tracks up to 90 miles behind the front, supply conditions are so bad that only the barest essentials can be brought to the front. . . .
> In these circumstances we must expect that in the foreseeable

future the enemy will succeed in breaking through our thin front, above all, Seventh Army's, and thrusting deep into France. Apart from the Panzer Group's sector reserves, which are at present tied down by the fighting on their own front and—due to the enemy's command of the air—can only move by night, we dispose of no mobile reserve for defense against such a breakthrough. Action by our air force will, as in the past, have little effect.

Rommel read over this dispatch before it was sent and changed a word here and there. It seemed to lack a decisive ending. He wrote at the end:

> The troops are everywhere fighting heroically, but the unequal struggle is approaching its end. It is urgently necessary for the proper political conclusion to be drawn from this situation. As C.-in-C. of the Army Group I feel myself in duty bound to speak plainly on this point.
>
> Rommel

It was done. Never again after reading this dispatch would Hitler have any use for Rommel. Plain speaking in defeat was not to his liking.

Before the message was sent, Rommel's staff persuaded him to omit the word "political" in the next to last sentence. It could have done no possible good. It would simply have brought on one of Hitler's tantrums of rage and prevented him from thinking about the message at all. Let the dispatch be on purely military grounds. Only a fool or a madman would fail to understand the political consequences of the collapse of the Western Front.

Hitler was no fool, but he was at this time almost certainly a madman. Certainly he was one of the supreme egotists of all time.

As the message went out by teleprinter, Rommel told his Chief of Staff, Lieutenant General Fritz Bayerlein, that the die was cast. "I have given him his last chance. If he does not take it, we will act."

But there was no time. Fate intervened, and on July 17 the one man who might—might—have been able to bring about a surrender in the field to the Allies was removed from the scene. But for those British aircraft the war in the west might have ended in the summer of 1944. No one will ever know.

Another group of conspirators was at work in East Prussia, and they had reached a more far-ranging conclusion. Nothing less than the death of Hitler and the installation of a responsible moderate—Rommel, for example—as head of state gave any promise of salvation for Germany. This group included some of the highest ranking officers in Germany. They laid their plans carefully, including the seizure of communication facilities and the arrest of SS leaders who were presumed to be more loyal to Hitler than to the German Reich.

On July 20, having returned to the Wolfsschantze from his headquarters in Berlin some days earlier, Hitler met with his leaders in a large wooden building in a routine war conference. Maps were spread out on a large table, and officers were crowding around looking at the situation on the Eastern Front. Among them was Colonel von Stauffenberg who was waiting to give his report on reserves on the Russian Front. His papers were in a briefcase he kept in his hand. Also in the briefcase was a bomb. Before he entered the building, he had set the time fuse for ten minutes.

Quietly von Stauffenberg set the briefcase on the floor next to Hitler, leaning it against a table leg. Then he excused himself on the grounds that he had to make a telephone call. He slipped from the room unobtrusively.

Unaware of his peril, Hitler moved a few feet down the table to look at another section of the map. Then the bomb went off in a terrible explosion, killing everyone near where Hitler had stood only a moment before. The Führer staggered out of the building, one trouser leg blown off, his right arm hanging stiff and useless, and his eardrums damaged so that he was partially deaf for months.

But he had survived, and the revolt collapsed.

Hitler met Mussolini as scheduled that afternoon and seemed calm and unshaken. After a period of conversation with the Duce, during which he gave a coherent and moderate description of the attack, Hitler suddenly flew into one of his rages. He ranted for thirty minutes or more, promising revenge on any and all who had had any part in the disgraceful, traitorous attack on his person.

That evening he spoke on the radio a brief message carried by all German stations.

> If I speak to you today it is first in order that you should hear my voice and should know that I am unhurt and well and secondly that you should know of a crime unparalleled in German history. . . .
>
> I am convinced that with the uncovering of this tiny clique of traitors and saboteurs there has at long last been created in the rear that atmosphere which the fighting front needs. . . .
>
> This time we shall get even with them in the way to which we National Socialists are accustomed.

He meant just what he had said. Not since the Roehm purge of 1934 had so many highly placed Germans lost their lives. No complete tally has ever been made of those who were executed for real or presumed complicity in the plot. A list containing 4,980 names has been compiled, but no one believes for a moment that it is complete. Some of the earliest arrested were simply shot out of hand. They were the fortunate ones. As soon as the Gestapo intervened, the persons arrested were often tortured to make them reveal others in the plot. The first formal trial took place on August 7, at which a field marshal, three generals and four lesser officers were condemned to death. They were executed by hanging with piano wire which cut into the flesh of their necks as they slowly strangled in excruciating agony, the blood dripping down their bodies. Motion pictures were taken of all eight executions and were shown to Hitler that evening in the Reich Chancellery. He savored every moment of the spectacle.

Hitler and Himmler used the excuse of the July 20 plot to eliminate either by imprisonment or death not only those who might have had some connection with the plot but also those who had displeased them or who showed too little enthusiasm for the Thousand Year Reich.

General von Stülpnagel, once he realized that the coup had

41

failed, attempted to blow out his brains, but only succeeded in blinding himself. As he was coming back to consciousness after an operation he called out the name "Rommel." That was enough for the Führer. Rommel was a doomed man.

After he had partially recovered from his injuries, Rommel had returned to his home at Herrlingen near Ulm on the Danube. There, cared for by his wife, Lucie Marie, and his son, Manfred, he made a rapid convalescence. He spent his waking moments trying to devise some means of bringing the war to an end. Hitler, he realized full well, meant to bring the Reich down in a senseless *Götterdämmerung* as he perished magnificently in the flaming ruin. "I am afraid," he told his doctor a week before his own death, "that this madman will sacrifice the last German before he meets his own end."

Hitler dared not bring Rommel to a public trial and execution. The evidence was too flimsy, and Rommel was too popular with the German people. He was the only officer whose name was a household word and whose reputation remained unblemished despite the long retreat from El Alamein and the landing in Normandy.

Yet Hitler hated Rommel as a man he had never been able to control. He was too independent and he had the infuriating trait of being right every time he crossed Hitler's will. He was too good, too popular. So he had to go.

Hitler had studied his Machiavelli, the cynically pragmatic Florentine political philosopher who, 400 years earlier, had written:

> The general whose skill has brought victory and success to the Prince, must stand in such high esteem with the soldiers, the people, and the enemy, that the Prince must not merely be grateful for victories. The Prince must secure himself against his general, do away with him, or strip him of his renown.

On October 7, Rommel was summoned to an "important conference in the Führer's headquarters." His doctors certified that he was not yet well enough to travel, so, a week later, on October 14, two generals came to his home at Herrlingen. They asked to speak to him privately. A quarter of an hour later, Rommel appeared alone in the room where his wife was waiting. "I shall be dead in a quarter of an hour. Hitler has given me the choice of taking poison or appearing before the People's Court."

There was really no choice for Rommel to make. If he were tried publicly, his family would either share his fate or would be sent to a concentration camp.

After saying farewell to his staff and his wife and son, Rommel entered a car and drove off with the two generals. After a few minutes the car stopped, and the driver and one of the generals got out. When they returned, Rommel was slumped over, the Field Marshal's baton having fallen from his hand.

Cause of death was announced as heart failure resulting from his wounds. No autopsy was permitted, but a state funeral was held in Ulm. Not even Hitler had the effrontery to attend. He sent von Rundstedt who read a speech which had been prepared for him. At one part the speech said, "His heart belonged to the Führer." Von Rundstedt, being an honest man, nearly choked over the words.

Rommel's last military success had been the successful containment of a major effort by Montgomery to break out through the Caen front. Although the climax of the battle came after Rommel was wounded, it was his plan that stopped the British drive in two-corps strength. No one at SHAEF Headquarters, from Eisenhower on down, had any doubt but what it was a major effort at a breakout, but when it failed, Montgomery was quick to state that he had planned it that way all the time, as a diversion for the Cobra operation the following week.

The tendency to revise fact was Montgomery's greatest weakness. He could never bring himself to admit that things had not "gone according to plan." At El Alamein and at the Mareth Line, his original plan failed. In each case he made a swift revision that did bring victory. So far, so good. This flexibility is the hallmark of a great general. But in each instance, Monty insisted that the improvised scheme was the original plan, records to the contrary notwithstanding.

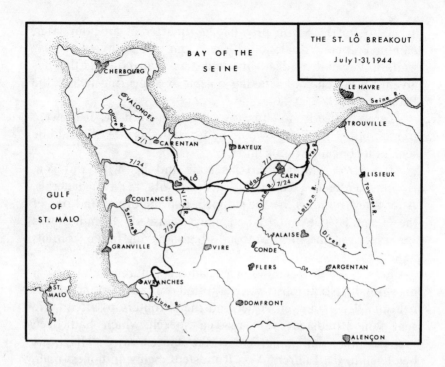

THE ST. LÔ BREAKOUT

July 1-31, 1944

So it was at Caen. Remember, Montgomery was in command of all land operations in Normandy at this time, and it would make no difference to his reputation whether the British Second Army broke out at Caen or the American First at St. Lô. From every point of view, a breakout at Caen was sounder, for it would have trapped a large number of German troops and made the subsequent operations much easier. Montgomery saw this clearly, but when his drive at Caen failed, he reverted to the original Overlord Plan, which subsequent events had made obsolete.

Operation Cobra, which jumped off on July 25, had the limited objective of getting out of the hedgerow country and trapping the Germans in the Brittany Peninsula. After Brittany was captured, the Allies would wheel to the east to begin a systematic advance across France.

Cobra went well, and after six days of fighting, Bradley's First Army had seized Coutances, Granville, and Avranches, the British VIII Corps protecting the flank as the Americans wheeled east.

The following day, Bradley became commander of the Twelfth Army Group, Lieutenant General Courtney Hodges relieving him as commander of First Army, and Patton bringing the newly formed Third Army into action on Hodges's western flank.

Patton then proceeded to turn the limited objective Operation Cobra into the decisive breakout which might have ended the war with Germany that fall. It was a very near thing.

Sending his VIII Corps to deal with Brittany, Patton used his others—XV, XX, and XII—to head for Le Mans, protecting his flank with the Loire River. Montgomery complemented this bold dash more cautiously by a slow advance with three armies—the Canadian First, the British Second, and the American First—in the Caen, Vire, Mortain area.

The contrast in the movement of these forces—Patton's and Montgomery's—reveals a fundamental difference between them. Montgomery demanded absolute superiority and more than adequate logistical support before he would move at all. Patton saw opportunities and exploited them with reckless disregard of logistical problems. He seems to have felt rather like Moses in this respect. If he needed water, he would only have to strike a rock, and if he needed food, manna would fall from Heaven.

Unfortunately a modern army needs more than food and water, and this fact was to prove fatal to Patton's hopes—but that came later.

In the second week of August, von Kluge, on the direct orders of Hitler, struck back at Mortain, trying to split Patton's and Hodges's armies. Patton swung north and Hodges sideslipped to close the gap, but von Kluge's Seventh Army, under General Hausser, threatened Avranches. Hitler had finally released divisions from the Fifteenth Army now that Patton was in France and the Pas de Calais was no longer threatened. Hitler's plan was to recapture Avranches, trap Patton in southern France, and wipe out the Normandy beachhead.

Von Kluge's thrust was too weak. Air attacks slowed down all German movement, and Patton's northward drive toward Argentan threatened to entrap the enemy between Mortain and Falaise. At first Hitler refused to authorize a withdrawal, but finally on August 10 he was persuaded. It would have been too late had not Bradley, worried about possible confusion, become overcautious and ordered Patton to stop. As a result, a large part of the German Seventh Army escaped the Falaise trap and was used later in the defense of the West Wall. Patton was disgusted, but moved quickly in a wider sweep toward Dreux, Paris, and Troyes. This was in conformity with Montgomery's plan to trap the remnants of the Germans in northern France against the bridgeless Seine.

Although the Falaise pocket was disappointing, netting only 50,000 German prisoners, while 10,000 German corpses dotted the battle area, it marked the last German resistance short of the West Wall itself. From there it was a matter of racing.

In Paris, anxious Frenchmen waited for liberation of their capital and national pride. Hitler was determined they should not have it. Although Paris had no military value, he ordered that it be burned to the ground, that the monuments of thousands of years of man's culture be destroyed, sacrifices to his vanity.

Fortunately for the world, Hitler's orders were ignored, and Paris was liberated on August 25 by Third Army's V Corps, the honor of the ceremonial entry given to the French Second Armored Division.

By this time, the Germans had more than northern France to worry about. Another Allied landing had taken place, this time along the French Riviera, between Cannes and Hyères.

The invasion of southern France was originally scheduled to be simultaneous with Overlord. Its code name, Anvil, suggests the strategic role it was to play; the Germans were to be crushed by the hammer blow at Normandy on the anvil of southern France. But it did not work out that way.

Shortage of troop-lift capacity and landing craft, plus Eisenhower's decision that Normandy would be a five-division assault, meant that Anvil had to be postponed, and once it was postponed, it got all tangled up in the opportunistic ideas of Winston Churchill.

If Anvil could not directly support Overlord, Churchill could think of a dozen better things to do with the troops—although his pet schemes for Rhodes and the Aegean had been firmly squashed. On April 19, after Anvil had been postponed, the Combined Chiefs issued a directive to General Sir Henry Maitland Wilson, now running the show in the Mediterranean, which told him to use his remaining amphibious forces "either in support of operations in Italy, or in order to take advantage of opportunities arising in the South of France or elsewhere for the furtherance of your object."

This was about as mushy a directive as was ever issued in modern war. Mr. Churchill seized upon the words "or elsewhere" to push his latest brainstorm, a drive from the head of the Adriatic at Trieste through the Ljubljana Gap through Yugoslavia to the Hungarian plain.

The plan had certain obvious advantages. It would maintain the momentum of Alexander's drive in Italy, which had by July gone almost a hundred miles beyond Rome. It would deprive the Germans of rich oil and mineral resources in the Balkans, and it would force the Germans to weaken both the Western and Russian fronts in order to deal with the new peril from the southeast.

But in war, as in so many other things, strategy has to be based on the possible as well as on the desirable. The decision not to seize the Brittany ports, which Bradley made just before Patton made his dramatic sweep around the Falaise pocket, meant that Marseilles was essential to sustaining operations in France. Then there was the question of terrain which lies above Trieste and Ljubljana and the political situation. It is by no means certain that Tito would have permitted the Allies to march through Yugoslavia, although the British planners took this for granted and even counted on his cooperation.

The name Ljubljana Gap sounds inviting, but for a modern army it was more likely to resemble the Donner Pass than the Cumberland Gap. Getting an army of over 100,000 men and their equipment through that area between the Julian and

Dinaric alps would be as difficult as it would be to spell Ljubljana without ever having seen the word! There is a 20-foot-wide road that winds through narrow defiles and across two 2,000-foot passes, both dominated by mountains well suited to military defense. At times the gradient of the road is 1 in 10, and in autumn, when the Allies were trying to go through, the rains would combine with military traffic to make the road impassable.

Despite these facts, the British continued to press for the Balkan project, driven largely by the political objective of getting into Hungary and Austria ahead of the Russians. If they had tried the operation, they would have been lucky to arrive by late 1945. And since the Russians reached Bucharest on August 31, 1944, the whole thing seems a pipe dream.

Roosevelt, Marshall, and Eisenhower all refused to have anything to do with the Ljubljana project. Brooke grew waspish in his diary, and Churchill refused to surrender until July, and then he insisted that the Anvil operation be switched to the Brittany ports, most of which had not been captured by that date.

This was too much even for the British commanders, who pointed out that the troops would have to be reloaded aboard different, larger ships, and that those ships were not available in the Mediterranean. So it was to be southern France after all.

There had been so much discussion of the operation that planners decided the code name might have been compromised. The story goes that Churchill suggested the new name himself, "Dragoon, because I have been dragooned into it." Whether true or not, it makes a good story.

Operation Dragoon came off with D-Day on August 15, 1944. For the first time in the Mediterranean theater, the Army consented to a daylight landing, with the actual landing areas concealed, as in northern Europe, by widespread bombing of several areas as well as the actual target. The U.S. and the Royal navies cooperated in the troop lift, in carrying supplies, and in support of the landing. Several ships and landing craft and vessels which had taken part at Normandy came around

through the Bay of Biscay, past Gibraltar, and into the Mediterranean to give their support.

Preliminary operations included Commando raids at various points east and west of the actual landing areas to control roads and high points. All but one went well. A French unit, trying to seize control of the Corniche road ran into trouble and was captured by the Germans. Their imprisonment did not last long, for they were released by the assault troops the next day.

A major threat to the landing consisted of gun emplacements on the two largest of the Îles d'Hyères—Île de Port Cros and Île

49

du Levant. The former had three old stone forts dating from Napoleonic days, and the thick masonry proved tough, eventually being reduced by naval gunfire on D-plus-one-day. But the Ranger attack, which began during the night of August 14/15, kept the Germans there too busy with their own woes for them to take any interest in operations on the mainland.

The Île du Levant today is probably the world's most famous nudist colony, but in the summer of 1944 it bristled with a three-gun 164-mm. battery which commanded the westernmost landing beaches. A special service force commanded by Colonel Edwin A. Walker, U.S. Army, landed during the dark hours before D-Day and quickly disposed of the Germans there. To their amazement they discovered that the Île du Levant was already nude. The guns of the battery were only dummies.

The main landings came off like clockwork the next morning as scheduled. The westernmost, called Alpha Beaches, were at Cavalaire and Pampelonne. The Third Division landed two Regimental Combat Teams on the target beaches right on schedule with practically no opposition and drove to close the thirteen-mile gap between them and to cut off the St. Tropez Peninsula. It was a perfect textbook operation.

The Forty-Fifth Division, called the "Thunderbirds" because it was mostly composed of Apache and Cherokee Indians, was responsible for landing on the northeast corner of the entrance to the Golfe de St. Tropez. Naval gunfire was so intense that no defenders were alive or in the region to oppose the landing. There were no casualties, and by 2100 that night, the Thunderbirds had joined up with elements of the Third Division on their left.

The Camel Force, which landed the Thirty-Sixth Division was the only one to run into any trouble. The resort St. Raphael overlooks the point where the Argens River flows into the sea. The Argens Valley is a natural invasion route to the Rhône Valley and the interior and has been so used for 1,500 years or more. It took no great imagination on the part of the German defenders to see that an invasion in southern France would use it as had those in days gone by.

Because of the strength of the defenses, the plan called for landings at Camel Yellow, Camel Green, and Camel Blue on either side of the Rade d'Agay in the morning, and then at 1400 that afternoon a combined sea and land attack would be opened against Camel Red at the head of the Golfe de Fréjus. The morning attacks went off with little difficulty, but Beach Red was another story. It proved such a tough nut for the naval gunners to crack, that on his own responsibility, Rear Admiral Spencer S. Lewis, unable to raise the Army commander, ordered the troops for Camel Red to be landed on Camel Green and to take Beach Red from the rear. When the division commander heard about Lewis's decision, he signalled: AP-PRECIATE YOUR PROMPT ACTION IN CHANGING PLAN WHEN OBSTACLES COULD NOT BE BREACHED X EXPECT TO TAKE RED BEACH TO-NIGHT NO MATTER HOW LATE X OPPOSITION IRRITATING BUT NOT TOO TOUGH SO FAR.

The Corps Commander, Lieutenant General Lucian K. Truscott, was irritated by the change of plan, but only because he had not been consulted. Even he had to admit that events fully supported Admiral Lewis's decision.

Once the beachheads were consolidated, events moved into high gear. The Germans had no such strength in depth as they had shown in Normandy. Most of those who had not been killed or captured were hightailing it for Germany, trying to get there before they were cut off by Patton's Third Army driving east.

The build-up in the south was rapid. General Alexander Patch, commanding the Seventh Army, took over ground command from General Truscott, who thereupon took his VI Corps up the Rhône Valley to join up with Patton in the region around Dijon. Meanwhile the French II Corps, supported by American units, set about taking Toulon and Marseilles.

Everywhere the Allies were greeted enthusiastically by the liberated Frenchmen. In the Overlord area, the reception had been restrained, for the Norman temperament is cold, reserved, and suspicious. But the men and women of Provence are Latin in behavior, and they cheered on the Americans as well as the French, tossing flowers into passing vehicles. Pretty girls dashed

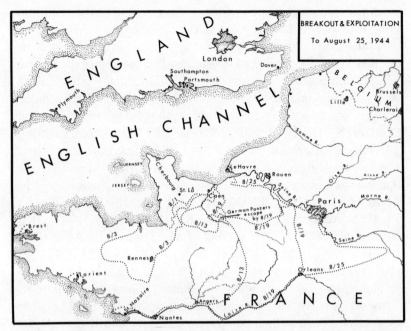

out to embrace and kiss the unshaven *poilus* and G.I.s, who were quick to respond in kind. Everywhere they went the soldiers were greeted with lusty singing of "La Marseillaise," which had been *strengst verboten* under German occupation.

Special hero of the day was French General Jean de Lattre de Tassigny, who had started with a tiny band of determined Frenchmen in Senegal and had brought more and more with him until he now commanded a corps in his own native land. In a few days a second corps would arrive, and he would lead French Army B.

Marseilles and Toulon were both captured August 28, and Marseilles, the largest French port in the Mediterranean, was soon in operation. The Germans had failed to destroy the port facilities the way they had done in Cherbourg, and on September 3, the first supply ships tied up and began to unload. As engineers went to work improving the port, its capacity went up amazingly. From November 1 on, Marseilles alone handled an average of 500,000 long tons of cargo and 54,000 troops per month. By V-E Day, May 8, 1945, 1,285,512 troops and

4,429,794 long tons of cargo had been landed in southern French ports, including the beachhead areas.

On September 11, Truscott's VI Corps, driving up the Rhône Valley, linked up with Patton's Third Army at Sombernon, thirty-five miles west of Dijon.

But by that time a great opportunity had been lost.

There was no reason why the war could not have been won in September 1944. At no place along the entire Western Front were the Germans organized for defense, nor had they any reserves which could be summoned swiftly.

On September 3, the Guards Armoured Division of the British Second Army dashed into Brussels as the climax of a seventy-five-mile march that day. The following day, the Eleventh Armoured Division, which had raced abreast of the Guards, seized Antwerp and captured the port facilities intact before the shocked Germans could set off the prepared demolition charges.

Farther south, the American Third Army that same day captured Namur on the Meuse, after passing Verdun four days earlier. On September 5, Third Army patrols were on the Moselle near Metz, with only another thirty-five miles to go to the great industrial area of the Saar on the German border, less than a hundred miles from the Rhine itself.

In both the British and the American areas there was nothing to stop the Allies. The way to Germany was unbarred. But the Allies failed to capitalize on the opportunity. By the time they started forward again, the opportunity had gone.

The swiftness of the German collapse caught the Allied commanders flat-footed. The original Overlord plan called for a broad sweep into Germany, dealing always with an organized military opposition. But when there was no major opposition ahead of them, Allied planning was too inflexible and too sluggish.

Montgomery and Patton both realized that a single, narrow advance in depth, delivered without pause and with telling force, might bring about unforeseen results, even the early end of the war. Bradley went along with Patton's ideas, and the result was to present mutually exclusive alternatives to Eisenhower. Naturally, each commander wanted his army or army group to be the one to deliver the knockout blow. As early as August 17, Montgomery proposed an advance northward to the Ruhr, with everything else being subordinated to his drive. This proposal meant that Patton would have to stop where he was so that the supplies he normally consumed could be diverted to Montgomery's thrust.

Bradley's and Patton's plan proposed that the main drive should be that of the Third Army into the Saar region and across the Rhine and into Germany near Frankfurt.

Could these have worked? Probably either one would have, if it had been promptly and properly carried out. General Siegfried Westphal, Chief of Staff on the Western Front, believed so:

> The over-all situation in the West was serious in the extreme. A heavy defeat anywhere along the front, which was so full of gaps that it did not deserve this name, might lead to a catastrophe, if the enemy were to exploit his opportunity skillfully. A particular source of danger was that not a single bridge over the Rhine had been prepared for demolition, an omission which took weeks to repair. . . . Until the middle of October the enemy could have broken through at any point he liked with ease, and would then have been able to cross the Rhine and thrust deep into Germany almost unhindered.

When the conflicting proposals reached SHAEF Headquarters, Eisenhower compromised. He still wanted to advance along a broad front, and he gave priority temporarily to Montgomery's plan, cutting supplies for the Third Army down to 2,000 tons a day. This meant that Patton received only 32,000 gallons of gasoline a day, instead of his daily requirement of 400,000. Patton came roaring into Bradley's headquarters, "To hell with Hodges and Monty. We'll win your goddam war if you'll keep Third Army going!"

Montgomery's advance started slowly after a pause to "refit, refuel, and rest." It quickly ran into trouble. The traditional pathway to Germany through the Low Countries is over ground that is often marshy and is cut up by small streams and canals. General Karl Student, suddenly assigned to hold in that particular front, scraped together everyone he could find who was capable of holding a gun, and the elderly men and young boys put up a defense out of all proportion to their numbers. Every day the defenses got stronger. An attempt to bypass them by means of an air drop near Arnhem ended in disaster for the British when the paratroops landed in the midst of two SS Panzer divisions and had to surrender after heavy fighting. Only 2,163 out of the 9,000 dropped managed to escape death or capture.

Hodges's First Army, which got the supplies denied Patton, was assigned the job of advancing on Aachen and protecting Montgomery's right flank. The front assigned the First Army was so narrow that its full strength could not be brought to bear, and the advance was again indecisive.

After the capture of Antwerp, Patton was once again given equal treatment with Hodges, but until the middle of September, this new policy afforded him no more than 2,500 tons a day. By this time, the defenses opposite the Third Army had strengthened. Von Rundstedt, out of the doghouse and reassigned as Commander in Chief West, had skillfully positioned what strength there was in Germany to block the two key thrusts. He could not have done so only a few days earlier if Monty had not paused to "refit, refuel, and rest," or if Patton had not been deprived of gasoline. As Patton said to Eisenhower on September 2, "My men can eat their belts, but my tanks have gotta have gas!"

Montgomery subsequently blamed the reallocation of supplies to Patton for the failure of his own offensive, and Patton never thought anything other than that the early victory was sacrificed to appease "Monty's insatiable appetite."

Probably the real culprit was the "war is won attitude" that permeated SHAEF Headquarters. There seemed little need for haste.

But momentum lost in war can seldom be regained. Those few crucial days lost at the end of August and the beginning of September meant that the war in Europe would go on another eight months and that millions more would die in the fighting and in the extermination camps before the end came in the fires of ruined Berlin. They also meant that Russia would have time to come west, to hold the line at the Elbe instead of in Poland.

No one on the Allied side in a high command position was mentally ready to deal with a sudden German collapse. No one could believe that the moment was at hand. When the commanders did realize it, the moment was already past.

# CHAPTER TWO

# One-Two Punches:
# New Guinea and the Marianas

*The rise and fall of Imperial Japan*
*depends on this one battle.*
*Every man shall do his utmost.*

Togo's message on the eve of
the Battle of Tsushima, 1905

G ENERAL Douglas MacArthur looked with small favor on the
Central Pacific drive that Nimitz had opened by capturing
Makin, Tarawa, Kwajalein, Majuro, and Eniwetok. Everything,
he felt, should be concentrated in his own advance along the
northern coast of New Guinea, through the Celebes Sea, and on
to Mindanao in the Philippines. Nimitz's way, he protested, was
"time-consuming and expensive in our naval power and
shipping," while his own way was easily "supported by
land-based aircraft which is utterly essential and will immediately cut the enemy lines from Japan to his conquered territory
to the southward." Nimitz and his carriers, according to
MacArthur's plan, would be relegated to supporting the right
flank of MacArthur's drive, aided by the Royal Navy which
would break through the Strait of Malacca to reopen the Burma
Road. In his grandiose manner, MacArthur envisioned himself
as leading this Anglo-American drive which would liberate
Burma, free the Philippines, and capture Hong Kong, from
which position Japan could be bombed by long-range bombers.

Nimitz, not unnaturally, objected to this scheme, which would relegate his powerful forces to a secondary role and would represent going the long way around to get at Japan. In addition he looked with disfavor on the idea of his large carrier forces operating in the restricted waters of the Celebes Sea where Japanese land-based air power could be added to the strength of the carrier air groups that he might have to encounter.

Why not, argued Nimitz, continue to drive along the second route that his forces had so successfully begun across the Central Pacific? MacArthur could continue to advance all he wanted along New Guinea, and the Pacific Fleet would even help out with timely air support as requested, if it did not interfere with its own operations. During the Sextant Conference the Combined Chiefs of Staff approved the principle of the dual advance across the Pacific, with MacArthur to continue as he was going, while Nimitz was to advance through the Marianas, Truk, Palau, and possibly Formosa.

It took the eye of a naval strategist to appreciate the importance of the Marianas in the drive against Japan. The Marianas are comprised of a chain of fifteen islands extending some 425 miles in an arc along the meridian of 145° east longitude. Only four of these islands, Saipan, Tinian, Rota, and Guam, all at the southern end of the chain, had any economic or strategic value.

Discovered by Magellan in 1521, these islands gained the name of Las Islas de los Ladrones (the Islands of Thieves), from the taking ways of the natives who threatened to strip his ships of everything they could carry away. Spain claimed these islands for centuries, but did little about them other than to replace the disgraceful name with one honoring Queen Maria Anna. After the Spanish-American War, the United States took possession of Guam for a coaling station, and could have bought the rest of the chain cheaply, but the McKinley administration was in an economical frame of mind, and Germany took advantage of the bargain in real estate. After World War I, the Marianas, like the Marshalls, were mandated to Japan.

American possession of Guam gave the United States a position from which they could keep an eye on what the Japanese were doing in the Marianas, and the Japanese resented the Americans as such close neighbors. Not that much observation of any military sort went on, for Guam was conveniently forgotten by all but a succession of naval officers sent out there as governors. The United States did much to improve the health and education of the native Chamorros, but the economic development of the island was almost entirely neglected.

Not so on Rota, Tinian, and Saipan. The principal product of these islands, sugar, was cultivated with improved methods, and refineries produced sugar for export and molasses for rum. The ingenious Japanese found ways of turning the rum into "Scotch whiskey" and "port wine." Roads were cut, and a narrow-gauge railroad was built on Saipan. For "cultural purposes" Aslito Airfield was constructed on the southern end of Saipan. It was only coincidence that the runways and repair shops were capable of handling military aircraft. From this airfield it is approximately 1,500 miles to Manila, 1,500 to Formosa, and 1,200 to Tokyo.

Naval and air bases in the Marianas would give the Americans an excellent opportunity to interfere with Japanese ships bringing vital materials from the Resources Area of southeast Asia, and they would also keep the Japanese guessing as to where the next blow might fall, for its nearly equidistant location from the Philippines, Formosa, and Japan itself made all logistically possible. Japan's puzzlement on this matter was reflected in the Sho Plan,* which was devised soon after the capture of the Marianas, which covered just those possibilities.

At a meeting on March 12, 1944, the Joint Chiefs of Staff rejected MacArthur's proposal to make the Southwest Pacific drive through New Guinea, Halmahera, and Mindanao the main effort and assigned first priority to Nimitz's Central Pacific operations. In a face-saving compromise, MacArthur

---

* Japan's desperate last-ditch plan for the defense of the Philippines, Formosa, or the Home Islands. See Chapter Five.

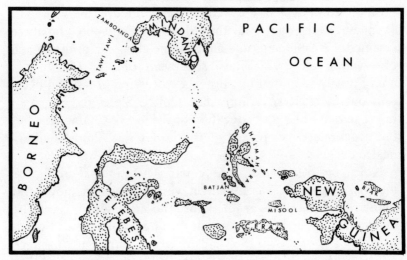

was directed to plan for the invasion of Mindanao on November 15, which, in a very real sense gave him a free hand to plan and execute intermediate operations along the way with the forces available to him and such forces as Nimitz could lend him from time to time.

General Henry H. Arnold, Chief of Staff of the Army Air Force, joined Admiral King in supporting the Central Pacific priority. He had a very good reason. Nearly ready to enter service was the B-29 bomber, half again as large as the B-17, and with far greater range and bomb-load. From the Marianas, B-29s could reach Japan. It would be a long, dangerous flight over water, past Japanese aircraft based on the Bonin and Volcano Islands, but it could be done and could shorten the war.

The compromise left General MacArthur discontented, but he was resigned on at least one count. His directive to invade Mindanao would enable him to keep his promise, "I shall return." He regarded this promise as a sacred pledge and bitterly opposed Navy plans to bypass the Philippines in favor of the invasion of Formosa.

Under the directive promulgated by the Joint Chiefs on

60

March 12, the bypassing strategy was to be applied in both the Central and Southwest Pacific campaigns. If Nimitz was to join MacArthur for the Mindanao operation in November, both he and MacArthur would have to hustle.

The Joint Chiefs' directive provided:

*For MacArthur's Southwest Pacific forces—*
Early completion of the occupation and establishment of bases in the Admiralties.

Bypassing rather than capture of Kavieng in New Ireland.

Occupation of the Hollandia area on the northern coast of New Guinea on April 15, to be supported by Nimitz's carriers.

Further operations at MacArthur's discretion along the northern coast of New Guinea to gain control of the Vogelkop (the western extremity of New Guinea).

Occupation of Mindanao starting November 15 with the assistance of Nimitz's Pacific Fleet.

*For Nimitz's Pacific Ocean Area forces—*
Support MacArthur's operations against Hollandia.

Capture of Saipan, Tinian, and Guam in the Mariana Islands starting June 15.

Bypassing of Truk and other Caroline Islands and the seizure of Palau starting September 15 in order to control the eastern approaches to the Philippines and Formosa.

Support MacArthur's invasion of Mindanao for the purpose of establishing air bases to knock out Japanese strength in the Philippines "preparatory to a further advance to Formosa, either directly or via Luzon."

Every one of these operations was subsequently carried out either on or ahead of schedule, except for the invasion of Formosa, which was later bypassed in favor of Okinawa.

The Japanese Imperial Headquarters could not, of course, know of these decisions, but they made some very shrewd guesses. They generally believed that the United States would follow a southern strategy, curiously similar to that proposed by

61

General MacArthur. This analysis of American intentions was to some extent based on wishful thinking, for it would ease the Japanese problems immensely to have the Pacific Fleet brought within range of land-based air from New Guinea, Biak, Halmahera, Celebes, and other islands in the general area. Also it would save precious fuel for the Japanese Navy, giving Combined Fleet a much shorter run from the source of oil in the Resources Area. And Japan was getting desperately short of oil. Marauding American submarines had so reduced the number of tankers that the most stringent emergency measures had to be taken to conserve all petroleum products in Japan and anywhere else outside of the Resources Area itself.

Admiral Mineichi Koga, who had succeeded to command of Combined Fleet on the death of Admiral Yamamoto, believed, along with most naval officers, in "the Decisive Battle." Ever since the revered Admiral Togo had defeated the Russians at the Battle of Tsushima in 1905 in an action so one-sided that it forced an end of the Russo-Japanese War, this concept dominated naval thinking. In the present war, it was to be the one decisive battle that would reverse the Japanese descent into defeat and force America to accept peace on terms acceptable to Japan. Being a practical man, Admiral Koga realized that the chances of success in such a battle were small, but there was nothing else to try. Accordingly, on March 8, three days* before the Joint Chiefs' directive, he issued his strategic plan, designating it Z-Go (Operation Z). Any time the Americans broke into the Philippine Sea, whether via the Marianas, Palau, or New Guinea, Combined Fleet would advance into battle to destroy the intrusive Americans. He concentrated most of the fleet in southern waters to be near the source of oil, in Palau, in Brunei Bay, and especially in Lingga Roads, just off Singapore. He transferred his headquarters from the *Musashi*, now back in Palau, to the Philippines. "Let us go out and die together," he remarked to his Chief of Staff, Admiral Shigeru Fukudome, as they were preparing to fly to Mindanao. He got his wish, at

---

* The dates are four days apart, but it was actually only three because of the International Date Line.

least as far as he was concerned, for his plane ran into a storm and was never seen again. Admiral Fukudome, flying in a separate plane, also crashed near Cebu. He made his way ashore and was captured by guerrillas, who held him captive for two weeks but were forced to turn him over to Japanese troops searching for him.

The brilliant, sarcastic, demanding Admiral Soemu Toyoda took over as commander of the Combined Fleet. Like Koga he believed in the "Decisive Battle," but he was not satisfied with Koga's plan for forcing one. The fleet, it seemed to him, was based too far from the potential combat zone. "No matter how strong the bow," he argued, recalling an ancient Chinese proverb, "an arrow in flight cannot tear the sheerest cloth." The Mobile Fleet, now at Lingga Roads, should be moved forward to Tawi Tawi, one of the southernmost of the Philippine Islands. If the Americans were so inconsiderate as to enter the Philippine Sea by means of an invasion of the Marianas, they should be lured south where Japanese land-based air power could hit at them and where the Combined Fleet would not have to expend so much fuel in reaching the scene of action.

These revisions in Koga's plan were accepted and it was renamed A-Go (Operation A). As Toyoda saw it, it was Japan's only chance of relieving the flood of disasters the Japanese were experiencing.

But Nimitz and MacArthur had further disasters planned for the Japanese.

No matter which plan the Joint Chiefs accepted in March, Hollandia was the first step for MacArthur's Southwest Pacific forces, and the planning for it was well advanced. The major portion of the Japanese Combined Fleet based at Palau formed a threat to the Hollandia operation, and MacArthur and Nimitz agreed it should be removed. Mitscher's fast carriers were available, and it was just the type of job their airmen liked to do. Judging from the type of job they had done on Truk in February, it seemed that the Hollandia operation would meet with little air opposition from Palau-based planes. The only other Japanese air bases in range from which powerful resistance might be expected were on the Vogelkop, and General Kenney's B-24s from Port Darwin could take care of them.

On March 22, three task groups of Task Force 58 stood out of Majuro Atoll and made a wide southerly sweep to avoid possible search planes from Truk. On the way, the force skipped March 24, and all hands were initiated into the Order of the Golden Dragon in honor of their crossing of the International Date Line.*

Admiral Spruance's hope for surprise was lost when Task Force 58 was snooped by a search plane from Truk in the afternoon of March 25, and again while engaged in fueling the next day. Annoyed by this premature flushing of the game, Spruance informed Mitscher that the attack would be set ahead two days and would take place on March 30 rather than April 1. On the afternoon of March 28, all destroyers were topped off, and the force began a high-speed run in to the target area.

American submarines were a vital part of the plan for attacking Palau. Seven of them were stationed off the passes leading from the lagoon to the open sea. They were spread out to increase the chance of interception. Then Fate took a hand and robbed Spruance of the full prize he sought.

On the evening of March 26, the submarine *Tullibee* was on patrol off Toagel Mlungui (West Pass), 60 miles northwest of Palau. Running surfaced, *Tullibee* picked up a small convoy of four *Marus* and three escorts. Commander Charles F. Brindupke maneuvered his boat into position for attack and at 3,000 yards fired two torpedoes. A few seconds later, *Tullibee* was blown apart by a terrible explosion as one of her own torpedoes circled back and hit her. The only survivor, Gunner's Mate C. W. Kuykendall, who was on lookout duty, was blown overboard and rescued by the Japanese the next morning. He spent the rest of the war laboring in a Japanese copper mine, and the story of the *Tullibee* was not known until his release in 1945.

*Tullibee*'s loss, of course, was not known to the skippers of

---

* Although Majuro is west of the 180° meridian, forces there kept West Longitude dates for convenience in communications with Pearl Harbor.

64

the other American submarines off Palau, so no effort was made to plug the hole in the patrol stations created by her absence. And it was just through this hole that most of the Japanese shipping in Palau escaped. *Tunny* got a shot at the super-battleship *Musashi* and hit her far forward in the chain locker, but the damage was repaired in Kure in three weeks.

The Japanese sent out a reception party to greet the American carriers on the night of March 28, when torpedo bombers circled Task Force 58, dropping flares and float lights. American fighters knocked some of the intruders down and the rest left for home after two hours of pyrotechnics. Not a ship was touched.

At dawn, March 30, the carriers had reached their launching point about a hundred miles from Palau and began to launch aircraft. All day, American Hellcats, Avengers, and Dauntlesses ranged far and wide over the islands of Palau, bombing, strafing, looking for ships, aircraft, and shore targets. Avengers from the *Lexington, Bunker Hill,* and *Hornet* had been especially equipped to lay mines in the harbor entrances, and, although they had little liking for this task, they did it efficiently and with spirit, even to the extent of calling themselves the "Flying Miners," and painting on their planes an emblem of crossed shovel and pick-axe. The Japanese flew every plane they could find from Peliliu and Yap, but they simply made more targets for the Hellcats. On the second day of the raid, one task group moved over to Yap, but found no planes there. They did shoot up the ground installations, but the pilots grumbled that they were missing the fun at Palau.

When Task Force 58 left Palau about noon on the last day of March, a large number of Japanese aircraft had been destroyed and thirty-six ships, including a destroyer and a naval repair ship had been sunk. Thirty-two more were bottled up in the harbor by the "eggs" laid by the "Flying Miners." No ship of Task Force 58 received a single hit.

On the way back to Majuro, Task Force 58 gave Woleai in the Carolines a going over; the atoll was so weakly garrisoned it was scarcely worth the bother. Lifeguarding submarines worked so efficiently during the three days of operations against

65

Palau, Yap, and Woleai that twenty-six men were rescued out of the forty-four that manned the twenty-five aircraft lost in combat.

Task Force 58 had only a week to rest in Majuro before going out again, this time to support MacArthur's Hollandia operation.

Hollandia is the name for a region on the northern coast of New Guinea. It is also the name of a small village at the head of Challenger Cove, an arm of Humboldt Bay, the only good harbor in hundreds of miles on the New Guinea coast. Tanahmerah Bay, 25 miles farther west, is too exposed to weather, but it would support an amphibious landing. The Japanese had constructed three airfields in the Humboldt-Tanahmerah area, and General Kenney's pilots had discovered another at Tadji, 8 miles southeast of Aitape, which lies about 125 miles east-southeast along the coast of New Guinea.

The Japanese believed that MacArthur's thrust along the northern coast of New Guinea would be the principal Allied move to break their defense perimeter, and they were much more worried about such a move than they were about the actual capture of Torokina on Bougainville and of Makin and Tarawa. They rushed reinforcements into the entire island, insofar as they controlled it. Responsible for the defense was Lieutenant General Fusataro Teshima, who had his headquarters at Manokwari on the Vogelkop Peninsula. In eastern New Guinea, Lieutenant General Hatazo Adachi had an army consisting of over 45,000 men, mostly at Hansa Bay and Wewak, 150 and 75 miles, respectively, from Aitape. Although Teshima ordered him to move his army to the Hollandia area, Adachi stalled, because he was convinced in his own mind that Hansa Bay, or possibly Wewak, would be MacArthur's target. This was just what MacArthur wanted him to think, and he did all he could to confirm the idea by sending air raids against these two areas. Destroyers bombarded Wewak, dummy parachutists were dropped, and generally a loud noise was made to keep the defenders of Hansa Bay and Wewak alert and in the wrong position.

66

MacArthur's plan called for simultaneous landings at Aitape, Humboldt Bay, and Tanahmerah Bay. Admiral "Uncle Dan" Barbey was in overall command except for the carriers borrowed from Nimitz, while Lieutenant General Robert L. Eichelberger, USA, victor of the Buna-Gona campaign, commanded the ground troops, which consisted of the I, or "Eye," Corps, built around the Twenty-Fourth and Forty-First Infantry Divisions, with elements of the Thirty-Second attached. The Aitape phase was designated Operation Persecution, and the Humboldt-Tanahmerah phase Operation Reckless, possibly an ironic comment by planners on such a long leap forward beyond the range of Allied fighter cover.

Operation Persecution at Aitape went so smoothly that when the troops stepped ashore at 0645, April 22, they met only scattered rifle fire. By nightfall, all objectives had been secured at a cost of two men killed and thirteen wounded. The assault troops were soon relieved to get ready for another assault, this time on Wakde, 120 miles west of Hollandia, and the Thirty-Second Division moved in as a garrison force. Intelligence reports of Adachi's activities caused the Aitape foothold to be built up to corps strength under Major General Charles P. Hall, USA, and it was just as well. On the night of July 10, Adachi attacked with some 20,000 troops. It was one of the wildest, bitterest jungle fights since the Buna-Gona campaign of late 1942. At one point, the Japanese forced a 1,300-yard gap in Hall's lines, but it availed them nothing. Although the heavy fighting was limited to one night, Adachi's forces kept things interesting along the Driniumor River near Aitape until August 9. He then withdrew back toward Wewak, having lost approximately half his force. It cost the U.S. Army 400 killed and about 2,600 wounded to stop him. His battered force was eventually finished off by Australians advancing overland.

We have got ahead of our story. While Operation Persecution was going off like clockwork, Operation Reckless at Tanahmerah Bay and Humboldt Bay was proving more difficult.

At Tanahmerah Bay the difficulties were those of nature. There were no Japanese defenders there when the troops went ashore on the morning of April 22, but the two beaches selected as landing sites were incapable of fulfilling their assigned functions. Because the Japanese defenses were supposed to be concentrated in Humboldt Bay (which was correct), the Western Task Force landing at Tanahmerah Bay was planned to advance swiftly over a road to Humboldt Bay and trap the Japanese between themselves and the forces landing at Hollandia. Unfortunately the road did not exist; there was only a jungle trail, marked by hairpin turns, which could be used only by foot soldiers. No vehicle, even the almost omnipotent Jeep, could traverse it. In addition, no road existed connecting the two beaches at Tanahmerah, nor could one be built for eight days. That afternoon, General MacArthur arrived in the cruiser *Nashville* to look the situation over and discussed affairs with General Eichelberger and Admiral Barbey. After moving over to Humboldt Bay to take a look there, everyone agreed to shift the main thrust to Hollandia and leave the forces at Tanahmerah with the single task of advancing overland to seize the airfield at Sentani. Because of heavy rain, and a few small groups of Japanese, it took four days to get there, but it took three months for Army Engineers to build a road capable of supporting vehicles connecting Tanahmerah Bay with the airfields at Lake Sentani.

Humboldt Bay held none of the terrain surprises that had caused the massive snarl of troops and vehicles at Tanahmerah, but conditions were far from easy. Only two possible landing beaches existed: White 1, on the west coast of Humboldt Bay, was the only one which could receive LSTs, and it was only 800 yards wide. Beach White 2 was on a long sandspit known as Cape Tjeweri, whose only exit was to the southeast, directly away from White 1. Therefore the troops would have to land on White 2, cross the spit, and embark in LVTs for a landing in a small village called Pim.

As at Aitape and Tanahmerah, heavy naval bombardment preceded the landings, and it caught the Japanese defenders completely by surprise. Troops hitting the beaches at 0700, April 22, found Japanese breakfasts still cooking. The Japanese had taken to the hills. "The headlong flight of the enemy at the

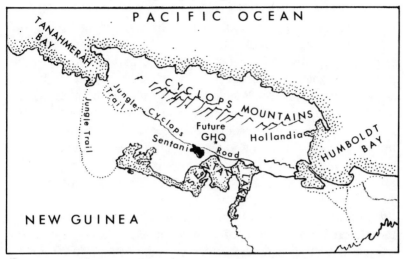

appearance of the Aitape and Hollandia Task Forces," noted Lieutenant General Walter Krueger, commander of all American troops under MacArthur, "was an event unparalleled in the history of our campaign against the Japanese. Not only did the majority flee without a show of resistance, but those who remained to fight failed to offer any type of resistance we have come to regard as characteristic of the Japanese."

Operations continued to go as smoothly as possible, even though the beaches were becoming crowded, and then jammed, with supplies because of the difficulties of getting them across the swamp that lay behind Beach White 1. The exit lanes became so rutted with the passage of heavy trucks that they were almost impossible to use.

A surprisingly large number of Japanese prisoners was taken, 611 at Hollandia, and 98 at Aitape. In addition a group of about 120 Sikhs, who had been captured at Singapore and had been used in forced labor at Hollandia, was released and eventually repatriated to India. A group of 125 nuns and missionaries was also rescued. There was no organized resistance anywhere.

While engineers toiled to develop roads, and shore parties

labored to deal with the mounting heaps of supplies, combat troops began a drive on Lake Sentani. They met no resistance until they got there, and then brisk fighting ensued, with the American troops on half rations.

A lucky bomb hit by a Japanese plane had solved the shore parties' problems temporarily by blowing up a Japanese ammunition dump on Beach White 1. The ensuing explosion destroyed large supplies of food and stores, twelve full LST loads, and the combat troops, being at the end of the supply line, were naturally the ones to suffer most. Air drops of supplies and food relieved the situation, and the troops were able to wipe out organized resistance in the Lake Sentani area. There was still a lot of mopping up to do, and this activity went on until June 6. General Inada, commanding the Japanese in the Hollandia area, decided to send the 7,200 men he had left westward to the Wakde-Sarmi area. Only about 1,000 got to their destination; the rest perished horribly in the jungle from wounds, disease, starvation, and the perils of the jungle.

Task Force 58 had only very little to do at Hollandia. Before the landing they had knocked out enemy strength at Wakde, Sawar, and Sarmi, some 120 miles west of Hollandia, meeting little resistance. They were not really needed for the landings, but they stood ready to intercept in case the Japanese fleet came out to oppose MacArthur. But this was not 1942, nor was it Guadalcanal; the Japanese fleet was being saved for a more serious threat.

On the way back to Majuro from Hollandia, Task Force 58 took another swipe at Truk. This time there was very little opposition, and Mitscher's aviators quickly eliminated what little there was. In fact it was so peaceful that on the second day of the strike, the Task Force replenished at sea and even received mail from home.

After that raid, Truk was eliminated as any kind of threat. Routinely, bombers from the Admiralties and from Eniwetok dropped a few calling cards just in case, but Truk was finished. Only seven vessels called there for the rest of the war—submarines bringing meager supplies for the garrison. The fourteen remaining aircraft were sent to Guam in June to add a little to the Marianas' air strength.

Still not satisfied, Task Force 58 paid calls on two islands in the Caroline group on the way home. Nine heavy cruisers bombarded Satawan Island on the afternoon of April 30, and the next afternoon, seven battleships gave Ponape a going over. The escorting destroyers joined in merrily. The only opposition was from antiaircraft guns, which did little good, as they could not reach the ships; and there were no planes over the target.

Its part done for the moment, Task Force 58 returned to Majuro to prepare for the Marianas operation.

Meanwhile, General MacArthur was on the move again.

It quickly became evident that the airfields around Lake Sentani were incapable of supporting operations of heavy bombers, and aerial photographs revealed that there was no site nearby which could be developed into a heavy-bomber strip. The nearest one was on Biak Island. The Joint Chiefs' directive of March 12 had included Hollandia on the assumption that it could function as a bomber base to neutralize Palau, Halmahera, and Vogelkop. Obviously, the assault on Biak had to be speeded up.

The first step was to take Wakde, 120 miles farther west. The name is a convenient reference for a section of the New Guinea coast about 18 miles long from the village of Toem to the village of Sarmi and to the Wakde Islands, Insoemoar and Insoemanai, just off Toem. On the larger island, Insoemoar, which the Americans called Wakde, the Japanese had constructed an airstrip which would be useful in the forthcoming attack on Biak. Three smaller airstrips on the mainland were of limited use.

The Japanese had some 11,000 men in the Wakde area, under Lieutenant General Tagami, but only half of them were combat troops, and they were scattered along the coast and on Insoemoar.

D-Day for the first phase of the operation, a landing about four miles west of Toem, was May 17. Rear Admiral William

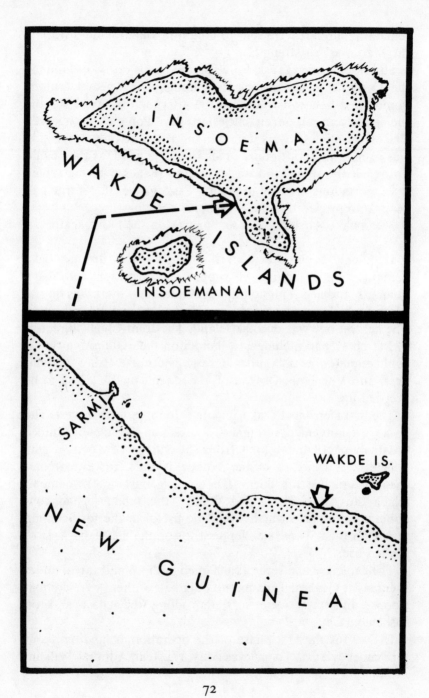

INSOEMAR

WAKDE ISLANDS

INSOEMANAI

SARMI

WAKDE IS.

NEW GUINEA

M. Fechteler, who had relieved Admiral Barbey in command of VII Phib, was in charge, and the assault troops were the 163rd Regimental Combat Team under Brigadier General Jens A. Doe, the same force that had taken Aitape. After the customary naval bombardment, the troops landed on time, meeting no opposition except for a little rifle fire. Again the enemy was caught completely by surprise. The same day, at 1100, a detachment of mortar and machine gunners landed on the smaller island, Insoemanai, finding it unoccupied. Here they set up their guns and commenced a leisurely working over of Insoemoar, which we will henceforth call Wakde, as it appears in almost all accounts.

Wakde proved a tougher nut to crack than anything MacArthur's amphibians had faced in a long time. The only practicable landing beach was on the west side of a small peninsula on the south coast, and to reach it, the boats had to pass through the bight between Insoemanai and Wakde, where they were exposed to fire on the port hand as they made their runs to the beach. The fanatical Japanese defenders fought well, and it took two and a half days to dig them out, foxhole by foxhole, strongpoint by strongpoint, bunker by bunker. By noon, May 21, the airstrip was in operation, and was a key airfield for the rest of the year.

It took much longer for the Army to clean out the area on the mainland opposite Wakde, and it was not until September that the fighting, for all practical purposes, ceased. It was a tough, nasty job, but eventually the Japanese withdrew to Sarmi, where they remained for the rest of the war, another isolated garrison which the war had passed by, and which had no hope of reinforcement or supplies from Japan.

The entire Wakde operation was but a stepping stone to the invasion of Biak, which followed ten days later. Although it could not be known at the time, the Biak operation would have far-ranging effects, not only on the Southwest Pacific campaign, but on the Central Pacific one as well.

Biak, the largest of the Schouten Islands, lies across the entrance to Geelvink Bay, which forms the neck of the

73

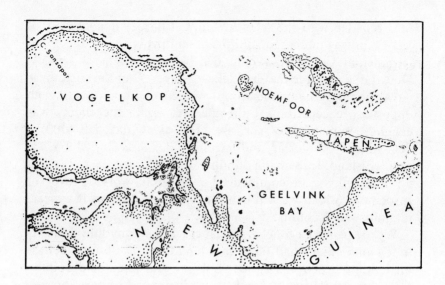

bird-shaped island of New Guinea. It is about forty-five miles long and twenty wide, characterized by low, flat-topped hills covered mostly by jungle forest. About 25,000 natives lived there and have been described as "a rather likeable race, well built, and pleasantly lazy. They had abandoned piracy and like to sit all day to watch waves break upon the coast. They work best in large groups, where two out of three can sit and offer technical advice on how to lift an axe or carry a bucket of water." As elsewhere, such people little appreciated the coming of the Japanese and the introduction of hard work.

On this rather pleasant tropical island, the Japanese had constructed three airstrips clustered within an area of six miles near the south coast, not far from the village of Bosnik. These were Mokmer, Borokoe, and Sorido.

Allied planners were hard put to discover a suitable landing beach, for the coral reef was more irregular than most encountered in Southwest Pacific operations, and it was doubtful whether they could be traversed by amphtracs and dukws. Also Army men wanted no more of being pinned on a narrow beach with the sea at their backs and a swamp in front of them. They had learned this lesson the hard way at Hollandia.

Finally they selected Bosnik as the site of the landing.

74

Although there is a coral cliff some 200 feet high behind the village, the 500-yard coastal plain gave room for maneuver. There was no swamp, there were stone jetties that could be used, and the coral reef was at least no worse than it was anywhere else. The greatest advantage was that the landing beach was close to the airstrips and the Allies could look toward an early change of ownership so they could be used to support further operations.

The Allied landing on Biak was no surprise to the Japanese high command, although its promptitude was. The large number of defenders indicated its important role in the Japanese defense perimeter. Colonel Kuzume was confident of his ability to defend the island, especially as he could expect regular and prompt reinforcements and adequate delivery of supplies.

On May 9, Imperial Headquarters astonished everyone by pulling back the perimeter line to Sorong and Halmahera. Biak was to be defended to the last man and then left to its fate. Colonel Kuzume made the best of a bad situation and prepared his defenses accordingly. He did not plan to waste the lives of his men in a futile beachhead defense nor in wild Banzai charges. He skillfully took advantage of the natural terrain and planned to make the enemy come to him. As a result, the assaulting forces initially had a comparatively easy time. Their troubles would come later.

While final preparations were being made for the sailing of the Hurricane Task Force, Army Air Force bombers from Nadzab on the northeast coast of New Guinea and from the Admiralties were busy working over Biak and other Japanese airfields farther west. These efforts were stepped up the three days before the landing by medium-range bombers from Hollandia and long-range bombers from Darwin. Fighter cover for the landings was to be supplied from elements of the Fifth Army Air Force based at Wakde.

At 0629 on Z-Day, Admiral Fechteler ordered, "Execute the landing plan." This order set off a forty-five-minute bombardment from the cruisers *Phoenix, Boise,* and *Nashville* and their accompanying destroyers. The Japanese response was comparatively light, although one 4.7-inch battery sited on high ground behind Mokmer airstrip proved to be more than a nuisance for several days. Destroyer fire would knock it out, but in a few hours it was back in action again.

The landings got off to a rather bad start. That morning a flat calm lay over Biak, and the clouds of dust and smoke from the bombardment hung over the landing beaches, completely obscuring the stone jetties and other landmarks intended to guide the troops ashore. The radars on the SCs which were controlling movements of the amphtracs and dukws were not sensitive enough to pick out the jetties. As a result, unknown to everyone, during the operations when the LSTs were disgorging the amphtracs and dukws, the entire formation had drifted westward in the 2- to 3-knot current. Thus the first five waves landed about 3,000 yards west of the intended beach in a mangrove swamp. A destroyer managed to pick out the jetties with her radar, and the sixth and subsequent waves landed in their proper places. There was no opposition, and by the end of the day, all initial objectives had been reached, while 12,000 men, 12 tanks, 28 artillery pieces, 500 vehicles, and 2,400 tons of supplies had been put ashore. The only Japanese response was in the form of three light air raids, one of which damaged *SC-699.*

Anxious to get control of the airstrips in order to support the forthcoming Marianas operations, General Fuller pushed his forces toward Mokmer. At first the going was easy, and then they ran into Kuzume's prepared defenses. Elements of the 162nd Infantry Regiment found themselves surrounded on three sides by the Japanese and had to be evacuated by sea and moved some 500 yards east to avoid being overrun. It quickly became evident that Biak would require more troops than the Forty-First Division had on hand, and arrangements were made to move more up from Wakde and Hollandia. It was not until June 7 that Mokmer was captured, and nearby Japanese artillery made sure that the Allies could make no use of it for another week.

Having once written Biak off, Imperial Headquarters changed its mind when faced with the actual Allied invasion of the island. One reason for the change may have been that Z-Day on Biak coincided with the thirty-ninth anniversary of the Battle of Tsushima. It was impertinent of the Allies to interfere with a national holiday in Japan. Toyoda's Chief of Staff saw a magnificent opportunity: "If we take it back," he observed, "that will draw the Pacific Fleet in sufficiently close so that we can have the Decisive Battle near Palau." Although other officers objected that MacArthur's occupation of Biak was secondary and that the big show would come in the Marianas, they were overruled, and Biak was restored to the defense perimeter. To take it back, a hastily devised operation known as Kon was thrown together. Kon called for the Japanese Navy to reinforce Biak with troops transported in warships from Zamboanga. In addition, the Japanese air strength in the area was beefed up from 16 to some 200 aircraft, including 70 flown down from the Marianas. This last contingent arrived at Menado on Celebes, and most of the pilots promptly came down with malaria.

The first reinforcement attempt failed when the three troop-carrying destroyers, escorted by cruisers and other destroyers, were sighted early. Reports of strong Allied naval forces, including a nonexistent aircraft carrier, caused Admiral Toyoda to suspend the entire operation, to try again a few days later.

The second attempt to implement Kon came during the period of June 7 to 9, after reconnaissance had satisfied Toyoda that there were no American carriers near Biak. This time 600 troops were loaded in three destroyers, and hundreds of others in barges towed by three other destroyers set sail from Sorong, escorted by the cruisers *Aoba* and *Kinu*. This force ran into an Allied Task Group led by Rear Admiral V. A. C. Crutchley, RN, and promptly decided to retire. Crutchley pressed on in pursuit but was unable to catch up before running into waters where Allied aviators had been told they could bomb anything that floated. Only one ship on either side was hit in this engagement, the *Shiratsuyu*, but the Japanese destroyers had promptly cast off their barges at the sight of Crutchley's ships, leaving the troops in them to their fate. The barges were destroyed, and only a handful of the Japanese reached shore.

Irritated by the failures of two successive attempts to implement the Kon operation, Admiral Toyoda decided to do it right on the third try. He assigned the job to Vice Admiral Matome Ugaki and told him to land the reinforcements at all costs. Flying his flag in the super-battleship *Yamato*, Ugaki left Tawi Tawi at 1600 in the afternoon of June 10, accompanied by *Yamato*'s sister ship *Musashi*, heavy cruisers *Myoko* and *Haguro*, light cruiser *Noshiro*, and three destroyers. At Batjan he picked up the *Aoba* and *Kinu*, and four more destroyers, as well as two minelayers and several subchasers and freighters.

Before this formidable force could leave Batjan, indications were piling up in Imperial Headquarters of something brewing in the Marianas. Carrier aircraft attacks on Saipan and Guam on June 11 and 12 made it abundantly clear that the main attack was coming in the Central Pacific. At 1820, June 12, Admiral Toyoda issued orders to implement Operation A-Go immediately and to suspend Operation Kon "temporarily." Like Operation Sea Lion, Hitler's intended invasion of England, once suspended, it was never reinstated. Toyoda would accept the "Decisive Battle" in the Philippine Sea rather than in the Southwest Pacific. The battleships, cruisers, and destroyers that had assembled for Kon were ordered to report to Ozawa west of the Marianas. Every aircraft that could fly was ordered from New Guinea to Palau so that they could be used against Spruance's forces in the Philippine Sea. In a Parthian shot, the Japanese aviators made a final raid on the American ships off Biak and seriously damaged the destroyer *Kalk*, but that was the end of air opposition at Biak.

It took until June 22 for the Army to finish up the job at Biak. Colonel Kuzume's cave-by-cave defense was hard to deal with, and General Krueger, not satisfied with the progress, relieved General Fuller with General Eichelberger, but the going was not much faster after the relief. Allied difficulties were compounded by the outbreak of a virulent epidemic of scrub typhus among members of the Hurricane Task Force.

On the night of June 21–22, Colonel Kuzume ceremonially burned his regimental colors and then either took his own life or went out to seek death in battle.

The importance of the capture of Biak in the Pacific war is too little realized. The fighting there sucked Japanese air strength out of the Marianas on the eve of the American invasion of Saipan, and the futile movement of ships for the abortive Kon operation disarranged Combined Fleet schedules and consumed precious fuel. Finally, Biak proved to be a very useful base in the capture of Noemfoor and Sansapor, the final stages of the New Guinea campaign and in the operations for the liberation of the Philippines.

Although it is getting ahead of our story, it will be well to finish up MacArthur's campaign in New Guinea before turning our attention to the operations of the Central Pacific Forces. The two principal remaining spots General MacArthur desired to take were the island of Noemfoor, almost midway between Biak and Manokwari, and Sansapor on the Vogelkop. Noemfoor is a circular island, about eleven miles across, and held three airstrips completed in mid-1944, largely by Indonesian labor imported from Java. The Indonesians were necessary because the natives of Noemfoor, appalled by the idea of work, had taken to the hills, and it was not worth the effort to hunt them down.

The landing on Noemfoor was the smoothest opposed landing of the entire Southwest Pacific campaign. About 2,000 Japanese defenders were concentrated around the village of Kamiri, where the most important airstrip was located. They were reduced to impotence by the massive bombardment that preceded the landing on July 2, and when the troops of the Cyclone Task Force came ashore, they encountered punch-drunk Japanese who wandered around neither fighting nor surrendering. They had to be mowed down by machine-gun fire to get them out of the way. There was little defense, even though each cave had to be cleaned out individually. Many were empty, many were filled with corpses of Japanese who had committed suicide with hand grenades, and in others the enemy offered no resistance. Most of the troops fled to the hills, and had to be mopped up in small units. Later that month, the native chiefs declared war on Japan and the natives enthusiastically joined in the hunt for Japanese in the hills and jungle. Since they knew the territory a great deal better than the Japanese, it was a rather one-sided affair.

The airfields were quickly placed in operation by Army Engineers, and they were a great help in the months to come.

MacArthur had real need of a base on the Vogelkop to support his forthcoming operations against Morotai on Halmahera and in the Philippines. At first Sorong had been the target, in order to take advantage of the installations the Japanese had constructed there and to seize the Klamano oilfield about thirty miles southeast. Nearby Waigeo Island was an additional objective, since it could support an air and naval base.

The acceleration of war in the Pacific caused MacArthur to change his plans. Before the Klamano oilfield could be developed, it would be too far to the rear. Instead the area between Sansapor and Mar on the northwest coast of the Vogelkop was selected. On July 30, the Typhoon Task Force went ashore north of Mar against no opposition, capturing at the same time the islands of Amsterdam and Middelburg, where airstrips and a PT-boat base were constructed. The next day, troops were ferried some ten miles southwest to Sansapor. Again there was no opposition. The month of August was employed in running down Japanese on the Vogelkop. From captives, MacArthur's intelligence officers learned that the Japanese had begun to evacuate Manokwari late in June, and that there was no organized Japanese opposition anywhere on New Guinea. The Japanese that were left in isolated pockets on that vast island survived as best they could until the end of the war. Most of them did not make it. In spite of everything, many of them still believed in the invincibility of the Japanese armed forces and waited for liberation. They could not know what was happening to their brothers hundreds of miles to the north on Saipan, Tinian, and Guam.

As Admiral Mitscher's Fast Carrier Task Force sortied from Majuro on June 6, 1944, halfway around the world American and British troops were spending their last night in the ships that would deliver them to the beaches at Normandy. The vastness of the war is sometimes lost as we concentrate on one or another theater. During the single month of June 1944, as MacArthur's New Guinea Campaign reached its final stages, D-Day in Europe took place, the Russians launched their great offensive against Germany from the east, and the American landings in the Marianas broke Japan's defense perimeter and led to the capture of the island from which the B-29 *Enola Gay* would take off to drop an atomic bomb on Hiroshima.

Once again the operation was entrusted to Admiral Spruance, with Vice Admiral Kelly Turner in charge of the assault forces. Vice Admiral Marc A. Mitscher, as usual, had Task Force 58, even more powerful than it had been in the Marshalls and Hollandia operations.

As usual, Kelly Turner decided to command one of the Attack Forces in addition to his responsibility for the Joint Expeditionary Force. He selected the Northern Attack Force, with V Phib, Major General Holland M. Smith, for his personal command, while the Southern Attack Force with III Phib, Major General Roy S. Geiger, was under Rear Admiral Richard L. Conolly. The Northern Attack Force had as its objectives the islands of Saipan and Tinian, while the Southern was assigned to the capture of Guam. In addition, there was a Floating Reserve commanded by Rear Admiral W. H. P. Blandy, which carried the Army Twenty-Seventh Division, reinforced, still under command of Major General Ralph Smith whom we came to know at Makin and Eniwetok.*

Only Operation Torch, the invasion of North Africa in November 1942, from the United States and the United Kingdom, can rival Operation Forager, the assault on the Marianas, as far as distances are involved. Saipan is about 3,500 miles from Pearl Harbor and about 1,000 miles from the nearest American base at Eniwetok. The troop-lift alone involved transporting four and a half reinforced divisions, some 127,500 men from places as far apart as Hawaii and Guadalca-

* See the author's *Years of Expectation* (New York: David McKay Company, Inc., 1973), pp. 301–2, 334.

81

nal. Naval forces came from those two places and from Majuro and Eniwetok as well.

While the troops were being assembled and trained, while the ships were drilling and brushing up on station keeping and gunnery, Admiral Nimitz made an important reorganization of the Pacific Fleet, reflecting the stepped-up tempo of the war. The South Pacific command, which Admiral Halsey had held so brilliantly, was reduced to a rear-echelon operation. Halsey was designated Commander Third Fleet, which put him on the same level as Admiral Spruance. The idea was that while Spruance and his staff were conducting one operation, Halsey and his would be planning the next. The designations Third Fleet and Fifth Fleet were endlessly confusing to the American public who wondered why husbands and sons did not come home when the Fifth Fleet was relieved by the Third. The answer was that the same ships went right on going. As Halsey put it, "Instead of the stagecoach system of keeping the drivers and changing the horses, we changed drivers and kept the horses. It was hard on the horses, but it was effective. Moreover, it consistently misled the Japs into an exaggerated conception of our seagoing strength."

Saipan and Tinian are ruggedly mountainous islands separated by a three-mile-wide channel. From Tinian to Rota, a sugarcane island, it is forty-six miles south-southwest, and thirty-three miles farther in the same direction lies Guam. The first American target, Saipan, is thirteen miles long and varies between two and a half and five miles in width, with a total area of seventy-one square miles. The Japanese were determined to defend every one of those square miles.

After World War I, during the period of their Mandate, the Japanese had developed Saipan into a little Japan, with about 80 percent of the 28,000 population being Japanese; the rest were Chamorros and about 1,000 Koreans. As on Tinian, these people were intensely loyal to Japan. There would be no native assistance as had been experienced in the Solomons and in New Guinea.

Responsible for the defense of Saipan was Lieutenant

General Yoshitsugu Saito, although he was nominally subordinate to two other officers in the Marianas. Lieutenant General Hideyoshi Obata, the area commander, found himself stranded on Guam during an inspection tour. He had just arrived there when the Americans attacked the Marianas; there he stayed. Senior to both of them was Vice Admiral Chuichi Nagumo, demoted since the Battle of Midway from commanding fast carriers to an area command consisting of small craft, barges, and ground troops. His headquarters were on Saipan, but it never occurred to him to interfere in the military operations Saito was running.

Saito disposed his 32,000 troops to cover all likely landing sites. He would have had more men, except for the depredations of American submarines, which had nearly cut off Saipan from the home islands. The *Trout* accounted for *Sakito Maru* on February 29, and only 1,680 of the 4,100 troops she was carrying ever reached Saipan. During the period of June 4 to 6, a Japanese troop convoy of seven ships bound for Saipan ran into an American submarine wolfpack known as Blair's Blasters, after its commander, Captain Leon N. Blair. The three boats of this pack, *Shark*, *Pintado*, and *Pilotfish*, managed to send five of these transports to the bottom before being forced to break off the action. The remaining ships picked up most of the survivors, but they arrived at Saipan minus most of their equipment, and many of the men badly burned. One might think that these units could have been usefully employed in strengthening the defenses of the island, but not according to Saito's Chief of Staff. "Unless," he reported, "the units are supplied with cement, steel reinforcements for cement, barbed wire, lumber, etc., which cannot be obtained in these islands, no matter how many soldiers there are, they can do nothing in regard to fortification but can sit around with their arms folded, and the situation is unbearable."

There was apparently too much sitting around with arms folded, for the Americans later found mines not emplaced, barbed wire not strung, and material unused. Not that they objected; Saipan was tough enough as it was. It was bad enough to have to meet the Japanese in difficult terrain. There were other perils as well. Offshore they might encounter sharks, barracuda, sea snakes, and razor-sharp coral, as well as giant clams and poison fish. Once they got ashore, if they survived the Japanese, the Marines would encounter poisonous snakes, giant lizards, together with the danger of exposure to leprosy, typhus, filariasis, typhoid, and dysentery.

"Sir," asked one man at a briefing session, "why don't we let the Japs keep the island?"

The landings were to take place along a three-and-a-half-mile front on the southern half of the west coast of Saipan, between Agingan Point and Garapan, a town of 10,000 souls. After advancing east to capture Aslito Airfield and on to the shore of Magicienne Bay on the east coast, the troops would execute a left wheel and drive toward the northern end of the island.

Intelligence estimates were shaky at best, for little was known of what the Japanese had been up to since they closed the island to foreign visitors years before Pearl Harbor. Photographic reconnaissance had been skimpy, partly as a result of cloud cover on the days when it was tried, and partly because Nimitz did not want to order too many flights over the Marianas for fear of tipping off the Japanese. Planners did know that there was a reef which amphtracs and dukws would have to overcome and that the southern end was comparatively flat and could be quickly exploited by the Marines.

No fewer than 535 ships were assigned to Operation Forager, although not all of them had anything directly to do with Saipan, for they carried the troops which would be used a little later against Tinian and Guam. Old battleships and escort carriers, accompanied by cruisers and destroyers, were to be on hand for direct support of troops, while Admiral Mitscher's Task Force 58 would roam the waters north and west of Saipan to deal with the Japanese Combined Fleet in case Toyoda decided to start something.

D-Day on Saipan was June 15, 1944, but well before that date, ships were on the move toward the Marianas, and by June 11, the Japanese were aware that something was coming their way.

Army Air Forces flew interdiction strikes against Peleliu,

Woleai, Yap, Truk, and other Japanese bases during the first days of June, but it was Admiral Mitscher's Task Force 58 that had the main responsibility for aerial chores commencing on June 11. For the first time since the Kwajalein operation, Task Force 58 was in full strength, for Nimitz and Spruance and Mitscher all hoped the Japanese Navy would come out and fight. For this operation, Task Force 58 included 105 ships, with over 800 aircraft flying from 7 large and 8 light carriers. It was divided into four task groups, with the carriers assigned as follows:

TG 58.1 CVs *Hornet, Yorktown;* CVLs *Belleau Wood, Bataan*
TG 58.2 CVs *Bunker Hill, Wasp;* CVLs *Monterey, Cabot*
TG 58.3 CVs *Enterprise, Lexington;* CVLs *Princeton, San Jacinto*
TG 58.4 CV *Essex,* CVLs *Langley, Cowpens*

Divided roughly evenly among these task groups were 7 battleships, 17 cruisers, and 66 destroyers.

Task Force 58 launched its first strike on the Marianas on the afternoon of June 11, after it had been snooped in the morning by Japanese planes, all of which were shot down by the combat air patrol. Intensive raids on June 12 and 13 succeeded in eliminating most of the Japanese air strength on Saipan, Tinian, and Guam, in addition to destroying a goodly number of ships. As always, there were losses, and on the carriers members of the air groups sadly inventoried the effects of airmen shot down.

There was a miraculously happy ending for Commander William I. Martin, the pilot of a TBF Avenger flying a dawn air strike from the *Enterprise.* His target was a small airstrip near Charan Kanoa on Saipan. Just as he released his stick of bombs, his plane was hit by antiaircraft fire. It began to tumble end-over-end, and Martin yelled to his two crewmen, Aviation Radioman First Class J. T. Williams, and Aviation Ordnance-man Second Class W. R. Hargrove to bail out. He released his seat belt and was thrown out of the spinning plane. As he jerked the ripcord he realized he was too low for his parachute to open, and in the few seconds before he hit the water of the lagoon, he thought of his wife and two sons, and let run through his mind the words of the Psalmist, "The Lord is my shepherd, I shall not want. . . ." There came the sudden remembrance of a pilot from the old *Hornet* who had survived a free fall from 2,000 feet by entering the water with his toes pointed like an arrow. He did the same and splashed down in four or five feet of water, unhurt except for a bruise on his hip acquired as he bailed out of his plane. There was no sign of Williams and Hargrove. Their funeral pyre was the blazing wreck of the Avenger a few yards away.

Martin was still in a bad fix. He was 200 yards from an enemy-held shore, with a reef between him and open water where he might get help from a lifeguard submarine or a float plane. And he was being fired on by Japanese riflemen.

Trailing his seat pack, which contained his life raft, Martin began a 1,000-yard swim to the reef, swimming under water as much as he could. Every time he surfaced for breath, he heard the "zing-blup" of bullets flying by and hitting the water. Once he glanced back and saw two small boats putting out after him. He could not afford to be captured; as a squadron commander, he had been fully briefed on plans for Saipan. He struggled on, but the boats came closer.

Rescue arrived in the form of two fighters who drove the pursuing boats away. Eventually Martin reached the reef. While he rested from the long, exhausting swim, he recognized just where he was and made mental notes of the condition of the reef, unknown enemy batteries ashore, the depth of water over the reef, the current, and other items of information that would be of intense interest to the Marines who would be crossing that same reef in two days' time.

Crossing the reef, Martin finally dared inflate his Mae West and swim slowly seaward until it seemed safe to inflate his life raft. He reflected that if he were not rescued soon, his next port of call was likely to be the Philippines.

Two planes roared overhead, and Martin attracted their attention with his signal mirror. One of them dropped an emergency kit, which he retrieved. It contained food, fresh water, a Very pistol, and first-aid supplies. To get out of range of the antiaircraft guns whose shrapnel was falling all around him, he rigged his parachute as a sail and was presently reported as making good 3 knots on course 290 degrees, not zigzagging.

Just before noon, two float planes from Admiral Spruance's flagship, *Indianapolis*, came over. One landed on the water and picked up the aviator-turned-raftman, returning him without delay to the *Indianapolis*. After a shower, Martin got into dry clothing provided for him, had a shot of whiskey thoughtfully provided by the medical officer, and reported to Admiral Spruance. After relating his information about the reef and beach conditions, Martin transferred by breeches buoy to the destroyer *MacDonough*. Later that afternoon he had the satisfaction of seeing the destroyer's guns demolish the very battery that had shot him down. The next morning, the *MacDonough* returned him to the *Enterprise*. On June 15, he was flying again, helping to support the Marines who had crossed the reef he had known all too well.

While Commander Martin was having his adventures, the seven battleships with accompanying destroyers pulled out of Task Force 58 for shore bombardment of Saipan. Although they blazed away with a will, the bombardment accomplished little, for their gunners had not had enough experience in this type of work, where the technique was quite different from a duel between battleships at sea. It was later described as "a Navy-sponsored farm project that simultaneously plows the fields, prunes the trees, harvests the crops, and adds iron to the soil."

The next day the old battleships arrived and took over the job of shore bombardment with far better results. The glamourous new battleships returned to their positions in Task Force 58, with the rising hope that they would have worthwhile targets in a sea battle.

While TGs 58.2 and 58.3 continued to support operations at Saipan, Rear Admiral Joseph J. Clark took his own 58.1 and Rear Admiral William K. Harrill's 58.4 north to eliminate Japanese air strength in the Volcano and Bonin islands so that their planes could not interfere with the business on Saipan. "Jocko" Clark was, as Samuel Eliot Morison put it, "part

Cherokee Indian and part Southern Methodist, but all fighter." Striking at Iwo Jima, Haha Jima, and Chichi Jima on June 15 and 16, his and Harrill's groups did a thorough job of eliminating danger from the north. WE GAVE THEM THE MERRY CHICHI HAHA he radioed Admiral Nimitz. Then he headed for an urgent rendezvous with the rest of TF 58, for the Japanese fleet had come out to fight.

On the evening of June 14, the transports carrying the Second and Fourth Marine Divisions which were to land the next day approached their assigned stations. As customary, many men were listening to radios tuned in to "Tokyo Rose," an American girl of Japanese descent, who had been caught in Japan when war broke out and had changed her allegiance. She was always popular with the sailors and Marines in the Pacific because she had a seemingly unending store of the latest hit records from America. Her propaganda they had learned to ignore.

"I've got some swell recordings for you," she broadcast that evening, "just in from the States. You'd better enjoy them while you can, because tomorrow at oh-six-hundred you're hitting Saipan . . . and we're ready for you. So, while you're still alive, let's listen to . . ."

The Marines were up early the next morning, and the eight battalions of the initial assault waves were embarked in 719 amphtracs which were carried in the maws of 64 LSTs. These ungainly vessels made their clumsy way up to the line of departure. At 0812 the LSTs opened their ponderous bow doors, and the clumsy amphtracs rolled down the well decks and splashed into the water and began the long swim toward the beaches. They crawled across the reef and, waterborne once again, crossed the lagoon toward shore, supported by aircraft and ships' gunfire.

So well had the lessons of Tarawa, Kwajalein, and Eniwetok been digested that the landing "went according to plan," even though the opposition was intense. A feint at Tanapag Harbor, north of Garapan and Mutcho Point, did not distract General Saito, and his gunners inflicted heavy casualties on the Marines. But they could not be stopped. The first wave hit the beach at

The Conquest of Saipan, June 15–July 9, 1944

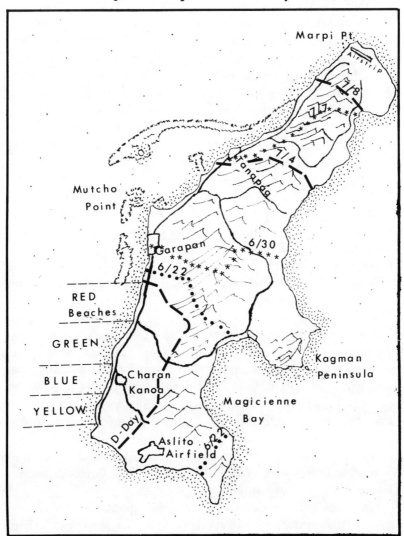

0844, and within twenty minutes there were 8,000 Marines ashore, and they were pushing on toward the village of Charan Kanoa. The fighting was heavy and grew heavier. It took three days for the American forces to reach the D-Day objectives and three weeks to end organized resistance on the island.

89

Aboard the *Rocky Mount* Admiral Turner watched the landing operation with satisfaction. Not yet had word reached him of the difficulties ashore. Everything seemed to be going so smoothly that he recommended to Admiral Spruance that W-Day for Guam be set for June 18. While Spruance was considering this, he received a radio report from the submarine *Flying Fish* of a Japanese carrier force entering the Philippine Sea through San Bernardino Strait. A few hours later, at 0400, June 16, he received another from the *Seahorse* of a second force steaming north off Surigao Strait. He postponed the Guam landing and rode over in his barge to the *Rocky Mount* for a conference with Admiral Turner.

By this time it was becoming clear that the going ashore was much tougher than Turner had supposed. Holland M. ("Howlin' Mad") Smith, the overall ground commander, also attended the conference, and he was vehement. Saipan was going to be no pushover.

As a result of this discussion, several changes in the plan were made. The floating reserve, the Army Twenty-Seventh Infantry Division would be committed to Saipan at once. Certain cruisers and destroyers assigned to shore bombardment duties were to be sent to augment the strength of Task Force 58 in the coming sea battle. Transports and cargo vessels would cease unloading after dark June 17 and withdraw to a safe position east of Saipan. The old battleships would move about twenty-five miles west to intercept the Japanese if they managed to get around Task Force 58. Only escort carriers would be left by Saipan for close air support of the Marines and G.I.s ashore.

In case things went really badly ashore, the Guam Invasion Force would be committed to Saipan also.

Once these basic decisions had been made, Spruance adjourned the conference and returned to his flagship, which then sailed to join Rear Admiral John W. Reeves' Task Group 58.3 to wait for the Japanese fleet to draw near.

The Philippine Sea in the month of June 1944 was neither the place nor the time Admiral Toyoda would have chosen for the

Decisive Battle. The waters west of the Marianas were too far from the oil supplies of the East Indies, and he needed at least another six months to train his carrier pilots. Most of Japan's highly trained pilots had been lost in the Battle of Midway; those that remained and their reasonably well trained replacements had been frittered away in the Solomons and against MacArthur in the Southwest Pacific. Now the Japanese carriers steaming toward the Battle of the Philippine Sea had very inexperienced air groups aboard. The three largest carriers had the "veteran" groups aboard; they had been flying six months. The other carriers had pilots who had only one or two months' experience.

In contrast, every carrier pilot in the U.S. Navy had been flying for at least two years and had over 300 hours in the air. Most of them had known combat, and even the greenest replacements were better than many of the Japanese squadron leaders. To make matters worse for the Japanese, fuel shortages kept the carriers immobile, so the pilots could not practice operations. The result was, as the Japanese analysis put it after the battle, the squadrons loafed in Tawi Tawi "for a month, decreasing the efficiency of their training."

The First Mobile Fleet, which included 90 percent of the combatant ships assigned to Combined Fleet, was to have the honor of meeting the Americans in the Decisive Battle. In command was Vice Admiral Jisaburo Ozawa, one of the best in the Japanese Navy. Although he was no airman, he understood better than most the use of naval air power and the employment of carriers. He had relieved the unfortunate Admiral Nagumo in November 1942, and assumed command of the First Mobile Fleet on March 1, 1944.

Because of the abortive Kon Operation, Ozawa's Mobile Fleet was divided. Ugaki's Kon ships sortied from Batjan anchorage on the morning of June 13 to rendezvous with Ozawa in position 11° 30′ N, 130° 30′ E, about 350 miles east of Samar and about 950 miles west-southwest of Saipan. The same day, Ozawa left Tawi Tawi and moved his carrier force up to Guimaras anchorage between Panay and Negros in the Philippines. Leaving there on the morning of June 15, he transited San Bernardino Strait where he was spotted by the *Flying Fish* at 1835 that evening.

Ugaki rendezvoused with oilers and refueled while continuing on his way to meet Ozawa. Once the two combatant forces joined, Ozawa also refueled, a process which was not completed until 2000 June 17.

During this time, aircraft reconnaissance reports kept coming in to Ozawa's flagship, the new carrier *Taiho*, the largest carrier in the world except for the *Saratoga*, which was not present for the battle. He had a very good idea of the strength he was running into, but he was undismayed. The Americans had had the weaker force at Midway and had been victorious; there was no reason the weaker force could not prevail again.

Mitscher had 7 large and 8 light carriers to his 5 large and 4 light. The rest of the line-up was: battleships, U.S. 7, Japan 5, but two of them were the monstrous *Yamato* and *Musashi* with their 18.1-inch guns; heavy cruisers, U.S. 8, Japan 11; light cruisers, U.S. 13, Japan 2; destroyers, U.S. 69, Japan 28.

Ozawa's inferiority in every category of ships except for heavy cruisers was paralleled by his 956 to 473 inferiority in all types of aircraft. Yet he had three advantages that gave him confidence. First, he depended on land-based aircraft from Guam, Rota, and Yap to cooperate with his carrier planes in destroying the American fleet. Second, his planes, which did not have protective armor for the pilots and were not equipped with self-sealing gasoline tanks, had a greater range than Mitscher's aircraft. Ozawa could send his planes out 300 miles to fight, while the Americans could not be employed in battle much over 200 miles. Additionally, Ozawa could stand even farther off and employ shuttle bombing, having his planes leave their carriers, attack the Americans, fly on to Guam, where they would refuel and rearm, attack the Americans on the way back, and reach their own carriers which were still outside the range of American attackers. Ozawa's third main advantage was that he had the weather. In the easterly trade wind that prevailed, Mitscher would have to turn back toward Saipan every time he launched or landed aircraft. It would be impossible for him to close the distance to Ozawa's force with any degree of speed. Ozawa, on the other hand, could close at will.

Spruance and Mitscher looked quite differently at the coming battle. Mitscher was anxious to push as far westward as he could in the hope of annihilating Ozawa's fleet, while Spruance, with wider responsibilities, felt his primary duty was to cover Saipan. He did not know that Ugaki had joined Ozawa; from the submarine sighting reports he had received, he assumed that two separate Japanese forces were coming at him, with one intended to draw him off while the other slipped behind him to attack the Americans on Saipan. He had ample reason for believing as he did, for in practically every other major action of the war, the Japanese had used multiple forces, and they would do so again at the Battle for Leyte Gulf.

Spruance's plan, accordingly, was to steam westward during the daylight hours and at nightfall turn back east toward Saipan to guard against a Japanese force slipping past him during hours of darkness.

About noon, June 18, Clark's and Harrill's task groups joined up, and Spruance formed a battle line by pulling the seven battleships and accompanying cruisers and destroyers out of the four carrier groups. This force, designated Task Group 58.7, was stationed fifteen miles west of TG 58.3. Clark's 58.1 was twelve miles north of TG 58.3, and Rear Admiral Alfred E. Montgomery's TG 58.2 was twelve miles south. The weakest carrier group, Harrill's TG 58.4, was positioned about twelve miles north of the battle line to give it air protection.

Although Vice Admiral Willis A. Lee's battle line was not needed in the Philippine Sea, it demonstrated the flexibility of TF 58 and it would have a role four months later off the Philippines.

After having made slow progress southwestward during the afternoon of June 18, TF 58 reversed course at 2030 that evening and moved back toward Saipan. Around midnight Spruance made his first controversial decision. Ozawa had broken radio silence to give instructions to bring about maximum cooperation between his airmen and those based on Guam and elsewhere. High-frequency radio direction-finders

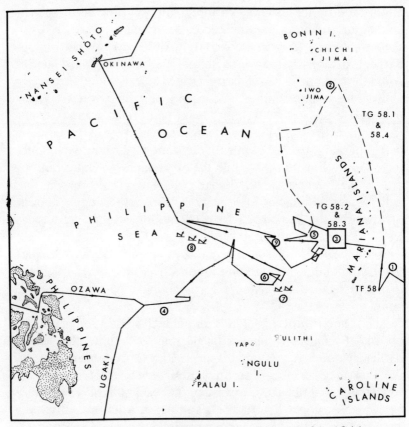

The Battle of the Philippine Sea, June 19–21, 1944

1. TF 58 strikes Guam, June 11–14
2. TG 58.1 and TG 58.4 strike Iwo Jima
3. Operating area for TG 58.2 and 58.3
4. Japanese refuel, June 16–17
5. TG 58.1 and 58.4 rejoin TF 58
6. Japanese attempt to shuttle bomb TF 58
7. *Shokaku* and *Taiho* sunk
8. *Hiyo* and two oilers sunk
9. Night recovery by TF 58

had picked up these signals and pinpointed his location within 40 miles. Spruance, however, preferred to believe a report from the submarine *Stingray*, which was operating about 175 miles east-southeast of the position given by direction finding. Actually *Stingray*'s report was routine, but ComSubPac had asked for a repeat as interference had distorted the signal, and it was interpreted as jamming. The only reason for jamming would be the nearby proximity of the enemy fleet.

Mitscher recommended that TF 58 turn around and head for the enemy, considering that the forces left near Saipan to support the troops ashore had enough strength to deal with an end run by the Japanese, but his recommendation was over-ruled by Spruance in a voice radio message: "Change proposed does not appear advisable. Believe indications given by *Stingray* more accurate than that determined by direction-finder. If that is so, continuation as at present seems preferable. End run by other carrier groups remains possibility and must not be overlooked."

A sighting by a Navy patrol bomber which might have changed Spruance's mind was victim of bad luck. The report did not reach him for seven and a half hours because of radio difficulties. By that time it was too late to do anything about it.

During the night Task Force 58 was snooped by a Japanese plane, probably based on Guam. It was safe to assume that Ozawa knew where the American force was and that he would make the first strike.

On the morning of June 19, the weather was beautiful, ideal for a tropical cruise or an air battle. There were few and scattered clouds, and the gentle 9- to 12-knot easterly wind scarcely stirred the surface of the blue sea. Atmospheric conditions created vapor trails, so it was easy for the shipborne sailors to watch their brothers in arms in the skies above. Dawn search, combat air and antisubmarine patrols were launched from the American carriers, and a little later fighters were sent over Guam to insure that the Japanese there would not interfere.

A few scattered planes from Guam bothered the task force

little, but at 0807 radar picked up a group of bogeys eighty-one miles southwest, which were reinforcements coming in from either Truk or Yap. Mitscher ordered thirty-six Hellcats out to deal with this threat, which they did efficiently, shooting down thirty fighters and five bombers.

The first big raid was detected at 0959 by radar when it was still 150 miles off to the west. The curtain-raisers were over. The main show was about to begin.

Some 380 miles west-southwest Ozawa was throwing everything he had into the battle. He had launched searches early, beginning at 0445, ninety minutes before sunrise, and at 0730, one of these planes sighted part of Task Force 58. That was enough for Ozawa. The pilots were hastily briefed, and at 0830 Raid I, consisting of sixty-one Zeke* fighters, forty-five of them carrying bombs, and eight Jills loaded with torpedoes, began taking off from the flight decks of the *Chiyoda*, *Zuiho*, and *Chitose*. They had a long flight ahead of them, and most of them did not live to see its completion.

Twenty minutes after Raid I was detected by radar, American pilots were taking off from Task Force 58. The old carnie cry of "Hey Rube!" recalled the fighters over Guam, and the Hellcats headed for the enemy, stacked at various altitudes in accordance with the battle plan. At 1036 the tallyho was sounded, and the Americans jumped on the Japanese planes from every conceivable direction. The greater experience of the American pilots paid off immediately. The Japanese were scattered or in loose formation, so that they could not help each

* In 1943 the U.S. changed the nickname "Zero" to "Zeke." The original name came from the last numbers of the model designation, but since other Japanese aircraft also had the designation "Zero," standardized nicknames were promulgated for the Allied forces. Chief designations were:
"Betty"—Mitsubishi Zero-1, Navy, 2 engines, medium bomber.
"Emily"—Kawanishi Zero-2, Navy, 4 engines, patrol bomber, flying boat.
"Helen"—Nakajima, Navy, 2 engines, medium bomber.
"Judy"—Aichi, Navy, single-engine, torpedo-bomber.
"Kate"—Nakajima 97-2, Navy, single-engine, high-level or torpedo-bomber.
"Pete"—Sasebo Zero-0, Navy, single-engine, float plane.
"Sally"—Mitsubishi 97, Army, 2 engines, medium bomber.
"Tojo"—Nakajima, Army, single-engine, fighter.
"Val"—Aichi 99-1, Navy, single-engine, dive bomber. This plane had nonretractable landing gears with "pants" [fairing to reduce drag] on the wheels.
"Zeke"—Mitsubishi Zero-3, Navy, single-engine, fighter, formerly known as "Zero."

other, and the fighters seemed more anxious to avoid their own destruction than to defend their charges. No fewer than twenty-five Japanese planes were shot down in this dogfight, and others were so badly damaged that they could not get back to their carriers, for only twenty-seven out of the sixty-nine returned. A few made it through and attacked Lee's battle line, and one of them made a bomb hit on the battleship *South Dakota*, killing twenty-seven men and wounding twenty-three, but the ship was unhurt. By 1057, Raid I had been repelled or destroyed.

Unconscious of the disaster that had struck Raid I, Ozawa was launching Raid II when another disaster hit from another direction—from beneath the sea.

Vice Admiral Charles A. Lockwood, ComSubPac, had carefully moved his submarines in a line across the projected track of the Japanese fleet, and his rewards were great this day. At approximately 0800, *Albacore* poked up her periscope and her skipper, Commander J. W. Blanchard, spotted a group of Japanese ships, including an aircraft carrier. As he maneuvered to gain attack position, a second carrier loomed up over the horizon, and Blanchard decided to go after her since she was in an easier attack position. At 0808 he ran up the periscope for a final observation, and it was obvious that the torpedo data computer was not indicating a correct solution. The carrier was already passing the optimum firing point, so Blanchard fired by a combination of computer and seaman's eye. Six torpedoes leaped out of the forward tubes and began their run toward the target which happened to be the *Taiho*, Japan's newest and largest carrier, proudly flying Admiral Ozawa's eight-rayed flag.

Blanchard could not know this. All he knew was that he had fired at a carrier, and with so many ships around it was time to get out of there. The sight of torpedo tracks would bring destroyers swarming on him. He pulled the plug and went deep. He heard a muffled explosion, but thought it was too little to have troubled a carrier very greatly. Cursing his TDC, he continued his patrol, and did not even bother to report his attack by radio.

He had done better than he knew.

On the flag bridge of the *Taiho* Admiral Ozawa was watching his flagship launch her contribution to Raid II. Suddenly a plane which had just taken off did a wingover and dived into the sea. Its pilot, Warrant Officer Akio Komatsu, had spotted one of *Albacore*'s torpedoes swimming toward the flagship and heroically crash-dived it to save his ship.

His sacrifice was in vain. Another torpedo struck *Taiho*'s starboard side. At first the damage seemed slight, and the carrier went on launching the forty-two planes she was contributing to Raid II. Although no one knew it, *Taiho* had received her death wound. The torpedo had ruptured one or more gasoline tanks, and an ill-trained damage-control officer ordered all the ventilating ducts opened and the fans operated at full blast in the belief that these measures would clear the gasoline fumes from the ship. All that he succeeded in doing was to distribute the deadly vapors into every nook and cranny so that she became a floating bomb that any tiny spark could set off. At 1532 the inevitable happened. She suddenly exploded with a terrific roar that turned the flight deck from a prairie into a mountain range, blasted out the sides and tore holes in the bottom. Everyone in the engine spaces was killed, and the ship began to go down. Admiral Ozawa, carefully taking the Emperor's portrait with him, shifted his flag temporarily to a destroyer and then to the cruiser *Haguro*. The stricken *Taiho* went down a few minutes later, taking with her some 1650 men and thirteen aircraft.

To return to Raid II. Launched at 0856, it was the largest one of the day, no fewer than 128 aircraft being assigned to the strike, with 2 additional ones to serve as scouts. We have already seen what happened to one of them. Engine trouble forced 8 others to turn back. On the way toward TF 58, they showed the poor judgment of flying over Vice Admiral Takeo Kurita's Van Force, which had been stationed 100 miles ahead. Kurita's green gunners opened up on their fellows and splashed 2 and damaged 8 more before officers could get them under control. While the damaged 8 turned back to their carriers, the

98

surviving 111 flew on together in a single group and were picked up by radar at 1107 when they were 115 miles from TF 58. When they still had 60 miles to go, they were given a warm reception by Hellcats which clawed some 70 of them from the skies. The undaunted remainder attacked Lee's battle line about 1145, and a good number were shot down. One of them crashed into the *Indiana* at the waterline, but her torpedo failed to explode, and the only damage was to the paintwork. Six Judy bombers eluded both the interception by fighters and the antiaircraft fire of the battle line and attacked TG 58.2. The *Wasp* and *Bunker Hill* were both lightly damaged, and three men were killed on the latter carrier. The two survivors of this attack flew on to the Marianas, where they landed on two of the few remaining undamaged airstrips.

Only thirty-one planes returned to the Japanese carriers from Raid II, and sixteen of them were those with engine trouble or damage from their own Van Force.

Raid III was far luckier than the first two, for most of the 47 planes that made it up were vectored in the wrong direction and found nothing but empty ocean. The smaller of the two sections ran into a flight of Hellcats and was lucky to get off with the loss of only seven. Most of the Hellcats were diverted to another radar target, which turned out to be a cloud. The Japanese got forty planes back from this raid.

There followed a lull in the battle for the Americans, for the radar screens showed no targets. Mitscher launched a search mission but it found nothing. Hellcats which had been long in the air landed on their carriers for the planes to be refueled and rearmed and the pilots and crewmen to get a bite to eat before taking off again.

Raid IV, launched between 1100 and 1130, was another big one, eighty-two planes strong, and it, too, headed in the wrong direction. Finding nothing at the designated point, it headed for Rota and Guam to refuel. The smaller group, one headed for Rota, spotted Montgomery's TG 58.2 and drove in to attack while the carriers were recovering aircraft. The *Wasp* and *Bunker Hill* were again the targets, but both escaped with nothing worse than superficial damage. At least ten planes were shot down. The larger group, which was bound for Guam, was picked up by radar, and a combat air patrol was sent to intercept. They were almost over Guam when the CAP leader, Commander Gaylord B. Brown, reported, "Forty enemy planes circling Orote Field at Angels 3 [3,000 feet], some with wheels down." Other Hellcats joined Brown's CAP, and together they succeeded in shooting down thirty of the forty-nine planes attempting to land. The other nineteen were so damaged that they could never fly again. Of this raid, Ozawa lost all but nine.

While the Hellcats were disposing of the planes in Ozawa's four raids, Helldivers and Avengers were working over the airfields on Guam. A captured Japanese diary tells how it felt: "The enemy, circling overhead, bombed our airfield the whole day long. When evening came our carrier bombers [from Raid IV] returned, but the airfield had been destroyed by the enemy and they . . . had to crash . . . I was unable to watch dry-eyed."

Ozawa's troubles for June 19 have not yet all been told. Once again disaster struck from below when his attention was on the skies. The submarine *Cavalla*, at 1218, fired a spread of six torpedoes at a Japanese carrier and hit with three of them. Her victim was the large carrier *Shokaku*, one of the six that had carried the Japanese planes that had attacked Pearl Harbor. Commander H. J. Kossler took the *Cavalla* deep as soon as he had fired and began twisting and turning his boat to escape the wrath of the infuriated Japanese destroyers. He counted 106 depth charge explosions. About two and a half hours after he dived, he heard rumblings and explosions which were the death throes of the *Shokaku*. Five of the Pearl Harbor carriers had been accounted for; there remained only the *Zuikaku* to finish off before America's revenge would be complete.*

This air battle, immediately dubbed "The Marianas Turkey Shoot," was the largest carrier battle in history. And never was

---

* The other four, *Hiryu, Soryu, Kaga*, and *Akagi*, were sunk in the Battle of Midway, June 4, 1942.

one so one-sided. American plane losses had been 23 shot down and six destroyed accidentally. Only 130 out of the 373 Ozawa had sent against the Americans returned to their carriers. Another 50 were destroyed among the force based on Guam. Others went down in the sunken carriers, and an unknown number were lost operationally. This one day, Ozawa had lost about 315 planes and two aircraft carriers. Japanese naval air power had been virtually destroyed.

Admiral Ozawa, however, was not ready to call it quits. He did not yet realize the extent of the disaster that had befallen him. True, he had lost two carriers, but he still had a formidable force of seven remaining. Only 130 planes had returned from his strikes, but he confidently believed that a large number of his missing birds were on Guam and Rota, ready to be called into action again when needed. He planned to refuel on June 20 and to renew the action the next day. He believed, at least in part, reports from his pilots that four American carriers had been sunk, another six set afire, and huge numbers of American planes shot down. That night Tokyo's Lie Factory claimed eleven American carriers and many other ships sunk.

Admiral Toyoda, however, saw the situation differently and ordered Ozawa to break off the action and withdraw. A-Go had failed.

By nightfall on June 19, Mitscher's carrier force was only twenty miles west of Rota. Detaching Harrill's TG 58.4, which was low on fuel, to rendezvous with oilers and at the same time keep the pressure on the Japanese airfields on Rota and Guam, Mitscher's other three task groups made good a northerly course while recovering aircraft, and then, at 2000, headed west after the Japanese fleet. Mitscher bent on 23 knots in hopes of closing the distance between him and the enemy. He wished he could order greater speed, but dared not, for that would leave his destroyers with too little fuel to fight the action he hoped for the next day.

It seems strange that Mitscher, hoping for a fight as early as possible the next day, sent out no night searches. Perhaps the reason was concern for his pilots who he believed were dog tired after a day of battle. But the Avenger pilots had not had a hard day and were ready to go. The probable reason was his realization that turning into the wind to launch aircraft would cost at least forty miles in his long stern chase after Ozawa. Whatever the reason, no night searches were flown.

The next morning, at 0530, a search was sent out covering the 40° sector from 275° to 315° for a distance of 325 miles. This search missed Ozawa by a mere seventy-five miles and might have found his ships steaming aimlessly around attempting to fuel. The oilers were at the designated rendezvous, but the scattered combatant ships had depended on the sunken *Taiho* as a reference point. During the early afternoon, Ozawa transferred his flag to the *Zuikaku* in order to have access to her superior communications equipment, and here it was he learned the sad truth that he had only 100 operational aircraft remaining on his carriers and 27 float planes on the battleships and cruisers. The 27 were useful for scouting but that was all. Despite this crushing news, Ozawa was not ready to throw in the towel. He had not received Toyoda's order to withdraw, and he believed the air strength on Guam and Rota had been reinforced by planes flown down from Iwo Jima and up from Yap and Truk. Tomorrow he would hit again.

Confusion still was the order of the day among the Japanese ships in their attempts to refuel, but the skies above remained empty of American planes. Perhaps the Americans had had enough. This notion was dispelled at 1615 when the cruiser *Atago* reported that she had intercepted a message from an American plane reporting the sighting of the Japanese fleet. Half an hour later, Ozawa cancelled the fueling attempts and ordered a retirement at 24 knots.

It was time that Ozawa got out of there. Indeed, he had left his withdrawal until too late.

At 1330, Task Force 58 launched another 325-mile search, again to the northwest. On through the beautiful afternoon droned the Hellcats and Avengers. At 1542, Lieutenant Robert S. Nelson, USNR, spotted part of Ozawa's force and flashed a voice radio contact. Aboard the flagship *Lexington*, Nelson's words came in so garbled that no one could make anything of it. All that Mitscher could know was that a pilot had seen something.

Wasting no time, he ordered the pilots to stand by and told Spruance that he intended to make an all-out strike, even though this would inevitably mean that his fliers would have to return to their carriers after dark. It was a risk he would have to take.

Fortunately for Mitscher, Nelson kept broadcasting his report over and over, and Mitscher received a complete copy at 1557. A few minutes later, Nelson corrected the report, which placed the Japanese in position 14° 30′ North, 134° 30′ East. This was about 275 miles from TF 58, some 75 miles farther than the range at which American carrier planes were designed to accept combat.

In the ready rooms of the carriers, large letters on the blackboards said GET THE CARRIERS! There was quick briefing, a few whistles from the pilots when they learned how far they would have to fly, and then the bullhorns blared, "Pilots, man your planes!" A few minutes later came the order, "Start engines," and the propellers of 216 Hellcats, Avengers, and Dauntlesses kicked over, the engines coughed, backfired, and began to run smoothly. The carriers swung into the wind at 1621 and broke all previous records by launching in ten minutes. All planes carried wing tanks or belly tanks for extra gasoline. Throttled back to 130 to 140 knots to conserve fuel, they set out on the long flight. There was time to wonder about the forthcoming battle, about whether they would spot the Japanese, about the fuel consumption curves, about the difficulty of the long flight back to their own carriers, with themselves or their crewmen possibly wounded, and of the difficulties of locating blacked-out carriers in the darkness and of landing aboard a carrier at night for the first time in their lives.

Yet theirs was a special privilege. They alone out of the 98,618 men embarked in Task Force 58 would have the chance to come to grips with the Japanese fleet. They nursed their throttles and flew on.

Just as the sun was touching the water, they came upon the Japanese. There was no time to organize—the fuel supply would not permit the luxury of doing so. They bored in for attack at once.

They were lucky. Ozawa had neglected to re-form his battle line or to put his ships in an effective antiaircraft disposition.

For twenty minutes the American pilots attacked everything they saw. The desperate Japanese maneuvered every ship independently, racing about with near collisions the order of the day, and throwing up intense antiaircraft fire that exploded in a dazzle of colors from dye-loaded shells—"blue, yellow, lavender, pink, red, white, and black," to quote the *Bunker Hill* action report. The first victims were the oilers *Genyo* and *Seiyo Maru* which were dive bombed and left ablaze. They were scuttled by their own crews that night.

"Get the Carriers!" The airmen did their best, and their best was very good, although not as good as they thought. Lieutenant George B. Brown, USNR, led the attack on the large carrier *Hiyo*, and his section got two torpedo hits on her at the cost of his own life. His two crewmen, who had bailed out in time, landed safely in the water and were spectators of the last throes of the *Hiyo*.* The carrier, blazing from stem to stern, went down about two hours after darkness had fallen. Carrier *Ryuho* was reported to be blazing, with flames 200 feet in the air, but whatever damage she incurred was more spectacular than real, for she was not listed as damaged in the Japanese records and did not have to go to a shipyard for repair.

The last survivor of the Pearl Harbor carriers, *Zuikaku*, was strafed and received several bomb hits that began unmanageable fires on the hangar deck. The order to abandon ship was given and then rescinded as damage-control parties began to

---

* They were rescued the next day when TF 58 passed through these waters looking for survivors.

get things in check. *Zuikaku* made it back to Kure and was repaired in time for the Battle for Leyte Gulf in October. The light carrier *Chiyoda*, the heavy cruiser *Maya*, and the battleship *Haruna* were also hit but survived.

While the bombers and torpedo planes were working over Ozawa's ships, the Hellcats were doing a job on his remaining planes. The determined Japanese had thrown everything they could into the air to defend their ships, and the pilots paid a heavy price. Of the even 100 carrier aircraft and 27 search planes Ozawa had remaining at 1800, the American fighters accounted for 64 of the former and 12 of the latter. A sad note appears in Ozawa's flag log for this date:

Surviving carrier air power: 35 aircraft operational.

This number was what remained out of 430 he had less than forty-eight hours earlier.

Twenty American planes were lost in this attack, but some of the pilots and crews were later recovered. The remaining 196 began the long, desperate flight home, the pilots keeping one eye on their gas gauges and the other on the horizon for any glimpse of American ships. Some planes, which had been engaged in heavy combat and had accordingly used more fuel, had no chance at all of making it. One pilot announced over the radio that he was going to splash down while he still had power. Another whole section of four planes went down at the same time so that they could help each other in the water. On flew the rest, some of them damaged, and some of the pilots wounded. But there was nothing else to do. It was that or go into the ocean.

In the *Lexington* Admiral Mitscher was making a hard decision. Most of the pilots in the air had never made a night landing on a carrier, and in the darkness there was little chance for them to spot the ships in any case. On the other hand, Mitscher was known throughout the Navy for his concern for his pilots. He would take enormous chances to save their lives, and he took one now.

Turning to his Chief of Staff, Captain Arleigh A. Burke, he said in his soft voice, "Turn on the lights."

In enemy waters, where Japanese submarines were known to be operating, Mitscher gambled his fleet to save his pilots. When he said, "Turn on the lights," he did not mean the deck-edge lights on the carriers which would faintly outline the landing area. He meant everything. Every ship turned on the red truck lights and those at the yardarms. Floodlights illuminated flight decks, red and green running lights were turned on, and some destroyers fired star shells. In each task group a 36-inch searchlight was turned on pointing directly up into the sky as a homing beacon.

The pilots began coming in. Inevitably there were foul-ups and scenes of confusion. Landing signal officers in their stations on the port quarter of the flight decks held out their illuminated paddles to coax the planes into the groove for landing. Some of the fortunate ones got "the cut," as the landing signal officers chopped down with the right hand in a signal to land. These pilots would chop their throttles and the planes would set down with a squeal of tortured rubber as the wheels hit the flight decks and their tail hooks caught the arrester wires. Too often the approach was wrong or the flight deck was foul, and the planes would get a wave-off and have to rejoin the landing circle to try again. Some of them didn't make it. They ran out of gas and went into the water. Fortunately, most of those who did were rescued by the destroyers which were running around like sheep dogs rounding up their flocks.

Some crack-ups occurred on the decks of the carriers, and if a plane looked badly damaged, deck crews would extricate the pilots and airmen and then plane pushers would manhandle the wreck over the side in order to permit others to land. Soon the order went out, "Any plane land on any carrier." It would be time enough to sort things out the next day.

Some pilots were understandably confused. An Avenger

made three passes over the destroyer *Owen* before running out of gas and splashing on her port bow. Commander Robert W. Wood backed his ship down emergency full and got the three men before they were really wet. As the pilot came up on the deck of the *Owen*, he looked up at her truck lights which were moving gently as the ship rolled in the slight sea. "So that's what those damned things were," he said. "I thought they were the paddles of the landing signal officer and couldn't figure out why I didn't get a cut."

By 2252 it was all over. Every plane had either landed or was down in the sea. The scene, perhaps the most spectacular operation in the Pacific war, was described by one pilot as "a Mardi Gras setting fantastically out of place here, midway between the Marianas and the Philippines."

Thanks to the destroyers, only sixteen pilots and thirty-three aircrewmen were lost of the 100 planes expended that day, twenty in attacking Ozawa, and eighty during the recovery. Mitscher's gamble had paid off.

The next morning, TF 58 began a long, stern chase of Ozawa's retiring force. It was a slow one, for Spruance still did not want to uncover the Saipan beachhead. Since Ozawa was making 20 knots toward Japan, and TF 58 only 16 in order not to miss any downed aviators, there was no chance whatever of Mitscher catching up. The only thing this westward sweep might accomplish was to find a few Japanese cripples which could be given the *coup de grâce,* and to look for American aviators down in the sea. They found no enemy ships, but they saved fifty-nine airmen who had gone down the previous night.

Admiral Ozawa had been given the chance to fight his great Decisive Battle, and he had lost at every turn. Three carriers and two oilers had gone to the bottom, and this was a small score which disappointed the men of the U.S. Navy, for they were out for blood. But the action really destroyed every carrier in the Japanese Navy, for there were practically no pilots left to fly from them. In the largest sea battle in the history of the world to be fought only four months later, the Japanese carriers would be reduced to the role of decoy, only a pitiful handful of aircraft aboard.

Ozawa fought the Decisive Battle, but the decision went against him.

CHAPTER THREE

# Victory Is Everywhere

*Victory is everywhere.*

Winston Churchill

*If the people command me to continue*
*in this office and in this war*
*I have as little right to withdraw*
*as the soldier has to leave*
*his post in the line.*

Franklin Delano Roosevelt

T HE Republicans gathered in the sweltering heat of Chicago in late June and early July for perhaps the most lackluster convention they had ever held. There was no trace of the excitement and drama that had been seen in Philadelphia four years earlier. It was all a foregone conclusion. While Thomas E. Dewey remained at home in Albany, his managers lost no time in getting the convention organized in their own way. Dewey's men came to Chicago with only 33 delegates officially pledged to him, but another 377 were "committed." Thus his early tally was only 120 votes short of the 530 required for the nomination. There was no question that he would find them among the 403 delegates reported as "leaning his way."

As the delegates sweltered and fanned themselves, Ohio's Robert Taft ground out the party platform. The only point of interest in it was the foreign policy plank which was drafted by Michigan Senator Arthur Vandenberg. Once an isolationist, Vandenberg had become one of the most respected experts on foreign policy in the Senate. The plank supported close ties with

109

America's allies and some kind of "peace-keeping" international organization after the war.

While the big shots worked, the rank-and-file delegates amused themselves watching the famous and the hangers-on who always came to conventions. There was Jeff Davis, "King of the Hoboes," and Mr. J. Worthington Scranton, who ruled over the Pennsylvania delegation. There was old Joe Grundy, also from Pennsylvania, arguing as ever for high tariffs and against reciprocal trade treaties. From the arguments of some of the delegates, one would wonder if they realized there was a war on.

The convention lasted six days, but its business might have been done in one. The delegates approved the platform—it was neither better nor worse than usual, and it meant as little. Then they came to the business of nominating the man who would carry the Republican banner until November.

Thomas E. Dewey, the "Racket Buster from New York," had come to national fame as District Attorney for New York County. Such unworthies as "Legs" Diamond, "Dutch" Schultz, and "Lucky" Luciano had found their underworld careers suddenly interrupted by Prosecutor Dewey's courtroom skill. During his term of office, he prosecuted seventy-three cases. He won seventy-two convictions.

Born in Owosso, Michigan, Dewey had been graduated from the University of Michigan, had then gone on to Columbia University Law School, joining a New York law firm when he had finished his studies. His rise in Republican politics in New York was rapid, and by 1938 he was ready for the job of District Attorney for New York County. His spectacular success against the racketeers indicated that he was ready for better things, and in 1942, he organized a superb political steam roller that installed him in the Governor's Mansion in Albany. He was only forty.

Now, at forty-two, he was ready to try for the highest stake of all.

Governor Dwight Griswold of Nebraska placed Dewey's name in nomination. A demonstration ensued. It was brief, but meticulously planned. Then John Bricker, who had hoped for the nomination, strode to the platform. It was the obvious wish of the convention, he said, to make the nomination of Dewey unanimous. He called for the vote.

The nomination was not unanimous. One delegate from Wisconsin had come to vote for MacArthur. He did so. The result: Dewey, 1,056; MacArthur, 1.

Later, after Dewey's choice for a Vice President had been made known, another vote was held. The result: Bricker, 1,057.

Two weeks later, in the same stadium, using the same lumber and the same seats, the Democrats moved in. Missing was one of the real old guard, Big Jim Farley, who had masterminded Roosevelt's first two Presidential campaigns. He had broken with F.D.R. over the third term issue, and now, with a fourth term in sight, he left the political arena.

There was no doubt about the nominee for President. Everyone knew that only Roosevelt could carry the country in face of the rising dissatisfaction with affairs at home. The war was not being won fast enough, and the shortages at home meant that someone was responsible. Any Democratic candidate except Roosevelt would have succumbed to the combination of discontent and the popularity of Tom Dewey with millions of voters.

Although it had been an open secret for weeks, F.D.R. broke the uncertainty just before the convention opened with a letter to the Chairman of the Democratic National Committee, Robert Hannegan.

> If the convention should nominate me for the Presidency, I shall accept. If the people elect me, I will serve.
> If the people command me to continue in this office and in this war I have as little right to withdraw as the soldier has to leave his post in the line.
> For myself I do not want to run. By next spring, I shall have been President and Commander in Chief of the armed forces for twelve years. . . . All that is within me cries out to go back to my home on the Hudson River.
> Reluctantly, but as a good soldier, I repeat that I will accept and serve in this office, if I am so ordered by the Commander in Chief of us all—the sovereign people of the United States.

After that, the Presidential nomination was a mere formality. The roll call of states ended at 6:57 P.M., Wednesday, July 19, with the final result: Roosevelt, 1,086; Senator Harry F. Byrd, 89; James A. Farley, 1.

The question of who would be the Vice Presidential nominee nearly split the convention wide open. Four years earlier, when Roosevelt had dumped John Nance Garner and rammed Secretary of Agriculture Henry A. Wallace down the conventioneers' throats, Wallace had come close to being the most disliked man in America, at least by the party leaders. Now in Chicago, he had surprising strength. The CIO Political Action Committee rallied behind the Wallace boom, for of all men in public office at the time, he was the farthest left, the most sympathetic to the needs and aspirations of labor.

The astute President Roosevelt, however, seemed to have sensed a shift to the right in the feelings of voters. Certainly the strikes and threats of strikes had not endeared Big Labor and labor leaders to men and women whose sons and husbands were fighting the enemies of the United States. Then, too, Wallace had embarrassed the administration over food shortages and squabbling with other food officials. His position was by no means secure.

Before he left Washington for Chicago, Wallace had a delegate-counting, showdown luncheon with the President. F.D.R. did not promise him the nomination. He did promise him he would send a letter to the convention.

When the letter came, it was addressed to the convention's permanent chairman, Senator Samuel Jackson of Indiana, and it was not what Wallace was looking for. The President wrote that if he were a delegate to the convention he would vote for Henry Wallace for Vice President. So far, so good. Then he threw Wallace to the wolves. He did not, he continued, wish to appear to be dictating to the convention. Obviously the convention would have to consider carefully the pros and cons of all the candidates.

This letter was the kiss of death for Wallace, although he didn't realize it. In refusing to state that he wanted Wallace,

F.D.R. threw the convention wide open—for a time. He would get it under control again later.

Prime candidates were James F. Byrnes, Alben Barkley, William O. Douglas, and, of course, Wallace. A name that was being heard with increasing frequency was that of Harry S Truman.

On July 20, Roosevelt delivered his acceptance speech by radio from Washington. He stressed the Democratic record of experience and accomplishment and doubted that the American people would wish to turn the job over "to inexperienced or immature hands."

As soon as the President's speech was over, and the dutiful applause had died away, the convention was supposed to turn to the nominations for Vice President. Then the galleries started chanting, and the chants were taken up on the floor. We Want Wallace! WE WANT WALLACE!

The party bosses, Bob Hannegan, Ed Kelly, Mayor of Chicago, and Ed Flynn of New York went into a huddle. Then Chairman Jackson strode to the rostrum and pounded on the gavel. The crowd refused to be quiet. Patiently Jackson kept on pounding but got nowhere. Finally he called for adjournment. A loud roar of "No!" shook the stadium, but Jackson murmured, "The Ayes have it," and adjourned the session.

Things had nearly gotten out of hand, and it had been touch-and-go whether the nomination of Henry Wallace would be shouted through in spite of all the bosses could do to stop it. Now there was time to regroup and reorganize.

Wallace still had the most delegates, but he did not have the President and he did not have the bosses. It was a question of who would have the nod.

Alben Barkley might have been the heir apparent had his defiance of the President over the tax bill not cooled their relations. Jimmy Byrnes was too valuable where he was as head of the Office of War Mobilization. Any chance he might have had evaporated when labor leaders Sidney Hillman and Philip Murray announced they would not support him.

That left Harry Truman. He was acceptable to labor and he

was acceptable to the President. The question was: Was he acceptable to the convention and to the American people?

Truman had come to Washington with the reputation of being something of a political hack. He owed his political life to Kansas City's old Pendergast machine. He had been rewarded for his faithful attention to political chores by a seat in the U.S. Senate. "I'm a Jackson County organization Democrat," he had once said, "and I'm proud of it."

Since the war had begun, however, Truman had chaired a watchdog Senate committee to keep an eye on war production, war producers, and on the way government money was spent in general. His committee had done such a magnificent job, completely without regard to politics, that it brought only praise to its chairman—except from those whose chicaneries it exposed. The record of the Truman Committee seemed good enough to offset the background of Pendergast.

When the convention reconvened the next morning, everything was organized. Mayor Kelly had increased the number of Chicago police on hand to keep things orderly. Every ticket was checked at least twice, and many of those who had set up the chanting the night before found that their tickets were no longer valid. Those who were admitted to the stadium were going to be more disciplined, or Mayor Kelly would know the reason why.

For four dreary hours nominating and seconding speeches droned on. Truman's name was placed in nomination by his fellow senator from Missouri, Bennett Clark. Wallace was proposed by State Supreme Court Justice Richard Mitchell of Iowa.

Then there were the nominations of those whose chances were hopeless, like Alben Barkley, and the favorite sons: Paul V. McNutt of Indiana, Scott Lucas of Illinois, Governor J. Melville Broughton of North Carolina, Senator John H. Bankhead of Alabama, Senator Joseph O'Mahoney of Wyoming, and Supreme Court Justice Frank Murphy of Michigan. None of these men had any chance, but, properly used, their delegate strength might mean future influence in the administration.

The first roll call began. No one expected it to be conclusive, as Wallace's delegates remained with him. When it was over, the leaders were: Wallace, 429½ votes; Truman, 319½; Bankhead, 98; Barkley, 49½; Lucas, 61; the rest scattered, including 1 vote for a Washington correspondent who regularly ran as a gag on a platform against the recurrence of the Johnstown Flood and the Chicago Fire.

Everyone knew the second ballot might be decisive, depending on which way the major states voted. If Truman failed to gain substantially on the second ballot, he was through, and Wallace would probably run away with the convention.

A quarter of the way through the roll call, Wallace was ahead of Truman 148 to 125. Seven important states passed in order to see which way the bandwagon was going. The break came when Ed Flynn swung New York's 74½ votes to Truman, putting him ahead 246 to 187.

Halfway through the roll call, Truman led 342 to 286 for Wallace, but the Wallacemen were not through. As they cajoled and pleaded with delegates, the gap narrowed until it was Truman, 400; Wallace, 395. Needed to win—589.

While the bosses watched and listened nervously, neither man was able to make any gain on the other. First Truman would gain and then Wallace, until the count stood at 477½ to 472½, Truman still holding a 5-vote lead.

The bosses conferred. Then Alabama's Bankhead withdrew and threw his 22 votes to Truman. South Carolina added another 18. The bandwagon rush was on. Governor Matt Neely of West Virginia added the final 13 votes to put Truman over. As state chairmen switched their delegations' votes, Wallace's count shrank and Truman's grew. The final tally was Truman, 1,031; Wallace, 105; Barkley, 6; Douglas, 4; McNutt, 1.

Once again, F.D.R. had forced the selection of a Vice Presidential candidate who clearly was not the first choice of the convention. It was of much greater importance this time than it had been in 1940, for few of the men whose influence really counted believed that Franklin Roosevelt had much chance of living out his fourth term. Their nominee for Vice

President might well become President of the United States. A good many delegates looked at Harry Truman and wondered.

Most Americans, when they could, listened to the conventions on the radio networks, but the only real moments of excitement were the roll-call votes. They also watched the proceedings a little later in the newsreel clips that preceded the feature movies at their local movie houses.

By this time war movies were distinctly on the wane. The people demanded and got escapism in the form of light comedy and musicals. A few exceptions to this fare were important, such as the screen biography *Wilson*, which was the most expensive film made to date, even without the mass battle and revelry scenes that were the trademark of Cecil B. De Mille. Alexander Knox starred in the title role.

The Hitchcock film *Lifeboat*, scripted by John Steinbeck, was less a war film than it was the study of the reactions of eight survivors of a sunken ship. The survivors were remarkably played by Henry Hull, Walter Slezak, William Bendix, Canada Lee, Mary Anderson, Tallulah Bankhead, Hume Cronyn, and Heather Angel.

Thrillers were also popular, and *The Lodger, Gaslight,* and *The Mask of Dimitrios* offered appropriate spine-tingling for the faithful. The best of the musicals was *Lady in the Dark,* with Ginger Rogers in the role made famous on Broadway by Gertrude Lawrence. Frank Sinatra took time off from the shrieking, fainting crowds of bobbysoxers to make his first movie, *Higher and Higher.* Sigmund Romberg's *Desert Song* was dusted off and given a new setting to capitalize on the public's recent awareness of North Africa.

Two of the most remarkable films of the year were *The Song of Bernadette* and *Going My Way.* The former was based on a novel by Franz Werfel about the French peasant girl whose vision of the Virgin Mary led to the shrine at Lourdes. Jennifer Jones gave an outstanding performance as Bernadette.

In *Going My Way,* one of the most extraordinary bits of miscasting led to a triumph. Bing Crosby played the part of a young priest sent as a trouble-shooter to a parish in difficulties because of the rigidity of Father Fitzgibbon, priest in charge. As the old priest, Barry Fitzgerald turned in his usual fine performance, but the real surprise was Crosby, who revealed greater depth of character and more sensitivity than had ever appeared in any of his previous screen roles.

Instead of fictional war movies, where Hollywood stars wiped out the Nazis and Japanese single-handed, real war scenes were shown in documentaries. Sometimes they were short features such as *Guadalcanal Diary*, which was partly fictional, or *In Our Time* or *Since You Went Away*, which dealt with noncombat parts of the war. A program called the *March of Time*, produced by *Time* magazine, gave regular short documentaries on the progress of the war.

No one could deny that the war was going reasonably well. By the time the Democrats had adjourned, the landing in Normandy was an accomplished fact, and the Americans were well on the way to finishing the campaign in the Marianas. Yet everyone knew that the war was not won, and it was going to take a lot more men to win it. And these new men would have to have the equipment and the weapons they needed.

There was a certain tendency among war workers and war producers to relax. Washington contributed to some extent to this feeling by canceling contracts for items no longer needed and allowing some factories to resume production of scarce civilian items. Some manufacturers deliberately cheated the government by falsified inspection records, but most of the cheaters were caught and went to jail. Harder to catch were the handfuls of workers in various plants who lay down on the job. Some would punch in at a shipyard and then find an empty compartment to sleep in for the eight-hour shift. Others played cards, or wandered about looking busy but doing nothing. Occasionally the goof-offs were protected by union leaders, but more often the union leaders saw to it that they got what was coming to them.

What hurt most was loss of deferment for work in an essential industry, and not a few of the men who had done nothing for a good day's pay found themselves doing a great deal more at considerably less pay in the Army.

The services were hungry as ever for men. The majority of the able-bodied men in the eighteen to twenty-six age group, most desired by the Army, had already gone into active service. Now the heat was on men who had been fathers at the time of Pearl Harbor. Only some 90,000 of them had been drafted. The Army looked with disfavor on the fathers, since most of them were over twenty-six. Where were the men to come from?

President Roosevelt suggested a harder look at deferments, and Draft Director Lewis B. Hershey issued appropriate instructions. Immediately industrialists howled, for where were they to get the men to keep production going? The Army and Navy leaders countered with the suggestion that they would settle for a little less production at the moment in order to get more men. Said an industrialist bitterly: "That's what they say now. In sixty days they'll be right back on our necks, yelling and raising hell about production, regardless of any agreements they make now."

It was estimated that Selective Service Draft Boards had fallen about 100,000 men behind quotas in the spring and would have to draft over a million men by mid-summer to catch up. Unless they could find the men from those classified as 4-F, some 250,000 would have to come from industry and agriculture. It was estimated that only some 200,000 of the 4-Fs would be acceptable to the Army. A surprising fact that had emerged was that of every four men reaching draft age, only three were suitable for unlimited service. A full 25 percent had disqualifying physical disabilities.

Nonetheless, the men had to be found, and they were. Factories trained older men and took more women. "Rosie the Riveter" became more than a song, and Tilly the taxi driver, and Bertha the bus driver, and Louise the lathe operator, and Sally the shipfitter and their sisters relieved their men to go to war.

A new difficulty—at least for smokers—was created by a sudden drying up of the supply of cigarettes. Almost overnight, all popular brands vanished. No more could a person ask for a pack of Luckies and get it. It took more than a mile-long walk to get a Camel. You could call in vain for Philip Morris. People had to make do with off-beat brands—Wings, Avalons, Spuds, and even less well known smokes.

An avid smoker would do almost anything for a cigarette. Cartons of the better brands became currency on the black market. You could get a steak or get a repair job done if you could come up with the proper number of cartons. Filter tips were not well known then, and they presented a particular hazard. Unwary smokers regularly lighted the wrong end. An agonized expression would come over the face of a person who did that. Then, with the realization that he could not afford to throw it away, he would grimace, break off the charred filter, and gamely puff on the burned-filter-flavored tobacco.

War was everywhere, it seemed, except in the Western Hemisphere. In Burma, Mountbatten's forces fought the heat and jungle in a campaign to reopen the way to China and capture Burma as well. It would not be until May 1945 that the victory would be won there.

The main attention of the American press was directed to the campaign going on in France, and there was little to spare for the rest of the world. Almost unnoticed was the surrender of Finland to the Russians after a short campaign extending from June 10, 1944, to September 4. Though the Finns fought heroically, they were hopelessly outclassed, and their German allies were less interested in the defense of Finland than they were in extricating their troops.

Following the capture of Rome, just two days before the Allies landed in France, there was high hope that the Italian campaign could be finished off quickly. At first the going was easy, and success was taken for granted. Civitavecchia fell on June 7, giving the Allies another seaport, and the capture of the Viterbo complex of airfields on June 9 insured absolute Allied air superiority. The French took the island of Elba in a surprise assault. General Alexander knew that Kesselring had been preparing a new defense line, called the Gothic Line, extending across Italy to take advantage of a mountain chain dividing central Italy from the Po Valley. It ran across from a point midway between Pisa and La Spezia on the west coast south of

Bologna to a point on the Adriatic south of Lake Commacchio. Alexander hoped to penetrate the line before its defenses were completed.

He might have done so had he not been forced to give up seven divisions in preparation for the forthcoming invasion of southern France. Further, he was stripped of a group of bombers and twenty-three squadrons of fighters, also reserved for the invasion. The result was that the Fifteenth Army Group remaining in Italy was too weak to force a decision. By August 4, two months after the capture of Rome, the Allies in Italy had advanced 270 miles in sixty-four days and had reached the Arno and had taken Ancona on the eastern coast.

As Alexander was stripped of forces, Kesselring got more. Hitler sent him eight additional divisions of varying quality, one each from Denmark, Holland, and Russia, two from the Balkans, and three reserve divisions from Germany intended for use on the Russian Front.

Alexander, nevertheless, had a plan. He moved the main weight of the British Eighth Army, now commanded by Lieutenant General Sir Oliver Leese, to the Adriatic side, hoping to slip around Kesselring's left end. To draw the German attention, Clark's Fifth Army made obvious preparations for an offensive in an effort to convince Kesselring that the main blow would be in the west.

The Eighth Army jumped off on August 25 and caught the Germans flatfooted. The attack carried through to Rimini, which was taken in early September. Using the excellent road network across northern Italy, Kesselring was able to rush reinforcements to slow the Eighth Army.

This movement enabled Alexander to implement the second part of his plan. The Fifth Army drove north from the Arno between Pisa and Florence and pushed Kesselring back to the main Gothic Line. When Kesselring moved to counter this threat, the Eighth Army was able to advance again. Ravenna was captured, and the Eighth Army moved up to the Gothic Line. Clark made a desperate effort to take Bologna, but was stopped only nine miles from the city.

By this time, the Italian weather was turning bad for military operations, and it became clear that no victory could be won that year. It was a bitter blow for the men fighting there, for they felt they could have won if they had not become the forgotten of the war in Europe.

The line was essentially stable during the fall of 1944 and into the spring of 1945. Small advances were made in the east, but both sides were waiting for spring before undertaking any significant military operations. During this time, most of the major commanders in Italy were changed. Kesselring was relieved by General S. von Vietinghoff in order to take command of the defenses of Germany. Alexander assumed command of the Mediterranean theater, and was relieved by Mark Clark as Commanding General of the Fifteenth Army Group. General Lucian Truscott took over the Fifth Army, and Lieutenant General R. L. McCreery replaced Leese in command of the Eighth.

By spring, the Fifteenth Army Group had become a polyglot organization. Some veteran divisions were transferred to the Western Front and had been replaced by Italian units. Also there was a Jewish brigade, and the Nisei 442nd Regimental Combat Team, and a Brazilian division. Before these additions, the Army Group had included American, British, French, New Zealand, Canadian, South African, Gurkha, Indian, and Polish units. The logistic and language difficulties are best left to the imagination.

Once the Allies got past the mountain range and into the Po Valley, armored units would be able to operate effectively. The drive began in April 1945. Vietinghoff's defenses were turned in the east by the Eighth Army and penetrated near Bologna by the Fifth. He could only fall back, constantly scourged by Allied air power. Italian partisans then rose, but since they were of widely differing political beliefs, they did as much damage to each other as they did to the Germans.

By late April, the German position in Italy was disintegrating just as it was everywhere else. On April 29, Vietinghoff agreed to an unconditional surrender to be effective May 2 at noon. This was the first major capitulation in Europe of large-scale German forces, but it was soon to be followed by others.

Ever since the landings in Normandy, the Italian campaign had become something of a sideshow as far as the Combined Chiefs of Staff were concerned. They were mainly interested in what was happening in France and what was about to happen in Russia.

Stalin had promised Churchill and Roosevelt that the Red Army would undertake a major offensive a few days after the Anglo-American forces landed in Normandy. On June 23, 1944, the promised offensive began, with its main thrust this time directed north of the Pripet Marshes.

Once again Hitler had refused to follow the sensible plan of shortening his line in Russia to one that could be held. A line running from Riga in the north, through Lwow, and along the Dniester River, with defenses in depth, would have given him a mobile reserve and very possibly enabled him to stop the Red Army. Instead, he looked at the map and saw that this plan would mean withdrawal of 200 miles or more in the north. He could not stand the idea. He designated certain positions as "fortresses" to be held to the last man. He forbade the construction of defenses in depth, thinking that such defenses would merely encourage the army units to fall back on them.

His orders were obeyed, with disastrous results for the Germans.

The Russian assault was initially directed against the German Army Group Center. The night before it began, Russian guerrillas rose in concerted attack in the rear of the German positions, crippling the communications facilities of Army Group Center.

The Russians opened with the largest artillery barrage the Germans had yet seen. It was reported that the Russians had massed 400 cannon or heavy mortars every mile along a 350-mile front—a total of 140,000 pieces of artillery. They had complete control of the air, since almost all of the Luftwaffe had been withdrawn to defend the Fatherland.

Most of Army Group Center units were drawn off in a futile defense of Hitler's "fortresses." The Red Army simply bypassed the "fortresses" and kept going. The isolated units were mopped up later by following troops.

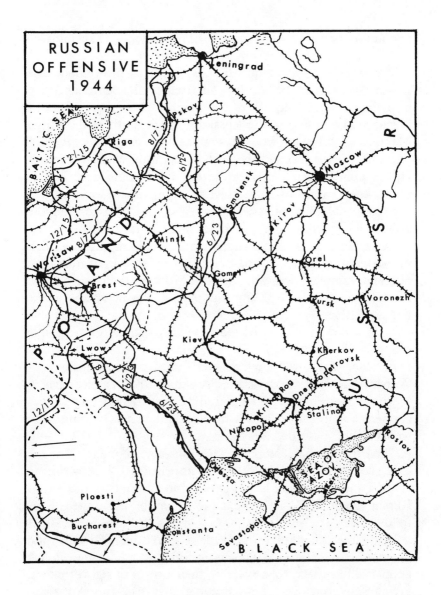

RUSSIAN
OFFENSIVE
1944

In ten days the Russians had driven a 250-mile gap in the German line, and Army Group Center had practically ceased to exist. Field Marshal Model, who was sometimes called "the Führer's fireman," took over in the center and rallied what was left and what was sent him. He was able to make a successful counterattack east of Warsaw at Radzymin, slowing the Russians temporarily.

The respite in the center did the Germans little good. The Russians struck in the north and reached the sea near Riga, trapping Army Group North in Estonia. Two days after the northern attack began, the Russians struck south of the Pripet Marshes on July 14. Two weeks later Lwow fell, and by August 1, the Reds had reached the Vistula south of Warsaw. Since a goodly number of the German forces in the south were Panzer units, they were usually able to fight their way out of encirclements. But they lost many men in doing so, and the ground they were giving up would never be regained.

By August 7, the line temporarily stabilized, the German positions running southward from Riga as far as Bialystok, then bulging ominously westward toward Warsaw, then south again for 150 miles, before turning southeast to the Black Sea at the Dniester River.

Then followed one of the most controversial and most tragic events of the war.

As the Russians were pushing toward the outskirts of Warsaw, the Polish underground seized control of some parts of the city. The Polish guerrillas fully expected that they would cooperate with the Russians in liquidating the Germans who were still trying to defend Warsaw.

Then the Russians stopped. Or were they stopped?

Irreconcilable versions of what happened at Warsaw during August and September have appeared in accounts of the war in Russia. Each side has blamed the other for the tragedy that followed.

Ever since the fall of Poland, a government-in-exile had operated from London, beaming broadcasts to the Polish people suffering the Nazi yoke. In the name of this government, Polish ships had fought alongside the British and American navies in convoys trying to meet the U-boat scourge. Polish troops had fought the Germans in Italy and elsewhere, men fighting without hope for loved ones left behind. They counted their families as good as dead.

But there was a powerful communist movement in Poland,

and its leaders saw their opportunity as the Russians began to move across their land. When Lublin was liberated on July 23, they were quick to act. The Soviet government announced that the only desire of the Russian people was to liberate Poland and help them establish an independent, strong, and democratic country. This was enough for the communist leaders who were on the scene. The government-in-exile in London could be ignored. Thus a Polish Committee on National Liberation was formed, representing "democratic elements inside Poland," and "recognized by Poles abroad—in the first place by the Union of Polish Patriots in the USSR and by the Polish Army formed in the Soviet Union." The government in London was denounced as "fascist" and "usurpers."

As in the case of most communist takeovers, the Committee of National Liberation commanded the allegiance of only a small minority of the Polish people. But it was backed by Moscow, and most of the territory of Poland was still in German hands. What was not was occupied by Soviet troops. The underground in Warsaw still looked to London for leadership.

On the strength of a Moscow broadcast at the end of July, General Bor-Komorowski heeded the Soviet call for patriots in Warsaw to rise and strike at the Nazi invaders. He called his underground fighters to the attack, fully expecting that Soviet troops would soon be in the city to finish off the Germans.

Instead, the Russians stopped a few miles from the city, and the Germans began to exact a horrible revenge on the members of the underground. For two months this fighting-massacring went on, until 300,000 Poles had been killed, the lucky ones while fighting, the others at the hands of the Gestapo and SS.

During this time the British and Americans dropped supplies on the city for the use of the Polish patriots, but they could carry only small loads because of the distance they had to fly. The Russian authorities refused permission for the Western planes to land on Russian airfields to refuel before the flight back to their own bases. Nor did the Russians advance on Warsaw. In fact, the city was not taken until January 1945, by which time nine-tenths of the city had been destroyed.

The Russian counter to the accusations of the West that they were deliberately permitting the Polish patriots to be destroyed was that their armies could go no farther. Although they had a foothold on the west bank of the Vistula, they lacked the strength to exploit it and were barely able to hang on in face of fierce German counterattack. All along the front, the Russians had run out of steam.

This claim is entirely possible. The Russian offensive lasted six weeks along a 350-mile front, and the logistic difficulties were enormous, despite the meager demands Russian soldiers made. But machines must have fuel and guns must have ammunition. Soldiers must have rest, and casualties must be replaced.

A man with no axe to grind as between the Russian and the Western view of what happened at Warsaw gives as good an answer as is perhaps available. He is General Heinz Guderian, who had taken over the German Army High Command. Guderian wrote:

> The question has frequently been asked why the Russians, who knew all about the Warsaw uprising, did not do more to help it and indeed stopped their offensive along the line of the Vistula. There can be no doubt that the Poles who had risen regarded themselves as owing allegiance to their Government-in-Exile, which was located in London, and it was from there that they received their instructions. They exemplified those elements in Poland which were conservative and which looked towards the West. It may be assumed that the Soviet Union had no interest in seeing these elements strengthened by a successful uprising and by the capture of their capital. . . .
>
> Be that as it may, an attempt by the Russian XVI Tank Corps to cross the railway bridge over the Vistula at Deblin on July 25, 1944, had failed with the loss of thirty tanks. The bridge could be blown in time. Further Russian tank forces were stopped to the north of Warsaw. We Germans had the impression that it was our defense which halted the enemy rather than a Russian desire to sabotage the Warsaw uprising.

The truth may never be known. The best guess this author

can hazard is that while the Russian drive was stopped just short of Warsaw by the Germans, the Soviets did not try very hard to get it going again with any rapidity. They may have appealed in good faith for the Warsaw underground to rise, but when their troops were stopped they saw a real advantage in letting the Nazis do what had to be done. After all, it would save trouble later when such dissident elements would have to be eliminated as enemies of the Polish People's Republic.

While the dreadful struggle continued in Warsaw, Stalin turned his attention to his two flanks. The great opportunity for a Balkan empire, which had tempted Russia for ages, beckoned. The Second and Third Ukrainian Fronts smashed across the Dniester River and broke the German hold on the Black Sea anchor near Odessa. This offensive began on August 20, and by August 25 most of the German Sixth Army and part of the Eighth were encircled and forced to surrender. Many Rumanian units that were serving alongside the Germans deserted and went over to the Russians. The Ploesti area was overrun toward the end of August, and Bucharest fell September 1.

The Bulgarian government had seen the handwriting on the wall as early as August 26 and had withdrawn from the war. This move failed to save them. The Russians ignored the peace negotiations in progress, crossed the Danube, and overran the country. A puppet government was quickly formed, and on September 8 it declared war on Germany.

Faced with the absolute necessity of shortening the defensive line on the Eastern Front, Guderian was finally able to persuade Hitler to withdraw Army Group F from Greece and the Aegean islands. This movement would take some time, and it was harassed all the way by the Bulgarians and Tito's guerrillas. The Russian capture of Belgrade on October 20 limited the movement of Army Group F to the rail and road routes through Sarajevo on the western side.

While this was going on, Guderian concentrated his attention in extricating Schoerner's Army Group North which had been cut off in Estonia. A successful campaign forced a link-up with Schoerner, and Guderian ordered him to withdraw west into East Prussia. Schoerner began to obey and got as far as Latvia when he suddenly stopped, probably on orders from Hitler. The twenty divisions that were trapped there remained until the end of the war.

Between his moves north and south, Guderian soon had to turn to meet yet another Russian drive, this one aimed through Hungary at Budapest and Vienna. Forcing a crossing of the Transylvanian Alps, they moved northwestward, reaching the outskirts of Budapest on October 29, and winning a foothold across the Danube below the city four weeks later.

By December 15, a temporary lull came to the Eastern Front. While the Russians regrouped and prepared for the final offensive, Hitler was busy transferring some of his best units to the west to be used in a final desperate gamble in the Ardennes, an attack which was to become known as the Battle of the Bulge.


It was a pleasant summer day in Hartford, Connecticut, and thousands of women and children, with a few men who had sneaked off from work, were enjoying Ringling Brothers and Barnum & Bailey's Greatest Show on Earth. In the Big Top, high-wire performers were swinging about the main ring, their feats bringing gasps and applause from the audience. No one noted a little tongue of flame crawling up the side of the tent near the main entrance. Suddenly the flame took hold and in an instant had erupted up the entire side and was spreading across the top.

The crowd panicked. Some dropped children in back of the bleacher seats so they could get out under the canvas. Others jammed the exits. Then great blazing pieces of canvas began to fall. Women's dresses caught fire and so did their hair. Then the main poles came crashing down, bringing with them the rest of the flaming roof. Dozens were trapped.

Fire department equipment arrived and began putting out the fire and sorting out the dead. It was the worst circus disaster in memory. Undertaking establishments were jammed dealing with the 169 bodies. Hundreds of families grieved.

War shortages and the scarcity of labor had prevented proper treatment of the Big Top to render it fireproof.

There was no shortage of campaign oratory during the summer. Thomas E. Dewey ran a campaign of military precision. His special train rolled into every stop precisely on time. (It was late only once, by a few minutes, in Des Moines.) A brief speech to the crowd at the station, then a ride to the leading hotel where a press conference had been set up to be followed by a thirty-minute conference with local bigwigs. Then back to the station, and the train would move on. If he had a major speech, of course, the routine took a little longer, but it was the same. There was no nonsense. He cracked no jokes, he slapped no backs. He hammered at the inefficiency of the Democratic administration.

Until October, Franklin Roosevelt played the role of the wartime statesman-leader, above partisan politics. Then he took off the gloves. He referred to the Republican love of Labor, a love that lay dormant three years and nine months out of every four years. He reminded his listeners that the country's unpreparedness before Pearl Harbor was a result of Republican isolationist votes in Congress. Then with a mockery that Dewey could not match and probably could not understand, he said, "These Republican leaders have not been content with attacks on me, or on my wife, or on my sons—no, not content with that—they now include my little dog Fala. Well, of course, I don't resent attacks, and my family doesn't resent attacks, but Fala *does* resent them. You know, Fala is Scotch, and being a Scottie, as soon as he learned that the Republican fiction writers in Congress and out had concocted a story that I had left him behind on the Aleutian Islands and had sent a destroyer back to find him—at a cost to the taxpayers of two or three, or eight or twenty million dollars—his Scotch soul was furious. He has not been the same dog since."

The Fala story probably cost Dewey at least a million votes.*

The campaign went on, Dewey ever more desperately attacking Roosevelt's record, and Roosevelt striking back with ridicule. The President also stood on the war record, and since victory was clearly in the air, the people listened.

* See p. 156.

When the votes were counted, Roosevelt had carried thirty-six states with an electoral vote of 432. Dewey had managed to win 99 electoral votes from twelve states.

At a press conference in Washington two days later, irrepressible Paul Ward of the Baltimore *Sun* spoke up.

"Mr. President, may I be the first to ask if you will run in 1948?"

While the campaigning was going on, the war had never let up. The Americans had broken out at St. Lô, and the Anglo-American troops drove across France. Paris fell, and the way to Germany seemed open.

In the skies over Europe, it was no longer a question of whether bombing missions would get through to their targets. The Germans had lost control of the air. The Luftwaffe was helpless to defend the Fatherland.

But the Germans had struck back by air—not with aircraft, but with pilotless guided bombs known as V-1, and later with rockets known as V-2. Somewhat irreverently, the British called them "Bob Hopes"—from "bob down and hope!"

The V-weapon attacks had begun just after D-Day, on June 13, and they had been demoralizing at first. The V-1 was an inaccurate weapon, so that one could never know where it might hit. It was as impersonal as a bomb and more destructive than most.

Its sounds had an important psychological impact. There would be a roar in the skies, but never where the bomb was. Its jet engine carried it faster than sound. Then there would be an eerie silence as the jet engine cut out, its fuel exhausted. That was the time to worry. Then came the blast. If you heard it, you were safe from that one.

As in the days of the Blitz, people went to the underground stations and to other air raid shelters. They watched the skies as they had done in 1940.

On Sunday morning, June 18, Divine Service was being held in the famed Brigade of Guards Chapel on the south side of Piccadilly near Green Park. A V-1 approached. Outside the Guards stood at rigid attention. They were spared, but the bomb crashed through the roof of the Chapel, killing many of Britain's finest soldiers.

On September 8, the V-2 entered service. Although it was even more destructive than the V-1, it was easier to bear, for no one could hear it coming. There would be an explosion, then the sound of the approaching bomb. If you heard the explosion, you were safe; if not, you had nothing more to worry about.

The V-weapons were never defeated in the air. Only as the Allied armies captured the sites from which they were launched did they cease to fall on London.

The German retreat to the borders of the Fatherland left disorder and chaos behind. In France civil authority was gradually established under a provisional government headed by de Gaulle. In Poland, the Lublin Committee of National Liberation was ruling unchecked. It seemed that the same pattern was about to be followed in Greece in the wake of the pull-back of German Army Group F.

The two principal guerrilla groups, the E.L.A.S. and the E.A.M., were both communist-dominated, and they managed to forget their mutual distrust and hatred in order to join in ousting the legitimate government of King George II, which was restored and backed by British troops on October 14. The British force, under Lieutenant General Sir R. M. Scobie, was too weak to go into the hinterlands after the dissidents, who gradually closed in on Athens. By December 3, they felt confident enough to defy the police of the capital. Soon there was civil war in the streets of the ancient city. Scobie was in a terrible dilemma. If he used insufficient force, he would surely lose and it were better he had not been there at all. If he used enough, he would be castigated for brutality. He chose the latter course, and was attacked by the press of the world, including British and American correspondents, who were stronger on abstract morality than they were on the facts of the situation. There was no doubt that the E.L.A.S. and the E.A.M. were a tiny minority who were trying to seize control of Greece through intimidation and terror.

Churchill would not let Scobie bear the opprobrium alone.

Challenged in the House of Commons for issuing the orders that authorized Scobie's harsh measures, he replied:

Democracy is not based on violence or terrorism, but on reason, on fair play, on freedom, on respecting the rights of other people. Democracy is no harlot to be picked up in the street by a man with a tommygun. I trust the people, the mass of the people, in almost any country, but I like to make sure that it is the people and not a gang of bandits who think that, by violence, they can overturn the constituted authority.

On Christmas Day, 1944, Churchill flew to Athens and had discussions with his leaders, including General Alexander. It was clear that the British and loyal Greeks did not have sufficient force to do any more than clear the Athens-Piraeus area. A political solution had to be reached.

Churchill set about finding one. In a conference the next day with all parties a compromise was reached by which Archbishop Damaskinos would be appointed Regent until regular elections could be held. Interestingly enough, the Archbishop's government did not include any communist members. It was by such a narrow margin that Greece was able to escape the fate of Poland, Bulgaria, Rumania, and Hungary.

As he sent his "State of the Union" message to the Congress in January 1945, President Roosevelt was already looking beyond the end of the war.

"This new year," he said, "can be the greatest year of achievement in human history. 1945 can see the final ending of the Nazi-Fascist reign of terror in Europe. 1945 can see the closing in of the forces of retribution against Japan. Most important of all, 1945 can and must see the substantial beginning of the organization of world peace."

# CHAPTER FOUR

# Return to the Philippines

*Thus much is certain; that he that commands
the sea is at great liberty, and may take
as much and as little of the war as he will.*

Francis Bacon, Essays

WHEN Task Force 58 triumphantly returned to Saipan after smashing the Japanese in the Battle of the Philippine Sea, the Marines and troops ashore felt a surge of relief. Having no knowledge of what was happening at sea, they had felt deserted on June 18 when the combatant ships disappeared over the western horizon and the transports and supply ships retired to the safer side of Saipan. Was it another case like Guadalcanal where Admiral Turner had been forced to abandon the Marines for a time as a result of the Battle of Savo Island?

The return of the Navy brought the answer. The Marines and the Army troops were going to get all the support they could get from carrier planes and from ships marauding the coasts and delivering call fire as needed.

By June 22, the Americans held all of the southern part of Saipan except for a pocket of 500 Japanese holed up on Nafutan Point, the southeastern extremity of the island. The line extended from a point on the west coast to about the center of Magicienne Bay. Aslito Field, now renamed Isely Field after Commander Robert H. Isely, a squadron commander from the *Lexington*, was in American hands. Isely had been shot down in attacking this very field before the landings.

Japanese defenses were centered on Mount Tapotchau, a 1,554-foot peak in the center of the island. General Holland

Smith, now established ashore, proposed to advance on a three-division front up and around Mount Tapotchau and push on to the northern end of the island. Leaving the Second Battalion of the 105th Regimental Combat Team to mop up on Nafutan Point, he pulled the Army's Twenty-Seventh Division out of reserve and assigned it to the center of the line with the Second Marine Division on the left and the Fourth Marine Division on the right. The commander of the Twenty-Seventh Division, Major General Ralph Smith, was directed to move his troops through the Fourth Division during the night of June 22–23 and join the attack on a corps front at dawn. Ralph Smith did not begin his move until there was light enough to see, fearing his men would go astray in the darkness, and as a result his battalions came into action as much as three hours and fifteen minutes late.

Things thus got off to a bad start. While the two Marine divisions were making good progress, Ralph Smith's troops fell farther and farther behind. There was no lack of courage on the part of the Army men; they were poorly led, and this lack of leadership was evident when this division had been employed at Makin and Eniwetok. A former National Guard division from New York, the Twenty-Seventh suffered from too much camaraderie and too little discipline. Company grade officers were older than most and were not up to the grueling strain of combat. Upper-grade officers were as much involved in politics as in military training.

There was also the difference in tactics. The Marines are trained to bypass pockets of resistance, leaving them to mop-up outfits. The Army doctrine calls for systematic, orderly advance, leaving nothing behind it. One of the Army's own officers wrote of this division:

Based on my observation of the Twenty-Seventh Division for a few days, I have noted certain things which give me some concern. They are, first, a lack of offensive spirit on the part of the troops. A battalion will run into one machine gun and be held up for several hours. When they get any kind of minor resistance they immediately open up with everything they have that can fire in the general

134

direction from which they are being fired upon. Second, at night if a patrol comes around their bivouac area they immediately telephone in and state they are under a counterattack and want to fall back to some other position. Third, I found that troops would work all day to capture well-earned terrain and at night would fall back a distance varying from 400 to 800 yards and sometimes 1,000 yards to organize a perimeter defense.

As a result of the laggard Twenty-Seventh, the front line developed a pocket resembling a capital U, which exposed the flanks of the Marines to the Japanese. Greatly dissatisfied, Holland Smith sent Major General Sanderford Jarman, who was to become island commander after the fighting was over, to talk to General Ralph Smith, as one Army man to another. Jarman reported back that Ralph Smith was dissatisfied too, that he had spent the day of June 23 at the lines pointing out mistakes to his officers. He promised to do better the following day.

The situation did not improve on June 24. The Twenty-Seventh moved but little, and the Marines had to slow their advance to avoid leaving gaps between themselves and the Army. That evening, Holland Smith went aboard the *Rocky Mount* to discuss the situation with Admiral Turner. Finding themselves in agreement, the two commanders went over to the *Indianapolis* to consult Admiral Spruance. "Ralph Smith has shown that he lacks aggressive spirit," Holland Smith stated, "and his division is slowing down our advance. He should be relieved." He went on to suggest that General Jarman take over temporarily, until the Army could send another officer to take command. Spruance concurred and issued the necessary orders saying that Holland Smith was "authorized and directed" to relieve Ralph Smith with General Jarman "in order that the offensive on Saipan may proceed in accordance with the plans and orders of the Commander, Northern Troops and Landing Force."

There ensued such a tempest that a quarter of a century after the event, it still attracts more attention than most of the other operations in the Marianas. The Commanding General, Army

Forces Pacific, Lieutenant General Robert C. Richardson, hastened out to Saipan and berated Holland Smith. No Marine officer, he contended, was competent to command large bodies of men, and Ralph Smith's relief had been completely unjustified. Holland Smith, controlling his temper and thereby belying his nickname of "Howlin' Mad," kept his tongue. Richardson went on board the *Rocky Mount* to continue his diatribe, and Kelly Turner reported to Spruance in no uncertain terms, calling Richardson's behavior an "unwarranted assumption of command authority."

The controversy did not die, and Richardson's actions threatened to bring interservice rivalry to an area where interservice cooperation was good and getting better. Fortunately Major General George W. Griner, who took over the Twenty-Seventh a few days later, was able to improve the performance of the division and to restore Holland Smith's confidence in it.

Meanwhile another unit of the Twenty-Seventh had failed to distinguish itself on Saipan. The Second Battalion of the 105th Regimental Combat Team had, as we recall, been given the job of wiping out the Japanese on Nafutan Point. Although there were only 500 Japanese there, the battalion advanced slowly, and on the evening of June 26 was holding a 3,000-yard front, too thinly as it turned out. A short advance would have cut that front in half because Nafutan Point narrows rapidly as one moves south.

The Japanese commander on Nafutan Point, Captain A. Sasaki, determined to try to break through the American lines and join other Japanese forces he still believed were holding out in the southern end of the island. Adopting the password "Shichesei Hokoku" ("Seven Lives to Repay Our Country"), Sasaki marched his men around the American right flank. Incredibly they got by without difficulty, scarcely a shot being fired. The Japanese then fell on Isely Field at 0230, June 27, where they were diverted, and then they tangled with two Marine regiments and were wiped out to a man.

General Richardson crowned his accomplishments on Saipan

by conferring on the Second Battalion a unit citation as a result of their actions on Nafutan Point!

Meanwhile, the fighting was going on to the north. The Twenty-Seventh Division redeemed itself and straightened out the line. On June 27, the Second Marine Division, after fierce fighting, won control of Mount Tapotchau, and from then on the fighting was literally all downhill.

Even though General Yoshitsugu Saito, the Japanese ground commander, had lost 80 percent of his troops, he was still determined to resist and make the Americans pay for every foot. He established a "final line of resistance" running east from Tanapag Village, but he could never establish a real line. Isolated forces fought splendidly when their time came to die for the Emperor, but the Americans were not to be stopped. On July 3, the Americans had reached a point where the island becomes so narrow that there was room for only two divisions, so the Second Marine Division went into reserve temporarily. The strongest point of Saito's "final line of resistance" was captured the next day and became known as "Fourth of July Hill." For two more days the hard fighting continued, and then on the night of July 6–7, came the biggest Banzai attack of the war.

Although both Admiral Nagumo and General Saito knew the situation was hopeless, they organized this attack as though they expected it had a chance. No one will ever know how many Japanese were involved, but the best estimates agree around 3,000, including the wounded who could walk or hobble. They were to jump off just before dawn, July 7. Saito would not lead his men. With Nagumo and Major General Keiji Igeta, the third-ranking officer on Saipan, he would commit suicide in his command post, a cave overlooking an area the Japanese called Paradise Valley. The Americans called it the Valley of Hell. Curiously enough, it adjoined another valley dubbed Harakiri Gulch.

The scene was curiously Japanese. The three ranking officers assembled in the main cave on the evening of July 6 and ate a last meal of canned crab meat and sake. General Saito read aloud a farewell message he wished to have distributed to all those who would be taking part in the final desperate attack on the morrow:

Our comrades have fallen one after another. Despite the bitterness of defeat, we pledge, "Seven lives to repay our country." Whether we attack or whether we stay where we are, there is only death. However, in death there is life. We must utilize this opportunity to exalt true Japanese manhood. I will advance with those who remain to deliver still another blow to the American devils, and leave my bones on Saipan as a bulwark of the Pacific.

At 2000, while sorrowing aides stood by, each of the three commanders inserted the ceremonial dagger into his bowels in the first step of *seppuku*. Behind each of them stood another officer with a pistol. As soon as the daggers had been thrust truly home, the officers stepped forward and shot Saito, Igeta, and Nagumo in the temple. The bodies were cremated, along with the regimental colors, by pouring gasoline over them and setting it alight. Later, when the battle was over, a captured Japanese officer identified Saito's ashes, and Holland Smith gave them a military funeral with honors appropriate to his rank.

Before this could happen, there were still scenes of horror to be experienced. At dawn came the Banzai charge.

Once again the brunt fell on the Twenty-Seventh Division, and once again the Twenty-Seventh was found wanting.

Holland Smith had been expecting just such a charge, and he personally warned General Griner to be ready. But once again, the middle-grade officers of the division let their outfit down. In particular the 105th Regimental Combat Team was not prepared. They bedded down for the night in comfortable positions with no regard for fields of fire in case of attack. There was even a gap the length of three football fields between two of their battalions, and it was through this gap that the Japanese hordes came.

There was no pretense at formation in the Japanese crowd. Able-bodied soldiers with rifles were accompanied by the maimed, hobbling on crutches and carrying only bamboo poles with bayonets lashed to the end of them. There were the blind, led by their fellows; there were civilians, for Saito had said, "There is no longer any distinction between civilians and troops."

On they came, straight into the muzzles of the American guns. "I didn't think they'd ever stop," recalled Major Edward McCarthy. "It was like a cattle stampede."

Under the pressure of this stampede, there was no stopping the Japanese at first. "If you shot one," continued McCarthy, "five more would take his place."

By no means were all of the officers of the Twenty-Seventh Division weak. The commander of the First Battalion, 105th, Lieutenant Colonel William J. O'Brien, refused to yield an inch and strode up and down his line, encouraging his men, and with a pistol in either hand he blazed away at the Japanese until his magazine clips were empty. Then he took over a .50-caliber machine gun mounted on a jeep. He kept on firing until he was overrun and killed.

The human wave passed on, leaving Americans dead and wounded behind them. They also left their own. Wounded Japanese who could go no farther committed suicide with hand grenades or opened arteries to let out their life blood.

By 1130, the Banzai charge had been stopped, and by late afternoon, the Americans were back in the positions they had held at dawn. It had cost 406 American lives to stop this charge, but 4,311 Japanese corpses were later counted in Paradise Valley and Harakiri Gulch. Some of them had undoubtedly been killed earlier by the naval bombardment and the bombing, but most had fallen in the futile charge.

Following these heavy casualties, the Twenty-Seventh Division went into reserve and the Second Marine Division took its place on the west side for the final push up to Marpi Point at the northern end of the island.

At 0430, July 8, there was a second Banzai charge, but it was weaker than the first and the Marines held their lines, disposing of several hundred Japanese in the process. The Fourth Division, meanwhile, was advancing toward Marpi Point, and the Second Division moved up along the west coast. On the next afternoon, Admiral Turner announced that Saipan was secure, and at 1000 the following morning, July 10, the official flag-raising ceremony was held at Charan Kanoa.

But there were still dreadful scenes to witness on Saipan.

Hundreds of Japanese civilians were holed up on the northern end of Saipan, and they had been well indoctrinated that they would suffer horrible deaths by torture if the Americans got their hands on them. At the very least, they believed, all the males would be castrated and all the women raped. Several hundred of them emerged and, despite the repeated invitations to surrender, began to commit suicide. Whole families met their deaths together. Fathers would dash out their babies' brains against cliffs and then would take their wives' hands and leap off the cliffs onto the rocks below. Older children played a grisly game of catch with armed hand grenades.

Not all the Japanese committed suicide. Gradually propaganda leaflets and loudspeakers manned by captured civilians attesting to good treatment had their effect, and the people began to come in. The final tally of the captured was 1,780 military and over 14,500 civilians.

Saipan was the costliest action to date in the Pacific, with 3,426 Americans killed ashore and 13,099 wounded. But there was no doubt of its importance. "I have always considered Saipan the decisive battle of the Pacific offensive," wrote General Holland Smith later. "Saipan was Japan's administrative Pearl Harbor, . . . the naval and military heart and brain of Japanese defense strategy." Its loss had far-reaching effects in Japan.

While mop-up troops busied themselves with isolated pockets of Japanese still holding out in caves, the scene of action shifts from that bloodied island to Guam and Tinian.

These last two objectives in the Marianas campaign were undertaken concurrently, with W-Day for Guam July 21 and J-Day for Tinian July 24. Each island was stubbornly defended, and each was overcome by the combination of bravery and

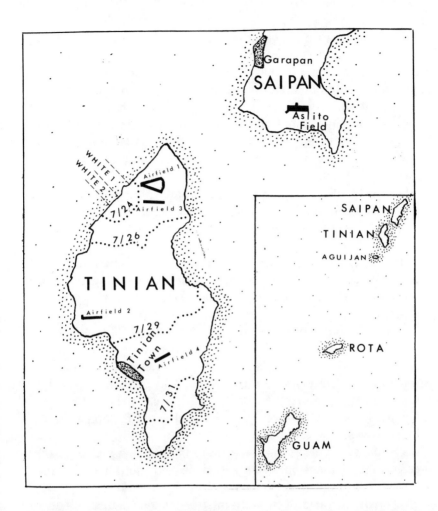

skilled application of amphibious technique that made the Central Pacific campaign possible.

Tinian Island lies three miles southwest of Saipan. It is ten and a half miles long from north to south and only five miles wide at its widest. Although the difficulties of getting ashore over the two narrow landing beaches were enormous, the operation was, in Holland Smith's words, "the perfect amphibious operation in the Pacific war."

In contrast to the lack of information about Saipan, knowledge of Tinian was thorough. The long duration of the fight for Saipan gave ample opportunity for photo-reconnaissance and for underwater demolition teams to explore possible beachheads. Also there was time for a really thorough naval bombardment. From June 14 on, not a day went by without some naval force coming by and throwing in a large number of shells. As J-Day approached, the number increased. On June 20, XXIV Corps Artillery completed its installations on the south side of Saipan and began regular bombardments of Japanese positions on the other side of the three-mile channel.

The particular difficulty about Tinian was the lack of any suitable landing beach. The best were in Sunharon Bay, opposite Tinian Town on the southwest side of the island, but because these were so obvious, Colonel Kiuochi Ogata, commanding the 9,000 defenders, had established his primary defense there.

Only two other possible landing sites existed. The rest of the island rises sheer from the sea with cliffs of rugged coral up to 150 feet in height. In Asiga Bay, on the center of the east coast, the cliffs drop down to about 10 feet, and this was a possible landing site. Planners designated the area Yellow Beaches. Ogata also knew they were possible and made his preparations there as well.

On the northwest coast there were two narrow breaks in the coral, one of them only 60 yards wide and the other 160, and these were designated White Beaches. They looked completely inadequate for assault in division strength, but tactical surprise might be achieved across them. It was an intriguing idea.

Obviously a choice would have to be made. Admiral Turner, discarding the obvious Tinian Town area, sent an amphibious reconnaissance battalion and two underwater-demolition teams to explore both White and Yellow beaches. The report on the Yellow Beaches was all negative. The cliffs were higher than expected, there were too many anchored mines, and barbed wire along the beaches was covered by numerous pillboxes to mow down men struggling through the barbed wire.

White Beaches, on the other hand, were undefended, and

there were no serious underwater obstacles. Once up the cliffs, which were only ten feet or so in height, the men could fan out easily and establish a perimeter. White Beaches were accordingly selected, and complete tactical surprise was achieved.

Admiral Turner assigned Rear Admiral Harry W. Hill to command the naval task force for this assault, and Holland Smith designated Major General Harry Schmidt, USMC, as ground commander. In addition to his own Fourth Marine Division, now commanded by Major General Clifton B. Cates, which would make the assault, Schmidt had the Second Marine Division (Major General Thomas E. Watson) for follow up.

The difficulties of landing two divisions through two such narrow passageways gave a unique feature to the Tinian landings. Not a single box of supplies was to be landed on the beaches. The LVTs and dukws would crawl directly up the slopes to supply dumps inland without ever letting anyone touch a bit of their cargo. Only in this way could beach congestion be avoided.

In addition to the naval bombardments preceding the landing, Tinian was softened up by carrier strikes. The Japanese had by this time no air strength left in the Marianas, and to keep the Japanese from sending in more, Task Force 58 cooperated with land-based air in shooting up such places as Iwo Jima, Chichi Jima, and Haha Jima, as well as Truk, Yap, and the Palaus.

In accordance with military logic, Colonel Ogata would have surrendered the day Saipan fell, but the Japanese did not fight according to military logic. It was to be another futile fight to the last man.

The assault troops were picked up in LSTs and landing craft from Tanapag Harbor and Charan Kanoa beaches. The Second Division, embarked in transports, staged a feint off Tinian Town that was among the most realistic of any in the war.

On J-Day, July 24, while the White Beaches were getting a heavy pre-landing bombardment, transports entered Sunharon Bay under the fascinated eyes of Colonel Ogata. They hoisted out boats and Marines crawled down cargo nets and entered the bobbing LCMs. Assault waves formed up and started for

Tinian Town under erratic Japanese gunfire. When they were a mile from the beach, the boats reversed course and went back to their ships, where the Marines re-embarked and the boats were hoisted aboard. Colonel Ogata congratulated himself that a landing had been repulsed.

Although the Japanese gunfire had caused no casualties among the Marines in the landing craft, it had not been so erratic against the naval ships which were supporting the "landing." The destroyer *Norman Scott* was hit six times by 6-inch shells, which killed her commanding officer, Commander Seymour D. Owens, and eighteen others, wounded forty-seven, and did considerable damage to the ship. The battleship *Colorado* was hit twenty-two times and lost forty-three killed and ninety-seven wounded. The feint, thus, was not without its cost, but it did keep Ogata pinned down until it was too late to do anything about it.

The landings on the White Beaches went off exactly as planned. Only scattered rifle fire opposed the Marines, and by nightfall there were 15,614 men on Tinian.

Colonel Ogata could respond only slowly and with difficulty. He quickly realized that the White Beach landings were the big show, but his communications were in such sorry shape from the bombing and shelling that he could not organize his defense in any hurry. He did, however, manage to mount a serious counterattack beginning at 0200, July 25. The Marines held their ground and the next morning found that they had suffered fewer than a hundred casualties while sending some 1,250 Japanese to join their ancestors.

On July 26, the Marines captured Ushi Point Airfield. From here, almost a year later, a B-29 took off for Hiroshima.

It took nine days from the landing until General Schmidt could declare the island secured, but it took until after the end of the war to dig out all the Japanese. They were not a serious threat unless one got too careless.

Guam was a considerably harder nut to crack than Tinian. Although the problem of landing beaches was much easier, the island was known to be much more strongly held. Including

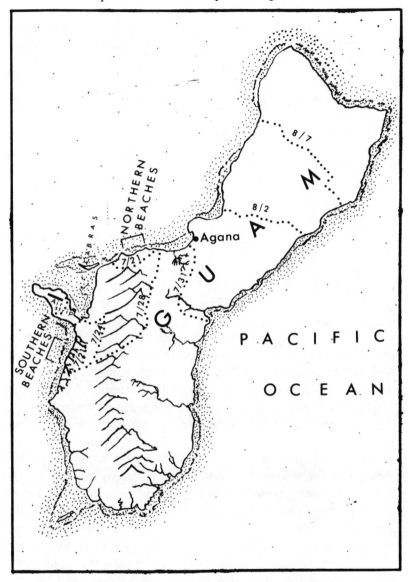

naval forces based ashore, there were about 19,000 Japanese on Guam under Lieutenant General Takeshi Takashina.

The original plan had been for the Americans to land on

Guam about three days after the assault on Saipan, but the Battle of the Philippine Sea and the unexpected length of the fighting on Saipan changed all that. The III Amphibious Corps, consisting of the Third Marine Division and the First Provisional Brigade, had been milling around in their transports for days, wondering what they were going to do. On June 25, Spruance sent the Third Division back to Eniwetok, keeping the First Provisional Brigade as a floating reserve. It was not until the last day of the month that he released the brigade as well.

Profiting from the experiences on Saipan, Spruance, Turner, and Holland Smith concluded that the seizure of Guam would require three full divisions instead of the one and a half first assigned. The capture would have to wait until the Army's Seventy-Seventh Infantry Division could be taken from general reserve on Oahu and be brought forward.

Rear Admiral Richard L. Conolly, who had commanded at Roi and Namur, was in command of Task Force 53, designated the Southern Attack Force. The ground commander was Major General Roy S. Geiger, USMC, who had won distinction on Guadalcanal. The two men got on extremely well together, and this cordiality communicated itself to all hands. "At no time," reported General Geiger, "was there a conflicting opinion that was not settled to the satisfaction of all concerned."

The beaches chosen for the landings were on either side of Apra on the west coast. Because the Americans wanted these facilities for their own use, and because the Guamanians were mostly loyal to the United States, there were particular difficulties for the pre-invasion bombardments and air raids. The Chamorros who lived on Guam had been under American rule for forty years, and had suffered miserably under the Japanese. They resented having to study Japanese in the schools, they resented having the name of their homeland changed to Omiya Jima (Great Shrine Island), and they resented being forced to work on military installations and port facilities at starvation wages. In early 1944, when the Japanese decided to fortify the Marianas, conditions became worse. Schools were closed, and everyone, young and old, was set to forced labor. Not a few were executed for displaying "American sympathy," which could manifest itself in looking up with a smile when an American plane came over.

Even though Americans had ruled Guam for four decades, the knowledge of the terrain of the island was not good enough for an amphibious assault. In particular, slopes and heights were not well known, and the maps delivered to the attack forces were badly in error, despite intensive air and submarine photographic reconnaissance.

Thirteen days of continuous bombardment preceded the landings on July 21, with 28,764 rounds of 5-inch or larger ammunition being hurled against the island. It was the most extended bombardment of the Pacific war. Combined with bombing raids, it was particularly effective. After the war, a Japanese colonel reported that all coast defense emplacements in the open and half of the concealed ones had been destroyed before a man set foot on shore.

The first elements of the Seventy-Seventh Division sailed from Pearl Harbor on July 1. This was a reserve division, inexperienced, but ready to learn. Most of the men were draftees from the metropolitan New York area, and they had been well led. They had undergone intensive amphibious training in Hawaii before setting out for the Marianas, and this training was to pay off. Holland Smith paid the Seventy-Seventh high (for him) tribute when he wrote that it "was a raw division, with no previous combat experience, but it showed combat efficiency to a degree one would expect only of veteran troops. Its aggressive patrolling, its close coordination with other units, and its superior conduct of assigned missions gave evidence of a high order of training, fine leadership, and high morale."

The key objective on Guam was the Orote Peninsula which forms the south side of Apra Harbor. On Orote were the chief military installations and an airfield. Since early seizure of Orote would mean that the Americans could use both the harbor and the airfield to support the rest of the operations, all tactical plans led to this objective. Two sets of beaches were selected, a northern assault between Asan and Adelup points, a little over a mile west of the city of Agana, and a southern assault south of Orote Peninsula, known as the Agat Beaches. Once these simultaneous landings had taken place, the troops would drive toward each other in a pincer movement to isolate and secure Orote. After that would follow the campaign to clean up the rest of the island.

As usual, underwater-demolition teams cleared beach obstacles. There were so many of them that Admiral Conolly afterward stated that no landing could have taken place without their skilled, dangerous work. As the swimmers left Asan, they left a sign in the reef, "Welcome Marines!"

The landing on the northern beaches went ashore on schedule between "the Devil's Horns," as Asan and Adelup Points were dubbed. The assault troops were the men of the Third Marine Division, thankful to set foot ashore after nearly fifty days in their transports. Hills and cliffs made this landing site a kind of natural amphitheater, rather like Salerno on a smaller scale, and the Third Division would have to fight its way out, but it would have powerful assistance from naval ships and planes.

By nightfall on July 21, W-Day objectives had been largely secured, and Major General Allen H. Turnage, the division commander, prepared for a counterattack. Casualties had been heavy, both in the amphtracs crossing the reef, and ashore. By the end of the day, the 20,000 Marines were packed so closely in the confined space that a projectile could scarcely fall without hitting someone.

The expected counterattack came at dawn, July 22, but it was beaten off. Then the Marines advanced steadily up the trails, passes, and defiles. By July 24 they had reached the ridges enclosing the amphitheater and were ready to advance and secure the Fonte Plateau.

On the night of July 25–26, however, came another heavy counterattack. This was a well-organized, coordinated attack by at least six battalions, supported by artillery. Except in the cases of a few small groups of frenzied Japanese, there were no Banzai charges. The Japanese came on, and it seemed nothing could stop them. One group of Japanese attacked a battalion command post, but it was beaten off, with the cooks, bakers, and clerks joining in the fray. Every Marine, regardless of his job, is trained in infantry tactics, and this training paid off here. Another detachment of Japanese reached the division field hospital, but were gunned down to a man. Patients who could, left their beds and fought in pajamas. Those too sick to get out of bed fired their rifles from where they lay, shooting through the gaps in the tent.

This counterattack cost the Japanese over 3,500 killed and broke the back of their resistance on Guam. General Takashina was killed on July 28, and the senior surviving officer was unable to do much toward organizing the troops that remained. The assault phase of the northern landings ended that same day when the Third Division linked up with the Seventy-Seventh east of Apra Harbor.

Casualties had been heavy, with 753 killed or missing and 3,147 wounded, a casualty rate of 19.5 percent. They would have been far worse had it not been for the expert gunnery, bombing, and strafing of the Navy.

On the southern beachhead, the First Provisional Marine Brigade, under Brigadier General Lemuel C. Shepherd, furnished the assault troops. The Army's Seventy-Seventh Division was in general reserve and then would follow the Marines ashore over the southern beaches.

In addition to the usual dangers of any amphibious landing, there was special peril from flanking fire of Japanese gunners on Orote Peninsula. Most of the guns there were knocked out by fire-support ships, the battleship *Pennsylvania* in particular doing a job on the Japanese defenders. A few, however, escaped detection, and gave the Marines a warm reception. In fact, the opposition at Agat was stronger than at Asan, but the issue was never in doubt. By afternoon, G.I.s of the Seventy-Seventh began landing. By 1830, July 21, W-Day objectives realized, Shepherd sent a message to General Geiger: "Our casualties about 350. Critical shortage of fuel and ammunition all types. Think we can handle it. Will continue as planned tomorrow."

The expected counterattack came that night, and it was beaten off with heavy losses on both sides, but the Japanese losses were far greater than those of the Americans.

The next two days were spent in consolidating the beachhead and establishing a perimeter. It was not until July 24 that the Marines were able to begin an advance toward Sumay which would seal off the 4,000 Japanese defenders of Orote Peninsula.

The first day they did not get very far, owing to road mines and pre-sited artillery, but by sundown July 25, Orote Peninsula was cut off.

The usual G.I. and Marine humor was always present. Anticipating a Banzai charge, someone passed out a mimeographed announcement:

TONIGHT
BANZAI CHARGE
Thrills    Chills    Suspense
See Sake-crazed Japanese charge at high port
See Everybody Shoot Everybody
See the Cream of the Marine Corps Play with Live Ammo
Come along and Bring a Friend
Don't miss the thrilling spectacle of the Banzai Charge
Starting at 10 p.m. and lasting all night
ADMISSION FREE

The Marines were not disappointed in the show. On the evening of July 25, Commander Asaichi Tamai, senior surviving officer on Orote, broke out all the sake, beer, and rum-based "Scotch whiskey" and issued it to his men, presumably to keep it from falling into enemy hands. The drunken, hopped-up Japanese swarmed out of the mangrove and fell on the amazed Marines. Yelling, screaming, they came on brandishing broken bottles, pitchforks, and even baseball bats in addition to their rifles. "Arms and legs flew like snowflakes. . . . Flares revealed an out-of-this-world picture of Nipponese drunks reeling about in our forward positions, falling into foxholes, tossing aimless grenades here and there . . . laughing crazily, to be exterminated in savage close-in fighting."

The next morning, burial squads had to dispose of over 400 mangled Japanese corpses.

It still took time to clean out Orote Peninsula, for isolated pockets of Japanese resisted strongly, but by 1400, July 29, the airfield was taken, and later that afternoon a patrol reached the end of the peninsula and found only two Japanese soldiers. That same afternoon, Admiral Spruance and Generals Holland Smith, Geiger, and Shepherd witnessed the flag-raising ceremony on the old Marine parade ground, "To the Colors," being played on a captured Japanese bugle.

Organized military operations for the liberation of Guam lasted until August 10. After the Third and Seventy-Seventh Divisions linked up, they pushed across the five miles to the east coast and then wheeled north, the Marines on the left and the Army on the right. Loyal Guamanians reported that the Japanese had pulled out of the southern half of the island, so the remaining task was to clean the Japanese out of the north.

The final Japanese strong point was Mount Santa Rosa, about five miles south of Pati Point on the northeastern coast. If General Geiger had known this, it would have facilitated his task enormously, but he had no way of knowing, and the expanse of jungle that makes up most of the northern half of Guam had to be explored as though it contained enemy forces. Small Japanese units were there, and they were an infernal nuisance. The G.I.s took Mount Santa Rosa on August 8, with unusually light casualties considering the strength of the defense. A combination of naval shelling and good training of the men was responsible for the low butcher's bill. Elements of the Seventy-Seventh reached Pati Point the following after-noon, while the Marines had arrived at Ritidian Point, the northwestern extremity, as the G.I.s were capturing Mount Santa Rosa.

Although the formal fighting was over officially, G.I.s on August 12 overran the last Japanese command post near Mount Mataguac to find that, after expending their last bullets, everyone had committed suicide.

Some 9,000 Japanese were still hiding out in the jungle, but they were disorganized. Some surrendered, others took their own lives, and most of the rest were hunted down. One unit of 113 officers and men came in only when they heard the broadcast of their Emperor's orders to surrender, while a major and a small group held out until 1947 before they were finally convinced that the war was over. In the spring of 1972, a lone survivor turned up and was repatriated to Japan.

The capture of Guam ended the long campaign for the Marianas, but there was no pausing for rest. The momentum of the Pacific war kept right on going. In fact, it was gathering steam.

The fall of Saipan brought about the collapse of the government of Prime Minister Hideki Tojo. Caricatures of his grinning face, buckteeth, and heavy glasses had made him perhaps the Japanese best known to the American people; this caricature often appeared with equally unflattering ones of Hitler and Mussolini. After Italy's surrender, the face of Mussolini was crossed out with a large X in such posters. Rather than lose a convenient symbol, American propagandists kept Tojo's face displayed until the end of the war.

His prominence in America could not save him. He had demanded enormous sacrifices from the Japanese people, and they had been borne with increasing resentment. It was no longer possible to pretend to the people of Japan that they were winning the war; the problem was to conceal from them how near at hand defeat was. Even the official Japanese communiqués could not hide the losses the Japanese were sustaining on all fronts, and the truth was far worse than the communiqués even hinted. The Emperor hinted that he sought an end to the war through diplomatic means, and Tojo was out. He was replaced by General Kuniaki Koiso, with Admiral Mitsumasa Yonai as Deputy Prime Minister. Although both men promised vigorous prosecution of the war, everyone knew that these were statements for the record, and they were really looking for a way out. Yet no official in Japan could bring himself to think in terms of defeat nor accept the blame for proposing peace negotiations. Every Japanese leader hoped for a miracle which would allow Japan to pretend she had won some sort of victory. Thus the war dragged on for another year.

"Where do we go from here?" This was a question which General Marshall asked of the British so often that it drove General Alan Brooke to a fury. Yet the Joint Chiefs had not realistically faced that same question when it came to the war in the Pacific. Although General MacArthur had been given the objective of taking Mindanao by November 15, and Admiral Nimitz bases in Palau on September 15, the final road to Japan was as yet unchosen. The directive of the Joint Chiefs, by which operations to date in the Pacific had been conducted, stated "that the most feasible approach to Formosa, Luzon and China is by way of the Marianas, the Carolines, Palau and Mindanao."

In other words, the Marianas, the Carolines, Palau, and Mindanao were the stepping stones, and Formosa, Luzon, and mainland China the next major objectives. But which one first? No one knew for certain, and the Joint Chiefs were divided. The Navy view was that except for Mindanao, the Philippines should be bypassed. A dual drive would be mounted against Japan itself, one by the capture of Formosa and then up through the Ryukyus, and the other north from the Marianas through the Bonins. MacArthur, on the other hand, believed bypassing Luzon would be nothing less than betrayal of the Philippine people. To a suggestion that he bypass Luzon, he heatedly cabled General Marshall:

THE PHILIPPINES IS AMERICAN TERRITORY WHERE OUR UNSUPPORTED FORCES WERE DESTROYED BY THE ENEMY. PRACTICALLY ALL OF THE 17,000,000 FILIPINOS REMAIN LOYAL TO THE UNITED STATES AND ARE UNDERGOING THE GREATEST PRIVATION AND SUFFERING BECAUSE WE HAVE NOT BEEN ABLE TO SUPPORT OR SUCCOR THEM. WE HAVE A GREAT NATIONAL OBLIGATION TO DISCHARGE. MOREOVER, IF THE UNITED STATES SHOULD DELIB- ERATELY BYPASS THE PHILIPPINES, LEAVING OUR

PRISONERS, NATIONALS, AND LOYAL FILIPINOS IN ENEMY HANDS WITHOUT AN EFFORT TO RETRIEVE THEM AT EARLIEST MOMENT, WE WOULD INCUR THE GRAVEST PSYCHOLOGICAL REACTION. WE WOULD ADMIT THE TRUTH OF JAPANESE PROPAGANDA TO THE EFFECT THAT WE HAD ABANDONED THE FILIPINOS AND WOULD NOT SHED AMERICAN BLOOD TO REDEEM THEM; WE WOULD UNDOUBTEDLY INCUR THE OPEN HOSTILITY OF THAT PEOPLE; WE WOULD PROBABLY SUFFER SUCH LOSS OF PRESTIGE AMONG ALL THE PEOPLES OF THE FAR EAST THAT IT WOULD ADVERSELY AFFECT THE UNITED STATES FOR MANY YEARS.

The impasse was resolved in a highly unusual way. President Roosevelt, who always loved a sea voyage, and who had not been in the Pacific since the war began, decided to bring the principal leaders of the controversy together and thrash things out with them. On the night of July 13, 1944, soon after he had announced his willingness to run for a fourth term, he left Washington by special train. After a day's stop at Hyde Park, the Presidential train made its slow way across the country, with a stop in Chicago. Since the Democratic National Convention was then in progress there, Mr. Roosevelt enjoyed some political conferences in the comfort of his train. After the train had left Chicago and was speeding across the plains, he revealed to those with him that Senator Harry S Truman had received the nod for Vice President.

It was an unusual group President Roosevelt was taking with him. Although he was going to discuss Pacific strategy with Nimitz and MacArthur, he took no member of the Joint Chiefs of Staff with him except for Admiral Leahy. He knew the views of the others, and he wanted to talk directly with the two men supposed to be at odds, perhaps with the idea of working some of the famous Roosevelt charm. As it happened, it turned out not to be necessary.

After arrival in San Diego on July 20, the President attended an amphibious rehearsal at a school and watched 10,000 men make a practice landing about forty miles north of the city.

Perhaps the smoothness of the landing encouraged the President in his discussions later in Hawaii.

At 2130, July 21, the Presidential party boarded the heavy cruiser *Baltimore* and sailed immediately, Mr. Roosevelt occupying the captain's day cabin, and Admiral Leahy the flag quarters. It was a pleasant voyage across the Pacific, with no incident other than the report of a Japanese task force reported 200 miles north of Hawaii. The *Baltimore* was so far distant that it caused no concern, but Pearl Harbor was in an uproar until the "task force" was diagnosed as moonlight reflected on the sea and spotted by a patrol plane at dusk.

Although the Presidential visit was top secret in Hawaii, the word had leaked and while the ship was still off Diamond Head, a large crowd had collected in the Navy Yard. Admiral Nimitz and a few others boarded the ship off Fort Kamehameha and paid their respects to the President as the ship stood slowly up the channel. When the *Baltimore* arrived at her berth at Pier 22-B, a long row of white-clad admirals and generals was waiting and marched aboard, following in rather ragged columns, which revealed how rusty their close-order drill had become.

Following the official ceremonies, Mr. Roosevelt asked to see General MacArthur, whose plane from Australia had landed just about the time the *Baltimore* was picking up Admiral Nimitz. After changing his clothes at Fort Shafter, MacArthur was driven behind a motorcycle escort to Pearl Harbor, sirens whining, to the pier. Coming aboard the *Baltimore* clad in his familiar khaki trousers, brown flight jacket, and cap of a field marshal of the Philippine Army, he smartly saluted the quarterdeck and the Officer of the Deck and was shown to the President's quarters.

The following day was devoted to inspections of military installations, but that evening, Mr. Roosevelt, Admirals Nimitz and Leahy, and General MacArthur got down to business. The major question was: should Luzon be bypassed. MacArthur and Nimitz took turns, arguing their cases to Mr. Roosevelt, using a long bamboo pole as a pointer to indicate one or another idea on a large map. Mr. Roosevelt, a student of geography, enjoyed the lesson. Gradually everyone present was convinced by MacArthur's arguments. "I think that decision was correct," noted Nimitz later. The United States would devote its next effort to the liberation of Luzon and the Philippine Archipelago.

On taking his leave of the President, MacArthur assured him that the reported differences between him and Nimitz were greater in Washington than they were in the Pacific. "We see eye to eye, Mr. President," he stated; "we understand each other perfectly."

After three busy days in Hawaii, the President and his party reboarded the *Baltimore* and sailed north for a visit to American military and naval bases in the Aleutians. It was a cold, miserable trip, and Mr. Roosevelt seemed fatigued when the ship finally reached Bremerton. After addressing workers in the Navy Yard, the President rode the cruiser to Seattle and boarded his special train for Washington.

Since this was an election year, Mr. Roosevelt's enemies made the most out of his trip. They grumbled about pleasure cruising and tying up large numbers of warships which could better be used in the war zones. Since the *Baltimore* sailed alone from San Diego to Pearl Harbor, and had an escort of only four destroyers in going through waters where Japanese submarines were known to operate, the criticism seems excessive. A more vicious story, which was based on malice, not fact, was that Roosevelt's little Scottie Fala had been left behind in the Aleutians and that a destroyer had been sent back several hundred miles to retrieve him. Such whispering campaigns were nothing new to F.D.R., but the story on Fala received such wide-spread distribution that Admiral Leahy issued an official statement that the dog had never been left behind and no destroyer had been sent back.

In spite of the fact that President Roosevelt was commander in chief, and in spite of the fact that the supreme commanders in the Pacific were in agreement, the Joint Chiefs of Staff continued to argue the Formosa–Luzon question for some months. On September 1, 1944, Rear Admiral Forrest Sherman,

Nimitz's Plans Officer, reported to them that the Central Pacific forces had no directive for anything beyond the Palau operation, now only two weeks off! Any decision was better than none. Still, the only decision made was to instruct MacArthur to go into Leyte with a target date of December 20. Gradually, however, the Formosa and China coast operations faded away and Luzon became established as a principal objective. The final decisions were not made until a top-level military conference was held in San Francisco the last week in September, and by that time plans for the Pacific had undergone a radical change, brought about by the man who had been responsible for the reversal in American fortunes at Guadalcanal—Admiral William F. Halsey, Jr.—now back at sea in command of the Third Fleet. As previously explained, the Third Fleet consisted of the same ships as the Fifth Fleet; only the drivers were changed. At 2359 one night the Fifth Fleet consisted of over 500 ships and the Third Fleet of the battleship *New Jersey* and three destroyers. A minute later those 500 ships belonged to the Third Fleet, and the Fifth Fleet consisted of the cruiser *Indianapolis* and three destroyers.

Although Halsey's responsibilities included more than Mitscher's TF 38, he usually rode in that force, his flagship forming part of TG 38.2. On August 28, 1944, he went to sea with TF 38 on an extended operation designed to cover the forthcoming operations against Morotai and Peleliu and to soften up Mindanao. One group took a sweep by the Bonins as a diversion, while the other three took on Yap, Palau, and Mindanao. Not a single Japanese plane opposed any of these southern strikes, and Halsey shifted to the southern Philippines, sometimes designated the Visayas. Again there was no opposition. In two days his carriers flew off some 2,400 sorties and destroyed about 200 Japanese aircraft in the air or on the ground. In addition they sank several ships and played hob with Japanese installations.

Halsey was so pleased that he sent a blanket dispatch to TF 38: BECAUSE OF THE BRILLIANT PERFORMANCE MY GROUP OF STARS HAS JUST GIVEN, I AM

157

CHINA

FORMOSA

PACIFIC

OCEAN

SOUTH CHINA SEA

LUZON

MINDORO

PANAY

NEGROS

CEBU

SAMAR

LEYTE

PALAWAN

SULU

SEA

MINDANAO

BORNEO

P H I L I P P I N E S

BOOKING YOU TO APPEAR BEFORE THE BEST
AUDIENCE IN THE ASIATIC THEATER. He had in
mind a raid on Manila.

Before his star performance came about, however, Halsey
made a recommendation which changed the course of the
Pacific war. He was impressed by the obvious Japanese
weakness in the Philippine area, and he began to wonder
whether the whole timetable might be advanced. "I sat in a
corner of the bridge and thought it over," he wrote. "Such a
recommendation, in addition to being none of my business,
would upset a great many applecarts, possibly all the way up to
Mr. Roosevelt and Mr. Churchill. On the other hand, it looked
sound, it ought to save thousands of lives, and it might cut
months off the war by hurrying the Nips and keeping them off
balance."

What he proposed was that the landings in Palau, Yap,
Morotai, and Mindanao be canceled and instead the troops
thus made available be used for an immediate invasion of
Leyte.

After consulting his staff, he said, "I'm going to stick my neck
out. Send an urgent dispatch to CincPac . . ."

As Halsey well knew, a great many people had to be
consulted before such a major change could be made in plans.
General MacArthur, the most concerned, was aboard the
cruiser *Nashville*, which was observing radio silence at sea, so he
could not give his opinion. His chief of staff, Lieutenant
General R. K. Sutherland, however, did not hesitate to embrace
Halsey's idea, knowing it was exactly the type of audacious
planning that delighted MacArthur. Accordingly, he informed
the Joint Chiefs and Nimitz that if Halsey's ideas were
approved, SouthWest Pacific forces would invade Leyte on
October 20, two months ahead of the original schedule.

There ensued a considerable flurry of radio traffic as specifics
were filled in, and after all had been said, staff members for the
Joint Chiefs entered the room where their bosses were having
dinner with Canadian hosts on the evening of September 15. It
was an easy decision. As General Marshall put it, "Having the
utmost confidence in General MacArthur, Admiral Nimitz, and

Admiral Halsey, it was not a difficult decision to make. Within ninety minutes after the signal had been received in Quebec, General MacArthur and Admiral Nimitz had received their instructions to execute the Leyte operation on the target date of 20 October."

The new plan eliminated the intermediate landings on Yap and Mindanao, but it did retain MacArthur's invasion of Morotai and Nimitz's invasion of Palau. Also the atoll of Ulithi was added; it was thought to be lightly held and would serve the purpose that Majuro and Eniwetok had done, that of an advanced base and anchorage for the fleet.

MacArthur's forces landed on Morotai and Nimitz's forces assaulted Palau on the same day, September 15, 1944. The first was a pushover; the second decidedly was not.

Morotai is a medium-sized island lying ten miles north of Halmahera. The Japanese had begun work on an airstrip on the southern side but had never completed it because of the boggy condition of the land. In American hands, Morotai could cut off the strong garrisons on Halmahera and subject them to the Nimitz–MacArthur specialty of letting them wither on the vine. Also, it was close enough to Leyte to permit medium-range bombers to be used in support of operations there.

Although only about 500 Japanese were on Morotai, 28,000 combat troops were assigned to its invasion. The landings were unopposed, and the chief problem was in rounding up the Japanese. About a quarter were killed or captured, some tried to escape to Halmahera and were eliminated by watchful PTs. The rest hid out in the mountains and were allowed to remain there.

Work began on the unfinished Japanese airstrip immediately, but the Americans encountered the same problems the Japanese had run into. A new site was selected, but construction was delayed by heavy rains, and it was not until the day before the Leyte landings that it was ready to handle medium and heavy bombers.

The Palau Islands were a different story. They are usually considered the westernmost of the Caroline group, and they have some of the characteristics of an atoll. They lie 470 miles east of Mindanao, and are 110 miles in length from north to south. Babelthuap, the largest island, and Peleliu had airfields and strong garrisons. They could be a threat to forthcoming moves against the Philippines unless they were eliminated. Admiral Nimitz felt that Kossol Passage north of Babelthuap and Peleliu would be useful staging bases, and he had not accepted Halsey's suggestion that the Palaus be neutralized by air power and bypassed. The writer believes that Halsey was right in this case and that the expenditure of American lives was too costly for the usefulness played by those two staging bases.

The American targets were Peleliu and Angaur at the southern extremity of the group. D-Day for Peleliu was September 15 with H-Hour set for 0830. The familiar pattern of bombardment, bombing, strafing, and rocket fire preceded the invasion, and the amphtracs and dukws took the troops across the coral reef to beaches on the western shore, near the airstrip. The Japanese, however, interjected something new. They offered slight opposition at the beach. They had learned that not once had they been able to stop a landing at the water's edge, and that naval guns offered too powerful a cover for successful defense. Instead, they offered only token resistance on the beach and prepared their main defenses farther inland.

Not that the defense was really token. The First Marine Division, which was assigned the job at Peleliu, ran into a nasty enfilading fire from concealed casemates at the end of Beach White 1, the northernmost of the five landing beaches. On the extreme left, part of Colonel Lewis B. ("Chesty") Puller's 1st Regimental Combat Team was held up by an unexpected twenty-foot-high coral cliff which was riddled with concealed Japanese positions. There was heavy fighting here all day, and little progress was made. In the center of the landing area the best progress was made, but by nightfall only half of the day's objectives had been attained.

The situation was somewhat eased by a fierce counterattack the Japanese put on late the afternoon of D-Day. Spearheaded by thirteen light tanks, the yelling Japanese penetrated the

161

Marine lines for some 150 yards before the tanks were knocked out by guns and bazookas. A few Japanese foot soldiers escaped, but most were killed where they stood.

That night the situation was miserable, for Japanese infiltrators kept everyone on edge. Destroyers fired star shells so that the Marines could spot the infiltrators, and the damage done to the men in the foxholes was more mental than physical.

For three days heavy fighting followed, and most of the flat ground on the southern end of Peleliu was taken. Then the Marines prepared to take on the Japanese real defense, Umurbrogol Ridge.

On this ridge the Japanese had emplaced guns at cave entrances, but the greatest danger lay inside the ridge. With the aid of professional miners, the Japanese had excavated the ridge so that the many caves which pock-marked its face were all interconnected. Carefully sited guns protected the cave entrances, and inside, men attempting to penetrate the labyrinth were easy targets for defenders who knew their way. There were only two ways the defenders of the caves of Umurbrogol Ridge could be overcome: seal them in or burn them out. Both ways were used. The most effective weapon was a newly developed long-range flame-thrower which shot out a tongue of flame some forty or fifty feet. The flame could bounce around corners, and if it did not kill men outright, it could exhaust the oxygen so that they died of suffocation. Hand grenades and other explosive devices were used to seal the mouths of other caves, and by these means the Japanese population of Umurbrogol Ridge was reduced to about thirty. It was not until February 1, 1945, that the last five survivors dug their way out of an inner cave and surrendered.

On adjacent Babelthuap, General Inoue had about 25,000 men, but he was not able to help out on Peleliu. American sea power trapped him there as effectively as if he had been a hundred miles away. Only about 500 men made their way across, too late to do any good on Peleliu.

The assault phase on Peleliu officially ended on October 12, but that was an administrative, not a real change. The Marines were relieved three days later by two regimental combat teams of the Army Eighty-First Division, and six weeks of bitter fighting lay ahead on the northern end of the island. On the southern end, the existing airstrip was improved and put to good use in helping out in the north.

Six miles southwest of Peleliu lies the island of Angaur, which the Japanese had developed because of its rich phosphate yield. The Americans wanted it for another reason; it was big enough and flat enough to support a bomber strip.

The assault forces for Angaur were to be furnished by the Army Eighty-First Division, but the assault was scheduled for a little after the one on Peleliu so that the Eighty-First could serve as a reserve there. Somewhat optimistically, on September 16, it was decided that the Marines could handle things on Peleliu, and the troops went ashore on Angaur at 0830, September 17. The landing was unopposed. Dense, almost impenetrable jungle aided the Japanese garrison of 1,600 men, but the defenders often gave up this advantage by coming out in futile counterattacks. On September 20, the island was declared secured, and the Eighty-First was able to send a regimental combat team to help out on Peleliu.

During the next few weeks, several atolls in the area were occupied, including Fais, Ngulu, and Ulithi. Most important by far was Ulithi, which served as the major forward base through the beginning of the Okinawa operation in April 1945.

Although the Japanese had occasionally used Ulithi as a staging area and fleet anchorage, they had abandoned it in early September, believing it would be of no use to anyone. They had taken most of the adult males to Yap to put them to work there, but a few had escaped and made their way back. Hating the Japanese, they welcomed the Americans, and when the G.I.s first stepped ashore, they were greeted by "King" Ueg in person. He readily agreed to the proposition that the native population be removed to Fassarai, midway along the east coast of the atoll, while the Americans developed installations on the northern islets.

An airstrip was set up on Falalop; Asor became administrative headquarters; Sorlen boasted a 100-bed hospital, and Mogmog, at the northern end of the atoll, became a fleet recreation area, with softball diamonds, volleyball courts, football fields, and horseshoe courts. Although Ulithi was no paradise, it was a blessed relief to put in for a few days, have a run ashore and a few beers, see a movie that night, and relax from the strain of one-in-three watch standing at sea.

But Ulithi was only a way station. The main business of the Third and Seventh fleets lay ahead, the invasion of Leyte, the making good of Douglas MacArthur's promise: "I shall return."

Landings in Leyte Gulf were scheduled for October 20, 1944, but there was much to be done first. Even while the fighting was still going on in the Palaus, ships and men were moving to get ready for Leyte.

One of the first orders of business was to smash Japanese air power on Formosa so it could not be used against the landing operations. A typhoon which brushed Ulithi on October 3 and 4 did not interfere with Task Force 38 as it moved against Formosa, but it did mean heavy seas and an uncomfortable time for the sailors in the destroyers. TF 38 rendezvoused October 7 about 375 miles west of the Marianas and refueled the next day under sea conditions that required the highest order of seamanship. A diversionary bombardment was made on Marcus Island on October 9, but the Japanese did not seem impressed. The main part of TF 38 then moved on toward the Ryukyus and on October 10 gave Okinawa and some smaller islands nearby a going over with 1,396 sorties, doing extensive damage—*mirabile dictu*, even more than the pilots reported!

The Okinawa strike thoroughly alarmed Imperial Headquarters, and Admiral Toyoda's Chief of Staff, Vice Admiral Ryunosuke ordered an alert for two phases of Japan's Sho Plan, of which more later. Also the remaining Japanese carriers were alerted to transfer their aircraft to land bases on Formosa.

Before hitting Formosa, TF 38 struck at the Aparri Airfield on the north coast of Luzon. This raid, as Admiral Halsey later noted, accomplished nothing and gave the forces on Formosa another day to prepare.

At dawn, October 12, TF 38 began a two-day strike on

Formosa. The first strike destroyed a third of the Japanese planes, and the second took care of the rest so that nothing came up to oppose the third strike. On the second day of the strikes, Friday, October 13, Admiral Halsey's old jinx day, the airmen concentrated on shipping. The results of the two days of attacks on Formosa were over 500 aircraft destroyed, forty or more ships sunk, and untold damage to shore installations, including ammunition dumps, hangars, machine shops, oil storage, and industrial plants.

Halsey's jinx had not left him, however, for at dusk a small group of Japanese torpedo-carrying Bettys came in low, undetected by radar. Most concentrated on the carrier *Franklin*, which escaped with light damage, but the new heavy cruiser, *Canberra*,* was hit by a torpedo which smashed into two firerooms, killing twenty-three men. Flames spread to the engine rooms and the ship slid to a stop. At that moment she was only ninety miles from Formosa.

Halsey was faced with a difficult decision. The wallowing *Canberra* had taken in about 4,500 tons of water; the normal procedure would have been to take off the crew and scuttle the ship. But Halsey was determined to save her. He ordered the *Wichita* to take her under tow and he ordered an unscheduled third day of strikes against Formosa in order to protect the cripple. Since the speed of the task force would be limited to that of the tow—4 knots or less—the crippled division (CripDiv, for short) could not be left to its fate.

The Japanese extracted a price for the extra day off Formosa, for on the evening of October 14, a dozen or so Fran torpedo bombers attacked TG 38.1, and one of them put a "fish" in the light cruiser *Houston*. She was even more sorely stricken than the *Canberra*. She seemed to be breaking up, and the skipper, Captain W. W. Behrens, prepared to abandon ship. Then he had second thoughts, so the cruiser *Boston* took her in tow.

Admiral Halsey declined to abandon either his mission or the crippled ships. Some quick calculations revealed that he could

---

* A U.S. ship named in honor of the Australian *Canberra* lost in the Battle of Savo. See the author's *1942: The Year That Doomed the Axis* (New York: David McKay Company, Inc., 1967).

165

carry out his schedule of strikes against Luzon and the Vasayas in the Central Philippines and at the same time protect the CripDiv, which by now consisted of *Boston* towing *Houston*, *Wichita* towing *Canberra*, and the cruisers *Santa Fe*, *Birmingham*, and *Mobile* along with eight destroyers. The next morning fleet tugs *Munsee* and *Pawnee*, summoned from an oiler group where they had been standing by for just such an eventuality, took over the towing chores, releasing the *Boston* and *Wichita* to join a light-carrier group assigned to give CripDiv 1 air cover.

On the afternoon of October 16, over a hundred aircraft attacked CripDiv 1. Although most were shot down or repelled, three penetrated the screen, and one of them put a torpedo squarely into the *Houston*'s stern. The tug *Pawnee* immediately signaled, WE'LL STAND BY YOU.

There was grave need. Nearly 2,000 more tons of water poured into the cruiser, but she stayed afloat.

The inexperienced Japanese aviators, most of them hurriedly trained since the Battle of the Philippine Sea, made fantastic claims of destruction, at least those who survived did. The amazing thing is that Imperial Headquarters swallowed these claims hook, line, and sinker. Any experienced commander learns to discount airmen's claims; there is simply too much chance for honest error. A pilot dodging antiaircraft fire cannot count accurately, and two planes often claim success on the same target. With greater experience comes greater accuracy. And the Japanese pilots were as green as the fields of their homeland. They "sank" ships where none existed, and the claims were solemnly added up to make the fantastic score which Tokyo announced in an official communiqué on October 16: 11 carriers, 2 battleships, 3 cruisers and 1 destroyer or light cruiser sunk, 8 battleships, 4 cruisers, 1 destroyer or light cruiser, and 13 unidentified ships heavily damaged and 12 more set on fire.

To be sure, 312 Japanese aircraft had failed to return, but that was a small price to pay for such a glorious victory.

Hearing these wild claims, Halsey got an idea. While two

166

task groups worked over Luzon, two others hid out over the horizon, leaving CripDiv 1, now renamed BaitDiv 1, to lure the Japanese fleet to come out and fight. Said the skipper of the *Birmingham*, still guarding the stricken cruisers, "Now I know how a worm on a fishhook must feel."

By this time the Japanese convinced themselves that BaitDiv 1 was all that remained of the Third Fleet, and the bait almost worked. Vice Admiral Shima sortied with three cruisers and a division of destroyers to eliminate BaitDiv 1, but unfortunately for Halsey's plans, a Japanese scout plane caught sight of one of the task groups, and Shima scurried back to port.

Slowly the cripples drew out of range of Japanese air power and reached Ulithi on October 27. After a brief stop, they were towed on to Manus for temporary repairs and thence to Pearl Harbor and the East Coast of the United States for complete overhauls.

Admiral Halsey, meanwhile, dropped down to give support for the landings on Leyte, only a few days off.

Leyte, one of the larger of the 7,000 islands of the Philippine Archipelago, lies north of Mindanao and is tucked in behind Samar. Leyte Gulf is formed by Samar on the north, Leyte on the west, and Dinagat on the south. Between Dinagat and Leyte is a passageway known as Surigao Strait, one of the principal passages through the Philippines into the South China Sea. The landings were to take place in the northwest corner of Leyte Gulf, south of the capital city of Tacloban and in the Dulag area, fifteen miles to the south. A-Day was set for October 20, 1944.

If we include the ships of the Third and Seventh Fleets, the array of naval power was the greatest ever assembled. It was larger and more powerful than that employed in the Normandy invasion. Yet, in the Pacific, where everything was under one national command, complications ensued that did not happen off Normandy where the powerful naval forces of the United States and Great Britain worked in harmony, assisted by ships of other nations at war with Germany. At this time, the Seventh Fleet comprised 738 ships of all kinds, and the Third Fleet, not counting oiler support groups, tugs, and other service ships, included 105 combatant ships.

The Seventh Fleet was commanded by Vice Admiral Thomas C. Kinkaid, whose immediate boss was General MacArthur, who reported to General Marshall on the Joint Chiefs of Staff. The Third Fleet was under Admiral William F. Halsey, Jr., who reported to Admiral Chester W. Nimitz. Nimitz was answerable to Admiral King, also on the Joint Chiefs of Staff. Thus forces of the Third and Seventh Fleets, operating in the same invasion, in the same waters, *had no common superior short of the President of the United States.* This division of authority nearly brought disaster. As General MacArthur later wrote, "Leyte came out all right, but the hazards would all have been avoided by unity of command."

The overjoyed Japanese celebrated the "Victory of Formosa," but Admiral Toyoda and the staff of Combined Fleet did not share the general optimism. Instead, they were taking a very hard look at the plan known as Sho-Go—Victory Operation. This plan had been drawn up in the last week of July, and since no one then could know where the Americans would go next, Sho-Go had four variants. Sho-1 dealt with a landing in the Philippines, Sho-2 with one in the Formosa–Ryukyu area, Sho-3 with one on Honshu or Kyushu, and Sho-4 with one on Hokkaido or the Kuriles. Once more the concept was the "Decisive Battle."

On October 17, reports of American activity in the Philippine area began to reach Combined Fleet Headquarters, and just after 0800 Toyoda issued the alert for Sho-1. He also ordered Admiral Kurita to leave Lingga Roads off Singapore and proceed to Borneo for fueling.

What caused this alert?

At 0630, October 17, a small group of eight destroyer transports and some landing craft approached Suluan Island off the mouth of Leyte Gulf and were sighted twenty minutes later by Japanese lookouts there. It was the report of the commander on Suluan that alerted Admiral Toyoda. The American ships stood in, and at 0800, the cruiser *Denver*, which with the *Columbia* and four destroyers was supporting this preliminary operation, opened fire on Suluan. This was the opening round in the liberation of the Philippines. A Ranger Infantry Battalion went ashore about 0820, the first Americans to "return." With the aid of delighted natives, they quickly dispatched the thirty-two Japanese on the island, and re-embarked the next day. They had disposed of a lighthouse and lookout station which might have given early warning of the approach of the landing force. Other preliminary landings were made on Dinagat and Homonhon on October 17 and 18. The next day, A-minus-1, was devoted to minesweeping, shore bombardment, and the clearing of obstacles by underwater-demolition teams. The twelve escort carriers of Rear Admiral Thomas L. Sprague's Task Group 77.4 provided strafing and bombing operations, assisted by planes from TF 38.

Just on midnight, the procession of transports entered Leyte Gulf and began to move to their assigned transport areas. On these transports and other vessels were two full corps, the X and XXIV, comprising the Sixth Army under Lieutenant General Walter Krueger. The Northern Attack Force, under Rear Admiral Daniel E. Barbey, was to land X Corps near Tacloban, while the Southern Attack Force under Vice Admiral T. S. Wilkinson would put the XXIV Corps ashore near Dulag.

Everything was quiet on the blacked out ships. Most of the troops preferred to try to sleep topside because of the intense heat in the troop spaces. There was still a nasty swell, a leftover from a typhoon which had passed near the Philippines on October 17, and there were some G.I.s who felt the motion enough to welcome dry land even if it meant going up against the Japanese.

As the sun rose through heavy clouds astern, the troops could begin to see land; Samar to starboard and later Leyte dead ahead. The hot, muggy day was oppressive, and as the sun dried up the humidity, it began to bake the men in its intense heat.

On shore, delighted Filipinos looked out and saw this huge armada approaching their shores. They could hardly believe their eyes. Deliverance was at hand.

Soon after entering Leyte Gulf, the transport forces diverged to move to their assigned areas off the two beach regions.

Leyte Landings, October 20, 1944,
and Operations to November 7, 1944

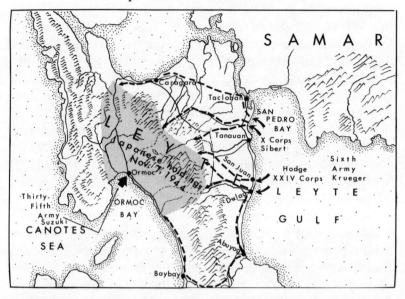

Battleships, cruisers, destroyers, and rocket-equipped landing craft bombarded likely Japanese strong points, and planes from the escort carrier groups and two of Mitscher's groups gave close air support. The landings were on two two-division fronts eleven miles apart. Off Tacloban the First Cavalry Division (Major General V. D. Mudge) landed on White Beach; immediately on their left on Red Beach came Major General F. A. Irving's Twenty-Fourth Infantry Division. The southern beaches were Orange and Blue, the responsibility of the Ninety-Sixth Division, and Violet and Yellow beaches, the responsibility of the Seventh Division. This assault, whose troops had come fifteen times the distance of those who landed in Normandy four and a half months earlier, was only a single division weaker than the initial landing on D-Day on Omaha, Utah, Juno, Gold, and Sword.

All landings came exactly on time, at 1000, October 20, 1944. Some hidden Japanese guns gave trouble, especially to the LSTs that were having difficulty in getting close enough inshore to unload. The beaches were too shelving, and the LSTs grounded some distance from the shoreline. All in all, however, it was one of the easiest landings in the entire war. The opposition would come later.

The comparative ease of the landing was a result of a basic change in Japanese defensive tactics. The Japanese had learned that no beach defenses could stand up to the naval bombardment that preceded an amphibious assault, and that to try to oppose the landing at the water's edge merely sacrificed troops uselessly. On Peleliu the tactics of digging in had delayed the American conquest of the island and made it more costly, and the Japanese decided to adapt these tactics to the Philippines. Lieutenant General Shiro Makino, who had responsibility for the defense of Leyte, had but one division, the Sixteenth, at his disposal. He was forced to divide it to meet both American thrusts. To add to his woes, the Sixteenth Division was one of the poorest in the Japanese Army. It was inexperienced, and was sneeringly referred to by army officers as being composed of men who were "better businessmen than fighters."

Imperial Headquarters realized that the situation must be remedied. Already Lieutenant General Tomoyuki Yamashita, conquerer of Singapore, had been assigned to Manila in overall command of the defense of the Philippines. This was a result of a decision to make the decisive land battle in the Philippines, in connection with the decisive sea battle. Although Yamashita had no illusions about the ability of Japan to hold the Philippines, his pessimism was not shared by subordinate officers. Obviously, a single division would not be able to repel the Americans, so plans were made for quick and heavy reinforcements. Lieutenant General Sosaku Suzuki, Commanding General of the Thirty-Fifth Army (which was about equal in size to an American Army Corps), was given responsibility for the defense of Leyte and the annihilation of the Americans there. So optimistic were some of the Japanese that they began to plan MacArthur's surrender. Suzuki stated sternly, "We must demand the capitulation of MacArthur's entire forces, those in New Guinea and other places as well as the troops on Leyte."

Unmindful of his enemy's plans for him, MacArthur was

preparing to keep a promise. Always the showman, he played the role he had been dreaming of for nearly three years: His return to the Philippines.

The Great Return took place on the afternoon of October 20. He and his staff had come up from Hollandia on the light cruiser *Nashville* and had watched the landing operations during the morning. After lunch, he changed to clean suntans and descended into an LCM and took his seat in the stern sheets, directly behind and above Philippine President Sergio Osmeña and Resident Commissioner Carlos Romulo. When the LCM grounded, MacArthur stepped out into the knee-deep water, followed by Osmeña, Romulo, and members of his staff, and waded ashore. The diminutive Romulo later noted, "The newspapers reported that I was right behind him [MacArthur]. Little did they realize that I nearly drowned. There was the tall MacArthur, with the waters reaching up to his knees, and behind him there was little Romulo, trying to keep his head above water."

Such jocularity was absent at the time. Although some fighting was still going on on Red Beach, five miles below Tacloban, where MacArthur stepped ashore, he ignored it. Using a portable radio transmitter, he made his famous broadcast to the Philippine people.

This is the Voice of Freedom, General MacArthur speaking. . . . *I have returned.* By the grace of Almighty God, our forces stand again on Philippine soil. . . . At my side is your President, Sergio Osmeña, worthy successor of that great patriot, Manuel Quezon. . . . The seat of your Government is now therefore firmly re-established on Philippine soil.

The hour of your redemption is here. . . . Rally to me. Let the indomitable spirit of Bataan and Corregidor lead on. As the lines of battle roll forward to bring you within the zone of operations, rise and strike! For future generations of your sons and daughters, strike! In the name of your sacred dead, strike! Let no heart be faint. Let every arm be steeled. The guidance of Divine God points the way. Follow in His name to the Holy Grail of righteous victory!

When the G.I.s and sailors heard rebroadcasts of MacArthur's "I have returned," they muttered, "Yeah! But what about the hundred thousand other guys it took to get him here?"

Yet MacArthur was right. His flamboyance was just what the moment called for, just what the Filipinos would respond to. They did rally to him. Obviously not yet in organized military units, but their guerrillas gave many a Japanese soldier an unhappy time on Leyte.

On the days following the landings, Sixth Army forces consolidated the beachheads and expanded the perimeters. Against stiff fighting, the two corps made contact with each other on October 25. During this time, the naval units were giving support and were paying a price for it. The light cruiser *Honolulu*, which had fought in many actions from Pearl Harbor on, had hitherto led a charmed life, never losing a man. Off Leyte on A-Day her luck ran out. A Japanese plane sneaked in through the mist and dropped a torpedo which caught her on the port side, killing sixty men and doing heavy damage. The next day the Australian cruiser *Australia* was the victim of a Japanese plane which crashed into her foremast.* Escorted by two destroyers, the battered cruisers retired to Manus for repair.

Engineers worked to get airstrips into use, but the heavy rains and the spongy soil hampered their work. Fields at Dulag and Tacloban were the first opened, although they were so soft that many planes cracked up on landing; they were literally lifesavers in the coming naval battle only a few days off.

By October 23, Imperial Headquarters had made a further decision. Already they had agreed that the decisive land battle would be in the Philippines. Now they decreed it would be on Leyte rather than Luzon. Forces were already in motion for the decisive sea battle, and if it was successful, the American ground forces could be destroyed at leisure on Leyte.

It was a big "if."

MacArthur's men had no intention of being destroyed. They

---

* This was not a Kamikaze attack. *Kamikazes*, which were formally organized suicide attack programs, were first used in the Battle for Leyte Gulf. There had been several cases of suicide attacks made by Japanese pilots on their own initiative.

were steadily grinding out territory held by the Japanese and were being embarrassingly warmly greeted by the Filipinos. Grinning natives handed out papayas, bananas, Japanese beer, even eggs, saying, "Thank you, thank you," as they did so. It was difficult to keep them out of harm's way.

One Filipino pointed to his home, saying, "My house, my house," as he indicated that there was a Japanese sniper inside. A G.I. went in. Eight shots rang out, and the G.I. emerged. He said it was OK to go in now.

"Thank you, sir. Thank you, sir."

By October 25, 132,400 men had been landed on Leyte with nearly 200,000 tons of supplies, enough to enable them to keep going for thirty days. Most of the ships had left, having completed unloading in record time. As the Battle for Leyte Gulf approached its climax, only three amphibious force flagships, one attack cargo ship, twenty-three LSTs, two LSMs, and twenty-eight Liberty ships remained in Leyte Gulf. The transports were retiring to rear areas, and the combatant ships were advancing to meet the Japanese.

CHAPTER FIVE

# The Battle for Leyte Gulf

> *. . . he which hath no stomach to this fight,*
> *Let him depart. His passport shall be made,*
> *And crowns for convoy put into his purse.*
> *We would not die in that man's company*
> *That fears his fellowship to die with us.*
> *This day is call'd the feast of Crispian.*
> *He that outlives this day and comes safe home*
> *Will stand a tip-toe when this day is named,*
> *And rouse him at the name of Crispian . . .*
> *And gentlemen in England now a-bed*
> *Shall think themselves accurs'd they were not here,*
> *And hold their manhoods cheap whiles any speaks*
> *That fought with us upon Saint Crispin's day.*
>
> Shakespeare, King Henry V

THE gentle brothers Crispin and Crispinian, who were martyred under Diocletian in the third century, were men of peace. Cobblers in life, they became the patron saints of the shoemakers, and their Saint's Day is celebrated October 25. Oddly enough, two decisive battles happened on this day, each ending an era. In 1415, English longbowmen crushed the chivalry of France at Agincourt, ending the dominance of the armored knight in battle. In 1944, the Battle for Leyte Gulf was the last conventional naval action, where ships fought ships, where two navies resolutely opposed each other with all the weapons of air, surface, and under water. The long, rolling thunder of battleship guns against battleship guns came to an end. It probably will never be heard again.

"Would it not be a shame to have the fleet remain intact while our nation perishes? I believe that Imperial Headquarters is giving us a glorious opportunity. You must remember that there are such things as miracles. What man can say that there is no chance for our fleet to turn the tide of war in a Decisive Battle?"

Vice Admiral Takeo Kurita was speaking to his commanders and their staffs aboard his flagship, the heavy cruiser *Atago*. From Imperial Headquarters had come the command to execute Sho-1. It was Japan's last chance. It was a scheme of desperation, which had no chance at all under any circumstances. And it came close to working, up to a point.

Sho-1 was literally a scraping together of all Japan's remaining naval strength in a desperate endeavor to drive the Americans from the Philippines. It was a jerry-built effort, for the Japanese could no longer operate their fleets as they would have liked. The reason? Lack of oil.

American submarines had concentrated on Japanese tankers as priority targets from the first. Hundreds of them had been sunk, reducing the supplies of fuel oil in Japan to such an extent that most of the naval ships had to move south to be near the source of oil. It could no longer come to them. Combined Fleet thus was split, with most of its strength in southern waters, and based at Lingga Roads, south of Singapore. With the exception of Japan's remaining aircraft carriers, only a few ships of combat worth remained in the Home Islands.

The order to execute Sho-1 set in motion four Japanese naval forces. Each was to coordinate with the others, yet command was badly divided, and no effective common control existed. Although Admiral Jisaburo Ozawa was still Commander in Chief Mobile Force, he was to be at sea with one of the weaker parts of it, so that whatever coordinated command function was performed was done by Admiral Soemu Toyoda, Commander in Chief Combined Fleet, from his headquarters at Tokyo. As it turned out, his orders were more hortative than helpful.

In order to follow the moves on the gigantic chessboard that was involved in the Battle for Leyte Gulf, we call to mind the cry of the hawker at a football game, "You can't tell the players

176

without a program!" Here, then, is the program for the Battle for Leyte Gulf.*

*On the Japanese side:*
Combined Fleet—This was the overall command, exercised by Admiral Toyoda in Tokyo.

Advance Force—This was a submarine command under Vice Admiral Shigeyoshi Miwa. Although Japanese submarines prowled around the battle area, they played only a small role in the battle.

Mobile Force—This force consisted of most of Japan's remaining combatant ships, under command of Admiral Ozawa. It was divided into two parts, the Main Body under Ozawa, and the First Striking Force under Vice Admiral Takeo Kurita.

Main Body—In spite of its impressive name, this force was nearly impotent. It consisted of four carriers with only a handful of planes and other ships, and was intended to lure Task Force 38 from the Leyte beachhead. Ozawa expected to lose his entire force. For clarity, we will henceforth refer to this as the *Northern Force.*

First Striking Force—This was the main attack force. It was divided into two sub-forces, the First Diversionary Attack Force, under Kurita's own command, and the Second Diversionary Attack Force under Vice Admiral Shoji Nishimura.

First Diversionary Attack Force—This was a powerful force indeed. It included 5 battleships, 10 heavy and 2 light cruisers, and 15 destroyers. Under Kurita's personal command, it was to transit San Bernardino Strait and attack Leyte Gulf from the north. We shall refer to it as the *Center Force.*

Second Diversionary Attack Force—This was a splinter force from Kurita's First Striking Force. It consisted of 2 old battleships, a heavy cruiser, and 4 destroyers. Its mission was to attack Leyte Gulf from the south after coming through Surigao Strait. We shall call it the *Southern Force.*

Southwest Area Force—This was an administrative com-

* Those who dislike organization tables should skip to page 179 where the narrative resumes.

177

mand under Vice Admiral Gunichi Mikawa. It controlled all Japanese naval air in the Philippines, which were divided into two parts—the Fifth Base Air Force under Vice Admiral Kimpei Teraoka,* and the Sixth Base Air Force and Second Air Fleet under Vice Admiral Shigeru Fukudome. There was also attached to this command, in a rather curious way, the Fifth Fleet under Vice Admiral Kiyohide Shima.

Fifth Fleet—Again, the name is deceptive. Also designated the Second Striking Force, this command had been so weakened that it comprised 1 heavy and 2 light cruisers and 4 destroyers. No one seemed to know what to do with it. Although it had been assigned to escort duties, Admiral Shima thought such a role would be demeaning for the forthcoming battle, so, having been given freedom of action by Admiral Mikawa, he decided to support Nishimura in the Surigao Strait. We shall refer to this force as *Southern Force II.*

*On the American side:*

In addition to Army Air Force commands which provided distant air support, and the Army troops ashore on Leyte, the principal naval forces concerned in the battle were:

Submarines, Pacific Fleet—Commanded by Vice Admiral Charles Lockwood at Pearl Harbor. Several American submarines were in the area, and two of them drew first blood in the battle.

Seventh Fleet—Commanded by Vice Admiral Thomas C. Kinkaid, under General MacArthur's Southwest Pacific Command, the Seventh Fleet included the transport forces, most of which had withdrawn, and the supporting forces, including old battleships and cruisers, destroyers and destroyer escorts, escort carriers, minesweepers, and smaller vessels including PT boats. There were two principal parts of the Seventh Fleet directly engaged in the battle: The Bombardment and Fire Support Group under Rear Admiral Jesse B. Oldendorf, and the Escort Carrier Group, under Rear Admiral Thomas L. Sprague.

Bombardment and Fire Support Group—This was formed after Japanese intentions to give battle became evident. It

---

* Relieved October 20 by Vice Admiral Tonosuke Ohnishi.

included the six old battleships which had been firing on the landing beaches, cruisers, and destroyers, and was intended to stop any penetration of Surigao Strait into Leyte Gulf.

Escort Carrier Group—This was a group of escort carriers and their screens intended to support the troops ashore with strafing and bombing runs. It was divided into three Task Units with six escort carriers each. We can most easily refer to them by their radio voice calls, "Taffy 1," "Taffy 2," and "Taffy 3." They were to bear the brunt of the battle.

Third Fleet—Commanded by Admiral William F. Halsey, Jr., under Admiral Nimitz, the Third Fleet was to protect the Leyte beachheads and to destroy the Japanese fleet if opportunity afforded.

Task Force 38—This was virtually the same as the Third Fleet. It was divided into four task groups. In all it included 8 fleet carriers and 8 light carriers, 6 battleships, and many cruisers and destroyers. Although it was commanded by Vice Admiral Marc A. Mitscher, Admiral Halsey's tendency to take over left Mitscher little more than a passenger in his own flagship.

Task Force 34—This was the source of one of the major confusions of the battle. It could be formed at Halsey's direction by pulling the battleships, some of the cruisers, and some of the destroyers from the groups of Task Force 38. Intended for surface action, it was under command of Vice Admiral Willis A. Lee. It did not exist when the battle began.

Even before the signal to execute Sho-1, Admiral Kurita had left Lingga Roads in Singapore and proceeded in company with Nishimura to Brunei Bay, Borneo, to refuel. In that area, the oil was so pure that it could be pumped directly from the wells into the ships' bunkers. This gave the Japanese a great advantage, since the crude oil did not have to be shipped to Japan for refining. On the other hand, the failure to crack off the elements which form gasoline and kerosene made the fuel oil highly volatile, greatly increasing the fire risk on the ships.

At Brunei, Kurita and Nishimura parted company, never to meet again in this world. At 0800, October 22, Kurita sortied

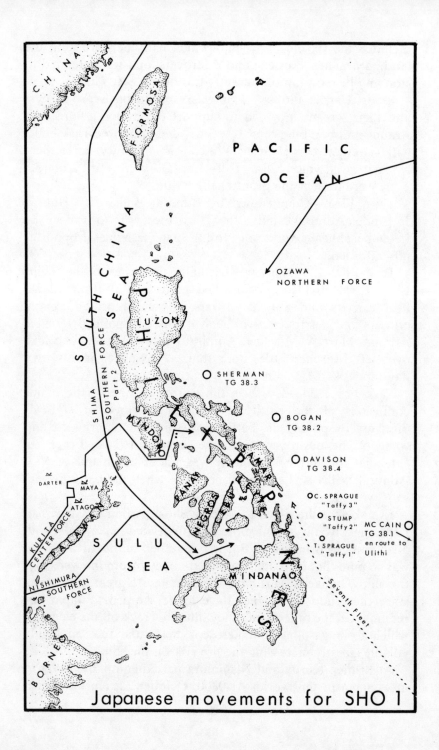

Japanese movements for SHO 1

and set a course for Palawan Passage, a twenty-five-mile-wide channel between Palawan and a shoal area of the South China Sea known as Dangerous Ground. For some reason, never explained, he neglected to have his destroyers assume an antisubmarine disposition. He was in battle approach formation, his heavy ships in two columns, and his destroyers in three, on either flank and between the heavies.

From the flag bridge of the *Atago*, leading the port column, Kurita could look out over his command. He had with him the two largest battleships in the world, *Yamato* and *Musashi*. Nearly half again larger than the *Iowa*-class American battleships, these vessels displaced 68,000 tons, and were armed with nine 18.1-inch (460-mm.) rifles. The secondary antiaircraft battery was formidable, and in addition each ship had 120 25-mm. guns. They were slower than the *Iowa*s, being able to make only 27 knots as opposed to 33, but the punch they could throw was deadly.

Kurita's three other battleships—the *Nagato*, with 16-inch guns, and the *Haruna* and *Kongo* with 14-inch guns—were less powerful but they could give a good account of themselves if challenged.

His ten heavy and two light cruisers were sleek and fast. The destroyers had full loads of the deadly Long Lance torpedoes. Kurita was spoiling for a fight. He knew it would not be easy, but he was ready.

The fight came sooner than he expected.

The U.S. submarines *Darter* and *Dace* were prowling Palawan Passage. En route to their station, they had sunk two merchant ships, but then they had seen nothing for ten days. All that changed at 0116, October 23, when *Darter* picked up a radar contact. The two boats were moving slowly along on the surface within hailing distance of one another. Commander David H. McClintock, skipper of the *Darter*, lost no time informing by megaphone Commander Bladen D. Claggett on the bridge of the *Dace*. "Let's go!"

Both submarines set off at flank speed in the direction of the contact, fifteen miles away. Soon it was apparent that there was something big. Soon they counted 11 heavy ships and 6 destroyers, which they promptly reported by radio. Then they got ready to attack.

Even though McClintock and Claggett had not seen all of Kurita's ships, they had seen enough of them to arouse the intense interest of U.S. Naval Intelligence. Admiral Halsey received the report early that morning and promptly set about preparing to deal with this menace.

It turned out that he had less to deal with than he might have had, for the *Darter* and *Dace* had cooperated to give Kurita a thoroughly bad time.

By dawn, the submarines had parted company, the *Darter* reaching attack position on Kurita's port column of heavy ships, and the *Dace* taking on the starboard column. At 0609, when she was only 980 yards from the leading ship in the port column, the *Darter*, which had submerged, fired all six of her bow tubes. Before the torpedoes could hit, McClintock swung ship in order to fire the stern tubes into the second ship.

Before he went deep, McClintock turned his periscope back to the first target just in time to see "the sight of a lifetime," as he put it. He had hit Kurita's flagship, *Atago*, which was already a mass of flame and smoke, and was down by the bow. Before *Darter* got deep, she heard unmistakable sounds of hits on the second cruiser, the *Takao*, and McClintock thought he had accounted for two in one attack. It was not to be, however, for *Takao*, although sorely crippled, survived the attack and made it back to Brunei.

While McClintock maneuvered *Darter* to avoid depth charges which were being dropped by four furious destroyers, *Dace* was getting into attack position. Her target was the heavy cruiser *Maya*, although Commander Claggett thought he was aiming at a battleship. At such close ranges it was hard to tell. They all looked big.

Just before firing, *Dace* ran up her periscope, and Commander Claggett took a look around. "Good Lord," he said, "it looks like the Fourth of July up there! One is sinking and another is burning!" At 0654 he commenced firing his six bow tubes, and two minutes later four of the torpedoes hit. *Dace* was scrambling for the depths when the explosions came and was so shaken Claggett thought he was the victim of a depth charge. It was the hapless *Maya* blowing up. She "exploded, and after the spray and smoke had disappeared nothing of her remained to be seen," wrote a Japanese observer later.

Meanwhile flagship *Atago* went down. It was just eighteen minutes after the torpedoes hit that she disappeared beneath the water, taking with her 360 officers and men. A destroyer had attempted to come alongside to take off Admiral Kurita and his staff, but before she could make it, the *Atago* went under. Kurita and his officers had to swim for it. The destroyer picked them up and became temporary flagship until Kurita could transfer to the *Yamato*.

This early morning swim was but the first in a series of woes for the sixty-two-year-old admiral. There was a great deal more to come.

Reduced by the loss of three heavy cruisers, Kurita's Center Force pressed on toward the Sibuyan Sea and San Bernardino Strait.

*Darter* and *Dace* concentrated on trying to finish off the stricken *Takao*, but had no success, as the escorting destroyers foiled every attempt to get into attack position. That night, *Darter*'s luck ran out, for she went hard and fast aground on Bombay Shoal in the Dangerous Ground. All efforts to free her were unsuccessful, and she was abandoned after secret publications had been destroyed. The crew transferred to *Dace*.

The *Darter*'s hulk was still pretty much intact on the shoal. The demolition charges had not been powerful enough to destroy her, and when *Dace* fired four torpedoes at her, they all exploded uselessly on the reef. Attempts to destroy her by *Dace*'s 4-inch deck gun had to be abandoned when a Japanese bomber came over. Fortunately the bomber pilot elected to pass up the submerging *Dace* in favor of attacking the motionless *Darter*, and he obligingly finished the job of destruction.

Alerted by *Darter*'s contact report a few minutes after midnight on the morning of October 23, Halsey and Kinkaid

183

began preparing for major battles. Although Nishimura's Southern Force was not sighted until the morning of October 24, intelligence reports indicated that a force other than Kurita's was on the way, and the two commanders took precautions accordingly.

At this time, only three of the four task groups of Task Force 38 were in Philippine waters. The strongest of all, Vice Admiral John S. McCain's TG 38.1 had been sent northeastward to Ulithi for rest and replenishment. The three remaining groups were spread out about a hundred miles apart, Rear Admiral Frederick C. Sherman's TG 38.3 farthest north off Luzon, Rear Admiral Gerald F. Bogan's TG 38.2 off San Bernardino Strait, and Rear Admiral Ralph E. Davison's TG 38.4 near Leyte Gulf. Even though Halsey knew the Japanese were on their way, he made no move to recall McCain's task group. He did move the other groups a little closer together.

Beginning at dawn, October 24, Hellcats and Helldivers went off from all three of the fast carrier groups. An *Intrepid* pilot spotted Kurita's force at 0812, and planes from *Enterprise* and *Franklin* sighted Nishimura less than an hour later at 0905. Shima's force, coming along behind Nishimura, was picked up about two hours later.

Clearly the powerful Center Force in the Sibuyan Sea was Halsey's responsibility, and he set about meeting it. He turned McCain's TG 38.1 around (about twenty-four hours too late in the opinion of this writer), arranged for it to refuel and rejoin Task Force 38 at best speed. He ordered a major strike from all carriers, issuing the orders directly to Admirals Sherman, Bogan, and Davison, bypassing Admiral Mitscher completely.

Before Halsey's strike order could be carried out, the Japanese drew first blood on Sherman's TG 38.3. Over Kurita's objections Admiral Mikawa had decided to use his 200 or so aircraft "offensively" to attack the American fleet rather than "defensively" to protect Kurita's. When Kurita was spotted on the morning of October 24, he sent an urgent request for air cover, but less than a dozen Zekes were sent to help him, and they could not find him! Everything else that could fly was sent in three fifty- to sixty-plane raids against the Americans. They concentrated on Sherman's group rather than Bogan's, which was the one in the best position to do Kurita the most harm.

Most of the attacking Japanese planes were shot down in a masterly fashion by fighters under Commander David McCampbell from the *Essex* and another group of fighters under Lieutenant Commander F. A. Bardshar from the *Princeton*. But they missed the one that counted. A single Judy which had been skulking behind the clouds broke through and planted a single 550-pound bomb on the *Princeton*'s flight deck. A holocaust ensued immediately on the hangar deck as the bomb penetrated deep within the carrier. Many men were killed instantly from the blast and scores of others were wounded. Destroyers *Cassin Young*, *Gatling*, and *Irwin* closed in to help and rescued many of the men forced into the water by the intense heat of the flames that were devouring the *Princeton*.

At 1004, less than half an hour after the carrier had been hit, the cruiser *Birmingham* came alongside to assist with the firefighting. Destroyer *Morrison*, on the other side, was wedged between uptakes on the *Princeton*'s starboard side and had the weird experience of having a jeep and a tractor fall onto her bridge and bounce off the main deck. It took nearly three hours to clear the destroyer from her "fly-in-flypaper" predicament.

A volunteer fire-fighting team from the *Birmingham*, under Lieutenant Allen Reed, assisted *Princeton*'s own men in fighting the flames and they were making good progress when an air raid was reported coming in, and the *Birmingham* had to cast off. The antiaircraft cruiser *Reno*, which had joined in the battle against the fires, took up an air defense position.

This raid was from Ozawa's Northern Force. Ozawa was anxiously trying to be discovered by Halsey, and he thought that sending his planes off would be a dead giveaway. It didn't work out. Most of the planes were destroyed, and those that survived landed on Luzon, leaving Ozawa's four carriers with only twenty-nine aircraft in all.

The raid disposed of, Captain Thomas B. Inglis took the *Birmingham* back to the *Princeton* to attempt to rig a tow. Approaching from the stern, the *Birmingham* passed along the port side of the carrier so they would have the maximum opportunity to pass the messenger line. Just as she was alongside, the fires reached the torpedo stowage in the *Princeton*'s stern. A tremendous explosion blew off most of her stern and all of the after section of the flight deck. Scraps of steel cut down men on both ships. The *Birmingham* was particularly vulnerable, since her open decks were crowded with men handling lines, fighting fires, manning antiaircraft guns, and preparing to rig the tow. Her War Diary tells the story:

The spectacle which greeted the human eye was horrible to behold. . . . Dead, dying, and wounded, many of them badly and horribly, covered the decks. The communication platform was no better. Blood ran freely down the waterways, and continued to run for some time. Said our Executive Officer, who inspected the ship immediately, "I really have no words at my command that can adequately describe the veritable splendor of the conduct of all hands, wounded and unwounded. Men with legs off, with arms off, with gaping wounds in their sides, with the tops of their heads furrowed by fragments, would insist, 'I'm all right. Take care of Joe over there,' or, 'Don't waste morphine on me, Commander; just hit me over the head.'" What went on below decks immediately following the explosion is well depicted by our Chaplain [who was in the Wardroom, which was the principal emergency battle dressing station]:—

"Within a very few minutes after the explosion, corpsmen and the only medical officer aboard the ship arrived from the sick bay. These in turn were assisted by officers and men in giving essential first aid. There was no sign of confusion. The wounded, even though suffering shock, in many cases probably in great pain until the morphine began to take effect, remained quiet and fully co-operative with those attempting to render first aid. Again and again I was urged by those horribly wounded to help others before themselves. There were no outcries and in cases of those with clean cuts which were not hemorrhaging too badly, when told that those who were bleeding more profusely must be tended first, agreed cheerfully in every case saying 'O.K. I'm all right, don't worry about me.' By the end of this first hour the care of the wounded was organized to the point at which plasma could be given to the most serious cases. At this point I was ordered by the Commanding Officer to make preparations for the identification and burial of the dead."

186

While the *Birmingham* ministered to the wounded and dying, Captain William H. Buracker reluctantly decided that the *Princeton* could not be saved. Although she still floated, there was danger of further explosions, and no other ship could be spared to tow her. The *Reno* gave her the *coup de grâce* with two torpedoes.

The *Princeton* was not the only ship to be lost that day. The Japanese were to pay dearly for their one success of October 24.

Weakened by the loss of three cruisers and four destroyers left to escort the crippled *Takao* back to Brunei, Admiral Kurita's Center Force resolutely pressed on to engage the Americans. Rounding the southern tip of Mindoro at 0625, they entered the Sibuyan Sea and headed northeasterly toward the approaches to San Bernardino Strait. They were in two groups, circular formations, seven miles apart. *Yamato* and *Musashi* were in the center of one group and the other battleships in the other. This daylight passage of the Sibuyan Sea was the most perilous part of the journey to the battle area. Kurita knew he could expect air attacks and he believed that submarines were stalking him as well. He was right on the first count and wrong on the second, for there were no submarines in the area at all. His experiences on the day before make his apprehension understandable.

At 0837, Halsey ordered by voice radio to all groups, "Strike! Repeat: Strike! Good luck!"

Bogan's force was closest, although the others were closing at best speed, and it was planes from his group that made the first attack. Planes from the *Intrepid* and *Cabot* hit the super-battleship *Musashi* at 1027, and they were but the first of many. By early afternoon she had fallen twenty miles astern of the rest of Kurita's ships. In desperation, she fired her main battery guns at the attacking aircraft, but to no purpose other than giving incredulous American aviators the shock of their lives as 18.1-inch shells exploded before them. But not a plane was knocked down by this expedient. The Americans simply spread out a little more and kept coming.

At 1520 another attack came in against the *Musashi*, and this

## Track of *Yamato*

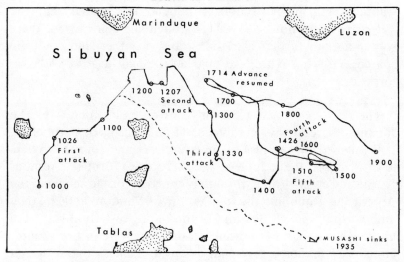

one did for her. In addition to the nine torpedo hits and five bombs the battleship had taken, this attack added ten more torpedoes and a dozen bombs. Her captain signalled: SPEED SIX KNOTS, CAPABLE OF OPERATION. DAMAGE GREAT. WHAT SHALL WE DO?

The ship was told to leave the battle area and head back to Brunei, escorted by two destroyers. The heavy cruiser *Myoko* had already turned back as a result of bomb damage. Little by little, Kurita's force was being weakened, but it still remained powerful: 4 battleships, 6 heavy cruisers, 2 light cruisers, and 11 destroyers.

It soon became evident that the *Musashi* could not make it back to Brunei. She was taking water fast. On learning this, Kurita ordered: MUSASHI GO FORWARD OR BACK-WARD AT TOP SPEED AND GROUND ON NEAR-EST ISLAND AND BECOME A LAND BATTERY.

She could not achieve even this ignominious goal. The ship was unmanageable and could move only in circles. She sank lower by the bow, and at 1935 rolled over and sank. Nearly 1,100 men and officers were lost; the others were rescued by destroyers and taken to Manila.

188

Shaken by these heavy attacks, Kurita temporarily reversed course in order to allow Japanese land-based air to come to his aid and to attack the American carriers. Land-based air, however, had shot its bolt, and there was no help forthcoming. Realizing that he was falling far behind schedule, Kurita, at 1714, once again reversed course and headed for San Bernardino.

An hour later, Toyoda sent a message: ALL FORCES WILL DASH TO THE ATTACK, TRUSTING IN DIVINE ASSISTANCE.

The Japanese kept coming.

Three hundred miles to the north of San Bernardino, Admiral Ozawa was doing his best to be discovered. Never, it seemed, was a man so plagued with ill-luck. He broke radio silence repeatedly, only to be foiled by a faulty transmitter in the flagship *Zuikaku.* He had sent off his carrier aircraft, only to have them interpreted as land-based from Luzon or Formosa. He sent a group on ahead with orders to "proceed southward and grasp a favorable opportunity to attack and destroy enemy remnants." Officially, Ozawa used the word "remnants," even though he well knew that Halsey had considerably more than that. What he really meant was go on and get yourselves discovered.

At length, Ozawa had his desire. His advance force was spotted at 1540 by planes from TG 38.4; his own force was discovered an hour later. He recalled the advance force and prepared to defend himself as best he could with only a handful of planes aboard his carriers. They would have to rely on the antiaircraft guns of the ships, including those of the *Ise* and *Hyuga*, hermaphrodite battleship-carriers, which had had the after turrets removed and replaced by short flight decks. They carried no planes.

Admiral Halsey received reports of Ozawa's presence during the later afternoon, and it caused him to rethink the entire battle. Already he had prepared to form a powerful surface force to deal with Kurita if he sortied from San Bernardino. At 1512 he sent a dispatch to commanders in the Third Fleet that 4 battleships, 2 heavy and 3 light cruisers, and 14 destroyers

WILL BE FORMED AS TF 34 UNDER VADM LEE, COMMANDER BATTLE LINE X TF 34 WILL ENGAGE DECISIVELY AT LONG RANGES.

*This dispatch was not addressed to Admiral Kinkaid.*

Halsey saw the coming battle as his great opportunity. He had missed everything. Although he had commanded in early carrier raids, he had met no opposition except from a few aircraft. He had missed commanding at the Battle of Midway because he had to go on the sick list just before it happened. Although ships under his command had fought the grim, bloody battles in the Solomons, he had commanded from Noumea, hundreds of miles away. He had had no part of the Central Pacific campaign. Now was the moment, and he did not intend to miss it.

At his insistence, a special paragraph had been added to the Operation Order for the invasion of the Philippines. His basic job was to "cover and support forces of the Southwest Pacific in order to assist in the seizure and occupation of objectives in the CENTRAL PHILIPPINES." The new paragraph read, "In case opportunity for destruction of major portion of the enemy fleet offer or can be created, such destruction becomes the primary task."

Halsey's problem now was to determine which was the major portion of the Japanese fleet.

Since all day he had been acting like a carrier task force commander, he now fell into the trap of his own making. He called for pilots' reports of their attacks on Kurita's fleet to be sent to him directly without being evaluated by the trained staff officers of each carrier group. These raw reports added up to a total of destruction far beyond that which Kurita had endured. To quote from his Action Report, which reflected his estimate at the time: "At least four and probably five battleships torpedoed and bombed, one probably sunk; a minimum of three heavy cruisers torpedoed and others bombed; one light cruiser sunk; one destroyer probably sunk and four damaged. . . . Some details of the foregoing information were not available at dusk, but flash reports indicated beyond doubt that the Center Force had been badly mauled with all of its

190

battleships and most of its heavy cruisers tremendously reduced in fighting power and life."

As Halsey saw it that evening in flag quarters in the *New Jersey*, all the pieces of the Japanese fleet had been discovered. The Southern Force could be safely left to Kinkaid. The Center Force had been so roughly handled in the Sibuyan Sea that it could constitute no menace. Although it was reported to be still advancing after a temporary retirement, Halsey did not seriously believe it was capable of winning a decision. The Northern Force was fresh; no attacks had been made on it, and it included carriers, which extended its effective range by hundreds of miles. Halsey had no way of knowing that it had no planes to speak of. This, as he saw it, was the great danger.

> We had chosen our antagonist [he wrote later]. It remained only to choose the best way to meet him. Again I had three alternatives:
>
> 1. *I could guard San Bernardino with my whole fleet and wait for the Northern Force to strike me.* Rejected. It yielded to the enemy the double initiative of his carriers and his fields on Luzon and would allow him to use them unmolested.
>
> 2. *I could guard San Bernardino with TF 34 while I struck the Northern Force with my carriers.* Rejected. The enemy's potential surface and air strength forbade half-measures; if his shore-based planes joined his carrier planes, together they might inflict far more damage on my half-fleets than they could inflict on the fleet intact.
>
> 3. *I could leave San Bernardino unguarded and strike the Northern Force with my whole fleet.* Accepted. It preserved my fleet's integrity, it left the initiative with me, and it promised the greatest possibility of surprise. Even if the Central Force meanwhile penetrated San Bernardino and headed for Leyte Gulf, it could hope only to harry the landing operation. It could not consolidate any advantage, because no transports accompanied it and no supply ships. It could merely hit and run.
>
> My decision to strike the Northern Force was a hard one to make, but given the same circumstances and the same information as I had then, I would make it again.
>
> I went into flag plot, put my finger on the Northern Force's charted position, 300 miles away, and said, "Here's where we're going. Mick,* start them north."

* Rear Admiral Robert B. "Mick" Carney, Admiral Halsey's Chief of Staff.

191

Such a presentation looks very neat and logical, yet there remains a nagging question in the historian's mind. Were these in fact his only choices? He had ten carriers in his three groups, and fifteen when McCain rejoined. Ozawa had four, as Halsey knew. Land-based air had accounted for the *Princeton* that day, but there had been no significant attacks since. The same evidence for enemy weakness in the air that had led Halsey to recommend moving up the whole Pacific schedule was before him that evening. He was taking his whole force to attack a weak one. He was using a cannon to stop a sparrow while he was expecting a bow and arrow to stop a charging rhinoceros.

Other possibilities suggest themselves:

1. Leave Task Force 34 and TG 38.2 to guard San Bernardino while TGs 38.1, 38.3, and 38.4 converged on Ozawa's Northern Force. This would have provided twelve carriers against Ozawa's four and would have given Task Force 34 air cover. Admiral Lee, incidentally, after the battle noted that he would have been glad to remain off San Bernardino without air cover at all.*

2. Concentrate on Ozawa with Sherman's TG 38.3 and McCain's 38.1, leaving the rest to guard San Bernardino. This would have been as close to an even split of Halsey's forces and would have given him more than adequate strength against both Ozawa and Kurita.

As it was, on the evening of October 24, the sixty-five ships Halsey had with him off the Philippines sped north at 16 knots to take on Ozawa's seventeen, leaving not so much as a picket destroyer to guard San Bernardino.

Aboard the *Lexington*, Admiral Mitscher, rightly assuming that Halsey intended to retain tactical command, turned in his bunk. His staff, however, was worried about reports from scout planes that the Center Force was "still very much afloat and still moving toward San Bernardino." Another contact at 2305 confirmed these movements of the enemy, and Commodore Arleigh Burke, Mitscher's Chief of Staff, decided to wake him

* The writer is just as glad this course was not selected, for the destroyer in which he served in the battle would have had the honor of participating in a planned torpedo attack on the Japanese battle line. The chances of surviving such attacks were not high.

up and urge him to recommend to Halsey that Task Force 34 be detached to return to the Strait. "Does Admiral Halsey have that report?" asked Mitscher.

"Yes, sir."

"If he wants my advice, he'll ask for it," replied Mitscher. Then he went back to sleep.

Before heading north, Halsey notified Kinkaid of his intentions. CENTRAL FORCE HEAVILY DAMAGED ACCORDING TO STRIKE REPORTS X AM PROCEEDING NORTH WITH THREE GROUPS TO ATTACK CARRIER FORCE AT DAWN.

This was all very clear. No one outside the Third Fleet was supposed to know of Halsey's plan to form Task Force 34, and everyone concerned in Task Force 38 knew very well that it had *not* been formed. But Kinkaid did not see it that way. He thought Task Force 34 had been formed, and Halsey's dispatch that he was proceeding north with three groups led Kinkaid to believe that San Bernardino was being guarded by Lee's battleships.

During the war, communication instructions were very clear. No one was supposed to decipher radio broadcast messages

---

The Battle for Leyte Gulf, Oct. 24–25, 1944
(Legend for maps on pages 194–195 and 206–207.)

1. TG 38.3 (Sherman) (Mitscher in *Lexington*)
2. TG 38.2 (Bogan) (Halsey in *New Jersey*)
3. TG 38.4 (Davison)
4. TF 34 (Lee) (Halsey in *New Jersey*)
5. Northern Force (Ozawa)
6. Advance Northern Force (Matsuda)
7. Center Force (Kurita)
8. Southern Force (Nishimura)
9. Southern Force II (Shima)
10. Seventh Fleet Battle Force (Oldendorf)
11. "Taffy 3" (C.A.F. Sprague)
12. "Taffy 2" (Stump)
13. "Taffy 1" (T. L. Sprague)
14. TG 38.1 (McCain)
15. Cruiser Attack Group (DuBose)
16. TG 34.5 (Badger) (Halsey in *New Jersey*)

1800
OCTOBER 24

0700
OCTOBER 25

unless they were addressed to him. Harried communication officers quickly learned, however, that their commanding officers and admirals wanted to know what was going on. Accordingly almost every ship, from destroyers on up, maintained a twenty-four-hour watch in the coding room and shamelessly snooped on everything it could break from the messages pouring into the ship from Pearl Harbor's Fox broadcasts to all ships at sea.*

In Kinkaid's case on the afternoon and evening of October 24, the snooping backfired. Kinkaid received Halsey's dispatch saying Task Force 34 "will be formed." He interpreted the words as an immediate imperative rather than a future indicative. Halsey himself cleaned up the ambiguity that afternoon when he broadcast by TBS (voice radio), "If the enemy sorties, Task Force 34 will be formed *when directed by me.*" Kinkaid, however, did not receive the TBS broadcast; he had only Halsey's original. Thus he reasoned: Task Force 34 had been formed. That made three groups and one task force off San Bernardino. Three groups were going north. By simple arithmetic, that left one task force off San Bernardino. *Ergo,* San Bernardino was being guarded, and he could turn his attention to other matters. So sure was he of this conclusion that he did not even send scouting planes to keep an eye on San Bernardino, just in case.

He had plenty else on his mind. Nishimura's Southern Force was reported at this time to be approaching the southern entrance to Surigao Strait.

Nishimura left Brunei a few hours after Kurita and steamed undisturbed through the Sulu Sea until the morning of October 24. Between 0918 and 0925 the Southern Force received several bombing attacks resulting in a hit on battleship *Fuso* which destroyed her float planes, and a hit on destroyer *Shigure* which knocked out one of her guns. He was spared further attacks that day by the withdrawal of Davison's carriers northward.

* Sometimes it paid off. The writer well remembers a fueling rendezvous being changed three times when his ship was rejoining from a detached mission. No one remembered to inform us, and if we had gone to the original rendezvous, we would have missed Task Force 38 by 150 miles.

About 1800, Nishimura's force passed between Negros and Mindanao and entered the Mindanao Sea, where a warm reception was being prepared for him. Although close timing between Nishimura and Kurita was essential for success of the Sho Plan, Nishimura seemed undisturbed when word reached him, about 1830, that Kurita had been delayed seven hours in the Sibuyan Sea. He replied that he expected "to penetrate to a point off Dulag" in Leyte Gulf at 0400, October 25. Although he later learned Kurita would not be there until 1100, he made no effort to accommodate his speed. Perhaps he felt that his only chance of getting through Surigao Strait was at night. Perhaps he did not want to wait for Shima to catch up, for Shima was senior and would have taken command of the Southern Force. One can only speculate, since Nishimura took the story of his decisions down with him to the bottom of Surigao Strait.

Apparently unruffled, Nishimura steamed on, very like a man about to run an Indian gauntlet course.

It was a fearsome gauntlet that Kinkaid was preparing. First to engage would be 13 sections of 3 PT boats each, patrolling between the islands south of Surigao. Attacks by the Peter Tares would be followed by destroyer torpedo attacks in the strait itself, and then, like a cork in the bottle, the battle line of veterans scraped off the mud of Pearl Harbor would be waiting to administer the *coup de grâce*.

Ever since noon on October 24, Admiral Kinkaid had been preparing for battle. Rear Admiral Jesse B. Oldendorf was given the job of stopping Nishimura. By combining the combatant ships present into a single force, Kinkaid was able to give Oldendorf 6 old battleships, 4 heavy cruisers, including one Australian, 4 light cruisers, and 28 destroyers, one of them also Australian. He might have had an additional light cruiser except for General MacArthur.

As on previous occasions, General MacArthur had used the light cruiser *Nashville* as command headquarters. Now, on the eve of battle, he refused to get off. Captain Charles E. Coney desperately wanted to take the *Nashville* into the coming action and put the problem to MacArthur.

"No, I do not desire to leave your ship, Captain," he said firmly. "I have never been able to witness a naval engagement and this is the opportunity of a lifetime. Proceed to the battle area when you wish."

Captain Coney thought things over and decided that it was too great a responsibility to go into battle with the Supreme Commander aboard. He put the matter up to Admiral Kinkaid aboard the *Wasatch*. Kinkaid invited MacArthur to share flag accommodations there.

MacArthur was outraged. He replied stiffly: "Transfer from a combatant ship to a noncombatant ship? Never! I have never been in the middle of a naval engagement and I would like nothing better than being in one tonight."

That finished the matter. Captain Coney did not get into the battle. Neither did MacArthur.

The absence of the *Nashville* made no difference in the outcome of the battle. Admiral Oldendorf had more than enough to settle the business, and he was prepared to use it. "My theory," he remarked later, "was that of the old-time gambler: *Never give a sucker a chance.* If my opponent is foolish enough to come at me with an inferior force, I'm certainly not going to give him an even break."

The preliminary engagement opened at 2250 when three PTs attacked Nishimura's ships, without success. They did, however, get off a contact report which was the first news of Nishimura since the previous morning. The report confirmed the wisdom of Oldendorf's dispositions.

1. Battle Line: *West Virginia, Maryland, Mississippi, Tennessee, California, Pennsylvania*
2. Left-flank Cruisers: *Louisville, Portland, Minneapolis, Denver, Columbia*
3. Right-flank Cruisers: *Phoenix, Boise,* H.M.A.S. *Shropshire*
4. DesDiv 108
5. DesRon 54
6. DesRon 56, Section 1
7. DesRon 24, Section 1
8. DesRon 24, Section 2
9. DesRon 56, Section 2
10. *A. W. Grant* disabled
11. *Yamagumo* sinks, 0319
12. *Fuso* explodes, 0338
13. U.S. battleships open fire, 0351
14. *Michishio* sinks, 0358
15. *Yamashiro* sinks, 0419
16. *Mogami* collides with *Nachi,* 0430
17. Shima abandons attack and retires, 0430
18. Track of *Mogami* and *Shiguro*

These attacks by Peter Tares went on until 0213, October 25, and although thirty-nine boats were involved, not a single hit was made on the Japanese Southern Force. One of them got a hit on Shima's Southern Force II.

At 0100, Nishimura was nearing Panaon Island and assumed

The Battle of Surigao Strait—Main Action, October 25, 1944

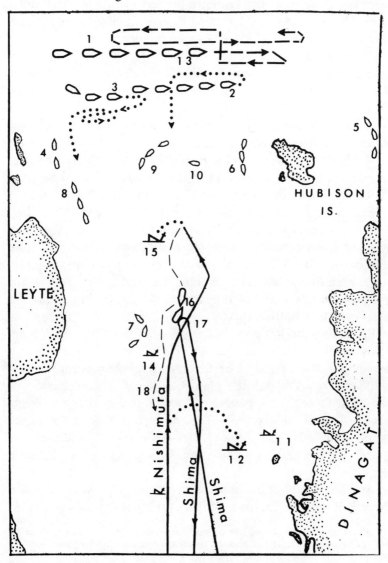

approach disposition. Destroyers *Michishio* and *Asagumo* led the way, followed at a distance of 4 kilometers by Nishimura's flagship, battleship *Yamashiro*. On either beam of the *Yamashiro* steamed the destroyers *Shigure* and *Yamagumo*, while the battleship *Fuso* and heavy cruiser *Mogami* followed 1 and 2 kilometers respectively astern of the flagship. On they advanced over the glassy sea, the visibility limited to two or three miles except when occasional lightning flashes illuminated the mountainous islands in a kind of Wagnerian spectacle.

Admiral Oldendorf was waiting for him. Across the northern entrance to Surigao Strait slowly steamed the old battleships *West Virginia* and *Maryland*, with 16-inch guns, and *Mississippi*, *Tennessee*, *California*, and *Pennsylvania* with 14-inch. Escorting were six destroyers. The force was under command of Rear Admiral George L. Weyler. There was only one concern as far as the battle line went. Did the ships have enough armor-piercing ammunition, the only kind that is of any use against a battleship. Since they had been loaded for shore-bombardment operations, their magazines contained 77.3 percent HC (High Capacity) ammunition, which explodes on contact. They had, moreover, expended over half their HC ammunition in shore bombardments at Leyte. In view of the shortage of armor-piercing ammunition, Weyler instructed his captains to use AP for the first five salvos and be prepared to shift to HC for any target smaller than a battleship.*

Protecting the left flank was a force of 5 cruisers and 9 destroyers under Admiral Oldendorf. On the right flank was a force of 3 cruisers and 13 destroyers, under Rear Admiral Russell S. Berkey. Oldendorf's plan was simple. The geography of the strait forced the Japanese to come at him in column. While the battleships crossed the "T" of the Japanese, the flank forces would deliver torpedo attacks with destroyers from either side as Nishimura came up the strait. It was a simple plan and deadly effective.

At 0230, October 25, the destroyers went to work. Captain Jesse B. Coward's DesRon 54 from the right flank force started

---

* According to best estimates, the six battleships had on board 1,637 rounds of AP and 1,602 rounds of HC ammunition. *California* and *Pennsylvania* were particularly low on HC, having 78 and 93 rounds respectively.

down the strait in two sections. The *Monssen* and *McDermut* went down the western side near the Leyte coast, while the *Melvin, McGowan,* and *Remey* stood down near mid-channel to attack Nishimura's starboard side. Coward ordered that only torpedoes be used in order to avoid giving their positions away. Once their torpedoes had been fired, the destroyers would turn away and retire near shore to prevent radar detection.

On sped the destroyers down through the night, eyes straining for a glimpse of the enemy. At 0240, *McGowan* reported, "Skunk 184°. 18 miles." A few minutes later, individual ships could be picked out on the radar screens. Nishimura was just changing into battle formation, a single column headed by his four destroyers, then the two battleships, and last the *Mogami.* It was an ideal setup for Captain Coward's anvil attack, a beautiful target.

Just before 0300, lookouts sighted the Japanese, and within two minutes or less, twenty-seven torpedoes left the tubes of Captain Coward's section of three destroyers. All were observed to run "hot, straight, and normal," as the ships turned radically away to get under cover of land. Shells from the *Yamashiro* began throwing up huge columns of water all around them, but the ships were not hit.

For the Japanese it was a different story. A torpedo from the *Melvin* slammed into battleship *Fuso*; she slowed down and sheered out of column to starboard.

A few minutes later, as Commander Richard H. Phillips's section was boring in for the attack, shells began dropping uncomfortably close. Escaping damage, the destroyers began launching their torpedoes at 0310. Even though only two ships were involved, the results were even more dramatic than those from the first section. A radio tuned to the Japanese command circuit began to squawk in what one radioman described as "verbal hysteria." Destroyer *Yamagumo* blew up and the remnants sank immediately. *Michishio* took a fish and was left in a sinking condition. *Asagumo* had her bow blown off but was able to withdraw from the action. It didn't do her much good, however, for she was sunk the next day in the mop-up phase. Nishimura's flagship *Yamashiro* took a torpedo but continued on course with no loss of speed.

The furious Japanese turned all their guns on Commander Phillips's retiring destroyers but managed to hit only the sea. Nishimura was not discouraged. Doggedly going forward, he sent his last radio dispatch: ENEMY TORPEDO BOATS AND DESTROYERS PRESENT ON BOTH SIDES OF NORTHERN ENTRANCE TO SURIGAO STRAIT. TWO OF OUR DESTROYERS TORPEDOED AND DRIFTING. YAMASHIRO SUSTAINED ONE TORPEDO HIT BUT NO IMPEDIMENT TO BATTLE CRUISING.

Now enter DesRon 24 under Captain K. M. McManes. There were six ships, including the Australian destroyer *Arunta*, and they were loaded for bear. Attacking in two sections, they fired a total of twenty-four torpedoes, finishing off *Michishio*. In the midst of all the excitement, *Fuso* blew apart, whether from a torpedo hit or from internal explosions no one knows. The drifting halves floated for some time, causing confusion on radar screens.

*Yamashiro* by this time was exchanging main battery fire with Oldendorf's battleships and was able to respond to another torpedo hit only with secondary battery against the pesky gadfly destroyers. The Japanese fire was more enthusiastic than effective, and no hits were made on McManes's squadron.

Still another destroyer attack came down the strait. DesRon 56, Captain R. N. Smoot, knifed through the water in three sections and fired thirty-one torpedoes and probably got two hits on the *Yamashiro*. It was difficult to tell, for the American battle line was lobbing 14- and 16-inch shells "like a continual stream of lighted railroad cars going over a hill." Just as the torpedoes were due to hit, two large explosions were seen on *Yamashiro* at 0411 1/2, but they could have been gunnery hits. The question is academic, for *Yamashiro* was done for. She attempted to withdraw but capsized and sank at 0419.

Smoot's squadron did not escape unscathed from this attack. Just as she was making a turn, destroyer *Albert W. Grant* had a rendezvous with several shells, whether Japanese or American is not certain. Both engine rooms were put out of action and the ship drifted to a stop midway between the forces with shells from both sides falling all around. She continued to fire all her remaining torpedoes in the general direction of the enemy. Admiral Oldendorf, who had feared just such an accident, ordered all ships to check fire until the *Grant* could be extricated. For some unknown reason, the Japanese stopped shooting about the same time, and an eerie silence fell over the strait, and pitch blackness descended as the gun flashes ceased.

Before the *Grant* could be assisted and before the rain of shells stopped, the unfortunate destroyer was hit eighteen more times; eleven of these shells were "friendly" from an American cruiser. It was small comfort to the men of the *Grant* that only seven of the hits were Japanese.

Destroyer *Newcomb* lashed herself to the *Grant* and pulled her clear. She survived and was repaired in time for the Okinawa operation.

So ended the destroyers' phase of the Battle of Surigao Strait. Now it was the turn of the big boys.

The battle line had been patrolling back and forth at 5 knots waiting for the Japanese to come in range. The flanking cruisers were farther down the strait. There was nothing for them to worry about, for the Japanese were coming into a sucker trap. It was the classic T-crossing situation, where all the American batteries could fire on the leading ship of the Japanese column while he could reply with only his forward guns. In fact, the only worry that Admirals Oldendorf, Weyler, and Berkey had was that there might be nothing left to shoot at after the destroyers had done their jobs.

At 0351 the cruisers opened fire on the Japanese survivors, and two minutes later the venerable battleships joined in. Five out of the six present had been sunk or damaged at Pearl Harbor. Now they were back and they were spoiling for revenge.

From 22,800 yards the battleship shells, and from 15,600 yards the cruiser shells were converging on *Yamashiro*, *Mogami*, and *Shigure*, the only effectives left of Nishimura's Southern Force. They did not remain that way long. Every ship was hit, but every one stubbornly returned fire as long as she was able. *Yamashiro* and *Mogami* were soon blazing. Lucky *Shigure* took only one shell, an 8-inch AP, which failed to explode. By common consent, the Japanese ships turned away soon after

0400, and to them the American order to check fire at 0409 must have seemed like a gift from Heaven, but it was too late to save *Yamashiro*, as we have seen. She went down off Bugho Point on the east coast of Leyte, taking with her Admiral Nishimura and most of her crew.

Blazing from stem to stern, heavy cruiser *Mogami* managed to get off her torpedoes as she turned away. A salvo of 8-inch shells had burst on her bridge, killing all the officers there, including Captain R. Tooma, and the executive officer. Further hits slowed her almost to a stop, but this ship, survivor of many a sea fight, had not yet reached the end of her course. Under some sort of control, she proceeded slowly down the strait. *Shigure*, with no one to give any orders, started down on her own.

Shima's ships now enter upon the stage. He had no idea of what to expect, but he knew it could be nothing good. He had not heard from Nishimura for several hours, since a vague message that Nishimura's ships had been attacked by torpedo boats. By this time, Nishimura was communicating with no one, so Shima was left to his own devices. His two heavy cruisers, *Nachi* and *Ashigara*, were accompanied by light cruiser *Abukuma* and four destroyers. Before long, *Abukuma* was no longer with him, having fallen victim to the only successful attack by the brave but unlucky PT-boat squadrons.

Undaunted, Shima increased speed to 28 knots and came to course north. He soon spotted what seemed to be two large ships on fire. On closer inspection, Shima decided they were the *Fuso* and *Yamashiro*, a rather depressing thought. They were actually the two halves of the *Fuso*. Passing to the west of them, Shima next picked up on radar two targets he took to be American ships, and both cruisers came to course 090° and fired sixteen torpedoes at them. The targets turned out to be the two Hibuson Islands, which survived the torpedoes with little damage.

At this point, Shima made the best decision of any Japanese commander in the battle. He decided to retire "temporarily" to take stock of the situation. Since he had attacked something, even though only a couple of islands, he was able to send a radio message: THIS FORCE HAS CONCLUDED ITS

ATTACK AND IS RETIRING FROM THE BATTLE
AREA TO PLAN SUBSEQUENT ACTION.

Then came a recognition challenge from the north. "I AM
THE NACHI" replied Shima's flagship.

"I AM THE SHIGURE," replied the other. "I HAVE
RUDDER DIFFICULTIES."

That was all. There was no suggestion that Shima might be
running into a hornet's nest up the strait; no report that
Nishimura was dead and that the entire force had been wiped
out except for the *Shigure.* Her skipper later explained: "I had
no connection with him and was not under his command."

Not quite everything had been wiped out, as Shima soon
learned. The blazing hulk of *Mogami* appeared, and everyone
scampered to get out of the way. Believing her to be dead in the
water, Captain Kanooka of *Nachi* managed to collide with her,
as she was actually making 8 knots. *Nachi* was heavily damaged
and her speed reduced to 18 knots. By some miracle, *Mogami*
managed to work up enough turns to fall in with Shima's
retiring force. *Shigure*'s captain was summarily told he was
under Shima's orders and instructed to take station on Shima's
retiring formation.

But Shima was not to escape so easily. The next day,
*Asagumo* was sunk by surface forces. *Mogami* came under
attack from Avengers flying off escort carriers. They left her
dead in the water before dashing back to join in the desperate
battle off Samar. A Japanese destroyer took off the survivors
and sent her down with a torpedo. On the morning of October
27, Army Air Force bombers came upon *Abukuma* west of
Negros and sent her to the bottom with several bomb hits.
Shima's flagship *Nachi* made it to Manila Bay, only to be sunk
on November 5 by Helldivers and Avengers from the *Lexington.*

Feeling well satisfied with the results of the night action,
Admiral Oldendorf ordered his ships to proceed down Surigao
Strait to polish off the cripples. While they were engaged in
giving the *coup de grâce* to *Asagumo* came the word they were
vitally needed off Samar. But they were deep within the strait,
over 100 miles from the scene of the crisis.

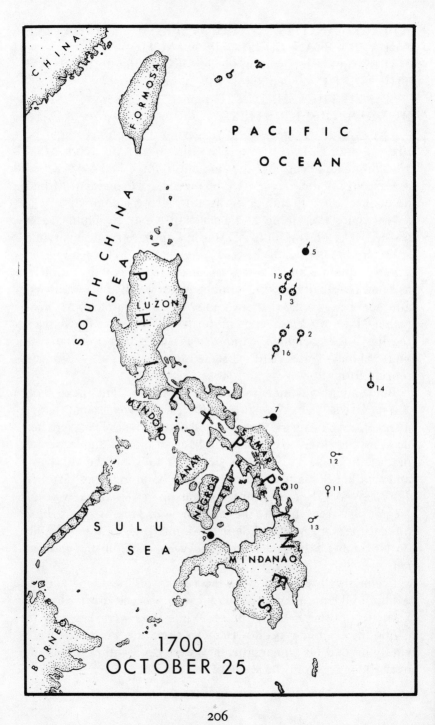

PACIFIC OCEAN

CHINA

FORMOSA

SOUTH CHINA SEA

LUZON

PHILIPPINES

MINDORO

PALAWAN

PANAY

NEGROS

CEBU

LEYTE

SAMAR

SULU SEA

MINDANAO

BORNEO

1700
OCTOBER 25

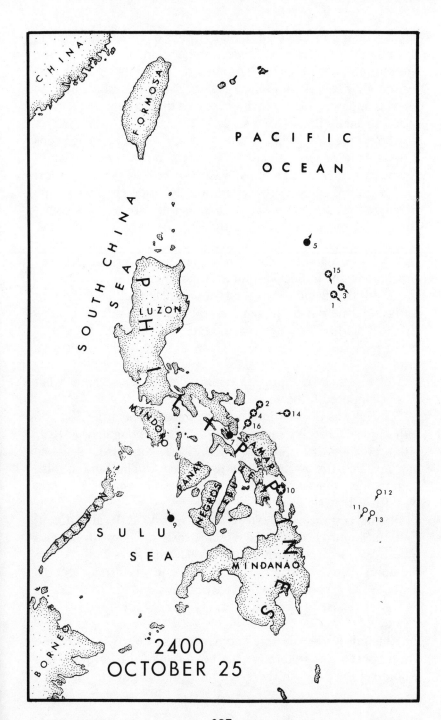

CHINA

FORMOSA

PACIFIC
OCEAN

SOUTH CHINA SEA

PHILIPPINE

LUZON

● 5

15
1
3

MINDORO

2
4
16

14

PANAY

SAMAR

NEGROS

CEBU

10

12

11
13

PALAWAN

SULU
SEA

● 9

MINDANAO

LEYTE

BORNEO

2400
OCTOBER 25

Off Samar and Leyte Gulf, St. Crispin's day was beginning to dawn in the eastern skies. On that same night, 529 years earlier, the outnumbered English "sit patiently and only ruminate the morning's danger; and their gesture sad, investing lank-lean cheeks and war-worn clots, presented them unto the gazing moon so many horrid ghosts."

Aboard the ships of Task Group 77.4, no such apprehensions haunted the American sailors. This was not a group of ships intended to fight other ships. Task Group 77.4 was an escort carrier group, and escort carriers were considered as not quite belonging to the Navy but were rather like reservists—something to be put up with during the war and then disposed of as quickly as possible. Escort carriers had done yeoman service in the Atlantic against submarines, but with wartime security restrictions, the public was not aware of them or their contributions. In the Pacific they had done such routine chores as antisubmarine patrol, ferrying replacement aircraft and pilots to the "fighting" carriers, and escort of convoy. They also performed the vital function of close air support in amphibious landings.

This was their role this St. Crispin's day. At least, that is what it was supposed to be.

TG 77.4 was divided into three task units, operating 30 to 50 miles apart. Farthest south, off northern Mindanao was Rear Admiral Thomas L. Sprague's TU 77.4.1, comprising 4 escort carriers, 3 destroyers, and 4 destroyer escorts. This Sprague also commanded the task group. The radio voice call of this unit was Taffy 1.

Off the entrance to Leyte Gulf was Taffy 2, Rear Admiral Felix B. Stump. It contained 6 escort carriers, 3 destroyers, and 4 destroyer escorts. Farthest north, off Samar, was Taffy 3, also including 6 escort carriers, 3 destroyers, and 4 destroyer escorts. Taffy 3 was commanded by Rear Admiral Clifton A. F. Sprague, whose nickname from Naval Academy days was "Ziggy."

All hands were expecting another routine day, flying off close air support strikes while the big boys fought the battles. They would get the dope on these actions from the guys in the radio shacks and from the inveterate spreaders of scuttlebutt who somehow always got the word, whether right or wrong.

During the night, Admiral Kinkaid ordered Thomas Sprague to conduct dawn searches to the north, just in case, but by the time the *Ommaney Bay* could respot her deck and get the search mission off, it was too late to do any good. By that time, no searches were needed. The enemy was there.

Other carriers began flying off combat air patrol, antisubmarine patrol, and other routine missions. The carriers of Taffy 3 took no part in the pursuit of Shima's survivors. They were too far north, so shortly before sunrise all ships secured from general quarters and men not on watch hurried to join the chow lines.

A quarter of an hour later some weird things began to happen. Antiaircraft fire was seen to the north. What ships did we have up there and why were they shooting at our own planes? *Fanshaw Bay* reported an unidentified radar surface contact, and a radioman heard some "Japs gabbling." Ensign Hans L. Jensen, flying antisubmarine patrol, reported 4 Japanese battleships, 8 cruisers and several destroyers only twenty miles from Taffy 3. Clifton Sprague yelled "Check identification!" into the radio microphone, but there was no need. His own lookouts reported the pagodalike superstructures of the Japanese battleships and cruisers looming up over the curvature of the earth. At 0659 brilliantly colored shell splashes began falling around Taffy 3.

How could it happen? The force Halsey had reported so badly mauled had pulled itself together, transited the dangerous San Bernardino Strait without being detected, and had emerged fresh and looking for a fight in the clear waters of the Philippine Sea. Air searches and radar had failed. No combatant force opposed their passage. The wolf was loose among the lambs.

Contrary to the usual result in such a story, these lambs had teeth and were prepared to use them. Perhaps these lambs were scrappy Bedlington terriers. In any case, scrap they did.

Admiral Kurita should have been elated. As far as his force was concerned, everything had worked according to plan. Ozawa had decoyed Halsey far to the north. But Kurita didn't know it. Reports came in to his flag bridge. All grossly overestimated the opposition ahead of them. Kurita's own chief of staff estimated that ahead of them was part of TF 38, including 4 or 5 fleet carriers, 1 or 2 battleships, and "at least" 10 heavy cruisers!

The events of the previous day had left Kurita with little faith in his antiaircraft gunners, and it was with a sinking heart that he saw carriers in front of him. He decided the best thing to do was to try to polish off the enemy as quickly as possible.

At the moment of sighting the Americans, he had been changing disposition from the single column used to transit the strait to a circular antiaircraft formation, but while this was going on, he ordered "General Attack." This meant that every ship was to operate on her own and chase the Americans down at best speed. This order lost him the battle. If he had formed battle line, he could have pounded the American ships to pieces at his leisure. As it was, his ships could not support each other and could be taken on piecemeal by the desperate American defenders.

What did Clifton Sprague have to throw against Kurita's 4 battleships, 6 heavy and 2 light cruisers, and 11 destroyers? His 6 escort carriers, *Fanshaw Bay*, *St. Lo*, *White Plains*, *Kalinin Bay*, *Kitkun Bay*, and *Gambier Bay*, carried a total of 97 Wildcat* fighters and 60 Avenger torpedo bombers. Not all of them were operational, and most of the torpedo planes were loaded with antipersonnel bombs, which were completely ineffective against ships' armor. His three destroyers were all new *Fletchers*, fast and sleek, armed with five 5-inch mounts and ten torpedo tubes each. They could put up a reasonable fight, but they were no match for battleships and cruisers.

As soon as Clifton Sprague saw what was happening, he changed course to due east, close enough to the wind to launch planes, and at the same time designed to give him sea room and prevent him from being boxed in the confines of Leyte Gulf. He stepped up speed to 17 1/2 knots, which left him with half a

---

* These were General Motors-built versions of the Grumman F4F Wildcat, obsolete as fighters, but still useful in close air support operations.

knot in reserve for emergencies. He ordered every operational plane into the air and every ship to make smoke. And he yelled for help in plain language, giving his position and that of the enemy.

Thomas Sprague's Taffy 1 was too far away to help immediately, but within a minute Stump of Taffy 2 had asked and received permission to send everything he could to help out. Planes began rising from the flight decks of Taffy 2 as he broadcast words of encouragement by voice radio to Ziggy Sprague: "Don't be alarmed, Ziggy—remember, we're back of you—don't get excited—don't do anything rash!" As he exhorted his friend not to get excited, his voice rose in crescendo, bringing brief smiles to the men of Taffy 3.

Gradually the superior speed of the Japanese ships was telling, and as they began to creep up on the port quarter, Ziggy Sprague was forced more and more to a southerly and then southwesterly direction. Dye-loaded shells landed all around, their brilliant hues causing a seaman in *White Plains* to exclaim, "They're shooting at us in technicolor!"

For long moments, not a ship was hit, and at 0706, the escort carriers were able to duck into a rain squall. This, combined with the smoke they had been making, threw the Japanese gunners off for a blessed fifteen minutes, and their shooting fell far from the mark.

By this time, Sprague's planes were doing everything they could to hit the enemy, but it was hell-for-leather, every man for himself. There simply was no time to form up organized air attacks in those first few desperate minutes. All during the individual ship actions to be related, the planes attacked the Japanese, dropping bombs, firing torpedoes if they had them, strafing, and making dummy runs to draw fire if they had nothing to drop or shoot. Some returned to their carriers for more ammunition; some landed at nearby Tacloban airstrip to refuel, rearm, and take off again to rejoin the fray.

At 0716, Sprague ordered his three destroyers to deliver a torpedo attack on the Japanese. This was practically a suicide mission for these ships, but there was no hesitation. Although they had immediately lighted off all boilers, there had not been enough time for steam pressure to build up, and they could not make their 36-knot rated speed.

The *Johnston*, being nearest to the enemy, was the first to comply with the order to attack with torpedoes. Her skipper, Commander Ernest E. Evans, conned his ship to within 10,000 yards of the cruiser *Kumano* and fired off a full salvo of ten torpedoes. With none left to shoot, he dodged behind his own smoke to retire. Two or three hits were heard on the *Kumano*—and the Japanese later admitted one—and the cruiser dropped out of action. But the *Johnston* had to pay for her success. As her senior surviving officer wrote later:

> At this time, about 0730, this ship got it. Three 14-inch shells from a battleship, followed thirty seconds later by three 6-inch shells from a light cruiser, hit us. It was like a puppy being smacked by a truck. These hits knocked out the after fire room and engine room, lost all power to the steering engine, all power to the after three 5-inch guns and rendered the gyro compass useless.

But the *Johnston* was not yet out of the fight. Her speed reduced to 17 knots, her deck a shambles, she managed to hide in a rain squall and take stock. During this respite, she managed to get two of her after guns operating again.

The *Hoel* was next in action. As screen flagship, she flew the pennant of Commander W. D. Thomas, who was attempting to coordinate the attack of the destroyers. Her skipper, Commander L. S. Kintberger, was able to give his whole attention to taking his ship in harm's way to inflict maximum damage on the Japanese. He picked out the battleship *Kongo* as his target, which was then 18,000 yards away. Closing rapidly, *Hoel* opened fire with her 5-inchers at 14,000 yards, and the *Kongo* answered in kind. A few minutes later, *Hoel* was hit on the bridge, which knocked out all radio communications but did nothing to stop her attack. At a range of 4,000 yards, Kintberger swung his ship around and launched a half-salvo of five torpedoes at the *Kongo* which the battleship evaded. The *Hoel* was not so fortunate, for the Japanese shells began hitting. Her port engine was knocked out, three guns were out of action, and her rudder was jammed so she headed right for the *Kongo*. Her action report noted, "Gun Nos. 1 and 2 continued to fire on the targets of opportunity."

Some opportunity!

Shifting steering control aft, *Hoel* managed to extricate herself and work around to attack position on the cruiser *Haguro*. At 0750 she launched her five remaining torpedoes and observed large columns of water rising from the target at the time the torpedoes were due. The Japanese deny that *Haguro* was hit, but something caused those water columns, and no planes were dropping bombs on her at that time, nor was anyone shooting at her.

The third destroyer, *Heermann*, was late in getting the word to join in the torpedo attack, but bent on knots to catch up, narrowly avoiding a collision with destroyer escort *Samuel B. Roberts* while pulling out of the screen. A few minutes later she had to back down to avoid the stricken *Hoel*, but those little episodes did not bother her skipper, Commander Amos T. Hathaway. At 0754, she launched seven torpedoes at the *Haguro*, all of which missed. While he was firing these, Hathaway spotted four battleships coming in his general direction and swung around to take on the bigger game. The Japanese opened up with everything, but he was able to dodge and at 0800 fired his three remaining torpedoes at the *Haruna*. He thought he obtained a hit, but it is doubtful. *Heermann* escaped unharmed by chasing shell splashes.

Kurita's flagship *Yamato* now found herself boxed in between two torpedo spreads which paralleled her wake. Daring to turn neither to port nor starboard, she ran almost due north for ten minutes, her outrider torpedoes accompanying her on either side until they ran out of fuel and sank. Only then could *Yamato* reverse course and rejoin the fray.

Time now ran out for the *Hoel*.

Wounded and operating on only one engine, she found herself unable to pull away from battleship *Kongo* on her port beam and the heavy cruisers to starboard. Presently *Yamato* came up from astern, and everyone who could took potshots at the hapless destroyer. Since the Japanese gunners classified her as a cruiser, they fired armor-piercing shells at her. These passed right on through without exploding, but there were so many of them that the ship soon resembled a colander. Still she managed to stay afloat for sixty-five minutes before the order was given to abandon ship. Twenty minutes later, at 0855, she rolled over and sank.

Not to be outdone by their big brothers, the destroyer escorts of the screen delivered the next attack. These four gallant ships, *J. C. Butler*, *Raymond*, *Dennis*, and *Samuel B. Roberts*, were of the long-hull type, powered by steam turbines and capable of 24 knots. They mounted two 5-inch guns and carried three torpedo tubes. So eager were they to get in the action that when the screen commander ordered the "Wolves" (code name for the destroyers) to attack, Lieutenant R. W. Copeland, skipper of the *Samuel B. Roberts*, asked, "Do you want Little Wolves to go in with Wolves?" At the moment the answer was "Negative," but a few minutes later the order came. Since the crews of the DEs had never been trained for torpedo attack, it was a case of every man for himself and the devil take the hindermost.

It was a gallant, futile attack, in that it did little or no damage to the enemy, but it did distract the Japanese for a time and prevented even worse damage being done to the CVEs, which were fighting for their lives the entire time. The *Butler* could not even get within range to fire her torpedoes, so heavy was the gunfire in front of her, but the other DEs got theirs off at the biggest game they could find. All nine missed, but they gave the Japanese something to think about.

The *Roberts* paid the supreme price for the intrepidity of all the DEs. About 0900 she was hit by two or three 14-inch shells which exploded on contact and nearly blew her apart. The abandonment was orderly, the wounded being placed on rafts before the crew left their shattered ship. After lolling in the sea with a list of about 80°, the *Roberts* went under, stern first, at 1005.

Having expended all torpedoes, except for the three remaining in the *Butler*, the survivors of the screen set about the business of laying all the smoke they could to screen the carriers. Their 5-inch guns fired when they could see anything.

Commander Evans of the *Johnston* saw a great deal. Light cruiser *Yahagi* and four destroyers were rapidly closing on the carriers, obviously to deliver a torpedo attack. Without asking for any help, Evans took it on himself to stop this particular threat. From about 10,000 yards, *Johnston* closed the range gradually, firing as she went, and receiving an intense return fire. Not all the shells missed, but Evans kept going. Suddenly *Yahagi* turned 90° to starboard and broke off. The destroyers kept on coming but soon made 90° turns of their own. Commander Evans believed he had driven them off. "Now I've seen everything," he marveled. As a point of fact, the turn of the Japanese ships was to launch torpedoes at the carriers.

*Johnston*'s bluff had forced the Japanese to launch the torpedoes prematurely, at too long a range, and all the Long Lances missed, even though the enemy action report stated, "three enemy destroyers and one cruiser [the *Johnston*?] were enveloped in black smoke and observed to sink one after another."

The ships were enveloped in black smoke, all right, but it was from their own funnels and intended to afford them some shelter from Japanese eyes. It was working, too.

GQ* Johnny, as her crew called the *Johnston*, was about to pay for her temerity. The destroyers that had launched their torpedoes unsuccessfully turned their guns on *Johnston*, and she was reduced to a wreck above the main deck, her mast trailing along the superstructure deck and fires blazing amidships. Several shells hit all at once, knocking out her remaining engine room, and the ship went dead in the water at 0940. Five minutes later, Commander Evans ordered, "Abandon ship." As the Japanese closed in for the kill, they kept pouring shells into the hulk until she went down at 1010. Several survivors in the water saw the captain of one of the Japanese destroyers salute as GQ Johnny sank.

Only 141 officers and men were saved, and Commander Evans was not among them. Like "Jocko" Clark, Evans was part Cherokee Indian and all fighter. Yet his sacrifice was not

---

* So-called from the frequency she went to GQ—General Quarters.

exceptional that day; it was typical of the courage of the men in all the "Small Boys," whether they survived or not.

Courage was a commodity not limited to destroyermen on St. Crispin's day. While the Wolves and Little Wolves were taking on the Japanese battleships and cruisers, the escort carriers were fighting for their lives, and their pilots were doing their utmost to save them.

The six CVEs of Taffy 3 were in circular disposition, making top speed of 17 1/2 knots. Admiral Clifton "Ziggy" Sprague had his flag in *Fanshaw Bay* in the northwest quadrant of the formation. Clockwise around the circle were *St. Lo, Kalinin Bay, Gambier Bay, Kitkun Bay,* and *White Plains.* All ships were making smoke, and Sprague several times found shelter in rain squalls, but gradually the Japanese were creeping up on him and boxing Taffy 3 into the restricted waters of Leyte Gulf.

As soon as the peril became evident, carriers from all the Taffys launched every plane they could to take on the Japanese, and throughout the running battle now being described, the planes were making what one Japanese officer described as "almost incessant" attacks on Japanese ships, dropping bombs or torpedoes when they could, and strafing and making dry runs when they could not. Since the carriers of Taffy 3 were forced to a southwesterly course, directly down wind, planes could not land on them and had to make their way to Tacloban Field, 100 miles away, but fortunately made operational only the previous day. Some landed on carriers of Stump's Taffy 2 to refuel and rearm. Admiral Sprague later paid tribute to these pilots:

> For two hours, with not so much as a machine-gun bullet to fight with, Lieutenant Commander Edward J. Huxtable (Air Group Commander *Gambier Bay*), glided his Avenger through the flak to make dry runs on enemy capital ships, once flying down a line of cruisers to divert them from their course and throw off their gunfire for a few precious minutes. . . .

> The Wildcat pilots were given a free hand to strafe, with the hope that their strafing would kill personnel on the Japanese warships, silence automatic weapons, and, most important, draw attention

from the struggling escort carriers. Sometimes two, or four Wildcats would join up for a strafing run. Again, a Wildcat would join up and run interference for an Avenger. Then, likely as not, it would turn out that the Avenger had no torpedo or bomb and was simply making a dummy run. When their ammunition gave out, the fighters also made dry runs to turn the pursuers. Lieutenant Paul B. Garrison USNR made 20 strafing runs, 10 of them dry.

In spite of these heroic diversions by destroyermen and airmen, the Japanese were slowly closing in on the CVEs. The peculiar wind conditions blew the smoke screen away from *Kalinin Bay* and *Gambier Bay*, leaving them in full view of the enemy. Shells soon began hitting them, nor were they the only ones to suffer. Every CVE was hit but *Kitkun Bay*, but even she suffered several casualties from shell fragments resulting from near misses. Fortunately for the Jeep carriers, the Japanese gunners were not up to their usual standards, and they persisted in using armor-piercing shells which passed through the ships without exploding.

The CVEs were armed with 5-inch guns installed for antiaircraft defense. No one ever dreamed that they would be employed against Japanese cruisers. But they were. As the range closed, "Ziggy" Sprague gave the somewhat unconventional order, "Open fire with the pea-shooters when range is clear."

Although every carrier was in mortal danger, *Gambier Bay* was the one whose luck ran out. When shells began dropping uncomfortably close to her about 0745, she successfully chased shell splashes and escaped injury until 0810. Once they had found the range, the Japanese gunners could not be denied. The rain of shells on *Gambier Bay* was incessant, and she soon came to a stop, burning, listing, and sinking. At 0850 her crew began to abandon ship, and at 0907 she rolled over and sank. The cruiser *Chikuma* stayed close to her, pumping shells into her until she went down. That proved to be a mistake, for *Chikuma* was hit by several shells from surface ships and sunk a little later by a torpedo attack, presumably by Avengers from Stump's Taffy 2.

217

Another victim of the combination of surface fire and air attack was heavy cruiser *Chokai*. Closing the *White Plains* to smash her out of existence, she suffered the humiliation of being knocked out of action by the single 5-inch gun on the carrier's fantail. It was rather like a mouse defeating a cat. She disappeared from radar screens about 0930.

Chief Gunner Jenkins of the *White Plains*, jubilantly watching the action, sang out to his crew, "Hold on a little longer, boys! We're sucking them into forty-millimeter range!"

By this time the battle had become so confused that Admiral Kurita decided to do something about it. In running to the north to evade the torpedoes, the *Yamato* had carried him so far from the scene of the action that he literally had no idea of what was going on. His ships were strung out over miles of ocean, with no pretense of coordination. He decided to break off and re-form his fleet before taking action to finish off the stubborn Americans who obviously did not have the sense to know when they were beaten. At 0911 he ordered, "Rendezvous, my course north, speed 20."

As the Japanese turned off, just as they seemed on the point of eliminating Taffy 3 entirely, a signalman on *Fanshaw Bay* yelled:

"Goddammit, boys, they're getting away!"

Although Kurita's intention was merely to retire temporarily and regroup, he soon began to have other ideas. The heroic fighting of the ships and men of Taffy 3 caused him to overestimate their strength. He believed that he was fighting one of Halsey's task groups, that the CVEs were fleet carriers, either *Independence* or *Ranger*\* class, that the destroyers were *Baltimore* class heavy cruisers, and the DEs were destroyers. In addition it was reported to him that the carriers were making 30 knots! This was no mean feat, since their absolute top speed was 18. "I knew you were scared, Ziggy," said a fellow admiral later, "but I didn't know you were *that* scared!"

---

\* There was no "*Ranger* class." The *Ranger* was the only one of her kind, and was too slow to be used in the Pacific. She saw extensive Atlantic service.

While Kurita was trying to decide what to do, the Japanese milled around aimlessly for nearly three and a half hours. It seems clear that Kurita was not thinking very clearly, and it is not surprising that he was not. He was in his sixties, and he had been two nights without sleep. On the night of October 23, he had had his flagship blown out from under him and had had to swim for his life. All the next day he had been under heavy air attack in the Sibuyan Sea, and had expected to have to fight his way out of San Bernardino Strait on the morning of October 25. He knew that Nishimura's force had been destroyed, and he had heard nothing from Ozawa because of a faulty radio transmitter in *Zuikaku*, the latter's flagship.

He knew that if he stayed very long, immensely powerful forces would close in on him. He knew very well that the U.S. Navy had ample forces to obliterate his fleet, and while he personally did not object to obliteration if it could accomplish something useful, he saw little to be gained by a further penetration of Leyte Gulf.

A mysterious report of a nonexistent American task force only 100 miles away led him to believe this new target might be a useful objective for his ships, and he headed in that direction for a time, reporting to Toyoda in Tokyo: FIRST STRIKING FORCE HAS ABANDONED PENETRATION OF LEYTE ANCHORAGE. IS PROCEEDING NORTH SEARCHING FOR ENEMY TASK FORCE. WILL ENGAGE DECISIVELY, THEN PASS THROUGH SAN BERNARDINO STRAIT.

The ordeal of Taffy 3 was not yet over, and this time Taffy 1, farthest to the south, suffered as well. For the first time, the Japanese employed a fearsome weapon, the Kamikaze.

No Westerner can understand the attitude of mind that made the Japanese Kamikaze Special Attack Corps possible. Soldiers, sailors, and airmen of all Western nations have shown incredible bravery against seemingly hopeless odds, but there is always that tiny possibility of getting away with your life in spite of all probabilities. But the Japanese Kamikaze pilot deliberately set out to die. Nor was it a policy imposed by the Japanese leaders;

the decision to employ the Kamikaze attacks arose spontaneously among the pilots themselves.

> This was not suicide! [wrote Saburo Sakai, one of Japan's foremost fighter pilots]. These men, young and old, were not dying in vain. Every plane which thundered into an enemy warship was a blow struck for our land. Every bomb carried by a Kamikaze into the fuel tanks of a giant carrier meant that many more of the enemy killed, that many more planes which would never bomb and strafe over our soil.
>
> These men had faith. They believed in Japan, in striking a blow for Japan with their lives. It was a cheap price to pay; one man, perhaps, against the lives of hundreds or even thousands. Our country no longer had the means to base its strength on conventional tactics. We were no longer possessed of such national power. And a man, every one of these men, who surrendered his mortal soul was not dying. He passed on life to those who remained.

The name Kamikaze was chosen because it means "divine wind." Its use commemorated the typhoon which destroyed a Mongol fleet bound for the invasion of Japan in 1570. These Japanese pilots now would create a typhoon made of their planes and their living bodies.

While "Ziggy" Sprague's men were fighting for their lives, "Tommy" Sprague's Taffy 1, some 130 miles to the southward was doing its best to help out. This meant that planes had to be recalled from morning strikes in support of troops fighting ashore and refueled and rearmed before they could be sent north. While the four CVEs of Taffy 1 were in the midst of this job, they were jumped by a group of six Kamikazes coming out of Davao. Somehow undiscovered by radar or by the CAP, the Japanese made their presence known by diving out of the clouds. One strafed carrier *Santee* and then about 0740 crashed into the flight deck forward, penetrating to the hangar deck, where spectacular fires raged in the immediate vicinity of eight 1000-pound bombs. By means of skilled fire-fighting, *Santee*'s damage-control party got the fires under control before the bombs could detonate.

Meanwhile two other Kamikazes were diving to attack. One

of them headed for the *Suwannee* and when hit by antiaircraft fire swerved to dive into the *Sangamon*. A direct hit from a 5-inch shell caused the plane to swerve and splash short of her target. *Petrof Bay* was near-missed by another Kamikaze just at the same moment.

While all eyes were turned on the skies, the next attack came from below. The submarine *I-56* just happened to be on the scene and put a torpedo into the unfortunate *Santee* on the starboard side forward. The carrier was sturdier than she appeared and within a few minutes after the hit, she was making 16 1/2 knots with only a slight list from the flooding.

The three remaining Kamikazes all took on the *Suwannee*. The carrier's gunners shot down two of them, but the third could not be denied. Although the plane was heavily hit and the pilot presumably dead, it kept coming and hit the flight deck forward of the after elevator. The bomb penetrated to the hangar deck space where it detonated, buckling the main deck and tearing a large hole in the hangar deck. Inside of two hours, however, temporary repairs had been made, and the *Suwannee* was able to resume flight operations.

On the surviving ships of Taffy 3, "Ziggy" Sprague's men were pinching themselves to see if they were still alive after Kurita's withdrawal. The carriers were trying to recover their own aircraft in order to be ready for what might come next. Most ships had secured from General Quarters to allow the men to get some coffee and something to eat. Nothing showed on the radar screens but friendly ships and planes.

Aboard the *St. Lo* an old sailors' superstition was about to be confirmed.

Every sailorman knows it is bad luck to change the name of a ship. It is not so bad for a merchant ship, for she seldom faces the danger of combat. But even the perils of the winds and the sea, of reef and shoal, are enough to make many men refuse to sign on a ship that has been rechristened. But for a warship—

*St. Lo* had originally been commissioned U.S.S. *Midway*, but later the Navy Department decided that a new class of big carriers should bear that name. She was rechristened in honor of another battle, the breakout at St. Lô in the Normandy campaign. Even worse, it was not a naval battle. There was much headshaking and talk of demanding transfers.

Still, *St. Lo* had had a creditable if unspectacular career. But this day, time ran out.

Captain F. J. McKenna was catching his breath on the bridge of *St. Lo* when five Kamikazes came out of nowhere and dived on the carriers of Taffy 3. One of them went for *Kitkun Bay*, catching only the port catwalk, but the explosion of the bomb did considerable damage. Two others went for *Fanshaw Bay*, but were shot down. The last pair picked on *White Plains*. The first kept on coming through a withering torrent of antiaircraft fire and at the last moment rolled over, missing the ship by inches, and exploded before it hit the water. Fragments of the plane and pilot rained on the flight deck, injuring eleven men.

The last of the five was also hit, but the pilot retained enough control to peel off from his attack on *White Plains*, and at 1051 smashed into the *St. Lo*. The explosion of the bomb set off the carrier's store of bombs and torpedoes spotted on the hangar deck for loading aboard the planes. No fewer than seven additional explosions followed, and great sections of the ship were hurled into the air. The ship could not be saved, and she went down at 1125.

By this time, Sprague had got a more adequate CAP in the air, so that the next group of fifteen Kamikazes received a warm reception. Only three were able to make attacks. The first picked on *Kitkun Bay*. It was shot down only twenty-five yards from the starboard bow. The others changed course at the last moment and dove into *Kalinin Bay*, but the damage was relatively slight and the fires were out within five minutes. Another pair headed for her, but were shot down.

So ended the first Kamikaze attacks of the war. There would be many others, both in the Philippines and off Okinawa. But in every case, Japanese fanaticism was met by the courage, discipline, and devotion to duty of the American sailors, most of whom had been civilians only a short time ago.

Following their ordeal, the Taffys were gradually withdrawn

after rescuing survivors, most of them going to Manus for rest and repairs. They were not to escape scot free, however, for the Kamikazes struck again the next day, near-missing *Sangamon* and *Petrof Bay* and making another hit on *Suwannee*. Although she was extensively damaged, she remained afloat and lived to fight another day.

Destroyer escort *Eversole* was trying to catch up with Taffy 1 when she was suddenly hit at 0228, October 29, by a torpedo from *I-45*. The explosion ripped her apart. Survivors in the water were decimated by an explosion about an hour later, presumably from the boilers as *Eversole* finally went down. Most of the rest were injured by the blast but were rescued after another hour by destroyer escort *Bull* following along the same general track. *Whitehurst*, another DE, detached from a nearby oiler group, helped out with the rescue work until she got a sonar contact. She attacked with hedgehogs and after the fourth run had the satisfaction of finishing off *I-45*.

After that, the submarines of the Imperial Navy found no more targets, and the Kamikazes devoted their attention to the shipping in Leyte Gulf, leaving the combatant ships alone for the time being.

The agony of the Taffy groups was not in vain. The thirty-five ships then in Leyte Gulf were saved, and the beachheads were spared a murderous shelling with practically no support except for a handful of land-based planes. The Taffys had turned back a truly formidable fleet, had outfought it and outbluffed it so that Kurita abandoned the mission for which all else had been sacrificed. As Admiral Clifton Sprague wrote later, "The failure of the enemy main body and encircling light forces to completely wipe out all vessels of this task unit can be attributed to our successful smoke screen, our torpedo counterattack, continuous harassment of enemy by bomb, torpedo, and strafing air attacks, timely maneuvers, and the definite partiality of Almighty God."

No one, of course, intended that Taffy 3 would have to stand off the chief strength of the Japanese navy. The two senior commanders, Admirals Kinkaid and Halsey, had miscalculated, and each was trying to do something about it.

Kinkaid, secure in the belief that Halsey had left Task Force 34 to guard San Bernardino, had concentrated his attention on the forthcoming battle with Nishimura to the south. After the battle, instead of pulling Oldendorf's battle force back to a central position to be ready for another threat, he allowed them to pursue the defeated Japanese deep down Surigao Strait. This accomplished nothing that could not have been done the next day with air power. Further, it exposed these ships to danger of mine fields or submarine attack to no purpose. It uncovered the beachhead just as surely as did Halsey's move to the north.

Admiral King criticized Kinkaid for failure "to use his own air squadrons for search at the crucial moment." Kinkaid, in fact, ordered two separate searches: one from the CVEs was too late, for the Japanese ships were sighted from the decks of Taffy 3 before search reports were received; an earlier search conducted by Black Cat Catalinas was ineffectual. He ordered five planes to be sent out, but only two actually took off, and the one who might have spotted Kurita flew all around him without seeing him. Kinkaid did nothing more about searches, seeming to share the view that permeated his staff that "Halsey would take care of the northern sector."

Halsey, as we have seen, took the view that Kinkaid could easily handle whatever stragglers came through from Kurita's force and that he could take care of the Nishimura–Shima approach as well. He was hypnotized by the carriers spotted to the north. He left with all three of his carrier groups to force battle the next morning.

During the night, Halsey finally did form Task Force 34. The three carrier groups did not rendezvous until 2345, October 24, and it was 0430, October 25, before the ships of Task Force 34 had pulled out of the three groups and taken station ten miles to the north. It was a formidable surface force indeed. From his flagship, battleship *New Jersey*, Halsey could look around to see five other battleships. *Iowa, Massachusetts, South Dakota, Washington,* and *Alabama.* All were armed with 16-inch guns, and all were capable of 30 knots or better. In addition were the heavy cruisers *New Orleans* and *Wichita* and the light cruisers *Biloxi, Vincennes, Miami, Santa Fe*, and *Mobile*, and seventeen destroyers. Everyone expected action momentarily, for garbled search plane reports placed Ozawa's ships much closer than they actually were.

As we have noted, Ozawa's was a sacrificial role. If he could decoy Halsey away from San Bernardino Strait, he would have accomplished his purpose, even though it cost every ship. And he had succeeded beyond his highest hopes. He had with him most of Japan's surviving carriers, including the last of those which had attacked Pearl Harbor, the 30,000-ton *Zuikaku*. There were the three light carriers *Zuiho, Chitose*, and *Chiyoda*. Of the 166 planes on board these four carriers when they sortied, 137 had been lost or diverted to shore bases; Ozawa had only a pitiful 29 aircraft remaining to him.

Two very curious ships accompanied Ozawa. They were the *Ise* and *Hyuga*, originally battleships, but now converted to hermaphrodite carriers. The after turrets had been removed and flight decks installed abaft the superstructure. They could launch aircraft but could not recover them. At this time, the question was academic, for they carried no planes at all. To complete the bait, Ozawa had with him 9 destroyers, 2 light cruisers, and 2 tankers, which were accompanied by 6 escort vessels.

Separated as he was from the carrier groups, Halsey turned over operational command of Task Force 38 to Mitscher, while Lee assumed the job for Task Force 34. Halsey had finally assumed his proper role as a fleet commander, responsible for coordinating the efforts of both task forces. Like everyone else, he was eagerly anticipating the coming battle.

At dawn, Mitscher launched deck searches from his flagship *Lexington*, but he did not await their reports before launching his first strike. He gave orders for the planes to orbit seventy to ninety miles up the line until the enemy was located.

It was not long until the searchers found their targets, and the orbiting planes began to bore in for the kill. At approximately 0800, the planes were over their targets and were attacking in accordance with the directions of Commander David McCampbell, commander of Air Group 15 from the *Essex*, who acted as target coordinator.

Only twelve to fifteen Japanese planes rose to meet the American attack; the rest were out scouting or were down with mechanical problems. The few that did make up the Japanese CAP seemed to McCampbell to be more interested in acrobatics than in protecting their own ships. Japanese antiaircraft fire was intense, but it did little good. *Zuiho* was hit by a bomb as she attempted to launch planes but was not seriously damaged. *Chitose*, her sister ship, took several bomb hits which finally did for her. She sank at 0937. *Zuikaku* was hit by a torpedo which did so much damage that Ozawa was forced to shift his flag to *Oyodo*, one of the light cruisers. A destroyer was sunk instantaneously by a bomb hit, and several Japanese planes were shot down before the first strike departed.

The second strike appeared on the scene about 0945, having been "given the dope" by returning pilots of the first. These planes accounted for carrier *Chiyoda*, which was abandoned around 1030 but stayed afloat until she was sunk by American cruisers later that afternoon. These planes also chased off a group of twenty to twenty-five Japanese land-based aircraft which were attempting to interfere.

Strike No. 3 concentrated on carriers *Zuikaku* and *Zuiho*. Although the latter was hard to sink, "Happy Crane" [*Zuikaku*] had reached her last mile. Three torpedoes slammed into her simultaneously, and at 1414 she rolled over and went down some 200 miles northeast of Cape Engaño. The last repayment for Pearl Harbor had been made.

Although badly damaged, *Zuiho* survived Strike No. 3, only to be finished off by Strike No. 4 at 1526. Thus Ozawa had lost all four of his carriers and a destroyer and was bent on extricating what was left of his force. By this time every ship had received some damage, and although the fifth and sixth strikes sank nothing, they contributed to giving the Japanese a thoroughly miserable day.

Admiral Halsey was not allowed to enjoy to the full the fruit of his battle, for he was being distracted by insistent calls for help from the south.

During the night, Kinkaid had decided to check on his assumption that Task Force 34 was guarding San Bernardino and he sent Halsey a message asking if such was the fact. Although he sent the message at 0412, October 25, Halsey did not receive it until 0648. He replied at once: NEGATIVE X IT IS WITH OUR CARRIERS NOW ENGAGING ENEMY CARRIERS.

Halsey was still not alarmed and continued to devote his attention to events to the north. He was eagerly looking forward to a surface action later that day. He had never seen one in his long naval career.

It was with some shock, therefore, that he read Kinkaid's next message at 0822: ENEMY BBS [battleships] AND CRUISERS REPORTED FIRING ON TU 77.4.3 [Taffy 3] FROM 15 MILES ASTERN. Before he had digested this message another came: URGENTLY NEED FAST BBS LEYTE GULF AT ONCE. Somewhat irritated at having to do what he conceived as Kinkaid's job, Halsey ordered McCain to break off fueling and STRIKE ENEMY VICINITY ELEVEN TWENTY NORTH ONE TWO SEVEN ZERO ZERO EAST AT BEST POSSIBLE SPEED.

On receipt of this message, McCain immediately cast off from the oilers and bent on 30 knots in a southwesterly direction. Even at that speed, it would take him until 1030 to reach extreme striking range, and it would take another hour and a half at best for the planes to reach the area where Kurita was engaging Taffy 3. Since McCain had by far the strongest of the carrier groups, including the large carriers *Hancock*, *Hornet*, and *Wasp*, and light carriers *Monterey* and *Cowpens*, it seems clear that they might have been called into the fray earlier. At this moment of time, the U.S. Navy had overwhelming strength in the Third and Seventh Fleets—all deployed where it would do the least good.

At 0900 Halsey received another urgent message, this one sent in plain language: OUR CVES BEING ATTACKED

BY FOUR BBS EIGHT CRUISERS PLUS OTHERS X REQUEST LEE [Vice Admiral Willis A. Lee, Commander TF 34] COVER LEYTE AT TOP SPEED X REQUEST FAST CARRIERS MAKE IMMEDIATE STRIKE.

Since Halsey had already sent McCain, and since the gunners of TF 34 were already scanning the horizon for a glimpse of the enemy off Cape Engaño, there was nothing Halsey could do except, as he put it, "become angrier."

Twenty minutes later another message clattered down the tube of Flag Plot in the *New Jersey.* CTU 77.4.3 UNDER ATTACK BY CRUISERS AND BBS 0700 11-40 N 126-25 E X REQUEST IMMEDIATE AIR STRIKE X ALSO REQUEST SUPPORT BY HEAVY SHIPS X MY OBBS [old battleships] LOW IN AMMUNITION.

The news that Kinkaid's battleships were low in ammunition rocked Halsey. He was even more shocked to discover that this vital bit of information had been held up somewhere along the line and that this was Kinkaid's third, not his sixth cry for help. Halsey could only repeat that he was too far away to help and that McCain was on his way.

Kinkaid was not completely candid when he stated that his old battleships were low on ammunition. At the heat of the moment, he did not have the full figures and had to depend on quick estimates. Of their stores of armor-piercing shells, Oldendorf's old battleships had expended only 285 rounds in dealing with Nishimura and Shima; they still had 1,352 rounds in their magazines, although only 299 of these were armor piercing. There had been a higher rate of expenditure of high capacity ammunition during the shore bombardments, but they still had 1,514 rounds aboard. Ammunition shortage, then, was not a real factor; the position of Oldendorf's force was.

Half an hour later, at about 1000, two messages arrived almost simultaneously. The first was a dramatic cry from Kinkaid in plain language: WHERE IS LEE X SEND LEE.

The second was from Nimitz, and it changed the course of the action.

Before we look at Nimitz's message, a little explanation is needed. Under normal circumstances in wartime, all radio messages are encrypted on the assumption that the enemy copies all broadcasts. The easiest points of attack for cryptanalysts are the beginning and end of messages, where phrasing may be stereotyped. To overcome this, officers in coding rooms employed padding—nonsense phrases—at the beginning and end to render the job of the cryptanalyst more difficult. There were certain rules for this padding: it must not employ well-known phrases or quotations, it must be separated from the main text by a double consonant, and it must not be capable of being read as part of the text. It was the violation of the last on the part of the coding officer at Pearl Harbor that led to the difficulty.

As broadcast, Nimitz's message read: TURKEY TROTS TO WATER PP WHERE IS RPT WHERE IS TASK FORCE THIRTY FOUR RR THE WORLD WONDERS.

Halsey's coding officer properly recognized that TURKEY TROTS TO WATER was padding and tore it off the message tape. But even though THE WORLD WONDERS was separated by RR, it seemed so plausibly a part of the message that it was left in the text Halsey read.

"I was as stunned as if I had been struck in the face," wrote Halsey later. "The paper rattled in my hands. I snatched off my cap, threw it on the deck, and shouted something that I am ashamed to remember. Mick Carney rushed over and grabbed my arm: 'Stop it! What the hell's the matter with you? Pull yourself together!'

"I gave him the dispatch and turned my back. I was so mad I couldn't talk. It was utterly impossible for me to believe that Chester Nimitz would send me such an insult." *

When Halsey had calmed down sufficiently, he completely revised his plan of battle. He ordered Task Force 34 and Bogan's Task Group 38.2 to reverse course and head back to Leyte, while Mitscher would use Sherman's Task Group 38.3 and Davison's Task Group 38.4 to finish off Ozawa.

* Although most accounts of this battle state that Nimitz was as much in the dark as Kinkaid over the whereabouts of Task Force 34, he informed Professor E. B. Potter of the U.S. Naval Academy faculty that he knew perfectly well where Task Force 34 was and that he intended the message as a nudge to Halsey to look at his orders again and remember his responsibilities at Leyte. The author well remembers how sharp Nimitz's mind was then and believes that his statement should be credited.

Halsey's heart nearly broke at turning away from the surface battle he longed for, but the greatest personal danger lay to the south, and that is where he went. It was a forlorn hope, for even at best speed, Task Force 34 could not arrive off San Bernardino until 0100, October 26. Even that proved impossible, for the destroyers had run too long at too high speed. They would have to be fueled before they could head back.

Reshuffling the forces and refueling the destroyers took until 1622. In order to have any hope of catching Kurita, who was reported to be still milling around off Samar, Halsey formed a light striking group, Task Group 34.5, to head south at high speed to delay the enemy until the rest could catch up. He went himself in the *New Jersey*, accompanied by the *Iowa*, the light cruisers *Biloxi*, *Vincennes*, and *Miami*, and the destroyers *Owen*, *Miller*, *The Sullivans*, *Tingey*, *Hickox*, *Hunt*, *Lewis Hancock*, and *Marshall*. This was too weak a force to engage the remaining Japanese battleships and cruisers, but it was the only one that had any chance of getting there in time.

Off it went at 28 knots, and the Battle of Bull's Run had begun.*

While all of this reshuffling was going on, the carrier strikes continued as has been told. At 1415 Mitscher ordered Rear Admiral Laurance T. DuBose to take a group of heavy cruisers *Wichita* and *New Orleans*, light cruisers *Santa Fe* and *Mobile*, and nine destroyers and pursue and polish off enemy cripples. After two hours they encountered a plane which led them to the *Chiyoda*, which was lolling dead in the water. The pilot, Commander T. H. Winters of the *Lexington*, obligingly spotted the fall of shot, and the *Chiyoda* went down after some thirty minutes of gunfire.

Just at the end of evening twilight at 1840, DuBose's ships encountered the large destroyer *Hatsuzuki* and two smaller ones. Engaging from an initial range of fourteen miles, the ships sped on through the night, the Americans gradually catching

---

* So called from the name "Bull" Halsey, as the press always referred to him. His friends always called him "Bill."

up. At 1915, DuBose ordered a torpedo attack which was successful in slowing *Hatsuzuki*, which proved to be no easy victim. Although she made no hits, she repeatedly straddled the *Santa Fe* until *Hatsuzuki* exploded and sank at 2059.

Admiral DuBose almost had a nasty shock in store for him, for Ozawa on learning of *Hatsuzuki*'s plight gathered up *Ise*, *Hyuga*, and a destroyer and had them accompany his own flagship *Oyodo* to help out. Although he continued southward until 2330, he had no luck and decided to retire. His force was spotted by night fighters later, but by this time they were so far away there was no chance to catch up before the Japanese ships came under protection of Japanese aircraft from Formosa. Regretfully DuBose turned away to rejoin Mitscher.

While DuBose was finishing off *Chiyoda* and *Hatsuzuki*, Halsey was steaming south in the *New Jersey*, a part of Rear Admiral Oscar C. Badger's Task Group 34.5. The phosphorescence of their wakes stood out clearly as the rushing ships sped to intercept Kurita's force. Unfortunately, they were already too late.

Kurita still held the vague notion of engaging the mythical force reported north of him and spent the better part of the afternoon looking for it. When McCain's planes began to arrive, further irresolution came over him, and at 1727 he sent word to Toyoda that he would head for San Bernardino Strait at dusk. At 2145 the Japanese were at the entrance of the Strait and started on through.

Halsey was to have his surface action in spite of everything. At 0028, October 25, destroyer *Lewis Hancock*, which was on picket duty twelve miles ahead of TG 34.5 reported a radar contact to the southward. The battleships and four destroyers peeled off on an easterly course, while the cruisers and remaining destroyers closed the target. At 0054 they opened up and the target was repeatedly hit. At 0103, when she was dead in the water and ablaze, destroyers *Owen* and *Miller* were sent in to administer the *coup de grâce*. The *Owen* fired a half-salvo of five torpedoes, one of which probably hit, for the target blew up shortly thereafter. Commander Carleton B. Jones, skipper of the *Owen*, remembering occasions where ships reported as sunk had turned up later as good as new, illuminated the scene with star shells. There was nothing to be seen. The enemy had gone down.

No one knew at the time what ship it was that had been destroyed. Estimates ranged from a battleship to a destroyer. After the war it was learned that the target was the large destroyer *Nowake* crammed with survivors of the *Chokai* and *Chikuma.*

This little action was Halsey's surface battle, and, except for mopping up, it was the last event of the Battle for Leyte Gulf. St. Crispin's Day was over.

Just as the English longbowmen at Agincourt on another St. Crispin's Day finished the chivalric armies of the French, so the Battle for Leyte Gulf finished the Japanese Navy as a fighting force. Only once more would its ships seek battle, during the Okinawa campaign, and that was a suicide effort, easily disposed of by air power.

The amazing thing about the battle is that the Japanese came so close to achieving their goal despite the overwhelming strength of the Third and Seventh Fleets. Mistakes by Kinkaid and Halsey were countered by the superb courage and skill of the airmen and sailors of the escort carrier groups, especially those of Taffy 3. Kurita's irresolution brought relief just at the time when courage and skill could do no more. When Kurita turned away at 0911, the last hope of the Japanese of avoiding total defeat was gone.

CHAPTER SIX

# Harmony to Discord

*Take but degree away, untune that string,
And, hark! what discord follows; each thing meets
In mere oppugnancy.*

Shakespeare, Troilus and Cressida

IT was quiet in Befort in Belgium, where a company of the U.S. First Army was in bivouac, waiting for something to happen.

It happened on December 16, 1944.

Suddenly the men resting in Befort were called out and loaded in halftracks and headed east. They didn't know where they were going or why. About a mile out of town they ran into a roadblock and a lot of Germans. Men began to die. The first one to get it was a twenty-one-year-old man from the Midwest. "Just before we pulled out," a survivor recalled, "I remember spotting his Christmas package on the table in the CP. He never even got a chance to open it."

In this scene, which was repeated many times over on a seventy-five-mile front between Butgenbach and Echternach, was the beginning of Germany's last, desperate gamble to survive, to win the war in the west. Historians know it as the Ardennes Offensive. It is better known as the Battle of the Bulge.

After the failure of Montgomery's offensive through Arnhem in September, Allied progress was disappointingly slow all along the front against Germany. The dramatic speed of the breakout and drive across France gave way to slow slogging. The stoppage of supplies to the Third Army in favor of

Montgomery's offensive may have added months to the war. Patton went to his grave convinced that it did.

Certainly there was little to stop the American forces in the Metz area, and a spearhead might have driven through the West Wall and on into Germany. But it was not to be.

Instead, gains during that disappointing autumn were measured by feet and yards, not by miles. The fault had to be shared by many people.

Most grievously to blame was SHAEF Headquarters which issued commands for all ground operations and in addition was responsible for the conduct of the entire campaign, including naval and air operations as well, insofar as they bore on the war in France and Belgium. Ensconced in comfortable offices in Versailles, they were too far away to be on top of the situation.

Eisenhower was having no easy time of it. He had no deputy commander for ground operations, and he had to coordinate the operations of three Army Groups from his forward headquarters or from his more elaborate ones in Paris.

And when one of the Army Group commanders was newly promoted Field Marshal Sir Bernard Law Montgomery, Eisenhower's task became difficult. It was made even more difficult by the fact that Lieutenant General Omar Bradley, commanding another Army group, was continually pressured by one of his Army commanders, George Patton. Bradley, normally quiet and tractable enough, was not going to take a back seat to "Miraculous Monty," nor was he going to let himself be led from below by his former boss, George Patton.

Of less nettlesome concern was the third Army Group commander, Lieutenant General Jacob L. Devers, U.S. Army, although, as we shall see, when Eisenhower gave him certain orders, they were immediately challenged by General de Gaulle, now acting as chief of state of liberated France.

High command is not an easy thing.

The British had little faith in Eisenhower's generalship and believed that an experienced general, Montgomery naturally, should be appointed deputy commander "to run Ike's war for him." On November 17, Montgomery had written the Chief of the Imperial General Staff, Sir Alan Brooke, a testy letter criticizing his superior and violating the chain of command in a magnificent display of insubordination.

"The directives he [Eisenhower] issues . . ." wrote Montgomery, "have no relation to the practical necessities of the battle. It is quite impossible for me to carry out my present orders. . . . Eisenhower should himself take a proper control of operations or he should appoint someone else to do this. If we go drifting along as at present we are merely playing into the enemy's hands and the war will go on indefinitely. . . . He has never commanded anything before in his whole career; now, for the first time, he has elected to take direct command of a very large-scale operation and he does not know how to do it."

Although Brooke agreed with Montgomery, he succeeded in preventing an open breach, while urging those in higher command to do something about the command situation. "Ike," he confided to his diary, "is incapable of running a land battle and it is all dependent on how well Monty can handle him."

There is little doubt that Montgomery and Brooke were right in their misgivings. Patton, an unlikely ally, if ever there was one, shared their sentiments in part. Eisenhower was inexperienced in handling forces in combat, and always before he had had a deputy commander, Alexander in Africa, Sicily, and Italy, and Montgomery in France. Eisenhower's great ability was in handling a coalition, but it was not so well suited to the balancing of troop needs, of strategic and grand tactical planning. And yet he would learn, and when the crisis came, he would prove himself inferior to no one.

Montgomery continued to press for a single offensive by his Twenty-First Army Group while Bradley's Twelfth Army Group covered his flank and Devers's Sixth Army Group held the line to the south. Emboldened by Brooke's support, Montgomery sent Eisenhower his understanding of a meeting held November 28, in which Montgomery had attempted to dominate affairs and win Ike to his own way of thinking.

We have definitely failed to implement the plan contained in the SHAEF directive of 28 October, [a directive calling for a broad-front advance] . . . and we have no hope of doing so. We have therefore failed; and we have suffered a strategic reverse.

We require a new plan. And this time *we must not fail.*

The need to get the German war finished early is vital, in view of other factors. The new plan *MUST NOT FAIL.*

In the new plan we must get away from the doctrine of attacking in so many places that nowhere are we strong enough to get decisive results. We must concentrate such strength on the main selected thrust that success will be certain. . . .

This letter infuriated Eisenhower, and he replied with some heat that he had not agreed to all these things, and that the Allies had not had a strategic reverse. Montgomery, meanwhile, had second thoughts, and wrote a more placating letter to Eisenhower, who replied more amiably, apologizing for "misreading" Monty's original letter. Thus the stage was set for an amiable opening of a major strategic conference held at Maastricht on December 7, 1944. Attending were Eisenhower, Air Chief Marshal Tedder, Montgomery, and Bradley, and their principal staff officers.

Once again Montgomery took over. Any idea of two drives into Germany was nonsense, he declared. Everything should be put into one, north of the Ardennes, in order to capture the Ruhr. Move the Twelfth Army Group north of the Ardennes and assign it the front between the Twenty-First Army Group and the town of Prüm. Both Army Groups would then drive through the Ruhr and receive "all support."

Montgomery then demanded once again that the entire operation be placed under a single commander. Somewhat feebly, he offered to serve under Bradley. Since Bradley was two grades his junior, lieutenant general as opposed to field marshal, he knew he was perfectly safe in making the offer.

Eisenhower rejected his plan. It was obvious to him if not to Brooke and Montgomery that if the Allies put everything into a single drive, the Germans would be able to mass everything they had against it, being able to hold in other areas with light forces supporting the West Wall. He did not disagree with Montgomery that the main effort should be made in the north, and, indeed, he was planning to place the U.S. Ninth Army temporarily in the Twenty-First Army Group in order to strengthen this drive. But, he insisted, it would not be the only drive. A strong thrust by the right wing of the Twelfth Army Group, spearheaded by Patton's Third Army would smash through toward the Saar through the Frankfurt–Kassel corridor. In Eisenhower's view there simply was not room in the north for all the strength Montgomery demanded there. Many divisions would be standing by useless for want of room for maneuver. Ike did not propose to weaken Patton's thrust to provide these unneeded divisions.

Eisenhower believed he had conceded a great deal to Montgomery at the meeting. He had confirmed that the northern drive under Montgomery would be the main one, and he had reinforced it with an entire American Army consisting of ten divisions, which would be under Monty's command. But Montgomery went away from the meeting in a frustrated frame of mind. He was ready for a latter-day Conway Cabal.* He hastened to confide in Brooke: "I played a lone hand against the three of them [Eisenhower, Bradley, and Tedder] . . ." grumbled Monty. "I can do no more myself. . . . If we want the war to end within any reasonable period you have to get Eisenhower's hand taken off the land battle. I regret to say that in my opinion he just doesn't know what he is doing. And you will have to see that Bradley's influence is curbed."

Brooke set to work to try to get the decision changed on the highest level. He proposed a meeting of the Combined Chiefs of Staff and/or a meeting of the President and the Prime Minister to overrule Eisenhower or cause his removal as Supreme Commander or inflict on him a subordinate ground commander. But his efforts came to naught. He invited Ike to attend a meeting in London with Mr. Churchill and the British Chiefs of Staff on December 12, and once Eisenhower arrived, Brooke pulled out all his big guns to make him change his mind. He thought he had an ally in Churchill, but he was

* The Conway Cabal was a plot originated by Brigadier General Thomas Conway in 1777 to depose Washington as commander at Valley Forge and replace him with General Horatio Gates. In spite of extensive scheming, it flopped.

mistaken. Despite all Brooke could do, the essential plan remained. Dejectedly that night he recorded in his diary: "I have just finished one of those days which should have been one of the keystones of the final days of the war. I feel I have utterly failed to do what is required, and yet God knows how I could have done anything else."

While the leaders squabbled, Patton had not been allowing his Third Army to sit idle. His frustrations at inadequate supplies had not kept him from aggressive patrolling and other activities designed to keep the Germans on edge. Then, in mid-November, he opened a campaign against the old fortified city of Metz, a necessary preliminary to his role in the forthcoming operations when he should make his drive against the Saar. By November 18, the city was surrounded, and four days later it capitulated.

Farther north, the First and Ninth Armies opened a drive against the West Wall in the region of Aachen and reached the Roer River, extending some bridgeheads across. Thus, by late November, American troops of the First, Third, and Ninth Armies stood on German soil.

In the south, Devers's Sixth Army Group made the most spectacular gains of all, capturing Strasbourg on November 23, and driving with French units to the juncture of the Rhine and the Swiss border. But the exhausted French were unable to clean out a dangerous German salient which came to be known as the Colmar Pocket. It would cause much worry in the days to come.

On the morning of December 16, Patton's Third Army had pretty well closed up to the Saar River. Its stiffest opponent had been the weather. It was one of the coldest and bitterest winters in recent history, and in the Third Army sector the rains never let up. There were practically no German organized forces ahead of him, and Patton planned to step off on another massive thrust at lightning speed into Germany. The jump-off date was December 19, and his attack was to be preceded by the war's heaviest bombing attack. Some 3,000 planes were to smash the West Wall ahead of him.

All that stood in the way were the rains.

Patton sent for Colonel James H. O'Neill, the Third Army Chaplain.

"Chaplain," he said, "I want you to pray for dry weather. I'm sick and tired of these soldiers having to fight mud and floods as well as Germans. See if you can't get God to work on our side."

"Sir," answered O'Neill, "it's going to take a pretty thick rug for that kind of praying."

"I don't care if it takes a flying carpet. I want you to get up a prayer for good weather."

Baffled, the Chaplain retired but did come up with a prayer just as Patton had ordered.

Almighty and most merciful Father, we humbly beseech Thee of Thy great goodness, to restrain these immoderate rains with which we have to contend. Grant us fair weather for battle. Graciously hearken to us as soldiers who call upon Thee that, armed with Thy power, we may advance from victory to victory, and crush the oppression and wickedness of our enemies, and establish Thy justice among men and nations. Amen.

There was no blasphemy in Patton's order. He was simply appealing through channels to the God in Whom he so firmly believed. As it turned out, the Lord took His time in answering the prayer, for it was not until December 23 that the weather cleared, and then it was in the nick of time to permit the Allies to deal with a situation which no one on their side had at that time foreseen.

Adolf Hitler had by no means conceded defeat. The summer and fall of 1944 had been disastrous from the German point of view, but he did not for a moment consider that all was lost. He had a plan, and it might have worked if he had had the strength and the reserves to carry it out. As it was, it caused consternation among the Allied leaders.

The plan is well described by one of the commanders, General Hasso von Manteuffel:

The plan for the Ardennes offensive was drawn up completely by OKW [Hitler's High Command Headquarters] and was sent to us

239

as a cut and dried "Führer order." The object defined was to achieve a decisive victory in the West by throwing in two panzer armies—the Sixth under [General Sepp] Dietrich, and the Fifth under me. The Sixth was to strike northwest, cross the Meuse between Liège and Huy, and drive for Antwerp. It had the main role, and main strength. My army was to advance along a more curving line, cross the Meuse between Namur and Dinant, and push toward Brussels—to cover the flank. . . . The aim of the whole offensive was, by cutting off the British Army from its bases of supply, to force it to evacuate the Continent.

Thus Hitler envisioned a second Dunkirk. The planned offensive was similar to the triumphant drive of 1940. It began at the same place, the Ardennes Forest, and was scheduled to sweep between the enemy main forces with the idea of cutting off part and causing surrender or evacuation. It was commanded by the same man, Field Marshal Gerd von Rundstedt.

There were differences, too. In 1940, von Rundstedt had had the advantage of a massive feint in the north to pull the French and British into the Low Countries so that the offensive could sweep behind them. Montgomery's arguments were almost, but not quite, having the same effect in December 1944.

But the most important difference was the relative German strength. In 1940, the German Wehrmacht was a finely honed machine, opposed by a demoralized French Army and an understrength and ill-trained British Expeditionary Force in little more than corps strength. Then the Luftwaffe ruled the skies over France. Now the Allied air forces were supreme. The Germans shrewdly planned to neutralize Allied air superiority by attacking in bad weather when nothing could fly. But bad weather could not last forever, even in France that December. Were Patton's prayers working?

Guarding the Ardennes was Major General Troy H. Middleton's VIII Corps, comprising four divisions. It was by far the weakest point of the Allied line. Each division held a front of some twenty miles as opposed to four or five miles both north and south of the Ardennes. There were several good reasons for accepting this risk. First, the Allies were thinking of the offensive, not of defense. Every available division was poised to support Montgomery's and Patton's forthcoming drives. There was nothing in strategic reserve. Also, there were no worthwhile military objectives east of the Ardennes, so no one dreamed of mounting an eastward attack from there. Although Allied leaders remembered the attack of 1940 in that region, they seriously underestimated the amount of German strength that Hitler would be able to gather for the last-ditch effort.

Intensive secrecy marked the German plans and troop movements in the weeks before the offensive. In fact, the plans were so secret that even Dietrich, who commanded the main effort, did not learn of his mission until a few days before the start. Some commanders did not know where they were going until they were on their way.

After his temporary disgrace for telling the OKW to make peace, von Rundstedt was restored as Commander in Chief West, but he took little interest in the forthcoming offensive. He had no faith whatever that it could succeed. "There were no adequate reinforcements," he remarked later, "nor supplies of ammunition, and although the number of armored divisions was high, their strength in tanks was low—it was largely paper strength."

He proposed a more modest plan, that of pinching off the Allied salient around Aachen, but Hitler would have none of it. The grandiose scheme would—must—succeed. Rundstedt thereupon retired into the background, leaving the details to Field Marshal Walther Model, now commanding Rommel's old Army Group B.

Model did succeed in convincing Hitler of the necessity for a few changes in the OKW plan, not in the objectives but in the methods. Since these matters were properly the business of the Army Group in the first place, Hitler accepted without any objection, particularly as Model was one of the few remaining generals he trusted. Even so, Model and his associates had to leave their side arms and brief cases outside the room where Hitler was receiving them. The Führer was taking no chances on another July 20 plot.

At 0530, December 16, a massive barrage opened up from

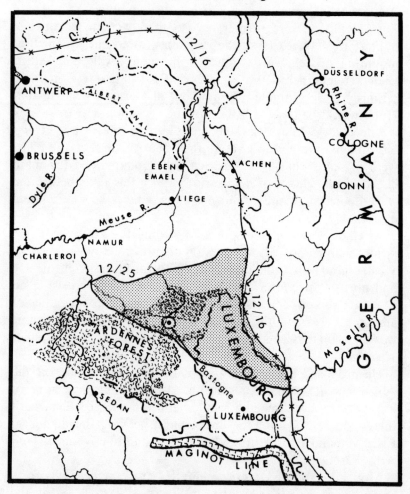

German guns on the troops of VIII Corps. Simultaneously a group of English-speaking German soldiers in American uniforms and driving captured American jeeps slipped out ahead into the darkness to spread confusion. Some forty jeeps got through and their riders had amazing success in misdirecting traffic, spreading rumors, cutting telephone lines, giving false reports, and creating chaos in any way they could.

Naturally, as the word got out, their numbers were greatly exaggerated in the minds of the American soldiers, and everyone was suspect. Before the Germans in American uniforms were captured and shot, nearly half a million American troops played games with each other, devising all sorts of tricks to show up imposters. On a short drive even General Bradley was stopped three times by suspicious sentries. The first time he was asked questions which a German would not be expected to be able to answer. The first question was to identify the capital of Illinois. Bradley correctly answered Springfield, which made the sentry even more suspicious. He thought it was Chicago. The next question, they agreed on, that the man in a football line between the center and tackle was the guard. Bradley flubbed the last question. He did not know the identity of Betty Grable's current husband.* Pleased at having stumped the boss, the sentry waved him on.

Even Eisenhower had his troubles. Rumors spread that these bogus G.I.s were planning to assassinate high allied officers, with the result that Ike was so closely surrounded by security troops he could scarcely move. He expressed his displeasure very forcefully, but it did no good. He could command the actions of more than a million men, but he could not call off his watchdogs.

The full extent of the German offensive was not immediately apparent at SHAEF Headquarters. It was regarded as a "spoiling attack," designed to throw off Patton's coming drive into the Saar.

On the afternoon of December 17, Bradley arrived at his headquarters in Verdun after a conference with Eisenhower. Looking at the situation map with his Chief of Staff, Major General Leven C. Allen, Bradley exclaimed, "Pardon my French, Lev, but just where in hell has this sonuvabitch gotten all his strength?" Already fourteen German divisions had been identified, half of them Panzer divisions.† It was obvious that there was more to come.

* Trumpeter Harry James.

† At that time, Army Group B included thirty-eight divisions, seven in reserve. The thirty-eight were organized into four armies—the Fifth, Sixth, Seventh, and Fifteenth. The Fifth and Sixth Armies were the attacking force, while the Fifteenth and Seventh

The Germans made fine gains the first day of the offensive, aided by vile weather that kept Allied air power on the ground. The outnumbered men of Middleton's VIII Corps held stubbornly, but were quickly driven back. Inevitably confusion developed, and men were cut off, left leaderless, and were overwhelmed by the enemy. But in general, all divisions fought well, and many Germans did not live to see another day.

It was not until December 17 that SS General Sepp Dietrich's Panzers got rolling in an attempt to outflank Liège from the south. The elite First SS Panzer Division was spearheaded by "Battle Group Peiper," named after its commander. Near Malmedy, Peiper's group surprised a battery of the American Seventh Armored Division. The Americans who did not escape were promptly rounded up, about 150 in all. A little later, Peiper himself having moved on, most of the prisoners were led into a field and massacred by machine gun fire. A few escaped by feigning death, but the Germans were particularly thorough. Walking among the slaughtered, they would put a bullet into the head of anyone who gave any sign of life.

Nor was the infamous Malmedy Massacre an isolated instance, even though it received the publicity. By December 20, Peiper's group had massacred over 300 American soldiers and more than 100 Belgian civilians, including women and children.*

As the picture began to develop in SHAEF Headquarters, it became apparent that this was no spoiling attack. Unless the Germans could be stopped at the Meuse or before, they might well break through to Antwerp. It was up to Eisenhower to stop them. At all costs, the crossings of the Meuse must be held. Meanwhile, an opportunity was developing to pinch out the huge salient by attacking its neck from north and south.

Armies had the job of pivoting to protect the flanks of the drive, the former in the north and the latter in the south. The Sixth Army had nine divisions, including four Panzer, the Fifth had three Panzer and four Volksgrenadier divisions, the Seventh Army four, and the Fifteenth eleven. There were no Panzer divisions in the latter two armies.

* Peiper later defended his actions, saying that the Führer himself had ordered the attacks to be marked by a wave of terror. Since Peiper's group was the only one to engage in such actions in the entire campaign, this defense made little impression on a military tribunal after the war, and Peiper was condemned to death. Later the sentence was commuted to life imprisonment, and by 1960 Peiper had been released.

Four key points developed, the so-called "shoulders" of the American defenses at Monschau on the right and Echternach on the left. If they gave way, the breach could be widened almost indefinitely.

A strong stand at St. Vith by the Seventh Armored Division denied this important road junction to the Germans until December 23, when the Americans withdrew to escape encirclement. By this time, the German offensive had failed, and it was merely a matter of how long they could hold in the Bulge. But the German failure was not yet apparent to the Allies.

The fourth key point was Bastogne.

On December 20, recognizing that the German advance had split Bradley's command in two, and that Bradley could not effectively coordinate the northern and southern parts, Eisenhower temporarily transferred the U.S. First and Ninth Armies on the northern side of the Bulge to Montgomery. This move had the additional advantage of making available to the Americans the British XXX Corps, which would otherwise be cut off by Army Group boundaries. Of course, as Supreme Commander, Eisenhower could have ordered Montgomery to make XXX Corps available to Bradley, but this would have caused a major furor with the British. Eisenhower took the simpler way.

Unfortunately, the repercussions were great in the other direction. Bradley, who was experiencing some difficulty in communicating with First Army, had few objections to the temporary transfer, but many American officers felt this was too much of an accommodation to the Brooke–Montgomery view of a single commander. The British press, which had an unfortunate tendency to belittle American military commanders and to paint Montgomery as the greatest general since Napoleon and Wellington, later published stories to the effect that Eisenhower had to call on Monty to retrieve his battle for him.

Certainly Montgomery's actions on December 20 did little to endear him to Eisenhower. As soon as he was informed by telephone of Eisenhower's decision to give him charge of the battle north of the Bulge, he set out to visit both First and

Ninth Army headquarters. One of his own officers remarked that he "strode into Hodges' HQ like Christ come to cleanse the temple."

This was simply Montgomery's way. He exercised much closer command of a battle than was customary in American military practice, and his bubbling confidence was irritating. But he and Hodges, commanding the First Army, had no real differences of opinion. The necessary regrouping went on, with men of the British XXX Corps advancing to fight alongside their American allies. Gradually the northern front began to straighten out.

In the south, events were advancing more rapidly than in the north.

From the first word of the German offensive, Patton had suspected that something big was afoot. Naturally he considered how this would affect his forthcoming Saar operation. It was quickly apparent that it would cancel it altogether. On December 18, Bradley called Patton to his headquarters and explained that the Saar offensive was off. Legend has it that Patton stormed at his boss, insisting that his own Saar operation go on and the First Army be damned.

Bradley tells a different story. When told that he would have to pivot 90° and attack north at the bottom of the bulge instead of east to the Saar, Patton merely responded, "What the hell! We'll still be killing Krauts."

Later that night, Patton was summoned to attend a meeting at Verdun the next day. Eisenhower would be there, as well as Bradley, Tedder, Devers, and others. Before he left, Patton had set his staff to work planning three possibilities for his attack to the north. "I want you," he told them, "to polish up the plan for each of the axes. I'm leaving a code name for each eventuality. . . . Be ready to jump with the one whose code name I'm going to phone back."

There was no sense of despair at the meeting in Verdun. Eisenhower had a firm grip on things, and was clear, lucid, and ready to make the essential decisions. Everyone else was equally confident. They were thinking in terms of attack, not of defense.

Their chief point of concern was Bastogne. This important crossroads was the key to the German penetration on the southern half of the bulge, and it was still holding out. The only reserve Eisenhower had been able to scrape up in the Twelfth Army Group area had been the 82nd and 101st Airborne Divisions. The 82nd was sent to the north to the First Army, while the 101st went to Bastogne under Brigadier General Anthony C. McAuliffe, in the absence on leave of its regular commander, Major General Maxwell D. Taylor. That very morning the division arrived at Bastogne. The next morning, they were cut off, but they gave no sign of giving up the position.

"George," said Ike, "I want you to go to Luxembourg and take charge of the battle, making a strong counterattack with at least six divisions."

"Yes, sir," replied Patton. He had three divisions available for this move. He wondered where he was going to get the others.

"When can you start?" asked Eisenhower.

"As soon as you're through with me."

The others stirred. This was obviously more flip Patton behavior. Would George never learn?

"I left my household in Nancy in perfect order before I came here," Patton went on, "and I can go to Luxembourg right away, sir, straight from here."

Eisenhower looked approving. "When can you attack?"

"The morning of December twenty-second." He paused. "With *three* divisions."

This statement was met with general skepticism. Every man there was a professional soldier and knew what would be involved. Patton had to withdraw three divisions then in combat, pull them back to a new start line, and move nearly 50,000 men a hundred miles over icy roads and engage in combat an enemy whose strength was still not known. He proposed to do all this within seventy-two hours.

Eisenhower was irritated. "Don't be fatuous, George," he said sharply.

"This has nothing to do with being fatuous, sir," he replied.

"I've made my arrangements and my staff is working like beavers this very moment to shape them up. . . . I'm positive I can make a strong attack on the twenty-second, but only with three divisions. . . . I cannot attack with more until some days later, but I'm determined to attack on the twenty-second with what I've got, because if I wait I lose surprise."

Eisenhower accepted the comment. It remained to work out with Devers how his Sixth Army Group could take over the area near Metz and the Saar which Patton would be leaving behind him. This was somewhat awkward because of the threat of the Colmar Pocket which the French had not been able to wipe out. If they had done so, then they could have held the entire line from the Swiss border to the Saar, releasing the Seventh Army to follow up Patton's attack. To make as many troops available as possible, Eisenhower authorized a withdrawal which would expose the city of Strasbourg to recapture by the Germans. This plan caused severe criticism from the French in later days, including a threat by General de Gaulle to appeal to President Roosevelt as one head of state to another. On January 3, matters came to a head, and Eisenhower was able to work out a compromise with the difficult Frenchman that assured the safety of Strasbourg and at the same time provided additional forces in Bradley's area to support Patton's attack.

When the conference broke up, Eisenhower saw Patton to the door and remarked facetiously, referring to his promotion to five-star General of the Army only a few days earlier, "Funny thing, George, every time I get another star, I get attacked." *

Patton, having won his point at the conference, grinned impishly. "And every time you get attacked, Ike, I have to bail you out."

The upshot of this conference and of the decision the next day to give the American First and Ninth Armies to Montgomery left Bradley with virtually nothing to do. Patton was in full charge of his own drive, and Bradley interfered with it as little as possible.

* Just after Eisenhower had received his fourth star in Tunisia had come the German attack at Kasserine Pass. Patton had taken over command in that area immediately after the battle.

248

Patton's three divisions started north on December 19. Not yet had the Lord seen fit to answer Patton's prayer, and the roads were barely passable. Icy winds swept down upon the men. Vehicles slid off the roads and had to be manhandled back or left where they were. Miserable, cold men marched on, but Patton's three divisions reached their goal on time. His promised offensive jumped off on schedule on the morning of December 22 at 0600, against steadily increasing resistance.

It was just in time.

Bastogne had been cut off by December 20, and was besieged by at least three divisions, with more on the way. Rommel's former Chief of Staff, Fritz Bayerlein, and General Heinrich Freiherr von Lüttwitz commanded the strongest forces. To them the American position seemed hopeless. It didn't seem so to McAuliffe and the G.I.s in the beleaguered city.

"So they've got us surrounded," said an unknown G.I.; "the poor bastards!"

Not knowing these sentiments, Bayerlein sent a note demanding surrender. As the *parlementaires* came in, the rumor began among the Americans that the Germans were asking to surrender!

McAuliffe took one look at the paper and dropped it on the floor. "Nuts!" he said. Then he decided to formalize his reply. Taking another scrap of paper, he wrote the following:

> To the German Commander:
> Nuts!
> The American Commander.

The officer who delivered the paper to the German *parlementaires* interpreted. "If you don't understand what 'Nuts!' means, in plain English it is the same as 'Go to Hell!' I will tell you something else—if you continue to attack, we will kill every goddamn German that tries to break into this city."

This episode happened on December 22. The next day the Lord decided it was time to answer Patton's prayer, for the skies cleared. Aircraft took off from bases in France, Belgium, and Holland, and drops of supplies—food and ammunition—were made on the cheering G.I.s in Bastogne. Also, planes were able to get in some good attacks on the German forces throughout the Bulge, much to the discomfiture of the Germans who were beginning to see the prize of victory eluding them.

Patton sent for Chaplain O'Neill, who was still in Nancy, to come to the new headquarters in Luxembourg. When the Chaplain reported, Patton greeted him with a firm handshake. "Chaplain," he said happily, "you're the most popular man in this headquarters. You sure stand in good with the Lord and soldiers."

Then he pinned the Bronze Star Medal on the chest of the surprised Chaplain.

Despite the clearing of the weather, there was still heavy fighting for the Third Army before Patton's men were able to force their way into Bastogne on December 26. At first the penetration was over a narrow road, and it was impossible for vehicles to follow with the needed food, ammunition, and fuel. The following day, the corridor was widened, and the seige of Bastogne ended.

The next stage in the Battle of the Bulge was a drive from south and north on Houffalize, to pinch off the German salient and trap as many Germans as possible in the pocket. Unfortunately for Allied hopes, von Rundstedt was able to extract most of his men before the trap closed. The reason? Patton did not have enough men to make rapid progress toward Houffalize, and Montgomery, wishing to "tidy up the battlefield" before he began, did not even start his offensive toward Houffalize until January 3.

Montgomery's role in this part of the Battle of the Bulge was professionally competent. He integrated the operations of the American First and Ninth Armies. He recognized the threat to the Meuse and the crossings of that river, and he sideslipped his British XXX Corps to avert that threat. Then, with his customary deliberation, he made his move in the direction of Houffalize to join up with Patton, moving with all deliberate speed. It was not fast enough, and von Rundstedt beat a successful retreat, extricating most of his men to fight again. On January 16, at 0905, the two Allied armies met, and the Battle of the Bulge was over.

Afterward Montgomery held a press conference which he believed would contribute to Allied unity. He thought he was heaping high praise on the Americans he had commanded in the battle, but to his listeners, his words sounded self-serving.

The battle has been most interesting [said Monty]; I think possibly one of the most interesting and tricky battles I have ever handled, with great issues at stake. The first thing to be done was to "head off" the enemy from the tender spots and vital places. Having done that successfully, the next thing was to "see him off," i.e., rope him in and make quite certain that he could not get to the places he wanted, *and also* that he was slowly but surely removed away from those places. . . .

But when all is said and done I shall always feel that Rundstedt was really beaten by the good fighting qualities of the American soldier and by the team-work of the Allies. . . .

American officers felt that Monty was claiming too much for himself, and his words to the press did little to enhance the Field Marshal's popularity in American circles. Stories appearing in the British press widened the split. Almost to a man, British journalists told the story of how Eisenhower's fecklessness had brought the Allies to the brink of disaster and how he had sent for Monty to save the day. This was too much for the American press, and their stories were not calculated to appease British sensibilities. The incident threatened to become the widest wedge between the British and Americans in the course of the war.

Then Brooke and Montgomery proceeded to widen it.

It was the old story. Montgomery took the occasion to bring up again the idea of a single thrust in the north under a single commander (Montgomery), which would cut into the Ruhr, while everything to the south stopped in its tracks in a holding action.

As the Battle of the Bulge was ending, Eisenhower reinstated his old plan of advancing to the Rhine along the entire front before undertaking *any* major thrust into Germany. His reasons were simple, although Brooke and Montgomery could not or would not see them. Devers's Sixth Army Group and Bradley's

Twelfth Army Group were not in positions which gave possibilities for easy defense. If they could clean out the Germans west of the Rhine, they would not have to fight those Germans again on the eastern bank and the swiftly flowing river would offer a natural defense against any renewal of a German offensive such as that at the Ardennes. Thus he could save approximately twenty divisions if he manned the easy defense lines on the banks of the Rhine rather than the difficult ones where Bradley's and Devers's men were at that moment.

Ike proposed to assign the American Ninth Army to Montgomery's Twenty-First Army Group. Since this would bring Montgomery's strength up to thirty-five divisions, all that could be logistically supported through the port of Antwerp, and all that could maneuver in the assigned area, Eisenhower would have a powerful force of fifteen to twenty divisions available for a secondary drive in the area between Cologne and Koblenz. Once the Rhine was crossed on such a broad front, the troops defending the west bank could come over, and, as Eisenhower wrote later, "We calculated that with the western bank of the Rhine in our possession we could hurl some seventy-five reinforced divisions against the Germans in great converging attacks. If we allowed the enemy south of the Ruhr to remain in the Siegfried [Line], we would be limited to a single offensive by some thirty-five divisions."

Riding high, as a result of the Battle of the Bulge, Montgomery tried again to get things his way. He suggested that Eisenhower's directive be revised to finish with this sentence:

12 and 21 Army Groups will develop operations in accordance with the above instructions. From now onwards full operational direction, control and co-ordination of these operations is vested in C.-in-C. 21 Army Group [Montgomery] subject to such instructions as may be issued by the Supreme Commander from time to time.

Then Montgomery got really nasty. In words that implied a complete lack of faith in Eisenhower's strategic ability, he went on.

I put this matter up to you again only because I am so anxious not to have another failure. I am absolutely convinced that the key to success lies in:

252

# The Rhineland Campaign, February–March, 1945

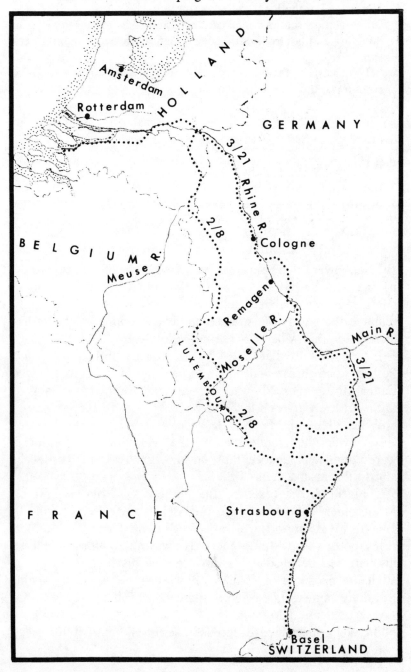

(a) all available offensive power being assigned to the northern line of advance to the Ruhr.

(b) a sound set-up for command, and this implies one man directing and controlling the whole tactical battle on the northern thrust.

I am certain that if we do not comply with these two basic conditions, then we will fail again.

The arrogance in this letter almost caused Eisenhower to explode. Still, he controlled himself and wrote back:

You know how greatly I've appreciated and depended upon your frank and friendly counsel, but in your latest letter you disturb me by predictions of "failure" unless your exact opinions in the matter of giving you command over Bradley are met in detail. I assure you that in this matter I can go no further.

Eisenhower concluded that he hoped their differences would not have to be put up to the Combined Chiefs of Staff. "The confusion and debate that would follow would certainly damage the good will and devotion to a common cause that have made this Allied Force unique in history."

Eisenhower was backed in his position by both Bradley and Patton. Each threatened to ask to be relieved if forced to serve under Montgomery. It was not national pride; it was lack of faith in Montgomery's leadership.

When General Marshall learned of the squabble, he sent Eisenhower a telegram explaining that Montgomery's proposals were completely unacceptable to him, to President Roosevelt, and to the Joint Chiefs of Staff.

That should have settled the matter. As a matter of fact, Montgomery had already accepted defeat and was preparing to give his loyal support to Eisenhower's plan. There was nothing really petty about Montgomery. He was no Achilles to sulk in his tent. He believed it his duty to give his best professional advice to his superior. If it was not taken, he would try again. But there came a time when a soldier must follow orders. As he saw it, that time had come.

Brooke, constrained by no such scruples, kept Montgomery

informed of every part of the controversy. He obtained a copy of Marshall's telegram to Eisenhower and sent it on to Montgomery, telling him to lie low, that he would carry on the fight at the highest level.

He did. In an unprecedented move, he submitted the controversy with a request for a formal review to the Combined Chiefs of Staff.

Nothing could have been more insulting to Eisenhower. As he well knew, Brooke was the most forceful member of the British Chiefs of Staff and the only soldier as well, with the exception of General Sir Hastings Ismay, who was Churchill's personal representative to the Chiefs of Staff. Although he knew Marshall backed his ideas, the whole thing could well turn into a major squabble on national lines.

But Eisenhower chose to ignore the insult. "I consider it," he cabled Marshall, "completely appropriate and even desirable that the Combined Chiefs of Staff should review the strategy in this theater, . . . The issues at stake are so great, and the consequences of victory or defeat so vital to our cause, that there should be achieved the greatest possible degree of conviction among all responsible parties as to the line or lines of action that should now be pursued."

As it turned out, Eisenhower did not have to justify his strategy to the Combined Chiefs. Eisenhower's directive was reworded to give priority to Montgomery's northern thrust, but leaving the way open for Bradley's smash into the center. This was thrashed out at a meeting in Malta of the Combined Chiefs of Staff, which was attended by Eisenhower's Chief of Staff, Walter Bedell Smith. The key paragraph read:

To deploy east of the Rhine, on the axis Frankfurt–Kassel, such forces, if adequate, as may be available after providing 35 divisions for the North and essential security elsewhere. The task of this force will be to draw enemy forces away from the North by capturing Frankfurt and advancing on Kassel.

Although the wording was British, it was in essence Eisenhower's plan from the beginning. A great many words had been wasted over a plan that was essentially unchanged. But as each side felt it had won the argument, perhaps all the passionate discussions did some good.

A great many things had happened by the time the plan was finally hammered out. The Russians had begun their promised winter offensive on January 12, forcing Hitler and the OKW to strip the German defenses in the West to meet the new threat from the East. Hitler had seriously weakened the Eastern Front in order to build up for the Ardennes offensive, and now he was paying the price.

With their attenuated forces, the Germans were holding a front of some 700 miles along the Vistula and Narev rivers. Behind them were the flat plains of Poland, offering little to aid the defending Germans. The Russians, on the other hand, would be able to exploit the plains, for the thousands of American vehicles which had arrived via Murmansk, Archangel, and the Persian Gulf ports were supplemented by the output of Russian factories. Tanks were in full production in Russian factories, including the new Stalin Tank, a monster that mounted a 122-mm. gun, far superior to the 88-mm. gun in the German Tiger Tank. In all the Russians enjoyed about a 5 to 1 superiority in man power and nearly a 2 to 1 superiority in vehicles and tanks.

To make matters worse, a limited Russian offensive in December had cut off Budapest in a miniature Stalingrad, and at the key moment Hitler ordered two Panzer divisions from the Vistula Front to help relieve the siege of Budapest. Thus, as the new year opened, Hitler was trying to do three things at once: defend the Rhine against the American, Canadian, British, and French forces, defend the Vistula–Narev Line against the Russians, and relieve the siege of Budapest. He lacked the strength to do any of them.

The Russian offensive was organized into three "Fronts." * In the north, opposite East Prussia, was the Third White Russian Front under General Chernyakhovsky. Next south came the Second White Russian Front under General Rokos-

* The Russians used the word "Front" to mean Army Group.

sovski. Its southern boundary was the Bug River. Opposite Warsaw was Zhukov's First White Russian Front. Facing Baranov was Koniev's First Ukrainian Front, while Petrov's Fourth Ukrainian Front held the area of the Carpathian Mountains. Not involved in the main offensive at first, Malinovski's Second and Tolbukhin's Third Ukrainian Fronts busied themselves with the siege of Budapest.

Already the German position in the east was as fragile as that of France in 1940. Already Army Group North under Vietinghoff was cut off in northern Latvia. Hitler stubbornly refused to permit evacuation by sea of the twenty-six divisions there for use in defense in the main thrust. Remnants of this army group held out until the end of the war, doing nothing to help Germany or to harm the Russians. It was another example of Hitler's fanatical desire to hold on to ground gained, no matter what the cost and no matter that a retreat would save men and would possibly make victory certain in another sector.

"Yield not a foot of ground!" Hitler had given this order in North Africa, in Sicily, in Italy, in France, and before in Russia. He gave it once again as the Russian offensive opened January 12. As a result the troops had to take the full shock of the offensive instead of absorbing it as they withdrew.

Although the Russians had some 225 infantry divisions and 22 armored corps facing 50 understrength German infantry divisions along the line from East Prussia to the Carpathians, they employed only 70 or so in the opening stages of the offensive. They were enough.

German high commander for the Russian Front was now General Heinz Guderian, Germany's foremost commander of armor. It was unfortunate that he had so little armor to work with.

From a thirty-mile bridgehead east of the Vistula at Baranov, Koniev began the offensive at 1000, January 12. It was hampered by fog hanging over the battlefield, which kept the supporting aircraft on the ground, but it covered the movements of the Russians from the German defenders. The fragile line of German positions collapsed, and in three days Koniev's troops had gained twenty miles, and they kept going.

257

Zhukov and Rokossovski jumped off on January 14, quickly capturing Radom and Warsaw in the south. As Rokossovski's troops approached Tannenberg, no one could have failed to think of the great Russian defeat there in 1914. There was no defeat this time. It was merely another position to be passed as the great offensive kept rolling.

It was really all a foregone conclusion. There was nothing to stop the Russians until they ran out of steam from overextended supply lines. Hitler stripped the Western Front, Greece, northern Italy to find troops to throw into the battle, but as fast as he threw them in, the Russians disposed of them.

It was grim, dirty fighting. The Russians were paying back for the atrocities the Germans had committed against the Russian people early in the war. Few prisoners were taken at first. They were simply shot or bayonetted as they tried to surrender.

Then the surrendering Germans became too many to be disposed of so simply, and hundreds of thousands of Germans disappeared into Russian prisoner of war camps. Only a small percentage was ever heard of again.

By the third week in February the Eastern Front had stabilized along the Neisse and lower Oder rivers. In some places the advance had been 300 miles. Budapest, Cracow, Poznan, and hundreds of lesser places were now in Russian hands. The Germans held out in a stubborn, futile defense of Breslau. The Russians simply bypassed the city. Danzig and Königsberg still held out, but the Russians were only forty miles from the outskirts of Berlin.

As the Russian offensive stalled, the German position improved. Instead of a 700-mile front, they now had only 200 miles to guard, and the natural defenses of the Neisse–lower Oder front were stronger than those on the Vistula. For two months, there was little activity except in the south, where Tolbukhin and Malinovski advanced from Budapest to Vienna, which fell April 13. By that time, the Russians were nearly ready to resume their advance.

As the Russians were driving westward, and as the Western Allies were poised to resume the offensive eastward, the Big

Three—Churchill, Roosevelt, and Stalin—were gathering in Yalta in the Russian Crimea for what would prove to be their last conference.

Roosevelt journeyed from the United States to Malta via the cruiser *Quincy*. Only a few days earlier, on January 20, 1945, he had been sworn in on the steps of the Capitol for his fourth term as President of the United States. The previous night snow had fallen, and it was a day of mud and slush in Washington. Following the swearing in of the new Vice President, former Senator Harry S Truman from Missouri, Roosevelt, hatless, and wearing a blue suit, made a supreme effort with his powerful arms and pushed up to his feet. His crippled legs with their braces held him erect as he took the oath of office administered by Chief Justice Harlan Fiske Stone.

His voice still clear and firm, his head still in the confident tilt, he made his last inaugural address. It lasted only five minutes, but Roosevelt had worked on it harder than on most of his speeches. "We have learned lessons—at a fearful cost—and we shall profit by them. We have learned that we cannot live alone, at peace. We have learned that we must live as men, and not as ostriches, nor as dogs in the manger. We have learned the simple truth, as Emerson said, that 'the only way to have a friend is to be one.' "

Three days later, the heavy cruiser *Quincy* got under way from Newport News, the President occupying the captain's quarters for the voyage. The ship set her course via Bermuda and the Azores in order to pick up air cover along the way, and passed through the Strait of Gibraltar. On January 30, 1945, Mr. Roosevelt celebrated his sixty-third birthday, his daughter, Anna Boettiger, acting as hostess and mistress of ceremonies. No less than five birthday cakes were provided, and the President gave every appearance of enjoying himself. Nonetheless, he was tired. The *Quincy*'s radio shack was kept busy with incoming messages which required his attention. Once or twice during the crossing, it was necessary to send replies back to Washington. The messages would be prepared and transferred to a destroyer which would drop out of formation. She would

259

then move some distance off the track of the *Quincy* and transmit the messages without fear that the *Quincy*'s position would be revealed.

One of the most worrisome things to Mr. Roosevelt was the furor in the Senate over the nomination of Henry Wallace to be Secretary of Commerce in Roosevelt's fourth administration. Although Wallace had been dumped as Vice President, Roosevelt had a political debt to him for his support and for the support of the CIO Political Action Committee, whose guiding star he was. Wallace's price was the Commerce Department. The firing of the incumbent, Jesse Jones, was a surprise to no one but a shock to a great many. To replace a hard-headed banker with a woolly-headed idealist, as Wallace was called, seemed the height of fiscal irresponsibility.

Part of the problem was that the huge Reconstruction Finance Corporation, with its vast lending power, was a part of the Department of Commerce. The idea of Henry Wallace managing all the millions available to the RFC was more than many Senators could bear. Although it seemed strange that the man who for four years had presided over the Senate should now be challenged for a Cabinet post, the challenge was there, and it was a problem of F.D.R.'s own making. It was a bother to the President during the crossing, but he took it in his stride. The upshot was that Roosevelt by executive action removed the RFC from the Commerce Department. Then Wallace's confirmation breezed through.

The *Quincy* arrived at Valetta Harbor in Malta on February 2, and the Eisenhower plan was finally approved by the President and by Mr. Churchill. Brooke felt quite grumpy about the whole matter, but put a good face on it. His editor, Sir Arthur Bryant, ends up his summary of these discussions by stating that the whole thing had worked out in accordance with Brooke's plan after all, and that the delay had enabled the American drive south of the Ruhr to be added once Montgomery's main assault was rolling. Since this was what Eisenhower had been urging all along, it seems that there was more emphasis on national reputations than on strategic considerations.

Many of those who saw Roosevelt at Malta were struck by his haggard look and his seeming lack of resilience. Admiral King, who had not seen him for some weeks, was struck by how ill he looked. Churchill's personal physician, Sir Charles Wilson (later Lord Moran) was much more explicit, writing in his diary:

> To a doctor's eye, the President appears a very sick man. He has all the symptoms of hardening of the arteries of the brain in an advanced stage, so that I give him only a few months to live. But men shut their eyes when they do not want to see, and the Americans here cannot bring themselves to believe that he is finished. His daughter thinks he is not really ill, and his doctor friends back her up.

Roosevelt and his party did not remain long at Malta. Starting at 11:30 that night, planes began taking off from Luga Airfield at ten-minute intervals, headed for Saki Field in the Crimea. Since there were over 700 members of the British and American parties, it took dozens of transport aircraft to do the airlift. The route lay past the southern tip of Greece, across the Aegean with its infinitude of small islands, along the length of European Turkey, across the Bosporus and the Black Sea to the airfield. Churchill's plane arrived before President Roosevelt's *Sacred Cow*, and when Churchill greeted him as the special elevator lowered him, he seemed "frail and ill."

It was a long drive from the airfield to Yalta, the first part taking the delegates across flat, barren lands where the Germans had destroyed everything they could before they had withdrawn. Abandoned vehicles lay gutted and burned. Nearly every building, including farm houses, had been destroyed. Entire freight trains sat on sidings, burned out and desolate.

Then the road began to twist and climb up the mountain range that lay between them and the coast. It became bitterly cold, and ice lay across the road in spots, but, as Admiral King pointed out, the Russians had no hesitation in traversing the treacherous road at top speed.

Then they came down into what seemed another world, a

world of bright sunshine, balmy breezes, and startling beauty from the mountains on the one hand and the sea on the other. It was the Russian Riviera. Roosevelt and his party were quartered in the Livadia Palace, two miles south of Yalta. The palace had been built in 1911 for Czar Nicholas. In deference to Roosevelt's difficulty of movement and his physical condition, all plenary sessions were held at Livadia.

Stalin and the Russian entourage were housed in the Yusupovski Palace at Koreis, four miles farther south. This palace had once belonged to Prince Yusupov, best known as the instigator of the murder of Rasputin. Churchill and the British party were assigned to the 100-year-old Vorontsov Villa, eight miles southwest of Livadia. Appropriately enough the villa had been designed by an English architect who let his fancy run free in a strange mixture of Gothic and Moorish styles.

These three buildings had been spared by the Germans, probably because there had not been time to destroy them in the retreat, since the high-ranking officers who occupied them would not leave their comfort until the last moment. Everywhere else there were signs of German attention in wrecked buildings and battered machinery.

The Yalta Conference was the largest of the war and has become the most controversial. It has been called Stalin's greatest triumph, and it has been called a success for Western Democracy. The truth lies somewhere in between.

Few military considerations were left to be decided, for the war was clearly won against Germany, and at that time the Soviet Union was not involved in the war against Japan. The political situation of the post-war world constituted the principal business of the conference.

It was a strange business, for there was a realignment of positions. In earlier planning and in earlier conferences, Roosevelt and Churchill had generally stood side by side when there had been disagreements among the Big Three. It had largely been a conflict between the Western views and the Eastern views. Now that changed.

Several times during the conference, Roosevelt seemed to be

closer to the Russian viewpoint than to that of Churchill. This was based on Roosevelt's almost instinctive dislike of colonialism in any form. At that time, the British Empire remained as the symbol of the greatest colonialism in the world and, rationally or irrationally, he seems to have regarded many of Churchill's arguments as desires to retain or even extend a discredited system. He had no way of knowing the path of ruthless imperialism on which Russia would embark in the years immediately following the war nor could he know that British colonial rule would prove itself a model of enlightened benevolence when contrasted to the stern repression shown by the Commissars in Hungary, Rumania, and elsewhere.

Five principal topics concerned the Big Three at Yalta: the question of German reparations, the problem of establishing the borders and a provisional government for Poland, the question of voting procedures in the new United Nations Organization, the occupation of Germany, and the price Russia would exact for joining the war against Japan.

As the only head of state, Roosevelt was asked to preside at all plenary sessions as he had often done in the past. At the first meeting, the Russians turned immediately to the question of reparations, demanding that Germany should be forced to pay for the destruction she had wrought and setting a figure of 20 billion dollars as the price, 10 of those billions to go to Russia. In addition, they demanded that Germany be stripped of her industrial potential for all time.

As it turned out, Stalin gained not one of these demands. Already it had been agreed that Germany should be divided into occupation zones, and the Soviet position was that these zones should be agricultural only. Churchill and Roosevelt realized that the balance of power required industrial and economic strength in the West to offset the massive power of the Soviet Union in the East. The only possible powers to fill this role were France and Germany, and the Western leaders successfully fought off Stalin's demands to keep those nations forever in the role of minor powers. The question of reparations was referred to a Reparations Commission with no specific figures mentioned. The President well remembered that the savage reparations following World War I had brought economic ruin to Germany. In the end American capital had to bail her out. Roosevelt did not propose to see the American taxpayer footing Germany's reparation bills.

The Polish problem was a particularly thorny one from the Western point of view, but the West had a losing hand. As the Big Three were meeting, Russian troops already held most of Poland, and they clearly intended to have their own way. There was not a great deal that Roosevelt and Churchill could do about it.

Pre-war Poland had been an enlarged state, its eastern and western borders carved out at the expense of Russia and Germany, and had included many people of German and Russian nationality who had looked on themselves as displaced minorities. Stalin intended to correct this error, at least as far as Russia was concerned.

The classic Russian position was to regard Poland as a buffer between Russia and Western Europe, and Stalin had stated that Russian involvement in war had come twice in the last thirty years "because Poland was weak." He intended to establish a "free, independent, and powerful" Poland which would be a real buffer, not a pathway to invasion from the West.

The words were agreeable to everyone, but their interpretation was not. Russia intended to have no Polish government that was not friendly to her, and this placed a curious meaning on the word "independent." Said Roosevelt, "We want a Poland that will be thoroughly friendly to the Soviet for years to come. This is essential." Churchill concurred. "I do not think," he said, "that the freedom of Poland could be made to cover hostile designs by an Polish government, perhaps by intrigues with Germany, against the Soviet."

Before considering the question of the Polish government, the Big Three took up the equally important problem of the Polish borders. In 1919, Lord Curzon proposed an eastern border for Poland which largely followed ethnic lines. The Treaty of Riga in 1921 had moved the actual border some 150 miles farther east, in response to perfervid nationalistic claims of the Poles. They were supported by Western diplomats who saw Poland as a *cordon sanitaire* against Bolshevism. The wider the *cordon* the better!

Stalin demanded that the eastern border of Poland be the Curzon Line, with a few variations in favor of Poland to the extent of 5 or 6 kilometers to solve local problems. This would return to the Soviet Union the great city of Brest-Litovsk and several millions of people, Ukrainians and Byelorussians, who had been forced to live under Polish rule between the wars, even though they outnumbered the Poles in the territory between the Curzon Line and that set by the Treaty of Riga.

There was no real argument over this point. In fact, it had been generally agreed as early as 1942 that the Curzon Line would be the basis for Poland's eastern frontier, so that item took little time for discussion.

It was then proposed that Poland be compensated by territory in the west at the expense of Germany. The Russians proposed the Oder–Neisse Line, which their troops would soon reach. To objections that this proposal would place many Germans inside the new Polish state, Stalin countered wryly that there were not many Germans in the areas in question. They had either been killed or had run away!

The issue no one could avoid, and the one the West could not win, was that of the provisional Polish government. In the collapse of their country in 1939, members of the Polish government had fled to Rumania, and thence to Paris, and finally in 1940 to London, where they set up headquarters and regarded themselves as the legitimate government-in-exile. Under their authority Polish warships joined the Royal Navy in convoying ships, and under their authority Polish military units fought alongside the British and Americans in the war against Germany.

The London Poles, as we shall call this government, were intensely nationalistic, intensely reactionary in political view (some of them were even feudal), and bitterly anti-Russian. They remembered the Katyn Massacre of 1940, and the photographs of the bodies of several thousand Polish officers who had been prisoners of war near Smolensk, all murdered, they believed, by the Russians. They remembered that the

Russians had halted before Warsaw in the summer of 1944. They had no doubt that this was deliberate in order to give the Germans time to slaughter all the Western-oriented Poles who had risen in response to urgings from the Soviet radio. They believed every story, some true, some false, of Russian pillage, looting, rapine, and murder that made its way from Poland to London.

As the Russians had driven west in the summer of 1944, they had seen to it that they would have a friendly government to deal with in Poland. In July of that year, the Kremlin had announced the formation of a Polish Committee of National Liberation, headed by a communist and by a left-wing socialist. It would set up headquarters in Lublin and administer the liberated areas from there. Only a month before the Yalta Conference convened, the Soviet Union had recognized the Lublin Poles as *the* legitimate government of Poland.

Thus there were rival governments, the London Poles—supported by Great Britain and less enthusiastically by the United States—and the Lublin Poles—supported, dominated, and recognized by the Soviet Union. And the rivals would have nothing to do with each other.

The London Poles seemed to live in a world apart from reality. They would agree to nothing that in any way compromised their position, authority, or well-being. They would agree to no diminution of the 1939 borders of Poland in the east or the west. When their Premier, Stanislaw Mikolajczyk, tried to persuade the others to agree to the Curzon Line, they forced him to resign. It was to be all or nothing. As it turned out, it was nothing.

Despite the Anglo-American forebodings, Stalin was quite amenable to discussion of the formation of the Provisional Government. Since the Lublin Poles, who had by this time moved to Warsaw, were actually functioning, Churchill and Roosevelt had to accept the *fait accompli*, but they hoped to get something better. As Roosevelt had written Stalin earlier, he saw "no prospect" of America recognizing the "Lublin Committee in its present form," since it was not established by any Polish popular choice. It was with some degree of triumph, then, that Churchill and Roosevelt found Stalin willing to accept this statement: "This Polish Provisional Government of National Unity [the Lublin Poles] shall be pledged to the holding of free and unfettered elections as soon as possible on the basis of universal suffrage and secret ballot. In these elections all democratic and anti-Nazi parties shall have the right to take part and to put forth candidates."

How were the British and Americans to know that within months Stalin and the Lublin Poles would violate every one of those provisions?

Most important in Roosevelt's mind of all the items considered at Yalta was the establishment of the United Nations Organization. Throughout the conference, Roosevelt had repeated the statement that the Big Three must stick together. He saw the United Nations as a means of assuring Big Three unity and bringing to other nations a voice in world affairs and giving them a means by which disputes could be settled without war.

Preliminary discussions at Dumbarton Oaks, near Washington, the previous summer had resulted in proposals the Big Three were ready to consider at Yalta. The Dumbarton Oaks conferees had proposed that the United Nations have a General Assembly and a Security Council, the first a deliberative body and an instrument of moral suasion. The Security Council they conceived as an instrument of force which would have authority to impose sanctions, both military and economic, as necessary. It would have eleven members, five (the United States, the United Kingdom, the Soviet Union, China, and France) as permanent members, and six to be elected for nonsuccessive two-year terms.

In the matter of voting in the General Assembly, Stalin demanded that the great powers have a larger voice than that of small nations. He had demanded that each of the sixteen republics which together made up the U.S.S.R. be given a vote on the ground that Britain would be able to control the vote of the British dominions and of India, while the United States would inevitably control those of Latin and South America and the Philippines!

By the time the Yalta Conference met, Stalin had retreated

from this position and now agreed to settle for three votes in the General Assembly, one for the U.S.S.R., and one each for the Ukraine and Byelorussia. Churchill could not oppose the suggestion because of the dominion status of Canada, New Zealand, and Australia, and the fact that India had been given a vote, even though she did not have full dominion status. Stalin offered to accept the United States having two additional votes, and Roosevelt agreed, feeling this to be the best compromise possible. He kept the two additional votes in his pocket, as it were, to be used if necessary when it came time for the Senate to confirm United States membership in the United Nations.

The Big Three agreed that membership in the United Nations should initially be limited to those who had declared war on Germany before the opening of the organizational meeting in San Francisco on April 25, 1945. Several nations, including Turkey, who had been neutral, hastened to declare war before the deadline.

The most difficult question concerning the United Nations considered at Yalta was that of voting in the Security Council. The agreement that emerged was substantially the one worked out earlier by Alger Hiss, and it separated procedural from substantive matters. The latter—questions involving the use of sanctions, condemnations, and any action against the interests of the permanent members—would be subject to a veto by any one of the permanent members. On procedural matters—such as whether a subject should be considered—no veto would exist. The Protocol of the conference spelled it out. "Decisions of the Security Council on procedural matters should be made by an affirmative vote of seven members. Decisions of the Security Council on all other matters should be made by an affirmative vote of seven members including the concurring votes of the permanent members. . . ."

In later years, Soviet abuse of the veto has caused the Security Council to be discredited by some people, and these critics have stated that the United States should never have agreed to such a restraint. However, it is clear that if the Soviet Union had not brought up and insisted on the veto, the United

States or Great Britain would. Without the veto, each nation would yield a part of its sovereignty. Suppose the Security Council voted to undertake military sanctions against a nation. Without the veto the United States would have been bound to contribute her share of troops. But only the Congress has the power to declare war. There was no chance that the Charter of the United Nations would have been ratified by Congress if the veto were not a part of the procedures.*

The dismemberment of Germany took little time. The original proposal had been for Germany to be divided into three occupation zones, one each for the Soviet Union, Britain, and the United States. Thinking of the time when the United States would withdraw most of its forces from Europe, Churchill proposed that France be given a zone to preserve the balance of power. Stalin at first opposed this suggestion on the ground that France was not a great power. She had contributed little to the war, the Soviet dictator went on, and she had opened "the gate to the enemy" in 1940. The next day, however, he withdrew his objections provided that France's zone was carved out of the territory already allocated to the United States and Great Britain.

The last major subject at the Yalta Conference involved the British very little. It concerned the matter of Russian entry into the war against Japan. "It was regarded as an American affair," wrote Churchill later, "and was certainly of prime interest to their military operations. It was not for us to claim to shape it. Anyhow we were not consulted but only asked to approve. This we did."

The question of Russia's entrance into the Pacific war had many ramifications. Stalin made it perfectly clear that he would have to get something out of it, for the Russian people had no such interest in it as they did in the defeat of Germany. Was Russia's participation worth what it would cost?

As viewed from the perspective of today, the answer is clearly no. It was obvious that Japan was defeated and was taking

* To be sure, the United States did send troops to Korea in 1950 at least in part as a result of United Nations actions. But the principal cause was in fulfillment of treaty obligations already approved by the Senate.

steps to surrender before the Russian declaration of war. Yet at Yalta, Mr. Roosevelt did not have the advantage of the historian's hindsight. What were the prospects for the early defeat of Japan as they appeared to Roosevelt in early February of 1945?

The Philippines had fallen. During the conference, F.D.R. had received a telegram announcing that MacArthur's troops had entered Manila. Not yet had the Americans landed on Iwo Jima, and Okinawa was nearly two months off. In another week or ten days American carrier planes would smash Tokyo, and American B-29s were conducting fire raids on Japanese cities.

At sea, Japanese merchant shipping had almost vanished. Submarines and carrier planes had done their work well. Japan was isolated from her resources in Southeast Asia, and a daring penetration of the Sea of Japan by American submarines threatened to cut her off from needed supplies in Manchuria.

At Pearl Harbor the previous summer, Nimitz and Mac-Arthur had told the President that Japan could be starved into surrender without actual invasion of the Home Islands. The sea blockade and the devastating air attacks would soon bring about her collapse.

The Joint Chiefs of Staff, on the other hand, were not in accord with this estimate. General Marshall and Admiral King believed that it would be necessary to invade the Home Islands, and that it would take at least a million men for a successful invasion. Some pessimists predicted a million American casualties!

In addition, President Roosevelt knew exactly how far along the scientists were in working on the atomic bomb. He had been told that a "practical" bomb would be available that summer, and that there would be enough for testing and for some to be used as weapons. The fact remained that no atomic bomb had ever been exploded, and no one knew just how powerful it would be if it were successfully exploded. Many military leaders were frankly skeptical. Admiral Leahy, Chairman of the Joint Chiefs of Staff, had no confidence in it whatever. "It sounds like a professor's dream to me," he said.

Russia's entry into the war against Japan would mean an

easing of the burden of the number of American troops. It would also mean that she would have a seat at the victors' table when the peace was finally written. Considering everything— the uncertainty of an atomic bomb, the recommendation of the Joint Chiefs of Staff that Russian help would be needed, and the desire they all shared to shorten the war even if the viewpoint of Nimitz and MacArthur should be correct—Roosevelt decided to pay the price.

In return for Stalin's promise to enter the war against Japan "in two or three months after Germany has surrendered," Roosevelt agreed to the following conditions: (1) that the status of Outer Mongolia as separate from China would be preserved; (2) that the southern half of Sakhalin should be returned to Russia from the Japanese who had taken it in the Russo-Japanese War of 1905; (3) that the Kurile Islands should be returned to Russia; (4) that the port of Dairen should be internationalized, "the preeminent interests of the Soviet Union in the port being safeguarded"; (5) that the Chinese-Eastern Railroad and the South-Manchurian Railroad be operated jointly by the Chinese and Russians; (6) that Port Arthur be restored to Russia as a naval base. As a concession, Stalin expressed his willingness "to conclude with the Nationalist Government of China a pact of friendship and alliance between the U.S.S.R. and China in order to render assistance to China with its armed forces for the purpose of liberating China from the Japanese yoke."

This was a pretty stiff list of demands, and part of it was not Roosevelt's to give away. It was reasonable enough to promise that Japan be required to give certain lands to the Russians, for the vanquished have no rights before the victors. But for the President to give away Chinese interests was a rather tall order.

Roosevelt undertook to get the consent of Chiang Kai-shek to this agreement and, indeed, there was little that Chiang could do. In the end it did not matter, for Russia paid very little attention to Chinese interests when the time came.

Critics of the Yalta Conference have seen in this agreement the sinister hand of Alger Hiss, later convicted of perjury, who engineered a sell-out, they say, to torpedo Chiang and install the communists of Mao Tse-tung in place of the Chinese Nationalist Government. To be sure, Hiss was there in Yalta, but he had nothing to do with the Far Eastern agreements, being fully occupied in working out problems of organization of the budding United Nations. He was in no policy-making position whatever.

Punctuating the talks were the usual state dinners, at which the Russian custom of frequent toasts in vodka was rather hard on the heads of those not forewarned. A Russian would propose a toast to someone at the table, rise from his seat and go to the man so honored. They would touch glasses and then toss the liquor down. Admiral King tells the story of how, at the end of the conference, Russian naval officials tried to ply him with food and drink in order to get him befuddled enough to sign a paper agreeing to transfer a long list of materials to the Russian Navy, including ships and aircraft. King felt sorry for the Soviet admiral in charge of this affair, for he believed his own abstemiousness would lead to the demotion of the Russian officer. Perhaps it did.

The conference ended on February 10 with a final dinner hosted by Churchill. It was a gala affair, with many toasts and many expressions of good will. It ended on a note of high hope for the world in the years to come.

The next day a final plenary session was held to announce the results of the conference to the world. The President, the Prime Minister, and the Premier posed for pictures.

It was the last time the three of them would meet.

That afternoon, Roosevelt left Yalta to drive to Sevastopol where the U.S.S. *Catoctin* was moored. She had served as a communication relay ship during the conference. Now she served as a refuge and resting place for F.D.R. who was tired, very tired. He enjoyed a steak dinner and went quietly to bed.

The following day he flew the 1,000 miles to Egypt where the *Quincy* was waiting for him in the Great Bitter Lake, which forms a link in the Suez Canal. With him was Harry Hopkins, as usual, who had been too ill to take his customary notes on the conferences and to attend many of the dinners, but who had faithfully been to every plenary session.

They were well satisfied with what had happened. Despite what later critics would charge, they honestly believed they had paved the way for a better world. They had no inkling that in the next few months and years, the Soviet Union would break nearly every agreement reached at Yalta.

We really believed in our hearts [Hopkins wrote later] that this was the dawn of the new day we had all been praying for and talking about for so many years. We were absolutely certain that we had won the first great victory of the peace—and, by "we," I mean *all* of us, the whole civilized human race. The Russians had proved that they could be reasonable and farseeing and there wasn't any doubt in the minds of the President or any of us that we could live with them and get along with them peacefully for as far into the future as any of us could imagine. But I have to make one amendment to that—I think we all had in our minds the reservation that we could not foretell what the results would be if anything should happen to Stalin. We felt sure that we could count on him to be reasonable and sensible and understanding—but we never could be sure who or what might be in back of him there in the Kremlin.

In Egypt, Roosevelt conferred with King Farouk, Emperor Haile Selassie of Ethiopia, and Ibn Saud, the King of Saudi Arabia. Discussions with the latter were especially frustrating, for Roosevelt hoped for a rapprochement between the Jews and the Arabs in Palestine, and was somewhat shocked when Ibn Saud said a simple "No!" to his request that more Jews be admitted. However, the King made a great impression on the President when it came to discussions about oil properties and the possibilities of a vast public works program to raise standards of living for the Arabs.

Churchill had been upset on learning that Roosevelt proposed to meet these Middle Eastern leaders without him, for he felt Roosevelt needed a guiding hand. Since Roosevelt did not invite him to the meetings, he made the best of a bad matter by visiting Greece in the aftermath of the civil war, and then by coming on to Egypt after Roosevelt had finished his talks. He came aboard the *Quincy* for an informal luncheon with the President, a luncheon at which no matters of state were discussed. It was just a meeting of old friends. Neither knew that it would be the last.

After Churchill had departed, the *Quincy* got under way from Alexandria on the afternoon of February 15 and set course for Algiers, where F.D.R. had expected to meet with de Gaulle. At the last moment, however, the prickly French general sent word that he would not come. He was punishing Roosevelt for not inviting him to the Yalta Conference.

Roosevelt refused to be upset. He shrugged off de Gaulle's discourtesy with the remark, "Well, I just wanted to discuss some of our problems with him. If he doesn't want to, it doesn't make any difference to me."

The voyage home was not a happy one for the President. Though the seeming triumph of the agreements of Yalta was fresh in everyone's mind, the inner circle team of the Roosevelt administration was reaching the end of the road. As the *Quincy* lay in harbor in Algiers, Major General Edwin M. ("Pa") Watson became critically ill. He was one of Roosevelt's closest friends and had served as his military aide for years.

While Roosevelt was sick with worry over Pa Watson, Harry Hopkins came to his cabin to say good-bye. Hopkins was so terribly ill and worn out that he dreaded adding seasickness to his woes and had decided to fly home and go to the Mayo Clinic for treatment. Roosevelt was far from pleased, for he had counted on Hopkins's help in preparing his reports to the Congress. Their leave-taking was not amiable. Roosevelt gave him a frosty farewell.

Two days out of Algiers, Pa Watson died of a stroke. Never before had Roosevelt shown such grief. When his mother had died, he wore a mourning band on his arm for a year, but he kept a reticence about his sorrow so that it was never revealed even to his closest friends. The same behavior had marked his reaction to the deaths of his other close associates, Missy LeHand, his trusted secretary of many years, Louis Howe, Marvin McIntyre, and others. But now, Roosevelt spoke openly of his grief, and his haggard face became more shrunken, the hollow look of his eyes apparent for all to see.

The sea voyage did nothing to restore his strength. Samuel Rosenman came aboard to help with the speech writing, but Rosenman had not been at Yalta, and the President had to do a great deal more of the work than was customary.

At the outset the weather was balmy, and the semitropical sun would have revived Roosevelt's spirits, had there been any reserve left in the President's body. But it was apparent to everyone that F.D.R. was near the end of the line. Still, he had been far down before, and somewhere he had found the strength to rise to the next effort.

The *Quincy* arrived in Newport News on February 27 in the evening, and the Presidential party embarked at once in a special train for Washington, arriving the next morning. General Watson's body was taken to Arlington, and at noon, in a cold, pouring rain, the committal service was held. The President attended, but did not leave his car; Mrs. Roosevelt joined the family and friends under the canopy.

The next day Mr. Roosevelt journeyed to Capitol Hill to deliver his report to Congress on Yalta. The address was broadcast to the nation by radio. It was a curiously lackluster speech for Roosevelt. It was delivered sitting down, for he no longer had the strength to support himself erect on his steel-braced legs. He began by asking pardon for "this unusual posture," but he continued by saying, "I know you will realize that it makes it a lot easier for me not to have to carry about ten pounds of steel around on the bottom of my legs; and also because of the fact that I have just completed a fourteen-thousand-mile trip."

Never before had Roosevelt made any reference to the infirmity which had crippled him in the midst of his career. Never before had he seemed to ask for pity.

Everyone agreed that the speech was not up to his usual standards. He ad-libbed parts of it, and it was far too long. He remarked that certain things, such as the voting procedures in the United Nations, could not yet be revealed. It is a mystery why Roosevelt kept the arrangements quiet, for when they did come out, they caused more of an uproar than they would have done if he had been frank and open. By the time they came out, Russia had openly violated the sovereignty of Rumania and Poland by imposing "friendly governments" on them.

As the President spoke, the hopes of men were for perfection in the peace to come, and the curious reservation in Roosevelt's report gave them cause to wonder. Even his conclusion was subdued.

> It has been a long journey. I hope you will all agree that it was a fruitful one. Speaking in all frankness, the question of whether it is entirely fruitful or not lies to a great extent in your hands. For unless you here in the halls of the American Congress—with the support of the American people—concur in the decisions reached at Yalta, and give them your active support, the meeting will not have produced lasting results.

The reaction set in almost at once. Even before the *Quincy* had reached the United States, the Soviets had forced King Michael of Rumania to dismiss the government, and a week later to install Communist Peter Groza as Premier. To be sure, Rumania had been a part of the Axis, and she had been overrun by Russia, but the Yalta agreements had provided for free elections in former enemy countries as well as in those which had been overrun by the Nazis. When Ambassador Harriman transmitted a request that Russia live up to the Yalta agreement in Rumania, the request was brusquely refused.

About the same time, the Russians insisted that the only "enlargement and reorganization" of the Polish government was to enlarge the number of Lublin Poles in it. Stalin excluded the London Poles on the ground that they would not accept the Curzon Line. Speciously the Russian argument went on that it had been agreed at Yalta that a government friendly to the Soviet Union was necessary to Russian security. Therefore, the only Poles who should be included were those who were "really striving to establish friendly relations between Poland and the Soviet Union." This clearly excluded everyone but the Lublin Poles.

These were dark clouds, almost buried in the newspapers, as

276

the Allied forces were driving in on Germany, the Rhine crossings now accomplished facts, as will be told later. But these clouds were ominous, and more people than the perfectionists were worried about them. What kind of a postwar world would exist if the Russians continued to act as though the temporary alliance with the West was over? What kind of a postwar world could exist if Russia replaced Germany as the enemy to freedom? Was the imperialism of the Hammer and Sickle to replace the imperialism of the Swastika?

No one longer doubted that the war would be won. Could the peace be won as well?

These were among the questions in Mr. Roosevelt's mind as he boarded his special train on the afternoon of March 29 to go south to Warm Springs. Tentative signs of the coming spring were in Washington; wisteria were in bloom on the South Portico of the White House, and the cherry blossoms were out.

But Georgia would be warmer, a place for a tired man to find rest.

# CHAPTER SEVEN

# The Road to Japan

*They that go down to the sea in ships,*
*that do business in great waters;*
*These see the works of the Lord,*
*and his wonders in the deep.*
*For he commandeth, and raiseth the stormy wind,*
*which lifteth up the waves thereof.*
*They mount up to the heaven, they go down again to the depths:*
*their soul is melted because of trouble.*

Psalm 107

"Our defeat at Leyte," observed Navy Minister Mitsumasa Yonai after the war, "was tantamount to the loss of the Philippines. When you took the Philippines, that was the end of our resources."

Taking the Philippines, even after the decisive defeat of the Japanese Navy at Leyte Gulf, was no easy matter. Although the Allied forces under MacArthur held an ever-expanding perimeter on the eastern shore of Leyte, the Japanese held the rest of the island and the rest of the Philippines. They could reinforce Leyte at will through the back door on the western side using the port of Ormoc to bring in troops from other islands. General Sosaku Suzuki, who was responsible for the defense of Leyte, was supremely confident. Believing the optimistic propaganda broadcasts of great Japanese victories at Leyte Gulf, he announced to his chief of staff:

"We are about to step on the center of the stage. There is no greater honor or privilege. We don't even need all the reinforcements they are sending us." He predicted that he would retake Tacloban in ten days.

Suzuki had a reasonable hope of success so long as the Americans could not maintain air control over Leyte and the Sibuyan Sea. He had real cause for optimism in this respect, for the Americans were having the devil's own time in getting a sufficient number of planes in the air to give their troops any support and to prevent the Japanese reinforcements from pouring in on the western side of Leyte.

The beleaguered escort carriers, having shot their bolt in the action off Samar, were gradually withdrawn, and by October 30 had left the area entirely. Army Air Force planes under General Kenney were supposed to establish bases ashore in order to release Halsey's carriers, but nature conspired against General Kenney's best efforts. The combination of monsoon rains and porous soil defeated the best efforts of Army Engineers and Seabees for a long time. The airstrip at Tacloban was available for operations on October 26, but could handle only two dozen planes or so. Plans called for quick development of the Japanese mud-and-grass airstrips at Bayug, Buri, Dulag, and San Pablo. The only one of these that worked out was Dulag, and it took until November 19 to put it in fit shape to handle the heavy American aircraft. Bayug and Buri opened briefly for fighter planes on November 3 and 5 respectively, but thirty-five inches of rain in forty days were too much and the strips had to be abandoned. Nothing the Engineers could do was of any avail. A truckload of heavy gravel would vanish without a trace in the mud. Another load in the same spot would likewise disappear. There seemed to be no bottom to the viscous mud. Steel mattings laid down to form runways would soon be waffle patterns in the slime, quickly fading from sight as they sank.

Eventually the Engineers and Seabees started over and constructed a good strip on the Leyte shore of San Pablo Bay at Tanauan, but it did not become operational until December 16, after the Leyte campaign was decided. Another base at Guiuan on the southern tip of Samar was ready December 18, and it came into full use at Christmas.

That left the big carriers. Halsey was anxious to get them ready for other things, and a certain tone of impatience creeps into his message to MacArthur on October 26: FOR GEN-

ERAL MACARTHUR X AFTER SEVENTEEN DAYS OF BATTLE MY FAST CARRIERS ARE UNABLE TO PROVIDE EXTENDED SUPPORT FOR LEYTE BUT TWO GROUPS ARE AVAILABLE TWO SEVEN OCTOBER X THE PILOTS ARE EXHAUSTED AND THE CARRIERS ARE LOW IN PROVISIONS CMA BOMBS AND TORPEDOES X WHEN WILL LANDBASED AIR TAKE OVER AT LEYTE X.

If Halsey had known the real answer to that question, he would have had a fit, but as it was he kept on supplying air support on a day-to-day basis, hoping that the next or the next would bring release. After rest and replenishment at Ulithi, Halsey hoped to lead his fast carriers in an attack on Tokyo, the first since the Doolittle raid in April 1942. But it was not to be. The carriers remained in the Philippine Sea. The glamour work would have to wait; there was dirty work to be done.

All during October 26, the ships of Task Force 38 searched for survivors of the Battle for Leyte Gulf while the planes went after stragglers from the various Japanese forces. First blood, however, was drawn by the submarine *Jallao*, which torpedoed and sank light cruiser *Tama* of Ozawa's force just before midnight on October 25. On the next day, carrier planes accounted for destroyer *Shiranuhi* of Shima's force and destroyers *Kinu* and *Uranami* which had just completed a troop run to Ormoc. Seaplane tender *Akisushima* and light cruiser *Noshiro* became victims of Sherman's and McCain's pilots, while heavy cruiser *Kumano* was damaged in the same attack that did in *Noshiro*. *Kumano* made it to Manila, and after temporary repairs, started for Japan. Four American submarines damaged her further, and she took refuge in Lingayen Gulf, where she was sunk on November 25 by planes from *Ticonderoga*. Earlier, on November 5, Shima's flagship *Nachi* was sunk in Manila Bay by Helldivers and Avengers from *Lexington*.

The Japanese were not always on the receiving end in the fighting around Leyte during the remaining days of October and all through November. Their Kamikazes and submarines were giving a good account of themselves.

It was manifestly impossible to maintain the full strength of Task Force 38 off Leyte indefinitely. Some provision had to be made for rest and replenishment, so Halsey began sending task groups to Ulithi on a rotation basis, keeping two off Leyte until October 30. During this time carriers *Intrepid*, *Franklin*, and *Belleau Wood* were all hit by Kamikazes. The last two had to be withdrawn for extensive repairs.

There was but brief respite for Task Force 38. There was too much at stake on Leyte, and the ships of the Seventh Fleet were catching it from Kamikazes, with little or no air power to oppose them. Task Group 38.2, which had not joined the general exodus, did what it could, but the Kamikazes kept coming. The reconstituted Task Force 38, now under command of Vice Admiral John S. McCain, was soon back on the job.

Halsey felt that the best way to deal with Japanese air power was to knock out the airfields whence came the attacking planes. Accordingly, on November 3, he set out with three groups* to strike at the Japanese air power on Luzon.

At 2330 that night the three groups were in formation well east of San Bernardino Strait. Suddenly, without any warning, antiaircraft cruiser *Reno* was rent by a violent explosion from a submarine torpedo. Although destroyers rushed around looking for the attacker, *I-41* made good her escape. The heavily damaged *Reno*, down by the stern, had to be escorted back to Ulithi. The rest of the force pushed on and by November 5 was east of Luzon. Out of respect for the Kamikazes, McCain kept his ships eighty miles or more offshore. During the two-day strikes, some 439 Japanese aircraft were destroyed and several ships were sunk in Manila Bay and elsewhere, including the heavy cruiser *Nachi*. Task Force 38 did not escape unscathed, however, for 25 planes were lost in combat and another 11 operationally. On the first day of the strikes, 4 Zekes made their way out to the force and eluded the CAP. Although three were shot down, the fourth crash dived McCain's flagship *Lexington*, inflicting moderate damage and heavy casualties. Within

---

* Davison's TG 38.4, since it contained the badly damaged *Franklin* and *Belleau Wood*, remained at Ulithi.

twenty minutes the fires were extinguished and "Lady Lex" continued flight operations.

For nearly three weeks, Task Force 38 stood by in support of Leyte operations ashore. Principal targets were enemy aircraft, air bases, and the Japanese convoys attempting to run reinforcements into Ormoc. On most days there were two or three carrier groups on the line, with one fueling. Bogan's Task Group 38.2 had a long-deserved respite in Ulithi but was back by the middle of the month.

The last operations of Task Force 38 in support of Leyte consisted of a two-group raid on the Manila area on November 25. This time the Kamikazes which had been held in check by raids on their bases put together an attack which hit four carriers in the space of ten minutes. *Hancock* was the first, and she was only lightly damaged by a piece of wing which fell on her flight deck as the Zeke was blown apart directly overhead. Next to get it was *Intrepid*, a hard luck ship if ever there was one. She, it seemed, could not stick her bow out of port without something bumping into it. She was known ruefully by her crew as the "Decrepit," or the "Dry I." This Kamikaze buckled her flight deck and caused severe fires. Almost at the same moment, light carrier *Cabot* was near-missed by one Kamikaze and had one plow into her flight deck. Temporary repairs were quickly made, and she was able to recover her own aircraft an hour later.

Just about the same time, *Essex* was launching aircraft when two Zekes jumped her at 1255. One was shot down, but the other crashed the flight deck forward, but the *Essex* was able to continue operations.

Before five minutes had elapsed, unlucky *Intrepid* caught it again. A Zeke struck her flight deck at a shallow angle; the bomb penetrated to the hangar deck and exploded as the plane disintegrated and "the engine and pilot continued on to the forward end of the flight deck." Casualties were very heavy, and it was impossible for her to continue operations. Other carriers had to accommodate the seventy-five aircraft she had in the air at the time.

These attacks on his carriers convinced Admiral Halsey that

enough was enough. He had already overstayed his intended time by four weeks. Since the force had really begun its operations against the Philippines in early September, its ships had been at sea almost continuously for eighty-four days. As Admiral Halsey wrote, "further casual strikes did not appear profitable; only strikes in great force for valuable stakes or at vital times would justify exposure of the fast carriers to suicidal attacks—at least until better defensive techniques were perfected."

Lest anyone think the carriers had been driven off, it should be pointed out that they had already done their part. After their departure on November 26, Japanese air activity did not suddenly increase, for they had little to increase it with. And Army Air Force planes on Leyte were getting things going more to their own satisfaction. The fast carriers hung on until they had completed their job. And their rest was not going to be a long one. They would be needed at sea to support MacArthur's next moves against Mindoro and Luzon.

On shore on Leyte things were going miserably for both sides. The torrential rains that caused airstrips to disappear into the mud were miring men and vehicles in sticky quagmires that had once been roads and trails. It made heavy going for General Krueger's Sixth Army as it attempted to advance on two Corps fronts across northern Leyte.

To the south XXIV Corps, under Major General J. R. Hodge, pushed westward from its Dulag beachhead against little opposition other than that provided by nature. In the foothills west of Dagami it ran into light opposition but overcame it by November 7. Its advance, however, was limited by the progress of Major General F. C. Sibert's X Corps, which was meeting the chief Japanese resistance.

General Suzuki hoped to make the chief point of his defense the town of Carigara on the north coast of Luzon. If he was successful, he planned to use the town as an alternate to Ormoc for bringing in reinforcement troops, thus sparing his men the long, difficult march up Highway No. 2 through the mountains. Unfortunately for him, the Americans got there first.

A few miles west of Carigara, between Pinamopoan and

Limon, is a steep watershed which became known to the G.I.s as "Breakneck Ridge." Here it was that the Japanese dug in, and here it was that the bitterest, most merciless fighting of the campaign took place. Time and again the Americans would try to cross the ridge, only to be driven back by heavy machine-gun and rifle fire from well dug-in defenders. The Japanese displayed an amazing aptitude for concealment. They camouflaged their octopus holes so well that a G.I. could not see them at ten feet. Patiently the Japanese would allow a body of men to pass and then rise and mow them down from the rear.

Even when not attacking, the Japanese gave the soldiers no rest, for they practiced their customary infiltration with a vengeance. Aided by the rain which often reduced visibility to a few feet, Japanese infiltrators crept into American positions to bayonet unsuspecting G.I.s huddled miserably in their foxholes.

It took until December 4 before the Battle of Breakneck Ridge was over and X and XXIV Corps made contact with each other south of Limon. By this time the Japanese were pinned down in two pockets, the San Isidro Peninsula northwest of Carigara and an enclave of a twelve-mile radius around Ormoc.

General Tomoyuki Yamashita, the "Tiger of Malaya," who held overall responsibility for the defense of the Philippines, wished to cut his losses on Leyte and preserve his remaining strength for the defense of Luzon. Field Marshal Count Hisaichi Terauchi, who commanded all defense forces in the southern area, decreed otherwise. In vain Yamashita argued that the battle for Luzon could be lost in the mud and mountains of Leyte. He wished to withdraw the 35,000 men remaining in his Fourteenth Area Army as quickly as possible, leaving only suicide units to trouble the Americans and defend the honor of the Army.

Terauchi was unimpressed. "We have heard the opinions of the Fourteenth Area Army," he said, "but the Leyte operation will continue."

Suzuki planned a drive across the center of Leyte, outflanking XXIV Corps on the south, but his power was blunted by the need to oppose the American Seventh Division which had made an amphibious landing about twelve miles south of Ormoc. The troops that did head for Burauen and points east encountered the same difficulty of movement that had so hampered the Americans.

Suzuki fully realized the importance of retaking the airfields on Leyte, for once they were established and fully operational, General Kenney's planes could range over the South China Sea and interdict all Japanese shipping from the Resources Area to the Home Islands. He planned, therefore, to use parachute and airborne troops to retake the key airfields. As with the Sho operation, the plan was ingeniously conceived and bunglingly executed. On November 27, in the early hours of the morning, a plane crash-landed on Buri airstrip so hard that all its occupants were killed by the impact. A second plane for the same target came down on the beach, but most of the survivors could do nothing but vanish into the hills. A third plane, landing at the same time, came down in the surf. A sentry, thinking it was a friendly plane, rushed into the surf to lend a helping hand, only to be greeted with hand grenades. His buddies finished off most of the Japanese, while a few escaped into the hills.

Buri caught it again on the night of December 5–6, this time by a group of some 150 infiltrators who came down out of the mountains. It took several hours to drive them off. This attack was supposed to be coordinated with a parachute drop which took place twenty hours later and was directed against several airfields. At Tacloban, all planes were shot down, and at Dulag a plane crash-landed, and once again everyone on board was killed.

About 600 paratroopers jumped on the Burauen complex during this same operation, and they created considerable havoc for two days before they were disposed of by the G.I.s. Ironically, the air complex had just a few days before been abandoned as hopelessly soggy. Only a field hospital and headquarters and service troops were left.

By this time, General Krueger was quite ready to finish off the Leyte campaign, and General MacArthur was more than impatient. The next phase of the Philippine operations, the invasion of Mindoro, had already had to be postponed from December 5 to December 15 because of the slow going on Leyte and the inability of Task Force 38 to return to the area in time. Since the Japanese reinforcements were largely coming in through Ormoc, the obvious thing to do was to seize Ormoc by amphibious assault.

American ships had been operating in the Camotes Sea to the west of Leyte for some time, catching hell from the Kamikazes, but dishing out quite a bit of their own against Japanese troop convoys. Little by little these Philippine versions of the Tokyo Express were eliminated.

The invasion force for Ormoc, Task Group 78.3, under command of Rear Admiral Arthur D. Struble, got under way from Dulag at 1330 the afternoon of December 6 and headed around the southern tip of Leyte. Although the ships carried a full division, the Seventy-Seventh Infantry under Major General A. D. Bruce, no ship was larger than a destroyer. Thus it resembled many another shore-to-shore movement of the Southwest Pacific forces, and it turned out to be just as successful.

For those who like to play the numbers game, we can note that the first wave of Seventy-Seventh Division landed at 0707 on December 7 on two beaches about five miles south of Ormoc. The Japanese were caught completely by surprise. Most of them were farther south, opposing the Seventh Division, which was driving north from Baybay. By nightfall the Seventy-Seventh had established its perimeter and had taken the little village of Ipil on the way to Ormoc.

The Navy then had to pay a price for this success. An approaching Tokyo Express was too far off for the destroyers of the invasion force to deal with, but it was given the best attention of Marine aviators recently moved up from the Solomons. All four transports were sunk as well as an LSV (the Japanese equivalent of an LST). Unfortunately they had already landed 4,000 fresh troops in San Isidro Bay.

While the Marines were thus engaged, bogeys appeared on the radar screens of the ships off Ormoc. At 0948, sixteen Japanese planes swept in and made for destroyer *Mahan* and destroyer transport *Ward.* In four minutes three Kamikazes hit *Mahan.* At first her skipper, Commander E. G. Campbell, believed she could be saved, but the fires spread rapidly and prevented anyone reaching the flooding controls for the magazines. Since she might blow up at any moment, Commander Campbell ordered her abandoned, and she was sunk by a torpedo from the *Walke,* a sad end to a gallant ship which had fought since the beginning of the war.

Although she was hit by only one Kamikaze, destroyer transport *Ward* was older and frailer than *Mahan* and could take the punishment less well. She shuddered to a halt, all power lost, with no way of flooding her magazines. Other vessels stood by to help, but she, too, had to be abandoned. Admiral Struble ordered *O'Brien* to put her out of her misery with gunfire.

By one of the ironies of fate, the commanding officer of *O'Brien* was Commander W. W. Outerbridge, whose first command had been the *Ward.* It was he who, from *Ward*'s bridge had given the orders for the ship's guns to open fire on a Japanese midget submarine off Pearl Harbor on the morning of December 7, 1941. These had been the first shots fired in the Pacific war.*

The Kamikazes were not through. Another attack came in shortly after 1100 and one plane crashed into destroyer transport *Liddle,* which survived, although severely damaged. She was able to join the other ships retiring from Ormoc, but was very nearly finished off by a third attack that afternoon. This time the Kamikaze hit destroyer *Lamson,* which was acting as fighter-director ship, attempting to vector the Army Air Force P-38s against oncoming Japanese planes. *Lamson,* too, survived, after a hard fight to save her. Other ships stood by, fighting off the Japanese with accurate antiaircraft fire. So intense was this fire that destroyer *Flusser* ran out of ammunition. Other ships were near-missed, but no more hits were made.

* See the author's *1942: The Year That Doomed the Axis* (New York: David McKay Company, Inc., 1967), pp. 27–28.

Resupply convoys for Ormoc proved to be costly, but none more costly than the "Terrible Second" which departed Leyte Gulf on the morning of December 11. Since the build-up for Mindoro was in full swing, only eight LSMs and four LCIs were available to carry supplies. Escorted by six destroyers, the "Terrible Second" headed down through Surigao Strait and around the southern tip of Leyte.

About 1700 a group of ten Japanese planes came in and four of them concentrated their attention on destroyer *Reid.* One was shot down, a second splashed near her bow, starting a fire, the third dropped a bomb or torpedo and went on, and the fourth crashed her port quarter. Under full power, she heeled over onto her beam ends and sank within two minutes. Only about half her crew was saved.

Almost at the same time, *Caldwell* was badly shaken by a near miss of a Kamikaze, but that was all—for the moment.

While the convoy was unloading at Ipil during the midnight hours of December 11–12, the Japanese were busily trying to land reinforcements themselves. Some made it at Palompon around the point west of Ormoc, but two Japanese ships and a barge attempted to land their load of troops at Ipil, right in the middle of the place where the American landing craft were unloading. There is always someone who doesn't get the word! A lively melee ensued before the Japanese were accounted for.

All night long the landing craft and the destroyers were harassed by planes and occasional gunfire. At 0400 the convoy got underway to return to Leyte, and on the way out destroyer *Caldwell* took a suicide plane with resulting heavy casualties. She kept afloat, however, and soon rejoined the formation. Every ship was attacked and bombed, but no further hits were made. A large number of Japanese aircraft were destroyed by the combination of Marine Corps CAP, ships' gunfire, and successful or unsuccessful Kamikaze attacks.

The opening of the Mindoro operation brought respite for the Ormoc resupply convoys, for the Japanese had more interesting targets to take on off Mindoro. At the same time, the attack on Mindoro convinced the Japanese that Leyte was lost and that the defense of Luzon would have to have top priority.

On December 22, Yamashita sent a message to Suzuki: REDEPLOY YOUR TROOPS TO FIGHT EXTENDED HOLDING ACTION IN AREAS OF YOUR CHOICE. SELECT AREAS SUCH AS BACALOD ON NEGROS WHICH ARE HIGHLY SUITABLE FOR SELF-SUSTAINING ACTION. THIS MESSAGE RELIEVES YOU OF YOUR ASSIGNED MISSION.

Although it took three days for this message to reach Suzuki, he had already made up his mind to fight a holding action in the Palompon area. Ormoc was taken on Christmas Day, and the San Isidro Peninsula was all that was left to the Japanese. That same day, General Bruce thwarted Suzuki's idea of a stronghold at Palompon by using part of his Seventy-Seventh Division to make a surprise amphibious landing there. Suzuki was driven into the hills.

That day, MacArthur announced that organized resistance had ceased in Leyte and that only mopping-up operations remained. As usual with the Japanese, that mopping up took a long time and cost a goodly number of lives, but the issue was never in doubt. The Japanese lost about 65,000 men killed on Leyte and had imposed only 13,500 casualties on the Americans, 3,500 of them killed in action. But they had lost another Decisive Battle.

Mindoro, which lies only seven and a half miles south of Luzon, was an essential stepping stone to the forthcoming landing in Lingayen Gulf. Since the airfields on Leyte had been so slow of development, they could not be used for air support on Luzon, and in any case Lingayen Gulf was beyond fighter range of the Leyte airfields.

Before the Allies could land on Luzon on January 9, 1945, they needed air bases closer, and Mindoro was the obvious answer. Another advantage of Mindoro was that it lies west of the monsoon belt that had turned so many of Leyte's airstrips into sponges. But there is a price on everything; the generally good weather off Mindoro gave a great opportunity to Japanese Kamikaze pilots. They were not slow to take advantage of it.

The landing was no problem. The Japanese had only 500 to

1,000 men on the island, and only about 200 in the landing area near San José in southwestern Mindoro. The problem was getting the troops there through the Kamikazes.

Rear Admiral Arthur D. Struble, who had handled the Ormoc landing, was given that job. As Commander Visayan Attack Force, he had under his direct command an Attack Force consisting of his flagship *Nashville*, 8 destroyer transports, 30 LSTs, 12 LSMs, 31 LCIs, 17 minesweepers, and 14 other small craft, all escorted by 12 destroyers. In addition he had a Close Covering Group of 3 cruisers and 7 destroyers and a PT Group with 23 Peter Tares.

Additional support was given by a Heavy Covering and Carrier Group of battleships, cruisers, destroyers, and escort carriers. The CVEs were again called on as at Ormoc because the target area was simply too far from the Leyte airstrips for efficient fighter coverage. It was a bold gamble and it paid off, but at a heavy cost.

The troops assigned to the job were a RCT of the Twenty-Fourth Division and the 503rd Parachute Regiment. In all over 16,500 men were landed during the assault phase and over 5,000 more in the follow-up operation.

In distant support the carriers of Task Force 38 gave the Luzon airfields a good going over and kept many Kamikazes out of Admiral Struble's hair.

The main force left Leyte on the afternoon of Tuesday, December 12, and proceeded through the Mindanao Sea to pass into the Sulu Sea south of Negros. Nothing developed that day or on the morning of the 13th. That afternoon the Kamikazes paid their first call.

The attack force had been snooped as early as 0900 that morning, but it was not until 1500 that the first attack developed. A "droopy drawers" Val* smashed into *Nashville* on the port side. The two bombs exploded, and all communications were knocked out. The ship shuddered from stem to stern,

* Val was an obsolescent dive bomber with fixed landing gear and fairing around the wheels for streamlining. It looked like a bird with pants hanging down. Since it was obsolescent, it was much used in Kamikaze attacks, but when it was coming at you, any Japanese plane could be a Kamikaze and probably was.

and no fewer than 133 officers and men were killed, including key staff officers. The admiral and General William C. Dunckel, the troop commander, shifted to a destroyer. *Nashville* had to return to Leyte for temporary repairs before proceeding to the United States for refit. Later that afternoon, the destroyer *Haraden* was visited by another Kamikaze and had to return to Leyte with fourteen dead and twenty-four wounded.

The Japanese were just warming up.

On December 14, the Japanese planned an all-out attack with 186 Kamikaze planes committed. Since the Japanese assumed that the invasion force was headed for Negros or Panay, they never did find Struble's ships. Instead they ran into planes from Task Force 38 and many of the Japanese failed to return without the satisfaction of crashing into anything but the earth or sea.

No further attacks developed until after the landings.

General Yamashita did not intend to waste any of his slender resources for Luzon in defending the island. He really believed that he had lost the battle for Luzon on Leyte, but there was still a chance. If he reacted to Mindoro, there would be no chance at all. The Kamikazes could do what they might, although they might better have been saved for Luzon.

The only difficulty in the landing at Mindoro was to persuade the friendly natives to get out of the way. Right in the middle of the prelanding bombardment area was a crowd of natives, waving and cheering. It took warning shots from the destroyers fired over their heads to get the embarrassing people out of the way.

The troops landed precisely on schedule to no opposition whatever. By noon they had entered the town of San José and were moving to establish the final perimeter. No effort was going to be made to take the entire island. A perimeter as at Torokina was the idea.* There could be established the airstrips and the PT base to support Lingayen Gulf operations three weeks later.

* See the author's *Years of Expectation* (New York: David McKay Company, Inc., 1973), pp. 242–57.

It was all too easy.

In fact, it wasn't easy at all for the naval ships. The CVEs, which had furnished air support up until 0800, were relieved by Air Force planes at that time and started back for Leyte. Just twelve minutes later, the Kamikazes started to come in. Destroyer *Ralph Talbot* and escort carrier *Marcus Island* were both superficially damaged by near misses.

Other Kamikazes went for the landing ships at the beachhead. *LST-738* and *LST-472* both were crashed and neither could be saved. The unloading continued, however, and by evening almost every ship was empty and headed back for Leyte Gulf.

Japanese propaganda was equal to the occasion. Lieutenant General M. Homma rallied the Japanese people with an ingenious theory that the landing on Mindoro was forced on the Americans because of the "terrific pressure exerted by our victorious forces on Leyte Island. We have the enemy in a position on Mindoro to deal him a stunning blow. Douglas MacArthur, having many times escaped our traps, will not this time slip away."

Kamikaze attacks were the curse of the Mindoro operation. They attacked regularly until January 4 when they found bigger game in the invasion convoys bound for Lingayen Gulf. By that time they had sunk three LSTs, three Liberty ships, an aviation gasoline tanker, and a PT boat. In addition they had inflicted more or less serious damage on three destroyers, two Liberty ships, and another PT. Additional damage was caused by bombing from conventional attacks.

The Japanese Navy made an attempt to knock out the beachhead in the manner so often tried at Guadalcanal and at Empress Augusta Bay. Rear Admiral Masanori Kimura sailed from Camranh Bay, Indochina, on December 24, wearing his flag in destroyer *Kasumi*, and accompanied by five other destroyers and heavy cruiser *Ashigara* and light cruiser *Oyodo*. The spanking new 27,000-ton carrier *Unryu* left Japan about the same time and may have been scheduled to join Kimura or to go to Lingga Roads. In any case, she was intercepted by submarine *Redfish* and sent to the bottom by two torpedo hits.

Kimura picked a bad time from the American point of view, for most of the combatant ships had been withdrawn from the Mindoro area by the time he was sighted at 1600, December 26. Kinkaid organized a group of two heavy and two light cruisers and eight destroyers to try to intercept, but there was no chance. PTs were sent out to intercept but were beaten off. Kimura did make it to the beachhead but delivered a perfunctory attack and did little damage before retiring shortly before midnight on December 26. On the way out he had to pay the price. PTs *221* and *223* intercepted him, and the latter Peter Tare fired two torpedoes at 0105, December 27. They leapt out of the tubes as Skipper Lieutenant (jg) Harry E. Griffin turned sharply away. A few minutes later the new destroyer *Kiyoshimo* went dead in the water and sank shortly thereafter.

Aircraft pursued Kimura back to Camranh Bay, but inflicted no more losses on him. The raid was a complete failure except for the morale boost it was able to give the Japanese people when highly inflated accounts were broadcast to them.

On shore, most of the fighting had been swiftly accomplished. Some mopping up remained to be done, and it was not until January 30 that the Americans turned what was left of it over to the Filipino guerrillas, who thoroughly relished the opportunity. The first airstrip, Hill Field, was operational on December 19 and the San José field was ready December 26. A third was ready January 26, and a fourth, heavy bomber field, was operational in early March.

Taking Mindoro was a tough affair for the Navy, but possession of the airstrips at San José enabled the Air Force to prevent worse during the passage to Lingayen Gulf in early January. The "Divine Wind" of the Kamikaze would still come in whirlwind force, but it would be less than it might have been.

Meanwhile, hundreds of miles to the east, quite another kind of wind would inflict on the U.S. Navy its greatest uncompensated loss since the Battle of Savo in August 1942.

The victim of the great typhoon of December 1944 was Task Force 38. Reorganized because of losses and the need for better concentration into three instead of four groups, Task Force 38 was now under command of Vice Admiral John Sidney McCain. On December 1, two groups sortied from Ulithi to join the third, already at sea. Their mission was to place an aerial umbrella over airfields on Luzon to keep planes there away from the Mindoro operation. Scarcely had the ships reached the open sea when news came in of the postponement of the Mindoro invasion from December 5 to December 15. Hearty rejoicing ensued, for this meant that the crews of the ships of Task Force 38 could have another ten days of rest and relaxation.

Rest and relaxation at Ulithi was better than being at sea where nearly everyone stood watches four hours on and eight off, but it was not to be confused with a peacetime vacation at the seashore. Ship's work for all hands continued until midday chow. Then, at 1300, say, a liberty section would be sent ashore to one of the barren coral islets where they could drink Coke or other soft drinks and two cans of beer per man. These were usually provided free of charge from the ship's welfare fund. Since some of the bluejackets did not drink beer, a lively market developed, a can of beer being traded for the "first liberty in Frisco," or several bottles of pop, or an unbelievable number of dollars. Money meant little out in the western Pacific, most of it being sent home or gambled away, so the price of essentials like beer skyrocketed.

Most liberties took place on the big island of Mogmog, at the northern end of the atoll. With the consent of their chief, the natives had been moved to a nearby island. On Mogmog, recreational facilities had been set up: basketball courts, baseball diamonds, football fields, and horseshoe pitches. Swimming was good if you avoided the coral. Most men swam with sneakers on, for coral wounds have a nasty tendency to fester and become infected.

The officers fared a little better, but not much. A bar was set up on Mogmog, where Scotch or bourbon sold for 20¢ a shot. Other refreshment was available also. Otherwise the officers existed much as the men.

Another welcome feature of Ulithi, at least to destroyermen,

294

was the chance to show movies. The larger ships had provisions for showing movies while they were under way, but not so the destroyers. At that time the only prints of feature movies available were 35-mm., and the equipment was too bulky for the mess hall. In Ulithi, destroyers nested in groups of four or five would rig the screen between the bows of adjacent ships. The projectors were located in the No. 2 gun mount and the films were divided to permit continuous projection. If it rained, as it often did, men would put on foul weather gear and the show would go on. Musicals were particular favorites, with Betty Grable's curvaceous figure especially admired. Westerns, especially Hopalong Cassidy, were to be endured. War movies, showing feats of derring-do, were great subjects for mirth, especially Navy war movies. Scenes which thrilled the folks back home convulsed their husbands and sons with laughter.

On December 11, Task Force 38 put away such things and stood out to sea to deliver preliminary strikes on Luzon. They began to put what was known as "the B.B.B." (Big Blue Blanket) of aircraft over Luzon to keep the Japanese planes pinned down. Except for one strike that left before the planes of Task Force 38 arrived, not a single Luzon-based aircraft hit Mindoro convoys during the period of December 14–16, and not a one came anywhere near Task Force 38. According to Admiral Halsey, 270 Japanese planes were destroyed those three days, with a cost of 27 planes in combat and another 38 lost to accidents.

On the evening of December 16, Task Force 38 retired eastward to refuel in an area comfortably out of range of Japanese aircraft in the Philippines. Unfortunately it brought the task force in range, in fact in the center of, a typhoon.

No one who has not experienced a typhoon in a small ship at sea can possibly know what it is like. No motion picture can do it justice, for in the theater one cannot feel the sickening lurches of ships tossed by the winds or smashing down in the sea as though dropped from a giant hand. The sheer struggle to stay erect during heavy rolling wears men to the point of exhaustion. Nor is there any relief. One cannot stay in his bunk or in a chair unless he is lashed down, and eating is limited to what can be held in the hand. It is possible to balance a cup of coffee so that one does not spill a drop.

Overall there is the fear. Rolling, even heavy rolling, does not frighten a sailor, but when a ship is caught in the trough of the sea and lies for minutes on end heeled far over to one side, the pressure of the wind and sea thwarting her every effort to right herself, it crosses the mind of everyone that she may not roll back. The chances for survival in those seas are practically nil. It takes the highest order of seamanship to bring a ship through such an ordeal. It all depends on the skill of the commanding officer and the strength and skill of the helmsman. The rest of the crew can only hang on and pray.

The typhoon that sneaked up on Task Force 38 was a small one as typhoons go, but because it was small its winds were concentrated and especially powerful. No ship, shore station, or weather plane spotted the small "tropical disturbance" that would grow and grow into a typhoon.

No suspicion of such danger was felt on any ship as Task Force 38 rendezvoused with the oiler group in 14°50′N, 129°57′E on the morning of December 17. It was heavy weather for fueling, with a stiff 20- to 30-knot breeze from the northeast. The sea had made up and getting the hoses across was hard work and it was difficult to keep the ships alongside the oilers. Hoses parted, spewing oil into the turbulence of the sea.

During the morning, Commander G. F. Kosco, Halsey's aerologist, concluded that something was up, and after destroyer *Spence*, which was refueling from Halsey's flagship *New Jersey*, had nearly slammed into the giant battleship, Halsey called a weather conference. Meteorological broadcasts from Pearl Harbor had just arrived, predicting a cold front that seemed to give some sort of a refuge, and Kosco recommended that they try again the next day in position 17°N, 128°E. Halsey agreed and fueling was delayed, except for destroyers *Spence*, *Hickox*, and *Maddox*, which were dangerously low on fuel. They remained with the oiler group while the rest of Task Force 38 set out for the new rendezvous.

Halsey made the decision to postpone fueling very reluctantly, for he was committed to make another strike on Luzon on December 19, and fueling all day on December 18 was cutting things rather fine. But he needed the replacement fuel, planes, and pilots that the oiler group had for him, and he meant to have them.

By this time the sea was too rough for the CVEs with the oiler group to launch their replacement aircraft and send them over to the fleet carriers. They would simply have to wait.

Dirty weather was obviously coming from somewhere, but what was it and where was it? Still no one forecast a typhoon. On every ship officers were trying to locate the storm, as it was still called. Everyone tried and no one got it right.

A typhoon, like a hurricane, is a vast whirlpool of air which circulates counterclockwise north of the Equator. At the center the "eye" may be calm, but extending out for a hundred miles or more in every direction are winds of hurricane force, sometimes over 100 knots near the center. Like a hurricane, a typhoon north of the Equator tends to move at a rate of 5 to 15 knots, but its movements are highly unpredictable. This particular typhoon was more tightly packed than usual, scarcely more than a hundred miles in diameter, and its winds were that much more destructive.

Even though no one knew just where the typhoon was, and by midafternoon they were beginning to call it one, everyone agreed that the rendezvous set for the next morning would be directly in its path. Halsey accordingly set a third rendezvous well to the south in position 14°N, 127°30′E. Unfortunately rendezvous No. 2 was clear of where the typhoon actually went; rendezvous No. 3 decidedly was not.

As Task Force 38 ran west that evening, it was outrunning the storm, and the wind and seas improved slightly, which cheered everyone. Still the lighter ships were making heavy weather of it, and some were suffering damage. Some were forced to slow down, and since they could not possibly make rendezvous No. 3 by morning, Halsey set yet a fourth in latitude 15°30′N, longitude 127°40′E. This turned out to be only thirty-five miles from where the eye of the typhoon would pass.

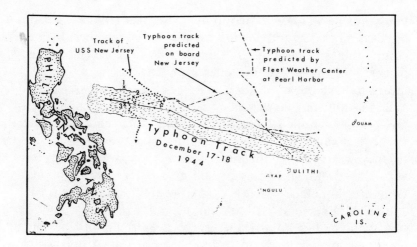

1. Last known position of *Monaghan*, 1007, December 18
2. Last known position of *Hull*, 1050, December 18
3. Last known position of *Spence*, 1117, December 18

It was not until 0400, the morning of December 18, after the weather had become much worse, that Halsey "for the first time" became aware "that the Fleet was confronted with serious storm conditions." After consultation with Commander Kosco, Halsey ordered by voice radio, "Cancel previous rendezvous; all groups come to course 180°. Commence exercise [fueling] when practicable. Suggest leading destroyers take it over stern, if necessary."

Halsey was suggesting that the destroyers fuel from astern of the oilers which would trail hoses to be picked up by the receiving ships.* However, the difficulties of rerigging the equipment prevented this from being carried out. In any case, the rapidly worsening weather would have made any such attempt impossible. No one could have lived on the exposed forecastle of a destroyer that morning.

Abandoning all efforts to fuel, Admiral Halsey at 0803 ordered base course of 180° to try to run out of the storm. By this time the barometer was dropping rapidly and the seas were

* Normally fueling was done with ships alongside of each other twenty to thirty yards apart.

going from "high" to "very high." By 1030 the crest of the waves towered sixty to seventy feet above the troughs where too many ships were trapped as though in stone walls. Winds were stepping up from 50 to 60 knots and kept on rising. Ships which were not caught in the troughs were laboring heavily, and the 45,000-ton *New Jersey* was tossed about "as if she were a canoe." The ships that especially caught hell were the light carriers, the destroyers, and the destroyer escorts.

The winds were now gusting to 90 knots or better and the barometer was going off the scale on some ships. An oiler recorded a reading of 27.07, and several ships reported even lower ones.* Torrential rain was falling steadily, except that the violent winds drove it nearly horizontal, as it combined with spray torn from the wave crests. It was impossible to see even the bow of one's own ship at times, and at the worst, when the wind rose to 125 knots (144 miles per hour), paint was scrubbed from exposed surfaces on some ships as though it had been done with a sand blaster. The screaming of wind in the rigging and the groans of the anguished ships made it hard to think of anything except fear. Yet the skippers kept their heads and most of the ships survived.

On the escort carriers, the greatest danger was from planes that broke loose. Even though they had been double and triple lashed, the lashings sometimes parted like thread or the pad-eyes pulled out of the decks. Twenty-thousand-pound aircraft would run amok on the hangar decks, crashing into others, and starting fires as spilled gasoline met sparks from scraping metal. At 0909, the light carrier *Monterey* had all this and worse.

She reported, "Cannot hold present 180° course. Am coming to 140° at fifteen knots."

She couldn't make it. Instead she was blown around in the opposite direction as the sea and wind took charge. A minute later she reported: "Present course 220°. All planes on my hangar deck on fire."

Flames were immediately sucked down into the lower spaces

---

* A normal reading at sea level is 29.12 inches.

of the ship and fires broke out below. On the hangar deck it was as much as one's life was worth to try to fight the flames while the ship was rolling 40° or more to either side. Yet there was no hesitation. Men broke out the hoses and set to work, their feet sliding out from under them as the wet deck took an unexpected pitch or roll.

The ship was saved by the magnificent courage of the fire fighters and the seamanship of Captain Stuart A. Ingersoll, who promptly hove to so that the ship yielded to the sea instead of trying to fight it. Although she still rolled and pitched heavily, the motion was gentler and it was possible for the men to approach the flames. Some, unfortunately, paid for their courage with their lives, and others suffered from burns and smoke inhalation, but *Monterey* came through.

Every ship in the storm had its tales of fear and courage that overcame fear and of seamanship that brought the ships through. But in three cases, even this was not enough.

U.S.S. *Dewey*, a 1,370-tonner destroyer of the *Farragut* class, was part of the screen of the logistics group, well to the east of Task Force 38, but the ships of all groups had been so scattered by the storm that she narrowly missed colliding with the laboring *Monterey*. In taking emergency action to avoid collision, she found herself in irons in the trough of the sea, and unable to get out with any combination of rudder and engines. Rolling heavily to starboard, she took the desperate chance of ballasting the weather side with 40,000 gallons of salt water and fuel oil pumped from the lee side to starboard. It worked. The rolls to starboard were gradually reduced to 60° and the ship began to respond to her helm. If the wind had suddenly changed, she would have capsized immediately.

She was still not out of trouble. Heavy seas short-circuited the switchboard for the steering-engine room and then the main switchboard. All lights and power were lost, and Lieutenant Commander C. R. Calhoun, her skipper, had to organize bucket brigades to keep enough water out of the steering-engine room so that men could keep the helm down by hand.

At 1210 the end seemed near. She rolled 65° to starboard,

recovered, and then rolled 75°and did not recover. Commander Calhoun lost his footing and clung to a stanchion which was normally vertical. He hung with his feet clear of the deck and clear of the bulkhead which was beneath him. He was about to order the mast cut away with acetylene torches when the sea smashed No. 1 stack and pulled it over the side completely flattened. With her "sail area" reduced, *Dewey* gradually regained stability, and by 1300 the center of the storm had passed probably only a mile or so away. Her barometer indicated that it was very close. It went off the scale at 27 and it was estimated that it reached 26.60.

Less fortunate was her sister ship *Hull.* She too was caught in irons and was pinned down on her beam ends by a wind estimated at 110 knots. Sea poured down the stacks and into the pilot house, and she foundered at about noon. Only 7 officers and 55 enlisted were rescued later from her crew of 18 officers and 246 men.

Another sister, the *Monaghan*, also capsized about the same time, but little is known of the details, for only six enlisted men survived.

U.S.S. *Spence*, a 2,100-ton *Fletcher*-class destroyer, was down to 15 percent fuel on the morning of December 18; all efforts to give her a drink the previous day had failed, and Admiral Halsey sent her over to the fueling group in hope of relieving a desperate situation. In the full fury of a typhoon, she had only enough fuel aboard for twenty-four hours steaming at 8 knots. Since she had attempted to take on oil from the *New Jersey* just before departure, she was not ballasted, and this lack led to her undoing. The normal precaution in heavy weather is to fill empty fuel tanks with sea water in order to lower a ship's center of gravity and increase the righting arm, the force which causes her to return to the vertical when rolling. Since it takes as much as six hours to pump the ballast out in order to take on fuel, it is natural that a destroyer skipper would be reluctant to ballast when there was any prospect of refueling. Lieutenant Commander J. P. Andrea, commanding officer of the *Spence*, left it until too late. She rolled heavily to port and water poured in.

301

Her rudder jammed and she rolled over two or three times and then went under about 1110. Only one officer and twenty-three enlisted men were picked up later.

Other ships had rough times, but no more were lost. The fleet entered the "safe semicircle" as the typhoon passed on its westerly course, and about 1500 the wind began to drop and the seas to moderate. By sunset the wind force was down to 60 knots and it kept dropping throughout the night.

The next day was spent fueling the desperately short destroyers and in searching for survivors. Because of the spread-out condition of the fleet and the frequent carrying away of radio antennas, no one knew the whereabouts of every ship, not even Admiral Halsey. In fact, it was not until 0225, December 19, that he knew any ship had been lost. Destroyer escort *Tabberer* then informed him that she was picking up survivors of the *Hull*. Halsey immediately intensified the search, and at the end of three days a total of eight officers and eighty-four men were rescued from the three foundered ships. Some of them had drifted sixty-six miles in the stormy seas. A few men who had been washed overboard from other ships were rescued through some miracle.

A Court of Inquiry later laid the blame for the storm losses squarely on the shoulders of Admiral Halsey. He was not accused of negligence but his mistakes "were errors in judgment committed under stress of war operations and stemming from a commendable desire to meet military requirements."

Since Task Force 38 could not meet its commitments over Luzon and search for survivors at the same time, the scheduled strikes for December 19–21 were canceled. They probably were not needed, for the typhoon moved over the northern part of the island and kept the Japanese on the ground, at least on the airfields located there. In addition the force was too battered to go right back into combat operations. Instead Task Force 38 retired to Ulithi for a Christmas whose joy was muted by the loss of ships and shipmates.

Damaged ships were repaired by December 29 when Task Force 38 sortied again in preparation for the landings on Luzon, the last major operation in the Philippine Campaign.

The landing area selected for the liberation of Luzon was Lingayen Gulf, where the Japanese had landed in 1941. Lingayen Gulf lies less than a hundred miles north of Manila and a broad plain between the mountains connects the gulf with the capital. In addition to offering relatively easy passage to troops, the plain offered good logistic possibilities as well containing, as it does, a railroad and a fine road network.

As at Leyte, General Krueger's Sixth Army was given the job. The XIV Corps, under Major General Oscar W. Griswold, comprised the Thirty-Seventh and Fortieth Infantry Divisions, and the I Corps, Major General Innis P. Swift, included the Sixth and Forty-Third Infantry Divisions. They were to land on two beach areas, the XIV Corps in the south near the town of Lingayen and the I Corps on the southeastern coast on either side of San Fabian town.

As at Mindoro, the Attack Forces would be accompanied by escort carriers and the old battleships. McCain's fast carriers were to work over Luzon and Formosa airfields before the landing and then move into the South China Sea in order to block an attempt by the Japanese ships at Lingga Roads and Camranh Bay to interfere.

S-Day was set for January 9, 1945.

While the troops were making the crossing from their staging areas to Lingayen, Admiral Oldendorf's heavy ships were moving through Surigao Strait into the Sulu Sea to conduct preliminary bombardments of the target area, and Task Force 38 was pounding the airfields of Luzon and Formosa. Though losses were heavy among carrier airmen, Task Force 38 was undisturbed during these strikes, which were extremely effective.

Admiral Oldendorf's Task Group 77.2, comprising 6 old battleships, 6 cruisers, 19 destroyers, and a host of other types, including 12 CVEs, decidedly was not undisturbed. Kamikaze attacks started almost at once. Escort carrier *Ommaney Bay* was the first to suffer. A plane crashed into her flight deck at 1712, January 4, starting fires that could not be fought since the crash had wiped out power to her fire mains. She was abandoned

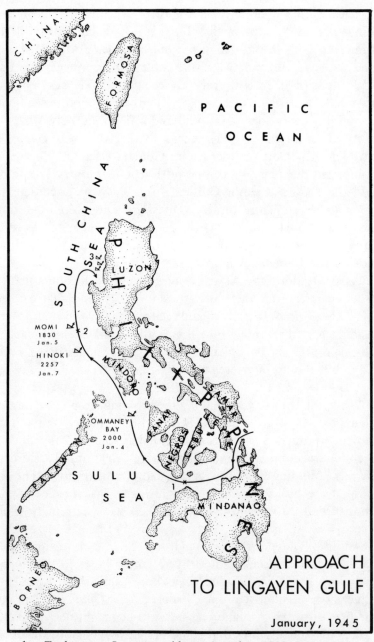

CHINA

FORMOSA

PACIFIC

OCEAN

SOUTH CHINA SEA

PHILIPPINES

LUZON

3

MOMI
1830
Jan. 5

2

HINOKI
2257
Jan. 7

MINDORO

OMMANEY
BAY
2000
Jan. 4

PANAY

SAMAR

NEGROS

CEBU

BOHOL

PALAWAN

SULU

SEA

1

MINDANAO

BORNEO

APPROACH
TO LINGAYEN GULF

January, 1945

1. *Taylor* rams Japanese midget submarine, 1530, January 5
2. Suicide raid on Oldendorf's groups, 1650–1750, January 5
3. *Palmer, Hovey,* and *Long* sunk in Lingayen Gulf, January 7

between 1750 and 1812 and sent to the bottom by a torpedo from destroyer *Burns.*

This was a bad omen, and worse was to come.

On January 5, the newly developed airstrips on Mindoro were socked in, so Oldendorf's ships had to depend on their own resources for defense against the Kamikazes. A CAP from the escort carriers managed to shoot down or chase off planes in two raids that developed around 0800 and noon. The afternoon brought a little excitement when two Japanese destroyers were spotted, and a lively stern chase by light Allied forces. They were unable to catch up, however, and Wildcats from the CVEs had to be brought in to do the job. One Japanese destroyer, the *Momi*, was sunk; the other got away to Manila, only to be sunk two days later by another American force.

Even as the Wildcats were looking for their quarry, and as Oldendorf's group was about a hundred miles west of Corregidor, the heaviest Kamikaze attack of the day developed, beginning about 1650 when a plane slammed into heavy cruiser *Louisville* from ahead. One man was killed and fifty-nine injured, including her skipper, Captain R. L. Hicks. About the same time H. M. Australian heavy cruiser *Australia* caught it from another Kamikaze with twenty-five killed and thirty wounded, but the damage was minor. Destroyer H.M.A.S. *Arunta* and escort carrier *Savo Island* were near-missed, but her sister *Manila Bay* was moderately damaged as another Kamikaze pilot joined his ancestors by crashing through her flight deck. She kept on going, however, and twenty-four hours later was able to conduct flight operations. Destroyer escort *Stafford* was forced to withdraw when a Hell Bird plowed into her, and destroyer *Helm* had six men injured when a Kamikaze brushed her lightly. In the minesweeping group some distance off, *LCI(G)-70* sustained moderate damage as one plane hit her and three others were splashed nearby.

Altogether it was a busy day for the ships bound for Lingayen Gulf.

At the end of the midwatch, January 6, Oldendorf's group and the minesweeping group were ready to round Cape Bolinao and enter Lingayen Gulf. The escort carriers peeled off to operate to the northwest where they had sea room, while the other ships moved toward their assigned stations for preliminary bombardments and minesweeping activities. Gunners were concentrating on shore targets, but a lot of watchful eyes were turned toward the heavens.

The first air attack came in just after sunrise, but it was disposed of by the CAP with no damage to any ship. Things were starting well.

They didn't stay that way long.

Beginning at 1122 a really heavy Kamikaze attack began. There were too many for the CAP to cope with, and it was, as one seaman put it, "one Helluva day in Lingayen Gulf." Just at noon, battleship *New Mexico*, which was bombarding the San Fernando area, was crashed on the port wing of the bridge. Rear Admiral George L. Weyler and the Royal Navy observer, former Commander in Chief Home Fleet, Admiral Sir Bruce Fraser, were on the starboard side and escaped injury. But Winston Churchill's personal liaison officer with MacArthur, Lieutenant General Herbert Lumsden, Captain R. W. Fleming, *New Mexico*'s commanding officer, the communication officer, an aide to General Lumsden, and *Time* magazine correspondent William Chickering were in the wrong spot at the wrong time. All were instantly killed, along with twenty-five others. In addition, eighty-seven men were wounded, but the ship kept all her assigned bombardment missions.

Within the next hour, four more ships were hit, destroyers *Walke*, *Allen M. Sumner*, and *Long*, and destroyer transport *Brooks*, with heavy loss of life. Skipper of the *Walke*, Commander George F. Davis, was drenched with flaming gasoline. Crewmen smothered the flames and he kept going, fighting to save his ship. When things were under control, and only then, would he let himself be carried below. He died a few hours later.

Toward evening of that gruesome day another Hell Bird attack came in. One plane finished off the stricken *Long*, which had been abandoned but which a salvage party was working to save. Two planes made a pass at destroyer *Newcomb*; one was shot down and the other veered at the last moment and ended up near the mainmast of battleship *California*, at a cost of 45 killed and 151 wounded. Light cruiser *Columbia* was victim of an attack which cost her use of 2 turrets whose magazines had to be flooded because of fires.

*Australia* was turning into a hard-luck ship, and that afternoon had a second Kamikaze drop in at a cost of another fourteen killed and twenty-six wounded. *Louisville* also took another Kamikaze which killed Rear Admiral Theodore E. Chandler and thirty-one others and forced her withdrawal, the first time in her thirteen years of existence that she had failed to carry out assigned duties. The last victims of this appalling day were destroyer *O'Brien* and destroyer minesweeper *Southard*, both of which were able to carry on despite their wounds.

January 6 is the day of Epiphany, the traditional date on which the Wise Men brought their gifts to the Christ Child. The gifts of the Japanese that day were of quite another sort, and if continued could threaten the entire course of the war in the Pacific. On that single day one ship had been sunk and eleven others damaged. A lieutenant general of the British Army, a rear admiral of the U.S. Navy and hundreds of others had been killed, some of them victims of "friendly" shells as over-enthusiastic gunners fired into other ships in their efforts to shoot down Kamikazes.

The attacks might have been worse had not Task Force 38 moved in to help out. Originally General Kenney's Air Force had the responsibility for southern and western Luzon; at MacArthur's request, Halsey devoted Task Force 38's attention to the airfields on Luzon. Weather reduced its effectiveness on January 6, but things improved on the 7th.

No one gave any consideration to withdrawing in face of Kamikaze attacks. The men in the invasion forces simply devoted themselves more completely to their antiaircraft duties.

January 7 started badly with minesweeper *Hovey* being sunk by a Kamikaze about 0430, but then events went quite smoothly until 1835 when another Hell Bird finished its career by dropping a bomb on minesweeper *Palmer* and splashing nearby. *Palmer* sank in six minutes, taking with her twenty-eight of her crew.

The day was devoted to bombardment and to clearing beach obstacles with underwater-demolition teams. There was little for the UDT men to do, for the Japanese had not defended the beaches with any barriers. They did pick up one mine.

On January 8, S-Day minus one, the Kamikazes returned in force. Two of them went for the unfortunate *Australia.* The first was shot down but skidded into her side, doing no damage. The second did exactly the same thing, but this one blew an 8-by-14-foot hole in her side, fortunately inflicting no casualties. The Aussies were considerably affronted when Admiral Oldendorf offered to relieve her of further duties that day. Four Kamikaze hits was usually enough for one ship.

As Oldendorf's battleships and cruisers worked over the beaches they had to be wary that they were not killing friendly Filipinos come down to see the fun and to welcome their liberators. At least once they had to suspend firing to enable a plane to drop leaflets warning the welcoming committees to clear the area.

Probably all this bombardment was unnecessary, for General Yamashita had adopted the strategy of not opposing the invasion at the beachhead but contesting it strongly once ashore in prepared positions of his own choosing. Only a handful of suicide troops was left near the water's edge for nuisance value.

The presence of the bombardment force had a different sort of value. By acting as bait it drew the Kamikazes which might otherwise have attacked the transports. A Kamikaze crashing into a crowded troop ship would have caused fearsome loss of life.

The Attack Forces, which included the transports, were comparatively unmolested. There was a scare on the afternoon of January 5 as the *Boise*, with General MacArthur aboard, suddenly had to maneuver radically to avoid mysterious torpedoes. They had come from one of two midget submarines in the area. One of them was promptly disposed of, but the other made good its escape. MacArthur was completely un-ruffled by the incident.

No air attacks developed on either the 5th or 6th; the Japanese were too busy with Oldendorf's ships, but a couple of bombs were dropped the next day, one near *Boise*. A Kamikaze ended up on the deck of *LST-912* but did little damage. Four men were killed.

On January 8 escort carrier *Kadashan Bay* and attack transport *Callaway* were both Kamikazied. Although only a few men on the carrier were injured, she had to return to Leyte because of extensive flooding. *Callaway* lost 29 of her crew, largely to flaming gasoline, but the ship was not severely damaged, and miraculously not one of the 1,188 troops aboard was even scratched. *Callaway* carried on with her mission.

Two more Kamikaze attacks were made before the landing. Escort carrier *Kitkun Bay* almost dodged but not quite. The crash blew a 9-by-20-foot hole in her side, giving her a 13° list before flooding could be controlled. She had to be taken in tow, but the next day was able to carry out her assigned mission after her engineers had made temporary repairs.

A few minutes after the hit on *Kitkun Bay* a Japanese plane made for H.M.A.S. *Westralia*. Although the Kamikaze missed, *Westralia*'s steering was thrown out temporarily.

Following these attacks, a curious peace descended on the gathering ships. No more Japanese appeared, and the mountains of the Philippines could be discerned in the fading light. All forces moved to their assigned positions during the night lighted by unusually brilliant stars and a last-quarter moon. On the bridges of the ships quiet commands were given to adjust course or speed as necessary. The squawk of the TBS could be heard from time to time. On the carriers machinists and gunners worked to get the Wildcats and Avengers ready to support the troops once they had landed. Cooks and bakers sweated in galleys getting breakfasts ready for the more than 100,000 men of the Army and Navy who would be having a very busy day. As usual before an amphibious assault, men cleaned their weapons, wrote letters home, shot the breeze, or sat quietly with their own thoughts. Chaplains did a land-office business in confessions and religious services.

Everything went like clockwork. The ships of Kinkaid's Seventh Fleet were old hands at amphibious operations and every officer in a key position was a veteran. By 0715 troops were loading into the boats and the attack waves began to form up soon thereafter. Battleships and cruisers were shelling suspected target areas and enemy installations. There was no response from the shore.

There was from the skies. Kamikazes put in their appearance a little after 0700. Two near-missed destroyer *Hodges* and amphibious command ship *Mount Olympus*, but unfortunate *Columbia* was hit yet a third time. Damage and casualties were moderate, and *Columbia* continued her bombardment assignments.

General Krueger's Sixth Army landed exactly on schedule on a two-corps front. In the Lingayen area, XIV Corps swarmed ashore from their amphtracs and pushed rapidly ahead with little or no opposition. In fact, a week later, when they had reached a point thirty miles inland, they had suffered losses of only thirty men killed and had encountered only a hundred or so Japanese. I Corps, landing two divisions abreast in the San Fabian area, had a little tougher sledding since they faced the flank of Yamashita's army drawing back into northern Luzon. Yet in the first week they lost only 220 killed and three times that number wounded.

A few Japanese guns along the shore did little to harass the troops, but they did turn their attention to the ships. They caused some damage and inflicted a few casualties but were silenced either by counter-battery fire or by being overrun by Army troops. That afternoon the Kamikazes came back. One hit *Mississippi*, causing slight damage but fairly heavy casualties. A Val, meanwhile, made for four-times-wounded *Australia*. It just missed the bridge, and the wing sliced off the top of No. 1 stack. There were no casualties and little material damage, but Admiral Berkey decided she had taken enough. She left, albeit reluctantly, with the first returning group of ships.

As night fell, everything had gone far better than anyone had

Invasion of Lingayen Gulf, January 9, 1945

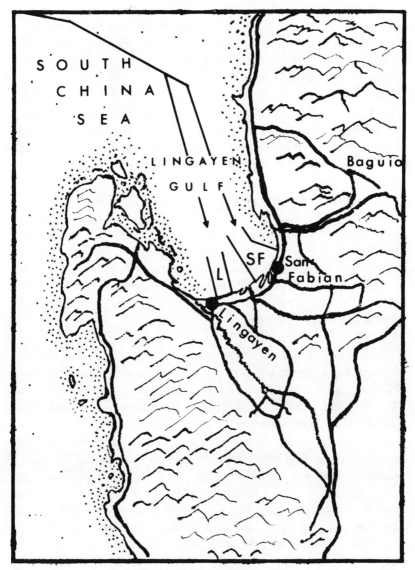

L = LINGAYEN LANDING AREA
SF = SAN FABIAN LANDING AREA

expected. A few guns fired in the darkness, and unfortunately, a 5-inch "friendly" shell killed eighteen men on battleship *Colorado*. Then the ships off shore were faced with a new menace—suicide boats. These were eighteen-foot plywood speedboats which carried two depth charges and a light machine gun. The two- or three-man crew stuffed their pockets with hand grenades and set out to sink Allied ships by dropping depth charges next to them. Most were victims of ships' gunfire or unknown hazards, but a few got through. An LCI(M) was sunk and eight other ships damaged. This single attack was all for the suicide boats, however, for the Japanese reported that they were incapable of further action.

The next morning was fairly quiet and the day's operations went along smoothly in spite of prowling Kamikazes, one of which damaged destroyer *Wilson* and another attack transport *Du Page*.

By January 12, everything was going so well that the two Corps commanders went ashore to set up their command posts. Most of the high naval commanders had departed and routine operations were going along as planned.

Then the Kamikazes returned.

That morning the destroyer escorts *Gilligan* and *Richard W. Suesens* were the first victims. A little later destroyer transport *Belknap* lost thirty-eight killed and forty-nine wounded and her No. 2 stack. A little later, off the west coast of Luzon, four Liberty ships were damaged by Hell Bird attacks as was attack transport *Zeilin*, returning empty in another convoy. In still another group *LST-700* was damaged slightly by a Kamikaze, while three others were shot down. As the convoy commander, Commander M. H. Hubbard remarked, "It is noted that the Japs expended four airplanes and four trained aviators to kill three men and damage one ship of an empty convoy."

The next day it was the turn of the escort carriers again. A single Kamikaze dove vertically, seemingly coming from no-where, on escort carrier *Salamaua* and penetrated the flight deck. Its bombs exploded below the hangar deck, spreading gasoline and fragments of the plane and pilot everywhere. The carrier was forced to return to Leyte.

After this attack, there were no more Kamikazes in Philippine waters. In fact, after January 12, there were no more Japanese planes in the Philippines, except for those unfit to fly. Evacuation of the remnants began as early as January 8, but only forty-seven planes made it to Formosa. Some were shot down on the way by Third or Seventh Fleet aircraft. Yamashita's ground forces were left to their fate.

MacArthur's success on Luzon depended on the lifeline from San José, Mindoro, to Lingayen Gulf. It had to be assumed that the Japanese would attempt to interdict it, and to keep them from doing just that, Admiral Halsey led his Third Fleet on a long-desired sweep into the South China Sea in order to destroy Japanese air and naval strength on the China and Indochina coasts.

Since the Japanese had carefully concealed the real extent of their losses at the Battle for Leyte Gulf, American planners had a more healthy respect for the remnants of Combined Fleet than they need have had. In home waters, the Japanese still had 3 battleships, 2 cruisers, 10 destroyers, and 3 aircraft carriers, but with only 48 planes to spread among them. In addition there were a submarine tender and 44 submarines based at Kure. At Lingga Roads off Singapore were hermaphrodite battleships *Ise* and *Hyuga*, 4 heavy cruisers, a light cruiser, 7 destroyers, and 4 DEs. At Formosa were about 400 naval and army aircraft.

Halsey set to work to cut down on that number at once. January 9, 1945, Task Force 38 aircraft plastered Formosa to knock out radar stations and shoot up aircraft that might interfere with the passage through Luzon Strait into the South China Sea. That night Task Force 38 passed in through the door it had blasted open. Captain J. T. Acuff, meanwhile, had taken an oiler group through Surigao Strait in order to refuel the big carriers and their consorts. Bad weather delayed operations until the 11th, but by noon every ship had had a drink.

The first and most important target in Halsey's mind was the magnificent harbor Camranh Bay on the coast of Indochina.

Intelligence officers believed that *Ise* and *Hyuga* and several other naval ships were there, and Halsey and McCain were anxious to finish them off. Bogan's TG 38.2 was beefed up with two heavy cruisers and five destroyers from Rear Admiral Arthur Radford's TG 38.1, and the plan was to peel off a surface unit from Bogan's group to make a coordinated gunnery and torpedo sweep in conjunction with the air attacks.

At 0600, TG 38.2 was within fifty miles of Camranh Bay, and a little later the surface group pulled out and began working up speed for its attack. Then came the disappointing word. Aircraft sweeps revealed that there were no naval ships in Camranh Bay. The Japanese had had the good sense to send them on to safer waters. Frustrated, the surface unit turned around, the ships rejoining their task groups.

There was plenty of merchant shipping, however, and the Japanese paid the price for exposing their freighters and oilers to McCain's pilots. That day forty-four ships were sunk, including the disarmed French cruiser *La Motte-Piquet*. The pilots either failed to spot the *tricoleur* or believed it was a Japanese trick. Over one hundred Japanese aircraft were destroyed in the air or on the ground, and Japanese opposition was feeble. Most of the pilots who were shot down were rescued by friendly natives and returned via Kunming.

The next day was spent in attempting to fuel, but it was very difficult because another typhoon came along to bedevil Halsey. This time, fortunately, the Third Fleet was able to escape the worst of its effects, which instead were visited on the Japanese in Indochina.

After fueling on January 13 and 14, TF 38 remained in intercepting position in case the Japanese tried to send any of their ships from the Home Islands. No attacks developed, and Halsey took the opportunity of dropping his calling cards on Takao and Toshien on the China coast and Mako in the Pescadores.

The 16th was spent in working over Hong Kong, Hainan, and Canton. The results were disappointing, but they hurt. A note of hysteria crept into the voice of Tokyo Rose in a broadcast that night when she stated that TF 38 was bottled up in the South China Sea. "We don't know how you got in," she said, "but how the hell are you going to get out?"

She did have a point. To sortie through Surigao Strait would take TF 38 a long way from the areas it wished to strike, while to go out the way it had come in was to expose it to the fully alerted Japanese on Formosa. Characteristically, Halsey, aided by the foul weather, chose the bolder course.

A 40-knot monsoon plagued efforts to refuel once more, for the shallow South China Sea responded more to the wind than would have happened in deeper water. It was not until January 19 that TF 38 was able to fuel in the lee of Luzon, and the next afternoon was headed for Balintang Channel, the southern part of Luzon Strait. Foul weather tended to keep enemy air attacks away from the force; although bogeys were constantly on the screens, no planes came anywhere near the force. Transit was completed during the night, and the morning of January 21, TF 38 began to plaster Formosa.

All during the ten days spent in the South China Sea, Halsey, McCain, and Company had had it all their own way as far as the Japanese were concerned. Now they had to pay the price. Although the strikes were very successful, destroying over a hundred aircraft and a dozen ships, the Kamikazes put on a return engagement, this time from Formosan bases. Light carrier *Langley* was the first victim, although to conventional bombing attack. The pilot sneaked in his blow while attention was being paid to Kamikazes after other ships.

A few minutes later a Kamikaze came out of the sun and slammed into fleet carrier *Ticonderoga*, starting an intense fire. The second raid of the day again hit *Ticonderoga*, this time on the island structure. A 9° list developed, and many planes were destroyed, but by midafternoon all fires were out and by evening she was ready to resume operations. The two attacks had cost her 143 killed and 202 wounded as well as 36 planes destroyed by fire or bombs.

Destroyer *Maddox* was also on the receiving end of a Kamikaze attack some twenty minutes after *Ticonderoga*'s second hit, but was able to keep on going after extinguishing the fires.

An accident did almost as much damage to carrier *Hancock* as some Kamikaze attacks. A 500-pound bomb broke loose from a landing plane and exploded, setting fires on the gallery, flight, and hangar decks. Several planes were destroyed and 52 men were killed, with 105 wounded.

After these mishaps, Halsey detached his cripples and proceeded northward for strikes on Okinawa. The bombing raids were really incidental cover for the photo-reconnaissance needed for the forthcoming invasion of the island. That job done, TF 38 retired to Ulithi, where Admiral Halsey relinquished command on January 27 to Admiral Raymond A. Spruance, whereupon the Third Fleet became the Fifth Fleet again and Task Force 38 became Task Force 58. As he left, he sent the following to the fleet:

> I am so proud of you that no words can express my feelings. This has been a hard operation. At times you have been driven almost beyond endurance but only because the stakes were high, the enemy was as weary as you were, and the lives of many Americans could be spared in later offensives if we did our work well now. We have driven the enemy off the sea and back to his inner defenses. Superlatively well done. HALSEY.

On Luzon, progress was not as rapid as MacArthur, now a five-star General of the Army, desired. Almost the entire strength of I Corps had to be used to contain Yamashita, who was directing operations in northern Luzon from headquarters at Baguio. This left only XIV Corps for the drive south to Manila, and the Japanese did all they could to make its path thorny. They blew up bridges and railways, they planted booby-trapped road blocks. Sixth Army was inexperienced in rapid movement over comparatively open ground. It had learned its ways in the jungles of New Guinea and the mountains of Leyte. It took time for the Engineers to learn. By January 29, XIV Corps had reached only as far as San Fernando.

That same day the situation was eased somewhat by an unopposed landing of XI Corps in Zambales Province. It took over the right flank of the advance, while XIV Corps side-stepped east. This left I Corps free to concentrate on Yamashita's northern forces, while the rest of the Sixth Army, supported by subsidiary landings in Nasugbu and Subic Bay pressed on to Manila and points south.

Since MacArthur was exceedingly worried over the fate of prisoners of war and American civilians in Manila, he formed a flying column to make a dash there as fast as possible. Its orders: "Go to Manila. Go around the Nips, bounce off the Nips, but go to Manila. Free the internees at Santo Tomás. Take Malacañan Palace and the Legislative Building."

The drive jumped off at 0001, February 1, supported by Marine aviators. On the afternoon of February 3, some of the 3,700 starving Allied prisoners at Santo Tomás prison were startled as nine Marine fighter planes buzzed them. An object fell from one of the planes; it proved to be a pair of pilot's goggles with a note attached: "Roll out the barrel. Santa Claus is coming Sunday or Monday." A moment later there was a tumult outside and an American voice could be heard shouting, "Where the hell is the front gate?"

The tank driver found the front gate and enlarged it by driving his vehicle, "Battling Basic," straight through to liberate the prisoners. Other points the General had specified fell, but the battle for Manila proved to be a long one. Although General Yamashita had ordered Manila to be abandoned, his subordinates disobeyed him, and the fighting was bitter, from house to house, from building to building, from tree to tree. The beautiful city, spared so long from the worst ravages of war, was nearly destroyed. It was not until March 4 that the city was finally cleared of Japanese, after suffering more damage than London, Cologne, or Hamburg.

Even before that moment, MacArthur had restored the Commonwealth Government. His voice broke as he looked around the city he loved so well and where he had lived so long. To a provisional Assembly he said:

More than three years have elapsed since I withdrew our forces from this beautiful city that, open and undefended, its churches,

317

monuments and cultural centers might be spared the violence of military ravage.

The enemy would not have it so. Much that I sought to preserve has been unnecessarily destroyed by his desperate action at bay, but by these deeds he has wantonly fixed the future pattern of his own doom. . . . My country has kept the faith. Its soldiers came here as an army of free men dedicated, with your people, to the cause of human liberty and committed to the task of destroying those evil forces that have sought to suppress it by the brutality of the sword. . . . Your capital city, cruelly punished though it be, has regained its rightful place—citadel of Democracy in the East.

As he spoke, he could see through a window the smoking ruins of his own house.

The campaign on Luzon lasted until the end of June, and even then Yamashita still had some 65,000 men holed up in the northern end of the island. When the Japanese surrender finally came, he made his own capitulation with the 50,000 survivors of the 170,000 men that had been on the island when Sixth Army stormed ashore in Lingayen Gulf that January.

It is not at all clear where General MacArthur got the authority to undertake campaigns to clean up the rest of the Philippines as well as move against Palawan and Borneo, but move he did. The directive from the Joint Chiefs of Staff called for the liberation of Leyte and Luzon. Mindoro was undertaken as a necessary preliminary to Luzon, but no reading of JCS directives can be seen as authorizing moves against the rest of the Philippines and the Dutch islands. Perhaps the Joint Chiefs simply ignored his actions, and he got away with them because his troops and his Seventh Fleet were not needed for the forthcoming invasions of Iwo Jima and Okinawa. In any case, MacArthur, never one to stand idle, undertook a series of landing operations which freed the rest of the Philippines before moving on to Borneo.

All these operations displayed the smooth cooperation of experts in the three services. Some hard fighting developed, but the Japanese, cut off from any hope of supply or reinforcement, had no chance whatever, even though some remnants managed to hold out until the final Japanese surrender. For the sake of completeness, it is convenient to show these operations in a table summary.

| Target | D–Day 1945 | Date Secured 1945 |
|---|---|---|
| Palawan | February 28 | April 22 |
| Zamboanga | March 10 | August 15 |
| Panay & W. Negros | March 18 | June 4 |
| Cebu | March 26 | April 18 |
| Bohol | April 11 | April 20 |
| S. E. Negros | April 26 | June 12 |
| Mindanao | April 17 | August 15 |
| Tarakan | May 1 | May 30 |
| Brunei Bay | June 10 | July 1 |
| Balikpapan | July 1 | July 22 |

MacArthur was not allowed, however, to move on to Java as he insistently urged, and he considered this prohibition as one of the greatest mistakes of the war, for it allowed Sukarno to establish his rule of tyranny in the Netherlands East Indies, renamed Indonesia. But that is to go beyond our story.

Before MacArthur had even started his campaign for the rest of the Philippines, another operation far to the north drove his name from the front pages of the newspapers, and Americans for the first time became aware of the name Iwo Jima, an ugly crag of rock 660 miles south of Toyko. It was a place where, as Admiral Nimitz later wrote, "uncommon valor was a common virtue."

CHAPTER EIGHT

# To the End in Germany

*Nothing now remains! nothing is spared me!*
*no loyalty is kept, no honor observed!*
*It is the end. No injury has been left undone!*

Adolf Hitler

Y ET once more the American, British, Canadian, and French
armies were poised to advance against the Germans.
Hitler's desperate offensive in the Ardennes—the Battle of the
Bulge—had failed, and all effects of it had been overcome by
the Allies. Germany would never recover from this failure, for it
cost her the last reserves which might have stopped the coming
drive through Germany.

In the east, German lines still held firm on the Oder–Neisse
Line, as the Russians waited to build up supplies to continue
their offensive. With the failure of his Ardennes offensive,
Hitler had stripped the west of reserves to meet the Russian
drive, and it had been stopped for the time being. But the only
real German strength remaining in the west was in the
Rhineland, separated from the rest of the Fatherland by the
swiftly rolling river.

Eisenhower's plan for the destruction of Germany, a kind of
rolling assault from the north to the south, now encompassed
three phases. First Montgomery's Twenty-First Army Group
would roll up to the Rhine in the north, then Bradley's Twelfth
Army Group would do the same in the center, and finally
Devers' Sixth Army Group would complete the picture in the
south. Then the Allies would cross the Rhine and roll through
country almost stripped of troops.

320

That was pretty much the way it happened, and it took almost exactly three months to do it. And there were some interesting moments along the way.

Following his usual meticulous preparations, Montgomery began his attack from Nijmegen with the Canadian First Army in what he called Operation Veritable. This began at 1030, February 8, following a five-and-one-half-hour bombardment and a heavy bombing attack by Bomber Command the previous night. The going was heavy, for the Germans had turned the towns of Cleves and Goch into major strongpoints, but the defenses were not strong enough. Despite the request that the bombers use incendiary bombs in the attack, the R.A.F. had employed demolition bombs, and the resulting wreckage, ruins, and bomb craters held up the troops more than did the German defenders.

So far, Montgomery had given the Germans north of the Ruhr a left hook. He proposed to follow this up with a right cross with Simpson's Ninth Army to cross the Roer River and advance toward Düsseldorf and Duisberg. This right cross was code-named Operation Grenade, and was set to begin February 10, two days after Veritable.

Yet Simpson could not advance so long as the dams of the River Roer were in German hands, and it was the job of Hodges's First Army in Bradley's Army Group to seize the dams before they could be opened and send waters roaring down on troops in the Roer Valley. One by one the dams were seized on February 10, and their control valves made secure. All but one, that is. In the last one they captured, the American soldiers discovered that the Germans had wrecked the valves, and the uncontrolled waters poured down the valley. The Ninth Army would not be able to move for two weeks.

This situation left the Germans free to concentrate against the Canadian First and British Second Armies which were now pushing on toward Wesel. Fanatic Nazis employed every device they knew to hold them back, but there was no stopping them. Foul weather aided the Germans, and some skirmishes were fought in waist-deep water.

Meanwhile Simpson's Ninth Army was taking advantage of

its enforced pause to get everything ready for the advance across the Roer. With only a brief preliminary bombardment, Simpson got a bridgehead across the Roer in the early morning hours of February 23, catching the Germans by surprise. The flood waters had not yet completely subsided, and the Germans had estimated they had another two or three days before they needed to worry about the Ninth Army. They were wrong.

Fighter-bombers protected the bridgeheads as pontoon bridges were set up to enable armored vehicles to cross, and two days later, the Americans were attacking out of their bridgehead positions. By February 28, they had broken out and were driving almost unimpeded toward the Rhine, most of the Germans having moved north to meet the British and Canadians.

Simpson believed he could force a crossing of the Rhine in the Düsseldorf-Duisberg area, but Montgomery refused permission to do so, saying it would "upset the plan." Also, Montgomery believed that the Ninth Army would be unable to do much except get bogged down in the "industrial jungle of the Ruhr."

Farther south, Bradley's Twelfth Army Group was grinding out the territory between the West Wall and the Rhine. It was heavy going through the West Wall, and Bradley had the further problem of keeping Hodges's First Army closed up with Simpson's Ninth so as not to expose a flank to a German counterattack. It was not very dramatic fighting, but it was nasty, and it had to be done.

Then, on March 7, something dramatic did happen. Leading units of the Ninth Armored Division in Hodges's First Army discovered that the Ludendorff railway bridge across the Rhine at Remagen was still standing.

Unbelieving, Sergeant Alexander A. Drabik, commanding the leading platoon, dashed toward the bridge, his men following at top speed. Drabik well knew that demolition charges must have been set, and he knew that if he and his men could stop them, it would be a heaven-sent opportunity for an early crossing of the Rhine.

He stepped on the bridge at 1550 that afternoon. He did not

know then that a German captain had ordered it blown up at 1600. The platoon rushed across, tearing loose every demolition wire they could find, all the while under small-arms fire. They missed a few, and when the Germans closed the switches, two small charges went off. The bridge shuddered but it did not collapse. While Drabik and his men took cover, hundreds of others rushed across, and hundreds more. By that time the next day, 8,000 men had crossed over, and within five days there was a bridgehead ten miles long and four miles deep on the eastern bank of the Rhine.

German counterattacks were disorganized and futile, for most of their attention was still taken up with Montgomery's operations in the north. German artillery and German aircraft set about destroying the bridge, and after ten days, it finally fell into the river, weakened by the pounding and by the heavy loads placed on it by the Americans. By that time, however, six Treadway bridges had been set up, and the Ludendorff bridge was no longer in use.

Patton's Third Army had driven across the Moselle River on March 13, and was pushing toward the Rhine despite the best efforts of the soldiers of the German Seventh Army. It was an army in name only, for it could offer little resistance. There was little ammunition, little food, and almost a complete absence of trained men. By March 21, Patton had reached the Rhine, having captured some 120,000 Germans along the way.

By that date, the Germans had been driven from the Rhineland except for one salient of the German First Army in the area between Karlsruhe and Mannheim. The Rhineland campaign was one of the greatest military defeats ever inflicted on Hitler, and it was such a vast defeat because of Hitler's stupid insistence never to yield a foot of ground. In the Rhineland campaign, he lost a quarter of a million men taken prisoner and an additional 60,000 killed, wounded, and missing. If these men had been placed on the east bank of the Rhine and had been given the proper arms, they could have made crossing Germany's greatest river expensive indeed.

But Hitler had given his usual order. The troops stayed where they were, and they were lost to Germany.

323

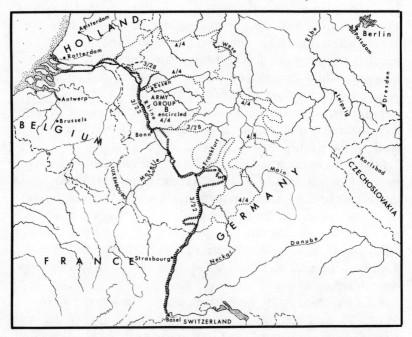

There were few others.

Most of what were left were engaged in the east against the Russians. On paper, there were sixty German divisions in western Germany to oppose the eighty-five fully effective divisions Eisenhower commanded. Most of the German divisions were shadows, manned by untrained, demoralized, mutinous recruits. Four of these divisions consisted of nothing but the division staffs. If the men had been reorganized, they might have been able to form twenty-five or so divisions, but they would have been untrained, unequipped, and demoralized.

This is not to say that nothing remained for the Allies but a victory parade east until they joined up with the Russians advancing west. There were still some German units that fought magnificently, and there was a lot of hard fighting ahead for some of the Allied units. But now it was only a matter of time.

The recurrent rivalry of Montgomery and Patton came out into the open once more, and this time Patton, who for so long had had to take a back seat to the demanding Field Marshal, emerged the winner. In fact, his name finally eclipsed that of the Britisher, although Montgomery was by no means a forgotten man.

On all sides the doomed Nazi Germany was pressed. A massive offensive was about to start in Italy, up the Po Valley, to be coordinated with risings by Italian Partisans in the major cities of the north. In the East, the Russians were closing in on Vienna, and had thrown a bridgehead across the Oder, only thirty miles from Berlin. In that bridgehead they were massing artillery, tanks, and men for the final drive on Berlin. In the West, there remained little that could be called organized defense. The last weeks were at hand.

Every German knew that the war was lost—all but Hitler and the tiny clique of fanatics around him. These included Martin Bormann, Goering, Himmler, and a few others. Even the fanatics were beginning to doubt.

Not Hitler. His eyes burned with the same intensity. His personal magnetism remained the same. Yet he appeared a physical wreck. The only doctor he trusted, Theodor Morell, was a quack, with the personal hygienic habits of a pig. He kept Hitler on various drugs, including four or five injections of "Ultraseptyl" a day. "Ultraseptyl" was a sulphonamide made in a factory owned by Morell, and had been condemned by the pharmacological faculty of Leipzig University as harmful to the nerves. Certainly Hitler's nerves were going. Faced with the necessity of a decision, he would sometimes sit and reminisce for hours on the early days of the Party and the great vision he had for Germany. Or he would react violently in the manner of Attila the Hun.

It was in the latter mood that Hitler reacted to the crossing of the Rhine. He ordered that the future conduct of the war should be "without consideration for our own population." "All industrial plants, all the main electricity works, waterworks, gas works" were to be destroyed in order to create "a desert" in the Allies' road. Minister of War Production Albert Speer protested vehemently, hoping to preserve the future of Germany. Hitler dismissed this with the terrifying logic of a madman.

"If the war is lost, the German nation will also perish. So there is no need to consider what the people require for continued existence."

Hitler's cruelty, never long subdued, broke out again in more virulent form. Gas chambers worked overtime in extermination camps. Political prisoners and prisoners of war were to be slaughtered. Officers and officials who crossed him were summarily sentenced to be shot. Like Attila, like Alaric, like Tamerlane, like Ghengis Khan, Hitler had to be appeased with blood.

He turned more and more toward the occult. He believed in astrology and had his horoscope prepared daily. A miracle would still save him and save Germany, for were they not one and the same? And so, amid the terrible scenes of destruction and despair, the Führer lived in his twilight, preparing the human sacrifices that would accompany him to the grave or that would appease the gods and restore "Ein Volk, ein Reich, ein Führer."

Not knowing the state of affairs in Berlin, Eisenhower continued to conduct operations for the final military obliteration of Germany. Bits of discomforting information began to reach his headquarters, all of which pointed to a "National Redoubt" the Nazis were building in the Austrian, Bavarian, and Italian Alps. An intelligence report stated that Hitler would command in person. "Here, defended by nature and by the most efficient secret weapons yet invented, the powers that have hitherto guided Germany will survive to reorganize her resurrection. . . . Here armaments will be manufactured in bomb-proof factories, food and equipment will be stored in vast underground caverns and a specially selected corps of young men will be trained in guerrilla warfare, so that a whole underground army can be fitted and directed to liberate Germany from the occupying forces."

Although the British did not take this report very seriously, the Americans did, and, as Bradley said later, "it shaped our tactical thinking during the closing weeks of the war."

Influenced by these reports, Eisenhower decided that Berlin

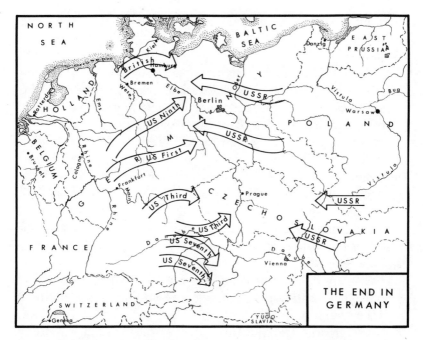

THE END IN
GERMANY

had no military significance, and that his responsibility was to
prevent any such National Redoubt from being formed.
Therefore, the armies under his command would operate to
attain three principal objectives. Montgomery's Twenty-First
Army Group, minus the U.S. Ninth Army, which was restored
to Bradley, would turn north, liberate Holland, and then drive
through Hamburg and on into Denmark. The main drive,
under Bradley, would move east along the Erfurt-Leipzig axis
to the Elbe and there await a link-up with the Russians. The
U.S. Third, the U.S. Seventh, and the First French Armies
would move into the Alpine region to prevent the formation of
the National Redoubt.

On March 28, in a personal message which had not been
cleared through the Combined Chiefs of Staff or through
Churchill and Roosevelt, Eisenhower communicated these
plans to Stalin. He felt that this action was proper, because he
had been expressly authorized to communicate directly with
Stalin on military matters. But, as Churchill insisted, this matter

was much more than military. It contained a political decision of the highest importance, that the Russians alone would take Berlin.

Although Eisenhower might argue that Berlin had become "nothing but a geographical location," its symbolic meaning was self-evident. Nor, despite the Yalta agreements, could anyone be sure that the Russians would adhere to them and permit Berlin to be governed by the Western Allies as well as themselves. So far, when the test had come, the Soviet Union had not lived up to a single agreement reached at Yalta pertaining to countries and territories taken from Germany.

Nevertheless, the decision had been made. Stalin, as might be expected, gave a cordial reply to Eisenhower's message, the only cordial note received by any Western leader from him in some weeks.

The irony is that the National Redoubt which weighed so heavily in Eisenhower's planning was nothing but a myth. It was the final triumph of the Nazi Propaganda Office. There was not enough war material in Germany to give such a redoubt one-tenth the strength that Eisenhower's intelligence section predicted, and the fanatic "Werewolves" who were to man it, turned out to be frightened little boys of ten to twelve years of age.

The National Redoubt was the last success of the Reich. But this success could not save Germany.

And so, March drifted into April, and the deaths and the dying continued in the rubble that the great German cities were becoming. And the spring flowers began to peep through the tortured land, but no one could pay any heed to them.

Far out in the Pacific a day was born as it reached the hour of midnight at the International Date Line. It was just like any other day, but it did not remain so. A few hours later, the sunrise came there and raced across the waters at 15° an hour. Soon the first light came to Tokyo, where the weary Japanese faced another day of labor, and to Okinawa, where Marines and G.I.s fought ashore and Kamikaze planes used that sunrise to cover their attacks on American ships. It crossed the Sea of

Japan and brought light to the Japanese and Chinese engaged in their fierce struggle. It crossed the long, long stretches of Siberia and on to the shining towers of the Kremlin. Still speeding on, it brought light to the Eastern and then to the Western front, which meant that by sunset, Germany would be a little smaller.

Soon the sunrise reached Paris and London, now rear areas, and began to cross the Atlantic, where ships brought more, ever more supplies, to keep the armies going in the final days. Soon it reached the New World, and along the east coast of the United States people rose and began to get ready to go to the office or to the factory. For some workers, it meant the end of the day, as the Graveyard Shift came to the end, and men who had worked since 11:00 P.M. or midnight prepared to go home to sleep.

Then the sunrise reached Warm Springs, Georgia. It was the dawn of April 12.

Every year President Roosevelt came to Warm Springs to strengthen his legs by swimming in the warm mineral water. He was well known to everyone in the town and an inspiration to the crippled men, women, and children who came for treatment in the sanitarium there. This time he was more tired than anyone could remember. But, as the days passed, he seemed to grow stronger, and his wit and spirit returned.

He loafed in the sun, and went for rides, and talked to friends in the old bantering way. But no one would dream of calling him robust.

Although his staff tried to ease his work as much as possible, there are certain things that only the President can do. Every day a pouch of mail and documents was delivered by special plane from Washington. Every day decisions had to be made, for the present and the future. He was pressured by the intransigence of the Russians. He was looking ahead to the peace, and to the world organization to keep that peace. He was making plans to attend the opening of the United Nations Conference in San Francisco to lend the prestige of his name and his office to that all-important meeting.

The mail was late that morning, and the President was able

to work on a speech to be delivered over the radio networks the next evening in honor of Jefferson Day. He looked over the typed draft, making sure, quick emendations here and there. He came to the last sentence: "The only limit to our realization of tomorrow will be our doubts of today." He didn't like that very well. It seemed weak. He crossed out the last three words and thought a moment. Then he wrote them back in and added the last sentence he would ever write for a public speech. "Let us move forward with strong and active faith."

He put the draft aside to work on the next day.

William Hassett, his confidential secretary, brought in the mail which had finally arrived. The President was seated at a card table near the fireplace in his cottage on Bowdell Knob. He turned to the mail at once, with his usual wisecracks. He came to a bill passed by both houses extending the life of the Commodity Credit Corporation. "Here's where I make a law," he joked as he did on all such occasions; he scribbled "Approved" and his signature and the date.

While he was working, Madame Elizabeth Shoumatoff, an artist, came in to paint his portrait as had been previously arranged. Mr. Hassett complained that she was a constant bother as the President was working, measuring his nose, asking him to turn this way or that, but F.D.R. didn't seem to mind.

At length the mail was finished, and Hassett left the room. Laura Delano and Margaret Suckley, both cousins of the President, were in the room watching Mme. Shoumatoff at work. The President was dressed in a suit, with a blue cape over his shoulders. A freshly lighted cigarette was in the long holder, and he was working through a sheaf of papers in his lap. Suddenly he raised his left hand to his temple, moved it across his eyes and nose. Then the hand fell limp. Margaret Suckley thought he might have dropped his cigarette and went over to him. His eyes were closed, but she heard him say, "I have a terrific headache." Then he lost consciousness. The time was 1:15 P.M.

The women summoned Arthur Prettyman, his Negro valet for many years. Prettyman picked the President up in his arms, and with the aid of a Filipino mess attendant took him to his

330

bedroom and got him into pajamas. Then the doctors arrived, but there was nothing to be done. Franklin Roosevelt had suffered a massive cerebral hemorrhage.

At 3:35 P.M. the awful, rasping breaths ceased.

Mrs. Roosevelt had not gone to Warm Springs. She was a guest of honor at the Sulgrave Club tea for the benefit of Washington's children's clinics, and she was chatting with Mrs. Woodrow Wilson when she was summoned to the telephone. She returned to make her apologies for leaving "in this way," and went to the White House. She had not been told what had happened, but she could make a shrewd guess.

In the White House, Admiral Ross T. McIntyre, the President's personal physician, met her, and with him was Press Secretary Stephen Early. "The President," he said, "has slept away."

Mrs. Roosevelt was composed. "I am more sorry," she said after a moment, "for the people of the country and the world than I am for us."

The government of the United States cannot stand still, even for an hour. There is no moment when there is not a President. From the moment of Roosevelt's death, Harry S Truman had been President of the United States, even though he did not know it.*

Summoned from the Senate, Harry Truman came to the White House and into Mrs. Roosevelt's sitting room. She stepped forward and said gently, "Harry, the President is dead."

He choked and asked what he could do to help.

"Is there anything *we* can do for you?" she asked. "For you are the one in trouble now."

Harry Truman knew she was right. Later he asked newsmen, "Did you ever have a bull or a load of hay fall on you? If you have, you know how I felt last night. I felt as if two planets and the whole constellation had fallen on me. I don't know if you

---

* Constitutional authorities have held that the swearing in of the Vice President is a symbolic act rather than a legal requirement for the transfer of authority, although it is popularly viewed as the latter. President Johnson had the same misunderstanding in Dallas in 1963.

boys pray, but if you do, please pray God to help me carry this load."

And an appalling load it was. Despite his failing health, President Roosevelt had told his Vice President literally nothing about what was going on. Except for what had appeared in the public press, Harry Truman knew nothing of what had gone on at Yalta. He knew nothing of the war plans against Germany and against Japan. He knew nothing of the myriads of details which Roosevelt kept at his fingertips.

There was one secret he had to know right away.

As soon as he was sworn in by Chief Justice Harlan F. Stone, he made his first decision. The United Nations Conference at San Francisco would go on as scheduled. A brief Cabinet meeting followed, at which the new President asked all officers to continue in their present posts. Then Secretary of War Harry Stimson took him aside. There was in progress a weapon so powerful that it could change the course of the war. That was all he felt free to say at the moment. The President must have a full briefing as soon as possible.

That was the first President Truman heard of the atomic bomb.

Mrs. Roosevelt and members of the family flew to Georgia by an Army plane, arriving at the Little White House about midnight. The President's body had already been placed in a massive bronze coffin.

The next morning, the coffin was taken in a procession to the railroad station to be placed in the special train that would bear it to Hyde Park, with a stop in Washington. On the way to the station, the procession passed by Georgia House, the main building of the Foundation. The patients were assembled on the portico, many of them with tears streaming down their faces. Graham Jackson, a Negro Chief Petty Officer in the Navy, stepped forward with his accordion. He had often played for Mr. Roosevelt, and he was giving his final tribute. He made no attempt to stem the tears as he played "Going Home" and "Nearer My God, to Thee." Then the procession moved on, and the coffin was soon loaded aboard the train.

All during the long ride to Washington, servicemen guarded

332

the body of the dead President. There was a soldier, a sailor, a Marine, and an Air Force man, one at each corner. At each village and city, the train slowed to permit mourning citizens to pay their respects.

The next morning, April 14, the train arrived in Washington's Union Station, and the military ceremonial for the Commander in Chief began. The flag-draped coffin was placed on a caisson drawn by six matched white horses. With full military escort and to the soul-numbing beat of muffled drums, the procession set out from the station across to Pennsylvania Avenue, up Fifteenth Street, and into the White House grounds through the Northwest Gate. Thousands of silent mourners lined the way.

Bishop Angus Dun conducted the funeral service, assisted by clergymen from the churches Roosevelt attended in Washington. At the President's often-expressed wish, the Navy Hymn, "Eternal Father, Strong to Save," was sung by the congregation before the ceremony began. "I am the Resurrection and the Life, saith the Lord . . ."

As he read Cranmer's words from the Book of Common Prayer, the men and women who filled the East Room looked on the closed casket, each with his thoughts of the man whose mortal remains lay there. There were the members of the family, and the members of the Cabinet, and of Congress, and the Supreme Court, and of the Army and the Navy, and of the Diplomatic Corps, all in strict protocol. Then there were the representatives of heads of state: Anthony Eden representing Churchill, and the Earl of Athlone representing the British Royal Family. Andrei Gromyko was there for Stalin, and many others. And then there was the new President.

As requested by Mrs. Roosevelt, Bishop Dun concluded with the words from the First Inaugural Address, "The only thing we have to fear is fear itself."

"As that was his first word to us, I am sure he would want it to be his last. We should go forward in the future as those who go forward without fear, without fear of our allies or friends, and without fear of our own insufficiencies."

Once more the mournful procession formed to bear the body back to Union Station and to place it aboard the train to begin

Franklin Delano Roosevelt's last journey. April 15, 1945, he arrived home at Hyde Park, where the grave had been prepared just where he had wished. William A. Plog, who had tended the grounds for nearly fifty years, supervised the digging of the grave to be sure that its sides were foursquare and firm, like the man he had served so long.

As the committal service was being read by Dr. Anthony, Rector of St. James Church in Hyde Park, William Hassett looked out toward the Hudson and noted that a lilac bush was just opening its blossoms. His mind went to Whitman's poem, "When Lilacs Last in the Dooryard Bloomed," commemorating the death of another great wartime President, Abraham Lincoln. It was exactly eighty years since an assassin's bullet had put an end to the life of the Great Emancipator.

Near Hersfeld, Germany, where Patton had temporarily established Third Army Headquarters in a trailer-truck, news of the President's death came by way of BBC radio near midnight. Patton immediately went to a small house nearby where Eisenhower and Bradley were spending the night after a visit to Third Army. Until 0200 the three men discussed the loss of the Commander in Chief and its meaning for the war and for the peace that was now so near.

The news of the President's death climaxed a day none of the three men would ever forget. In the morning they had visited a salt mine near the village of Merkers where a huge cache of Nazi loot and treasure had been hidden. Descending 2,100 feet in an elevator to the mine floor, they had seen some $250 million worth of gold, most of it in ingots, but part in the form of rings, watches, brooches, and fillings from the teeth of murdered Jews and others who had incurred the displeasure of the Nazis. There was some $2 million in American currency and lesser amounts of British, French, Norwegian, and other European monies.

The custodian of this treasure trove, a captured German, pointed out bundles amounting to 3 billion Reichsmarks, saying that they would be needed to meet the German army payrolls.

"Tell him," said Patton to the interpreter, "that I doubt the German army will be meeting payrolls much longer."

There was also a large collection of stolen art objects, most of which Patton dismissed contemptuously as the type suitable for ornamenting bars in America. Some, Patton notwithstanding, were of tremendous value.

From the salt mine, the generals went on to a concentration camp at Ohrdruf, the first that any of them had ever seen.

Ohrdruf was a minor camp as concentration camps went. It could not be compared with Buchenwald, Belsen, Dachau, Erlau, Auschwitz, to name the most infamous. But it was bad enough to turn the stomachs of the three men. At one point, tough old "Blood and Guts" Patton had to stumble over to a corner to vomit.

The first thing they noted was the stench. It was a miasma which greeted them before they reached the gates of the camp. Unburied bodies had been lightly covered with lime, but, as Patton noted, "As a reducer of smell, lime is a very ineffective medium."

Bodies were piled like cordwood. Some of the victims had been dispatched by a single shot in the back of the head. Others had been beaten to death or had starved, or had died of neglected disease. Some had had part of the flesh stripped off or showed toothmarks as maddened starving men had turned to cannibalism.

A guide showed off the gallows. The cord used was piano wire, and it was adjusted in length so that the victim's feet just touched the ground. The drop was too short to break the neck, and it usually took about fifteen minutes for him to die in agony. It turned out that the guide, far from being one of the inmates, was a guard. He was discovered the next day, murdered by the people he had terrorized. No investigation into his death was made.

A few days later, Patton's troops came to Buchenwald, and the grim story of Nazi atrocities began to unfold. There had been tales of Nazi terror, but the reality was worse than the wildest story. The liberation of France and the Low Countries had revealed the whole ghastly picture of the measures the Germans had used in occupied countries. The knock on the door at night, the rounding up of hostages to be executed at the rate of a hundred hostages for each German killed by the resistance, the slave labor—all these were known. But the Allies were not prepared for what the Nazis had done to their own people.

Concentration camps had been a part of German life since the Nazis had taken over the government, but they continued and grew in importance during the war years, for they housed not only German political prisoners and Jews. Now they contained unfortunates from conquered territories—Jews, resistance fighters, those who disobeyed the rules of the occupying authorities, those who offended the Nazis in any way.

All concentration camps were alike. The names of the brutes who ran them were different, but the inmates were all the same, so far as their guards were concerned. Everything was done to strip every trace of human dignity from the inmates. Those who could were forced to work at hard manual labor eleven or twelve hours a day. Those who could not were encouraged to die and were usually helped if they did not do so promptly.

On arrival at a concentration camp, men and women were segregated and taken off for "medical inspection." There they were forced to strip naked and were deloused. Heads were usually shorn, because the Germans could use the hair for manufacturing mattresses and upholstered furniture. Then a doctor or a medical orderly passed down the line, often making obscene remarks as he went. Those who were pronounced fit to work were given clothes and had a number tattooed on the arm and were led to the barracks where they would exist until they became too weak to work any longer.

Those too infirm or too sick to work were taken off in another direction. They were useless mouths and the precious food of the Reich could no longer be wasted on them. Most of the time they were executed by a pistol bullet in the nape of the neck. Later on as the numbers of victims grew, gassing in bunches of 150 or more was common.

At Buchenwald, Ilsa Koch, wife of the camp's commandant, had a hobby. Any prisoner of either sex who had a tattoo was pulled out of line and taken to her, still naked. If she approved, the unfortunate person was executed at once. The skin containing the tattoo would be carefully removed from the corpse and delivered to her. She would clean it, removing any bits of flesh clinging to the skin, and then tan it. From this human leather with the interesting designs tattooed upon it, she would make lamp shades, wallets, gloves, and book bindings. She was quite proud of her collection.

Those who survived "medical inspection" often wished that they had not. The life they led was one of deliberate degradation. Every effort was made to break them physically, mentally, and morally. Barracks were so terribly overcrowded that often there was not room for everyone to lie down at once. There were no sanitary facilities. Buckets were provided, but there were never enough and they were usually overturned in the night, so that in the morning the inmates were smeared with excreta. The barracks were unheated, and in the winter no cover was provided. At dawn each morning, after a breakfast of a bowl of ersatz coffee, the men and the women lined up in front of their respective barracks for roll call, standing in their thin cotton rags in the icy cold of winter or in the heat of summer. There were always those who did not answer roll call, for invariably some had died during the night.

Every form of disease was prevalent in these concentration camps, but those afflicted rarely received any treatment. It was usually much simpler to assign them to the groups that were to be disposed of that day. If they were taken to the camp hospitals, their treatment was usually a disgrace to the medical profession. They were untreated, attended by half-trained personnel, or actively mistreated. Often abdominal operations, such as the removal of the appendix or the gall bladder, were performed by first- or second-year medical students. If the patient did not die on the table, he usually perished in a few days as a result of complications.

Punishment was frequent and brutal. It had to be to exceed the brutality of daily life. No one really cared if the punishment maimed or killed the victim. There were official regulations in some camps that beating with an axe handle was to be

337

restricted to twenty-five blows at a time, under the supervision of a doctor, and that a week must pass before a second beating could be given. No one seems to have paid much attention to that regulation.

Sometimes prisoners were placed in solitary confinement in total darkness in cells where they could neither stand, sit, nor lie. Often they would be kept in such conditions for ten or twelve days; usually when they came out they were completely mad. Sometimes there were public floggings, and sometimes public executions which the inmates were required to witness.

Worst of all were the men and women who as inmates curried favor with the guards in order to ease their own lot. They had no hesitation in reporting real or fancied offenses by the prisoners. Some even were released to join the guard force. Such a one was Vera Salvequart at Ravensbrück, a concentration camp for women. After a few months there, she won favor and was assigned to the guard force. At first her duties consisted of helping to pick out those who were to be exterminated; later she began a little extermination program of her own with poisons she delighted in administering to those she disliked. In her trial after the war, she offered as a part of her defense that she frequently helped some of the women by providing them with boots or clothing from the bodies of those she had killed!

Another degrading story is that of the medical experiments conducted at Buchenwald, Belsen, and elsewhere. Sometimes healthy young men and women would be forced to undergo operations in the name of medical science. A piece of shin bone might be grafted elsewhere in the body. Germs of gas gangrene were sometimes introduced so that the doctors could try various compounds to cure the resulting infections. Most of those victims, if they did not die in the treatment, were maimed for life.

At Belsen experiments in the cure of malaria were carried out on 1,200 unwilling human guinea pigs. Many of them died from the malaria itself, many more from other causes as a result of their being weakened by the ravages of the malaria, and not a few were poisoned by overdoses of the drugs prescribed as cures. It made no difference to the doctors. There were plenty more "patients" available.

Another experiment conducted at Belsen was that of the effect on the human body of swift, high compression and decompression. The excuse was to determine how to protect men falling in parachute drops or men forced to work in high pressure in U-boats when something went wrong with the air system. A special van was constructed in which the air pressure could be quickly increased or decreased. Most of the victims of this experiment underwent agony. An inmate forced to work on this experiment has described what he saw:

> I have personally seen through the observation window of the decompression chamber when a prisoner inside would stand in a vacuum until his lungs ruptured. . . . They would go mad and pull out their hair in an effort to relieve the pressure. They would tear their heads and faces with their fingers and nails in an attempt to maim themselves in their madness. They would beat the walls with their hands and heads and scream in an effort to relieve the pressure on their eardrums. These cases usually ended in the death of the subject.

Sigmund Rascher, the same doctor who conducted the decompression experiments, was also interested in the problem of cold. To his orderly mind, two questions arose: how much cold and exposure could a person stand before he died? and, how best to revive a victim of freezing?

Some victims were immersed in full flying suits in icy water in varying depths. The nape of the neck, the doctor found, was the most vulnerable part of the body to cold, the victim invariably dying when that part reached a certain temperature. He suggested a heated head and neck protector for flying uniforms.

Others were exposed naked throughout winter nights. Others were covered by sheets which had been dipped in icy water first. Every hour a bucket of cold water would be poured on them. He discovered that those who remained naked survived better than those in the sheets.

Because German soldiers, sailors, or airmen might find

themselves exposed to icy cold, Dr. Rascher conducted experiments into reviving victims of freezing. The tests have been described by a Czech doctor who was an inmate and unwilling aide to Dr. Rascher.

The subject was placed in ice cold water and kept there until he became unconscious. Blood was taken from his neck and tested each time his body temperature dropped one degree. . . . The lowest body temperature reached was 19° centigrade (66.2° Fahrenheit) but most men died at 25° or 26° (77° and 78.8° Fahrenheit). When the men were removed from the icy water attempts were made to revive them with artificial sunshine, hot water, electro-therapy, or by animal warmth.

The use of animal warmth was suggested to Dr. Rascher by Heinrich Himmler, who was much interested in the subject and brought parties of friends to see the experiment. The victim was chilled in the usual way until he lost consciousness. Then his naked body was placed on a wide bed and two naked women were told to snuggle up to him as closely as possible. All three would then be covered with blankets. Once the victims gained consciousness, they recognized the situation and cooperated in snuggling close. Their temperatures rose at a predictable rate.

An exception which gratified Himmler and surprised Dr. Rascher was noted in four cases where the victim, on regaining consciousness, found the strength to engage in sexual intercourse with one of the women. In those instances the temperature rise was faster and the men made a speedier recovery.

The most ghastly tale of all yet remains to be told, that of the extermination camps. The "Final Solution of the Jewish Problem," a policy adopted by Hitler during the war, was a euphemism for the planned extermination of all European Jews. There were some ten extermination camps where the "Final Solution" was implemented, but the greatest of all was Auschwitz in Poland. It had four huge gas chambers and adjoining crematoria for disposal of the corpses.

The commandant of Auschwitz for a time was Rudolf Hoess, and he set about his work with the enthusiasm of a young executive sent to improve the performance of a faltering manufacturing plant. He visited Treblinka, another *Vernichtungslager*, as the Germans called the extermination camps. He watched the process with interest and saw weaknesses which he set about to correct at Auschwitz. His statements have a weird sense of detachment. They read as though he were talking about increasing efficiency in production, not in the taking of human lives. "Another improvement we made over Treblinka was that we built our gas chambers to accommodate 2,000 people at one time, whereas at Treblinka their ten gas chambers only accommodated 200 people each."

On arrival at Auschwitz the people would be taken from the freight cars in which they had been locked for days on end, traveling hundreds of miles from France or Holland or Greece or Russia. Those who were to perform slave labor would be sent in one direction and those destined for the gas chambers, the Jews and the children and the elderly, would be taken to another.

They had no notion as yet of their fate. Sometimes they were given picture postcards with a printed inscription on the back saying:

> We are doing very well here. We have work and we are well treated. We await your arrival.

After they had addressed and signed the postcards, the Jews and the other condemned were led up tidy walks bordered with flowers and well-kept lawns to the gas chambers, which were low, pleasant looking buildings, giving no hint of their grim purpose. An orchestra was seated in a bandstand nearby and it played light airs from *The Merry Widow* or the *Tales of Hoffman* or some other light opera. On arrival, the men were segregated from the women and children and led to an adjoining gas chamber. But it was called a bath house. The victims were told to strip because they were to be given showers and delousing after their long journey. Often they were handed towels to make the deception complete.

Once inside the shower room they may first have suspected

something was wrong, for 2,000 of them in the room all at once would make any washing difficult. But it was too late. The huge door slid shut, creating a hermetic seal.

As the prisoners were wondering what was going to happen next, if they had not already suspected, orderlies poured crystals of hydrogen cyanide or Zyklon B into vents leading to the chamber. Then they quickly sealed the vents.

It took some time for the gas to work, but when it did the people went mad, rushing for the exit and piling up in mounds of flesh as they tore at each other in an effort to reach the door. For perhaps twenty or thirty minutes the struggles went on, and then pumps drew out the poisonous air and the work of clearing out the bodies began. This noisome task was performed by Jewish males, inmates who had been promised their lives for doing it. Of course, those promises were never kept, and every so often they would be replaced and sent to the gas chamber themselves.

When the corpses were dragged out they would be inspected. Any gold teeth would be extracted and the gold retrieved. Hair would be shaved or clipped off. Any rings or watches or bracelets that had survived earlier thefts by guards would be added to the pile of gold or other valuable metals. Then it was time for the crematoria.

Even German efficiency was unable to create crematoria which were able to keep up with the supply of corpses to be burned. As many as 6,500 bodies a day had to be disposed of during the summer of 1944, so mass graves had to be excavated. The ashes from the crematoria were gathered and scattered in the nearby Sola River. Sometimes they were sold as fertilizer. There was even a recipe for making soap out of human fat: "12 pounds of human fat, 10 quarts of water, and 8 ounces to a pound of caustic soda . . . all boiled for two or three hours and then cooled."

Eisenhower was determined that such horrors should not be dismissed as "just war propaganda," and he urged both Washington and London to "send instantly to Germany a random group of newspaper editors and send representative groups from the national legislatures" to see for themselves the bestiality to which the Nazis had descended.

The final act was about to be played with all the Wagnerian drama that the sick minds of Hitler and his remaining faithful—and unfaithful—could bring to it. In the north, Montgomery's British and Canadians had moved through Bremen, crossed the Elbe, and had seized the ruins of Hamburg and moved across the base of the Jutland Peninsula to take Lübeck and thereby keep the Russians out of Denmark. The Americans, once having reached the Elbe, had turned southeast into Czechoslovakia and Austria and to the German border of Switzerland. In Italy, the Anglo-American armies and the Polish contingent which had joined them crossed the Po on a broad front. At the same time, the Russians opened their attack across the Oder and advanced on a 200-mile front. They met the Americans at Torgau on the Elbe on April 25 amid scenes of noisy demonstrations. Germany—what remained outside of enemy hands—was split in two. The end could not be long delayed.

During these days of disaster closing in from every side, Germany's evil genius, Adolf Hitler, was in the ruins of his capitol, in a bunker fifty feet below the ruins of the Reich's Chancellery where so many ceremonials of Nazi splendor had taken place. The broad, stately rooms of the Chancellery were all smashed now, and the remnants of the Nazi government lived a mole-like existence in the bomb-proof bunker that had been built for an emergency.

It is hard to depict the last days of the Third Reich as they went on in that bunker, not because the facts are not available, but because they are so incredible. In the cramped underground quarters the remnants of Nazi leadership continued to behave as though they had choices, as though any action of theirs could alter the course of the war. Somehow the Führer's genius would rescue them. Somehow a miracle would reverse reality and the Reich would be saved.

Hitler was now a physical wreck. An army captain has described his appearance:

His head was slightly wobbling. His left arm hung slackly and his hand trembled a good deal. There was an indescribable flickering glow in his eyes, creating a fearsome and wholly unnatural effect. His face and the parts around his eyes gave the impression of total exhaustion. All his movements were those of a senile man.

Some of his followers turned to astrology, among them the loyal Joseph Paul Goebbels, Propaganda Minister, who was to follow his deity in death. He was reading to Hitler one night from Thomas Carlyle's *History of Frederick the Great*, and the passage told of Frederick's despair during the darkest days of the Seven Years' War. Frederick had announced that if nothing happened to improve his fortunes by February 15, he would take poison. Then came the dramatic passage, written in Carlyle's best omniscient narrator style, which Goebbels read for all it was worth:

"Brave King! Wait yet a little while, and the days of your suffering will be over. Already the sun of your good fortune stands behind the clouds and soon will rise upon you." On February 12 the Czarina died, the Miracle of the House of Brandenburg had come to pass.

To Goebbels this passage seemed inspired, and he sent for horoscopes drawn up on the date of the birth of the Weimar Republic and on the date of Hitler's accession to office as Chancellor. The results were conclusive to a man of Goebbels's mentality.

An amazing fact has become evident [he wrote], both horoscopes predicting the outbreak of the war in 1939, the victories until 1941, and the subsequent series of reversals, with the hardest blows during the first months of 1945, particularly during the first half of April. In the second half of April we were to experience a temporary success. Then there would be stagnation until August and peace that same month. For the following three years Germany would have a hard time, but starting in 1948 she would rise again.

In mid-April the miracle happened, or so the Nazis thought.

On the late evening of April 12 Goebbels returned from a trip and found the capital again aflame from yet another bombing raid. On the steps of the Propaganda Ministry he was greeted with momentous news. He quickly phoned the *Führerbunker* to tell Hitler.

"Mein Führer," he said, "I congratulate you! Roosevelt is dead! It is written in the stars that the second half of April will be the turning point for us. This is Friday, April 13th. [It was by then after midnight in Berlin.] It is the turning point!"

Neither Goebbels nor anyone else in the Nazi hierarchy ever understood the principle of orderly transfer of power as it exists in Britain and the United States. In their thinking, Roosevelt had been the guiding spirit of the United States. With his death, Americans would lose all sense of direction, of purpose. Germany might yet be saved!

But the death of Franklin D. Roosevelt brought no letup in the war. Those who could afford the time to mourn the dead President did so, but for the soldier, sailor, or airman, there was no time. If they grieved, it was while they got on with the job.

On April 15, Hitler's mistress of many years' standing arrived at the bunker. No one more disappointing to historians and romancers has ever been the mistress of a world figure. A Pompadour she was not. Her name was Eva Braun, and she was the daughter of lower-middle-class Bavarian parents. From her photographs she appears to have been a pleasant enough looking woman, but certainly no great beauty. No one would have given her a second glance in a crowd. And she was certainly no intellect. She liked sentimental music and sentimental novels, movies of no particular merit or content. She enjoyed skiing and swimming. She even liked to dance, although Hitler disapproved of that activity.

Probably the reason she appealed to Hitler was that she made no demands on him, either materially or intellectually. It is by no means certain how much—if any—passion they shared. Hitler's physician, the quack Dr. Morell, hinted: "They slept in different beds; nevertheless, I believe . . ."

Now she had come to the bunker to share her lover's fate. From this determination she never wavered, even though Hitler urged her to leave. She had no desire to live in a Germany without Hitler. "It would not be fit to live in for a true German," she said.

April 20 was Hitler's fifty-sixth birthday, and it was passed quietly in the bunker as every front disintegrated even further. Most of the Old Guard was there—Goering, Goebbels, Bormann, Himmler, von Ribbentrop, as well as the military leaders, Dönitz, Keitel, Jodl, and Krebs, the last just appointed as Chief of the Army General Staff.

Hitler responded confidently to their congratulations and good wishes, expressing the belief that "the Russians were going to suffer their bloodiest defeat of all before Berlin." This was so patently absurd that the generals had difficulty in restraining themselves. They urged Hitler to escape to the south, for in two or three days they expected the encirclement of the city to be complete.

Hitler would not make up his mind at that moment. Perhaps he could not conceive the terrible truth that the Russians would actually take Berlin. The symbolic significance of the capital of the Third Reich gave it a kind of invincibility. One might as well talk of capturing Valhalla.

Yet Valhalla fell, and the *Götterdämmerung* would soon come to Berlin.

After the birthday party, a good many of the guests left Berlin. Ribbentrop got out and so did Goering and Himmler.

The last two had special reasons for leaving for safer parts. Each felt that the Führer had only a few days to live. Each expected to become the new leader of the Third Reich.

Neither of them considered the plain fact that the Third Reich had only a few days more to live, that there would be nothing to be leader of.

Hitler now turned his attention to the military defense of Berlin. He ordered SS General Felix Steiner to make an all-out counterattack in the southern suburbs, and he made available to Steiner every available soldier, including Luftwaffe ground troops. "Any commanding officer who keeps his men back," Hitler stormed, "will forfeit his life within five hours!"

Hitler gave his orders, but nothing happened. The Steiner attack never got started.

When Hitler finally realized that nothing had happened, and when he was told that his orders had weakened the north to support the nonexistent southern defenses, there was an explosion. All witnesses agree that it was the greatest rage of his life. All his orders had been ignored! He had been betrayed on all sides! The others could go if they liked. He would stay on to direct the defenses of Berlin to the end. He would die in the ruins.

Despite the protests of everyone, Hitler was adamant. He refused to listen to the pleas of his officers that the road out was still open. He had made his decision and there he would stay. The next day a propaganda broadcast announced to the world that the Führer would never leave Berlin.

There was one man Hitler knew would stay with him to the end, the faithful Goebbels. He invited him and his wife and six children to move into the *Führerbunker* to share his fate. Goebbels accepted with great emotion. Of all the faithful, he and his family had received the highest of all possible honors— the privilege of dying with the Führer.

Hitler ordered Keitel and Jodl to get out as fast as possible to take command of the remnants of the German armed forces in the south. Goering, he said, would take over the political leadership down in that area. "There is no question of fighting now," he went on; "there's nothing left to fight with. If it's a question of negotiating, Goering can do that better than I can."

Everyone still had the illusion that there was negotiating to be done. There was a question of just how to get the most favorable treatment for the German people. But Hitler had no interest in this goal. He had been deserted by everyone, and it was only right and proper that all Germany should go down with him in the Wagnerian finish.

Heinrich Himmler, meanwhile, was busily at work scheming on how he would take over the Reich at the proper time. As head of the SS, he had been responsible for the deaths of millions of persons in concentration camps, in extermination camps and by means of the *Einsatzgruppen*, Special Action Groups, which had massacred millions of Poles and Russians when the Germans held those lands. Still he thought he was the proper person to negotiate with the Allies for the surrender of Germany and that he would remain as head of the German government after the war had ended.

Through SS General Walter Schellenberg, who was even more stupidly optimistic than he, Himmler was put in touch with Count Bernadotte of Sweden, who was attempting to act as go-between for the Allies and Germany. He had several meetings with Bernadotte, but was torn by his loyalty to the Führer. So long as Hitler was alive, Himmler felt he could make no definitive offer. But how long would the Führer remain alive?

When Hitler's intention to remain in Berlin to the last was broadcast, Himmler felt free to act. In a meeting with Bernadotte in the Swedish consulate at Lübeck on April 22, he stated his position. It was a weird scene. All electricity had been knocked out by the bombing, and the men sat in candlelight. No sooner had they started than another air raid drove them to the bomb-proof cellars, where they continued to talk.

"The Führer's great life," said Himmler, "is drawing to its close." Himmler was now able to make the following proposition without being disloyal. He would surrender to the Western Allies, but not to the Russians. In the East he would continue the fight until the Western Allies had advanced to meet up with the Russians. By this time, every German military unit would have made its capitulation to the British and Americans and would be spared the destruction that would come upon them if they yielded to the Russians. He even wrote a personal letter to Bernadotte confirming all this so that Bernadotte could show it to the Swedish government as proof of his good faith.

Himmler left the meeting well satisfied. He could not conceive how the Americans and British could turn down such a fair offer. His only remaining problem was whether to bow, salute, or shake hands when he was introduced to Eisenhower!

Goering, the other man preparing to receive the mantle of succession to the Führerdom, was now in Obersaltzberg near

Munich. Luftwaffe General Karl Koller, who had not heard of Hitler's determination to remain in Berlin, was told by Jodl to fly at once to Goering's headquarters with the word that the fat *Reichsmarschall* should take over negotiations. After all, Hitler had just given that order. Also, by Hitler's decree of 1941, Goering was officially heir apparent to leadership of the Party and Reich. To be sure, Goering had been out of favor with the Führer, who held him personally responsible for the failure of the Luftwaffe, but the decree of succession had never been revoked. Now, with Hitler's statement that Goering should negotiate with the Allies, it seemed clear that he was back in favor.

When Koller arrived with this astonishing news, Goering was in a quandary. He wanted to act, but he knew that if he made the wrong move, he would be in peril of his life. His deadliest enemy, Martin Bormann, was still in the *Führerbunker* and would be quick to urge Hitler to accept the worst possible interpretation of any word or action of his. "If I act now," he said, "I may be stamped as a traitor; if I don't act, I'll be accused of having failed to do something in the hour of disaster."

He sent for his copy of the decree of succession and he and his legal advisers studied it carefully. It provided that he was to take over on the death of Hitler or his incapacity to act. Everyone agreed that with the Führer determined to remain in Berlin to die, the time had come for Goering to assume the powers given him in the decree.

Goering, however, wanted to make very sure. With extreme care, he drafted a telegram to Hitler.

My Führer!
    In view of your decision to remain at your post in the fortress of Berlin, do you agree that I take over, at once, the total leadership of the Reich, with full freedom of action at home and abroad, as your deputy, in accordance with your decree of 29 June 1941? If no reply is received by ten o'clock tonight, I shall take it for granted that you have lost your freedom of action, and shall consider the conditions of your decree as fulfilled, and shall act for the best interests of our

349

country and our people. You know what I feel for you in this gravest hour of my life. Words fail me to express myself. May God protect you, and speed you quickly here in spite of all.

Your loyal
Hermann Goering

Before this telegram was received, another man with a troubled conscience appeared. This was Albert Speer who had deliberately countermanded Hitler's orders for the destruction of everything in the Ruhr. In the dying moments of the Third Reich he had come to make his peace with the man whose will he had frustrated for the survival of the German people. He had no doubt in his mind of the correctness of his action, for if he had followed his orders, millions of people would have been doomed to suffering and death from exposure and starvation in the months ahead. Yet such was the fascination that Hitler still held over his followers that Speer felt he had to have a kind of absolution after confession. He had no way of knowing what his fate might be. At best, he expected to have to listen to one of the long tirades for which Hitler was now famous. At worst, the Führer might simply order him taken out and shot.

To his surprise, Hitler listened to his confession calmly. He neither reproved Speer nor ordered his execution. It was the calm before the storm.

While Speer was still in the bunker, Goering's telegram arrived. It seemed open in its purpose and loyal in its tone until Bormann interpreted it. The deadline of ten o'clock Bormann explained was an ultimatum and the whole thing an attempt to usurp power while the Führer was still alive.

Hitler immediately ordered the decree of succession rescinded. He dictated, under the influence of Bormann, a telegram to Goering saying that the *Reichsmarschall* had been guilty of treason in his actions and was worthy of death, but that in view of his long service to the Party and to the Reich his life would be spared if he resigned all his offices at once. He was ordered to reply immediately by telegram with the single word "Yes" or "No."

This was not enough for the malevolent Bormann. When he

350

took care of sending Hitler's telegram, he sent one of his own to SS headquarters in Berchtesgaden ordering Goering's arrest.

Two days later two visitors arrived at the *Führerbunker*. They were General Ritter von Greim and the famous woman test pilot Hanna Reitsch. General Greim had no idea of why he was summoned and Hanna Reitsch, always curious and anxious to be at the scene of power, had agreed to help him fly there.

Hanna Reitsch was a woman who needed a god. She had been an ardent Nazi all during the regime, but in the last few months her personal god had shown weakness. Her devotion to Adolf Hitler had turned to a worship of Ritter von Greim, a Luftwaffe general of no particular distinction. To her he embodied German honor, and she willingly set out on the journey with him.

In the final approach to Berlin, the plane came under antiaircraft fire and Greim's right foot was shattered. He was piloting at the moment, with Reitsch stuffed into the fuselage behind him, for it was a single-seater plane. She reached over him and brought the aircraft to a safe landing on the East-West Axis, a main street between the Chancellery and the Tiergarten.

In the *Führerbunker*, Greim had his foot dressed, and while the doctor was working on him, Hitler came into the surgery.

"Do you know why I have called you?" asked the Führer.

"No, my Führer."

"Because Hermann Goering has betrayed and deserted both me and his Fatherland. Behind my back he has established contact with the enemy. His action was a mark of cowardice. Against my orders he has gone to save himself at Berchtesgaden. From there he sent me a disrespectful telegram."

Warming to his subject, Hitler burst out: "Nothing now remains! nothing is spared me! no loyalty is kept, no honor observed! It is the end. No injury has been left undone!" The tirade went on for some time. Then Hitler got himself under control and astonished the wounded Greim by appointing him the new Commander in Chief of the Luftwaffe.

He could have made the appointment by radio and spared Greim a shattered foot and enabled him to remain at headquarters where he could direct what little Germany had left for an air war. But Hitler preferred to be dramatic, to see the expression of gratitude on the faces of the recipients of his favor. This action tied up the new Commander in Chief uselessly for three days, for every plane sent to bring him out was shot down by the Russians.

There came yet another blow. By April 28, the Russians were shelling the Chancellery and now it was practically impossible to get in or out of the *Führerbunker*. Still Hitler had faith, for he believed in a new relief campaign by General Wenck's army which would rescue Berlin. But Wenck's army had already been liquidated, and the only remaining troops in the region under General Heinrici were moving westward as fast as they could so that they could be captured by the British or Americans rather than the Russians.

Then the radio picked up a BBC broadcast which told of Himmler's dealings with Bernadotte. This was the most telling blow of all. Faithful Heinrich—Hitler often referred to him as *der treue Heinrich*—had stabbed him just as Brutus had plunged the dagger into Caesar's breast. Everyone agreed that the scene which followed was terrible. "He raged like a madman," wrote Hanna Reitsch. "His color rose to a heated red, and his face was almost unrecognizable . . . After the lengthy outburst Hitler sank into a stupor and for a time the entire bunker was silent."

When he had recovered, Hitler took speedy action. He ordered the arrest of Himmler on grounds of high treason. He had Himmler's liaison officer to Führer Headquarters, General Hermann Fegelein, taken out and shot. "A traitor must never succeed me as Führer," he shouted.

Now that he had been deserted by his oldest friends, all except Goebbels, Hitler began to make preparations for his death. First he granted Eva Braun's greatest wish. He formally married her. The marriage ceremony took place some time between 1:00 A.M. and 3:00 A.M., April 29. It was conducted by a certain Walter Wagner and was a civil ceremony. The two parties swore they were of pure Aryan descent and were free from hereditary disease. After congratulations the couple retired into Hitler's private apartment for a wedding breakfast, where they were shortly joined by Goebbels, Bormann, Frau Goebbels, and two of Hitler's secretaries.

It was a nostalgic occasion. They talked of old, happier times, of friends departed, of hopes unrealized. Hitler spoke of his approaching suicide and announced what they already knew, that Eva would accompany him in death. So would the devoted Goebbels and his entire family.

Martin Bormann had other plans.

Hitler occupied the next few hours in writing a "Political Testament" and his will. The "Political Testament" was almost a rehash of *Mein Kampf.* It told the same lies, it admitted no failure. Hitler had never failed. He had been betrayed.

In the second part of the "Political Testament," Hitler gave his instructions for the future. He named Grand Admiral Karl Dönitz, Commander in Chief of the Navy, as his successor and dictated who was to be in the new Cabinet. He berated Goering and Himmler and explained their ouster. He closed with a typical order.

> Above all, I enjoin the government and the people to uphold the racial laws to the limit and to resist mercilessly the poisoner of all nations, international Jewry.

Next he turned to his personal will. It was a simple affair, as Hitler had never used his position to amass a vast personal fortune as others had done. Eva Braun would die with him, so there was no need to make provision for her. He left everything to the State except for a few modest sums to provide a simple living for a few relatives.

Exhausted from the long night, Hitler went to bed for a few hours. Outside smoke hung heavy over the city, and out into this pall went messengers bearing copies of the "Political Testament."

There was a great deal of activity in the bunker that day, most of it meaningless, reflex actions of the dying state. That afternoon came the report of the death of Mussolini. The Duce had been captured by partisans while trying to escape from Como in Italy into Switzerland. He and his mistress, Clara

Petacci, had been shot and their corpses brought back to Milan in a truck. The next day they were hung up by their heels from a balcony and later cut down and thrown into a gutter. Vengeful Italians spat upon the bodies and threw garbage until at length they were taken away to paupers' graves in the Cimitero Maggiore in Milan.

It was soon after he had learned of Mussolini's death that Hitler began to prepare for his own. His favorite dog, Blondi, was killed by a lethal injection; the other two were shot. He handed out capsules of poison to everyone who wanted one, including his two women secretaries.

By this time it was evening, and Hitler sent word from his apartment that no one was to go to bed until further orders. No record exists of what happened in the hours that followed, as the tension mounted in the rest of the bunker. At length, about 2:30 A.M., he emerged and shook hands with the twenty or so people gathered there. He mumbled a few inaudible words to each one and then retired back to his apartment.

Then a curious thing happened. It was as though all obedience was unloosed. The Führer had made his final farewell, so no further obedience was due him. The Russians might appear at any moment, so enjoy the passing moment to the fullest. Dancing began and singing, and it grew so loud that a message came from the apartment requesting them to be less noisy. But even this did not quell the weird revelry. The people kept on dancing throughout the night.

Hitler surprised everyone by making an appearance the next day. Eva Braun did not appear, and, it seems, had no appetite for lunch. Hitler took his meal with his two secretaries and his cook. Once he had finished, Hitler sent for Eva Braun and took another farewell of his closest intimates. Then he and his new wife went into the apartment for the last time.

Meanwhile, Erich Kempka, Hitler's chauffeur had received instructions to take 200 liters of gasoline in jerricans to the Chancellery gardens. It was difficult to find so much fuel on such short notice, but he did manage to produce 180 liters. That would have to do.

Outside the Führer's apartment, Bormann, Goebbels and a handful of the faithful waited. In a few minutes there was the sound of a single revolver shot. After a few minutes they entered the apartment and found the two bodies. Hitler had shot himself through the mouth. Eva Braun had not used her revolver. She had taken poison instead.

The bodies were carried up into the garden and the gasoline was poured over them and set afire. It was a Viking funeral, to the accompaniment of Russian shells falling nearby. Later that night the bodies were buried in a shell crater. Subsequent efforts to identify Hitler's remains were useless. They were probably obliterated in the shelling.

Back in the bunker, Bormann and Goebbels still had work to do. The most important thing was to notify Dönitz of the death of Hitler and of the fact that he was now Führer of Germany. But Bormann could not bear to give up even the symbol of power. He knew he would be nothing in Dönitz's government. He would preserve his position as long as possible. He sent a strange radio message to Dönitz.

Grand Admiral Dönitz!
In place of the former Reich Marshal Goering the Führer appoints you as his successor. Written authority is on its way. You will immediately take all such measures as the situation requires.

It would take an astute reader to gather from this message that Hitler was dead.

This message was the first inkling Dönitz had received that he was to succeed Hitler. He was thunderstruck. Unlike the politicians, he had no desire for such responsibility, but he would obey orders.

From his headquarters on Ploen in Schleswig, he sent the following reply, firmly believing that Hitler was still alive.

My Führer!
My loyalty to you will be unconditional. I shall do everything possible to relieve you in Berlin. If fate nevertheless compels me to rule the Reich as your appointed successor, I shall continue this

355

war to an end worthy of the unique, heroic struggle of the German
people.

Dönitz

It was almost a pity that Hitler was not alive to read Dönitz's
message. It would have delighted him.

Goebbels and Bormann then tried to make a settlement with
the Russians, but they did not like the answer they received.
General Chuikov demanded the surrender of all troops in
Berlin and of everyone in the bunker.

Goebbels, having no need to be devious, sent the first
straightforward message to Dönitz, informing him of Hitler's
death. The power once and for all shifted from the bunker to
Ploen.

One last scene took place in the bunker. This was the deaths
of Goebbels, his wife and their six children. Early on the
evening of May 1, he administered poison to the children while
they were playing. Then, after making arrangements for his
family's and his own cremation, he joined his wife and the two
of them mounted the stairs from the bunker into the garden. At
their request, an SS orderly dispatched them with a single shot
into the back of each of their necks. Their bodies were found
the next day by the Russians.

Bormann, however, had no intention of dying just yet. He
and one or two others made their way out of the bunker and
attempted to penetrate the Russian lines to reach Dönitz's
headquarters. Perhaps after all he might still have some
influence.

He never got there. He was reported by a companion to have
been killed along the way.*

At Ploen, Dönitz took stock of the situation. He knew that he
must act quickly to save Germany from further destruction.
Already, on April 29, all German forces in Italy had capitulated, and on May 4, all the forces remaining in the Low

* Persistent reports keep turning up that Bormann escaped to South America by
U-boat. All accounts of the discovery of his identity there lack convincing proof. On
April 11, 1973, the West German government declared Bormann officially dead. This
declaration was based on the identification of a skeleton recently discovered in war
ruins.

Countries, Denmark, and northwest Germany yielded to Montgomery.

But the death throes of the Third Reich had to be done with all proper ceremonial.

On the evening of May 1, the Hamburg radio warned the people to stand by for an important announcement. There followed appropriate Wagnerian music and the slow movement of Bruckner's Seventh Symphony. At 10:20 P.M. came the crash and roll of military drums. Then the German people heard the voice of an announcer introducing their new Führer, Grand Admiral Karl Dönitz.

> Our Führer, Adolf Hitler, fighting to the last breath against Bolshevism, fell for Germany this afternoon in his operational headquarters in the Reich Chancellery. On April 30 the Führer appointed Grand Admiral Dönitz his successor. The Grand Admiral and successor of the Führer now speaks to the German people.

> It is my first task [proclaimed Dönitz sententiously] to save Germany from destruction by the advancing Bolshevik enemy. For this aim alone the military struggle continues. As far and as long as the achievement of this aim is impeded by the British and Americans, we shall be forced to carry on our defensive fight against them as well. Under such conditions, however, the Anglo-Americans will continue the war not for their own peoples but solely for the spreading of Bolshevism in Europe.

After repeating the Nazi lies that Germany had never sought the war, and ignoring the Nazi-Soviet pact of 1939 which had given Germany a free hand to attack Poland, the Grand Admiral concluded: "God will not forsake us after so much suffering and sacrifice."

The lies which had begun and sustained the Third Reich continued right up to the end. Dönitz, of course, knew better, and he was even then making his plans for a capitulation. It was only a question of how to do it.

Knowing full well that German atrocities in Russia might well be repaid manyfold when the Russians got their hands on the German soldiers, Dönitz was anxious to have as many units as possible surrender to Britain and America. Eisenhower saw through this scheme immediately and would have none of it. He authorized surrenders in the field but no capitulation by the Reich except to the Allies as a whole. The terms remained what they had been: Unconditional Surrender.

On the afternoon of May 6, Dönitz gave up trying to wangle an advantage where there was none to be had. He sent a delegation to Eisenhower's headquarters to arrange for the surrender on the Allied terms. The delegation was headed by Colonel General Alfred Jodl, new Chief of Staff of the Army, and included Admiral Hans Georg von Friedeburg, new head of the Navy, and Major General Wilhelm Oxenius, Jodl's aide. Eisenhower's testy Chief of Staff, "Beetle" Smith, presided for the Allies, assisted by General François Savez of the French Army and General Ivan Suslaparoff of the Russian Army.

It took hours to work out all the technical details, but the substance was never in question. The details dealt with where each German unit would lay down its arms, not whether. Finally the last signature was appended to the document at 0241, May 7.

The formal signing took place at 2330, May 8, in Berlin. Hostilities ceased at midnight. The war in Europe had lasted 5 years, 8 months, 7 days, 18 hours, and 45 minutes. The number of dead can never be counted.

Nor was the peace an easy one. Opposed ideologies and the follies of men would not allow a real peace. The hating and the dying went on.

And there was still the war to be won in the Pacific.

CHAPTER NINE

# To Tokyo Bay

*O Lord! Thou knowest how busy I must be this day:*
*If I forget Thee, do not Thou forget me.*

*Sir Jacob Astley.*
*Prayer before the Battle of Edgehill, 1642.*

Issued to Marines before Iwo Jima

"I WO, this is Nine Baker Able. We are running low on gasoline. Can you give us a bearing to Iwo?"

"Course one six seven for two eight miles. Do you prefer to ditch or try to land on the strip?"

The huge Superfort circled twice around the smoking island where men were still fighting and dying. Then its pilot, Lieutenant Raymond Malo, USAAF, spotted the short narrow runway. He set his plane down on the first few feet and stood on his brakes. Even so, the silvery bomber, just· back from Tokyo, rolled 3,000 feet before it came to a stop. Less than 500 feet of the runway remained.

That was what it was all about.

Iwo Jima, a small, volcanic island, where smouldering volcanic fires still pushed sulphur up through cracks and crannies to the surface, had nothing but geography to recommend it. It was needed as a way station for B-29s based on the Marianas in their aerial campaign against Tokyo and other targets in the Home Islands.

Iwo Jima was almost ideally suited for this purpose. Situated 625 miles north of Saipan and 660 miles south of Tokyo in the Volcano Islands, it was the only island of proper size and proper terrain to serve the purpose of a half-way house.

359

Damaged planes returning from Japan could land on Iwo Jima for repair. All could carry heavier bomb loads, for they could refuel at Iwo before returning to the Marianas. Fighter planes based on Iwo could accompany the bombers all the way to Japan and thus cut down losses over the target.

The advantages were obvious. It only remained to take it.

In October 1944, even as Allied forces were preparing to move against Leyte, the decision on the final route against Japan had been made. Admiral King, exponent of the Formosa and China route, had been convinced by the cogent arguments of Admiral Nimitz and Admiral Spruance that the smaller islands offered the better way. The first step would be to seize Iwo Jima or Chichi Jima, "up the Bonin ladder," and then move to Okinawa in the Ryukyus. After that would come the landings in Japan itself.

Iwo Jima would come first after Luzon, because it was believed to be easier. It was, but not much.

To begin the story of Iwo Jima at the beginning, it is necessary to back up in our narrative to the summer of 1944. Scarcely had the fighting died down on Saipan, Tinian, and Guam, than Seabees and Engineers were at work on airstrips, lengthening runways, building fuel-storage facilities, hangars, barracks, repair shops, and all the other installations necessary for an airbase. All of these would have been of little use but for the development of the largest bomber in the world at that time, the B-29. This plane would have the range to fly from the Marianas to Japan and back without refueling and to carry a two-ton bomb load.

The Superfortresses were twice the airplane of the famous B-17 Flying Fortress and the B-24 Liberator. They had the latest radar and automatic fire-control equipment to drive their power turrets. Carrying a crew of five officers and six enlisted men, these planes had pressurized cabins permitting them to operate at 30,000 feet.

B-29s were never used in the European war, but their long range made them ideally suited to the vast distances of the Pacific. In August 1944, Lieutenant General Millard F. Harmon became commander of Army Air Forces, Pacific Ocean Area, which included XX Air Force, B-29s operating from China, and XXI Bomber Command, B-29s flying out of the Marianas. In December, Nimitz broadened Harmon's responsibilities to include all land-based aviation in the Pacific, with the title Commander Strategic Air Force, Pacific Ocean Areas.

On October 12, 1944, while engineers on Saipan were still working on the job of lengthening Isley (formerly Aslito) Field, the first B-29 touched down and rolled to a stop. It was "Joltin' Josie, the Pacific Pioneer," piloted by Brigadier General Heywood ("Possum") Hansell, first commander of XXI Bomber Command. Just over a week later Brigadier General Emmett "Rosie" O'Donnell brought in another B-29, and the build-up was on. O'Donnell was commander of the 73rd Bombardment Wing, and he set about an intensive training program as other Superfortresses arrived. They flew practice missions against Truk and Iwo Jima, and it was an open secret that the first raid against Tokyo was set for November 17.

When that day rolled around everyone was disappointed, because heavy rains washed out the strike. It was the same the next day, and the next, and the next. It was not until November 24 that the skies cleared.

At 0615, "Dauntless Dotty," with General O'Donnell in the left-hand seat, roared down the runway and climbed slowly on course for Tokyo. Behind came 110 other B-29s, each one barely lifting before the runway ran out. Heavy loads of bombs and fuel made the climbing slow, but an unexpected tailwind brought their speed up to 445 miles per hour. Although 17 turned back with one trouble or another, the others raced on through the skies.

Over Tokyo, an undercast obscured the target, the Nakajima airplane-engine plant at Musashino, some ten miles from the Imperial Palace. The plant was not heavily damaged, but the psychological impact was severe. Over a hundred fighters rose to exact their vengeance, but only one B-29 was knocked down when a damaged Zeke rammed its tail. Another had to ditch on the way home.

Three days later the B-29s were back. This time the cloud

cover was so thick that they had to go after secondary targets. Japanese consternation grew for both emotional and practical reasons. American bombs were falling on Japanese soil; worse, they were falling near the sacred Emperor. On the practical side, Japanese economy was so shaky as a result of submarine depredations, which starved Japanese industry of supplies, that the B-29s threatened to grind things to a halt. The Japanese could not depend on cloud cover forever. Since their fighters could not reach the heights where the Superforts operated, there seemed no way to stop them. The only way was to go after the source.

Orders went out to Japanese air forces on Iwo Jima and they hit back hard. Beginning November 27, even as the second strike against Tokyo was taking off, bombers from Iwo roared in on Saipan and destroyed a B-29 and damaged eleven others. Six hours later another raid destroyed three and damaged two more. The raids were continued until January 2 and succeeded in destroying eleven Superforts and damaging six. It would have been worse had not B-24s and P-38s combined with B-29s in plastering the air installations on Iwo. The Navy helped out with several bombardments by cruisers and destroyers.

Terribly exposed to B-29 raids was the giant aircraft carrier *Shinano*. She was nearing completion in the Yokosuka Navy Yard. Sister ship originally of battleships *Musashi* and *Yamato*, she had been converted following the Battle of Midway to an aircraft carrier and, at 68,000 tons, she was the largest in the world. Every safety device had been built into her, including the latest fire-fighting equipment. She was coated with a special fire-resistant paint, and she had hundreds of watertight compartments.

Unfortunately for the Japanese, they were not yet watertight. In many compartments watertight doors had not been installed, and air tests had been made on only a few spaces. Packing glands had not been set up around cables and steam lines where they passed through bulkheads. All these things are comparatively minor tasks in the building of a ship, but they are vital to her watertight integrity.

Despite these obvious deficiencies, Commander in Chief,

Combined Fleet, decided she should be moved to safer waters. On the afternoon of November 28, she got under way with 1,900 persons aboard. They were not yet a crew, and they did not know their ship. Among them were a number of navy yard civilian workers who continued their jobs as the ship moved south out of Tokyo Bay headed for the Inland Sea where she would be safe.

A hundred miles to the south, Commander Joseph F. Enright, skipper of submarine *Archerfish*, was bored with his assignment. His boat had been given the essential job of lifeguard for B-29s which might have to ditch after a raid on Tokyo.

Then came the good news. The strike scheduled for that day had been scrubbed, and *Archerfish* was free to do a little hunting. Joe Enright decided that his best bet would be off Tokyo Bay, and he moved in that direction, patrolling leisurely on the surface, doing the routine jobs of charging batteries, refilling air tanks, dumping garbage, while keeping watchful eyes on the horizon and on the radar screens.

For an hour and a half this procedure continued, while life-giving amperes flowed into the batteries that propelled *Archerfish* under the water.

The time was 2048. Suddenly the words rang out: "Radar contact!"

There was enough moonlight for Enright to make out a long, low shape about nine miles away to the north. It appeared to be a tanker, and *Archerfish* soon was pounding along on the surface at 18 knots to deliver a torpedo attack from the starboard beam of the target.

It was a stern chase, and the target was making about the same speed as the submarine, but her zigzag course allowed *Archerfish* to gain slowly. By this time, Enright had correctly identified his target as an aircraft carrier escorted by four destroyers.

The hours passed slowly, and then the target, which was the *Shinano*, picked up speed and *Archerfish* began to fall behind. Enright ordered the last possible revolution for the screws of his boat, even at the risk of damage to his electrical system. It was no use. The *Shinano* continued to pull away. In the hope that some other submarine might pick up the chase, Enright reported to ComSubPac, Vice Admiral Charles Lockwood, at Pearl Harbor: URGENT FOR COMSUBPAC AND SUBS IN AREA X TARGET COURSE TWO SEVEN FIVE SPEED TWENTY X AM TRAILING LEFT FLANK X DO NOT EXPECT TO REACH FIRING POSITION BY DAWN X CONTINUING CHASE. He added his position.

Replied Lockwood: KEEP AFTER HIM JOE X YOUR PICTURE IS ON THE PIANO.

Enright kept after him, and about 0300 his patience was rewarded. *Shinano* changed base course again, this time almost due south, directly for the racing *Archerfish*. It was too good to be true. This time the problem was to avoid getting too close.

"Lookouts below! Clear the bridge! Dive!" ordered Enright. *Archerfish* slid beneath the waves, and the periscope rose into the skipper's hands. There were anxious moments.

"I see him," said Enright quietly. "Distance to track?"

"Five five oh yards," replied the exec, "Bobo" Bobczynski.

Much too close. The torpedoes would not have room to arm, and *Archerfish* would be almost beneath the target at the firing moment.

"Left full rudder! Left to course zero nine zero!"

That was better. Still, at her submerged speed, *Archerfish* was not opening the range fast enough. If *Shinano* continued her present course, it would have to be a "down the throat" shot with the least possible chance of hitting. If she should zigzag she would present a fine target for either bow or stern tubes depending on the direction.

*Shinano*, unconscious of what lay ahead of her, but her skipper, Captain Toshio Abe, understandably nervous in submarine waters, suddenly zigged to the left. It put the *Archerfish* in an ideal position to use her bow tubes.

"Down scope!" ordered Enright. "Escort passing overhead."

There was no need for listening gear in *Archerfish* as the crew could hear the thum - thum - thum - *thum* - *thum* - *thum* - THUM - THUM - THUM - *thum* - *thum* - *thum* - thum - thum - thum of the unsuspecting destroyer passing above.

364

Back up went the periscope. At 0317 Enright gave the order, "Fire!" At eight-second intervals, six torpedoes sprang from their tubes and raced toward the target, running "hot, straight, and normal." They were spread to hit along the entire length of the target.

After forty-seven seconds, Enright's efforts were rewarded. Two torpedoes hit near the stern, and he could see a ball of fire climbing the victim's quarter. There was no time to see any more, for the furious escorts were converging on *Archerfish*.

"Take her down!" *Archerfish* clawed for the depths. "Rig for silent running! Rig for depth charge!" The counterattack would be on them at any moment.

Four more hits were heard, and then the depth charges began to go off. It was a curiously ineffectual depth charging, and *Archerfish* was scarcely shaken.

It was far different with *Shinano*.

At first Captain Abe was not worried. His ship had been designed to survive twenty torpedoes. But that was when she was ready for sea. Her designers had not contemplated her taking any torpedo hits in her present state of watertight integrity. Captain Abe continued on course.

His inexperienced damage-control teams could make no progress against the flooding. In fact, they lost steadily. Pumps were not connected or broke down. Bucket brigades were tried, but the undisciplined crew dropped out and climbed up to the flight deck where they stood waiting for rescue.

When dawn came, *Shinano* was doomed, but Captain Abe would not admit it just yet. He could have beached her, but he kept on going, and she listed more and more.

Finally Abe yielded to the inevitable. A destroyer came alongside, and the portrait of the Emperor was reverently passed across. Then and only then Captain Abe gave permission to abandon ship.

Shortly before 1100, November 29, *Shinano* sank stern first, taking with her Captain Abe and 500 men. She had been at sea for less than twenty hours, and she had never fired a gun or launched a plane.

Fate, not content with having brought *Archerfish* and *Shinano* to their rendezvous, the following week played another dirty trick on Japan. An earthquake struck Honshu, tearing up rail lines and crippling or destroying factories needed for the war machine. As if this were not enough, the weather over Japan improved, and B-29s were able to hit the Mitsubishi Aircraft Engine Works at Nagoya so effectively that the Japanese started to move it underground.

All of these disasters made little difference to Lieutenant General Tadamichi Kuribayashi, who was responsible for the defense of Iwo Jima. He had arrived in June 1944 to prepare the defenses, and he meant to make them impregnable.

One of his staff members, Major Yoshitaka Horie was not so sanguine.

"When I saw this island from the air today," he said, "I thought the best thing to do would be to sink it to the bottom of the sea."

He had a point. The island was of little use to Japan except that it was important to keep the Americans from getting it.

Iwo Jima is a pork-chop-shaped island with its broad end toward the north. About 1,200 civilians lived there, but they were removed before the Japanese began the big build-up of defenses. Some farming had been done around the main village, Motoyama, located a little north of the center of the island. For the most part, however, Iwo Jima is an unlovely excrescence on the surface of the sea, its craggy rocks covered with soft volcanic ash and cinders so light and loose that they offered little footing. A man would sink to his knees in the stuff on the beaches.

From the sea, the island looks something like a monstrous whale with an overgrown tail. The northern—head—end is a plateau, which rises to 382 feet. Then comes the low-lying waist, and finally Mount Suribachi, an extinct volcano which rises 556 feet in the south to form the tail.

The only possible landing beaches were in the waist area, either on the east or west coast, and General Kuribayashi knew it as well as the American planners did.

366

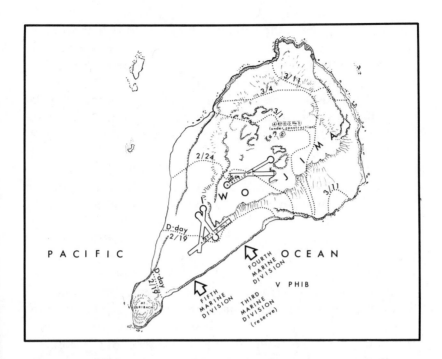

In line with the new strategy employed at Peleliu, Leyte, and Luzon, Kuribayashi did not plan to defend the beaches. He would let the Americans land and destroy them as they moved against his strongpoints. And he intended every yard to be a strongpoint. After all, the five-mile-long island had only eight square miles of area, and he had 21,000 men to use for defense.

Imagine the combined difficulties of Tarawa and Peleliu. That is what faced the American planners as they set about drawing up the operation order for Iwo Jima. Blockhouses, well camouflaged, combined with underground bunkers in overlapping fields of fire to make movements above ground as costly as possible. There was practically no natural cover on Iwo Jima, and there was no way to avoid the fire of Japanese defenders. They would have to be blasted out or burned out.

In addition to the gun emplacements—800 of them—Kuribayashi set his men to work supplementing the natural caves in Mount Suribachi and in the plateau area to the north with tunnels and underground bunkers. Each was to have a right-angle turn to prevent the entrance of shells and bullets and fire from flamethrowers. All the caves were to have several entrances, and many of them were interconnected. Everything must be nearly invisible from the air.

The Japanese suffered untold misery in digging these tunnels and artificial caves. In some places, the heat from the volcano beneath drove the temperature to 140 degrees and a man could work only ten minutes or so before being overcome by the heat and the sulphur fumes. Water was strictly rationed, for there were no springs on the island, and the porous rock absorbed rainfall before it could collect into pools. Large cisterns formed the only means of water storage, and with 21,000 men, a cup per day per man made extreme demands on the supply. Bathing had to be done in the sea, and the Japanese beloved daily hot bath was a luxury that could only be dreamed of.

Still the Japanese remained confident. Although Kuribayashi knew there was no hope once the Americans landed, in Japanese fashion he reconciled himself to death without question. "The life of your father is like a flicker of flame in the wind," he wrote his son. "It is apparent your father will have the same fate as the commanders of Saipan, Tinian, and Guam. There is no possibility of my survival."

To his troops he issued orders:

> Above all else, we shall dedicate ourselves and our entire strength to the defense of this island.
> We shall grasp grenades, charge enemy tanks and destroy them.
> We shall infiltrate into the midst of the enemy and annihilate them.
> With every salvo we will, without fail, kill the enemy.
> Each man will make it his duty to kill ten of the enemy before dying.
> Until we are destroyed to the last man, we shall harass the enemy by guerrilla tactics.

Still unaware of how warm the reception would be, American forces were closing in on Iwo Jima.

Overall command was held by Admiral Raymond A.

368

Spruance, who flew his flag in cruiser *Indianapolis*. The Joint Expeditionary Force was commanded by the veteran amphibian Vice Admiral Richmond Kelly Turner, while Commander Expeditionary Troops was the victor of the Gilberts and of Saipan, Lieutenant General Holland M. Smith. The actual assault was to be made by the V Amphibious Corps, under Major General Harry Schmidt, USMC, and it comprised the Third, Fourth, and Fifth Marine Divisions. The Third and Fourth Divisions were veterans, and the Fifth, while it had never been in combat, was formed around combat veterans. Rear Admiral Harry W. Hill commanded the Attack Force, and Rear Admiral William H. P. Blandy the Support Force. Task Force 58, now reconstituted into four groups, acted as cover, and some of its ships pitched in to help out Blandy's supporting operations.

As everyone agreed Iwo Jima would be a tough nut, one of the heaviest pre-invasion bombardments of the war was scheduled, but in the opinion of Howlin' Mad Smith the three days allotted were not enough. He asked for a full ten, which was obviously impossible without replenishing ammunition for the battleships at sea. Operations analysts figured out that after three days the law of diminishing returns would set in so long as general area fire was used, and that three days would give 90 percent of the results of the ten Smith demanded. Three days it remained, therefore, but Smith never ceased to blame the Navy for the high casualties his Marines suffered as they went ashore.

As the various forces converged on Iwo Jima, Admiral "Pete" Mitscher, once more in command of the Fast Carrier Task Force, took his ships out of Ulithi on February 10, bound for the first carrier attack on Tokyo since the Doolittle hit and run raid of 1942. This time he was going in overwhelming force. In addition to the nine large and five light carriers in the four groups of Task Force 58, he had the large carriers *Enterprise* and *Saratoga* as the nucleus of a fifth group, which had the responsibility for night-fighter operations.

There was more than interservice rivalry in this raid on Tokyo. If the Japanese were free from disturbance, their aircraft could play hob with the invasion force at Iwo Jima.

Since a powerful counterattack was only to be expected, the fighter complement of the carriers was strengthened at the expense of dive bombers and torpedo planes. After refueling on February 13 and topping off destroyers on the morning of the 15th, the task force began a high-speed run-in that evening to reach launching position at dawn February 16, 125 miles southeast of Tokyo and only 60 miles from the Honshu coast. Except for a few submarines, this was the closest to Japan any American ship had been since the outbreak of war.

As a result of thick weather, Task Force 58 was undetected, and the Japanese had no warning until the planes approached their coast. About a hundred fighters rose to intercept, and forty or so were shot down. Most of the rest showed an un-Japanese reluctance to engage in combat, and the Americans were able to go about their business of strafing and bombing. One aircraft plant was almost completely destroyed in this and the subsequent raid on February 25.

By late afternoon planes were recovered and TG 58.5, the night operations group, launched night-fighters to cover Japanese airfields throughout the night.

February 17 dawned with the weather deteriorating. It was cold on the exposed flight decks, even with foul-weather gear, for sailors who had spent the past year in the tropics. Still the planes went off and continued to hit at targets around Tokyo. Instead of improving, the weather got worse, and at 1115 Mitscher decided to call it a day. After recovering aircraft, Task Force 58 set a southerly course to help out at Iwo Jima.

This raid showed the pass to which the warlords had led Japan. Extensive damage was done to factories, and several ships were sunk in Tokyo Bay, including a 10,500-ton *Maru*. Approximately 340 planes were shot out of the air and another 190 destroyed on the ground for an American loss of 60 in combat and 28 more operationally.

Not one Japanese plane came within forty miles of Task Force 58.

Off Iwo Jima the pre-invasion bombardment had already started. Six battleships, including *Nevada, Texas,* and *Arkansas,* which had participated in the landings at Normandy and in Southern France, and four heavy cruisers began firing their big guns at the shore on February 16, supported by light cruiser *Vicksburg* and destroyers and kept it up all day. The result: "Little damage was apparent."

The next day, things went better, but the enemy responded, and the heavy cruiser *Pensacola* was hit six times and had to retire temporarily to fight fires and tend her wounded and dead. They broke off shooting at 1025 to allow UDT (Underwater Demolition Team) operations to proceed. While the frogmen took to the water, the LCI(G) flotilla, which was supposed to give protective fire, caught it from Kuribayashi's guns. Twelve LCI(G)s were engaged in these activities, and all twelve were hit, and one was sunk. *Nevada* conveniently disregarded the order to withdraw and worked over the offending battery for two hours. All but one of the frogmen were recovered, but the loss among LCI(G) crews was heavy.

It was during this minor episode before the landing that Kuribayashi made his first mistake. Convinced that the UDT operations were the actual assault, he ordered two well-concealed batteries which were in position to enfilade the landing beaches to open up. No one on the Allied side suspected their existence, for they had not shown up on aerial photographs, nor had they been spotted from the sea.

They quickly became high-priority targets in the hastily revised bombardment plan for February 18.

When the UDT men re-embarked and the supporting ships turned away, Kuribayashi was elated. He believed he had repulsed the landing attempt. He joyfully sent the news to Admiral Toyoda in Tokyo, who replied with hearty congratulations.

DESPITE VERY POWERFUL ENEMY BOMBINGS AND SHELLINGS, YOUR UNIT AT IWO COOLLY JUDGED THE ENEMY INTENTIONS AND FOILED THE FIRST LANDING ATTEMPT AND SERENELY AWAITS THE NEXT ONE, DETERMINED TO HOLD IWO AT ANY COST. I AM GREATLY ELATED TO KNOW THAT, AND

I WISH YOU TO CONTINUE TO MAINTAIN HIGH MORALE AND REPULSE THE ENEMY, NO MATTER HOW INTENSE HIS ATTACKS, AND SAFEGUARD THE OUTER DEFENSES OF OUR HOMELAND.

Now that the batteries enfilading the beach were revealed, the bombardment forces really went to work on them on the 18th. Blockhouses and pillboxes were literally blasted out of the ground. Any suspicious hummock in the ground was given a pasting in case it concealed a pillbox or a burrow. Most of them did, and a good many were eliminated. But plenty remained.

Monday, February 19, dawned fair and clear off Iwo Jima, with a calm sea that caused no problems for the landing craft, amphtracs, and other amphibians which would soon be making their way toward the beaches on the southeastern coast of the island, between Mount Suribachi and an inlet known as East Boat Basin.

The beautiful day, with its fleecy white clouds and light northerly breeze, was soon turned to a horror with the black smoke and pungent smell of cordite that resulted from the heaviest pre-invasion bombardment of World War II. Task Force 58 contributed battleships *North Carolina* and *Washington* and three cruisers to help out the bombardment force. Tons of explosive shells crashed ashore while the Japanese in their bunkers and pillboxes covered their ears to keep out the noise and concussion. But most of the garrison remained secure deep underground in their caves and dugout shelters.

At 0645, Admiral Turner gave the order, "Land the Landing Force," and ships, boats, and men began to move to their assigned stations. LSTs opened their ramps and the LVTs swarmed out loaded with Marines, "like all the cats in the world having kittens," as novelist-turned-correspondent John P. Marquand remarked.

At 0830 the first wave left the line of departure, preceded by a rolling barrage which moved inland as the men hit the beach. Exactly on time, at 0900, the first Marines hit the beaches and began to move inland.

Up to that point everything went like clockwork. Then the trouble began.

The landing was made on a two-division front, with the Fifth on the left and the Fourth on the right. The Third Division formed the floating reserve. The original plan had called for the Third to be held in reserve at Guam to be called up if needed, but Howlin' Mad Smith had a hunch that they would be needed sooner than they could get there from Guam. He was right.

Although the Japanese did not contest the landing, the troubles came from the soft volcanic ash which mired vehicles and slowed the run of a man to a walk. Behind the beaches was a fifteen-foot-high terrace of the same sort of ash mixture. The terrace could not be climbed by man or vehicle, for it offered no footing. In some places there were holes blasted through by shell bursts. A call went out for Marston mats, steel lattice-work strips, which would give the vehicles traction. They were slow in coming and when they arrived they were quickly chewed up by the caterpillar treads of tanks and other tracked vehicles.

While the Marines were contending with these difficulties, the enemy opened up with a withering fire and men began to die. The Japanese emerged from their shelters and manned their pillboxes and protected positions, waiting for a target to come within the field of fire commanded by the narrow slits designed to be invisible and to keep out grenades and shells. The preliminary bombardment had not knocked these out, nor could it except by a direct hit. There were too many of them, and they were manned by fanatics.

The advance of the Marines was slowed to a crawl, and men began to pile up on the narrow beaches, so closely packed that a shell or a bullet could scarcely fail to find a target.

The Fourth Marine Division on the right had an especially rough time. Its job was to hold the pivot with one regiment and advance inland with the others in conjunction with the Twenty-Seventh Regiment of the Fifth Marine Division. On the left of the Twenty-Seventh, the Twenty-Eighth had the job of driving the 700 yards straight across the island to isolate Mount Suribachi and secure the left flank for the advance northward.

It was slow, rough going, and the hideous sounds of guns, exploding shells, the crack of rifle fire, and the thud of a bullet in a buddy's body made the place "like Hell with the fire out," as one correspondent put it. Shortly before noon the Twenty-Eighth Marines had reached the runway of the southernmost of the airfields, halfway across the island. By 1500 they had reached the western cliff and isolated the southern end of the island.

Despite the intense enemy fire, 30,000 troops were landed on D-Day at a cost of 519 killed or missing and 1,901 wounded. The Marines had reached less than half their D-Day objectives, but they were ashore and intended to remain there.

"Whether the dead were Japs or Americans," wrote correspondent Robert Sherrod, as he surveyed the scene on D+1-Day, "they had died with the greatest possible violence. Nowhere in the Pacific war had I seen such badly mangled bodies. Many were cut squarely in half. Legs and arms lay 50 feet away from any body. I saw a string of guts 15 feet long. Only legs were easy to identify; they were Japanese if wrapped in khaki puttees, American if covered by canvas leggings. The smell of burning flesh was heavy."

No one quit. There were no spectacular charges to raise the morale of the men and bring quick success. It was a case of yard-by-yard, even foot-by-foot, advance, digging out pillboxes and blasting them with grenades or flamethrowers. Battalions were reduced to company strength and companies to platoon size.

Iwo would have been worse if it had not been for the constant support of ships' guns and carrier aircraft which were both controlled by the men ashore. A unit in trouble could call down a barrage from a ship or a bombing run from a carrier plane to help eliminate one more of the many obstacles that still lay ahead.

By the third day, the slash across the southern sector of the island had widened, and the front established facing both north and south. The Twenty-Eighth Marines, under command of Colonel Harry B. Liversedge (Harry the Horse), faced the slopes and caves of Mount Suribachi, which had been given the appropriate code name of "Hot Rock."

Unfortunately for unloading supplies, the weather turned bad on D+1, and the ugly surf, combining with a steep-to gradient, made it all but impossible to hold landing craft and even landing ships in place. The congestion on the beach, already serious, became near chaos with the hulks of wrecked boats and vehicles cluttering up the area. Bulldozer operators had to be ruthless in their efforts to clear the beaches so the men in combat could be kept supplied with ammunition, food, and water.

One bulldozer operator sat in his seat with the engine running. The way ahead had to be cleared, but directly before him was a pile of American bodies, Marines, and a few Seabees. He hesitated, but it had to be done. He let in the clutch and closed his eyes. The dozer lurched forward and drove ahead to complete its job. Behind it left a grisly purple and red mess of crushed bodies.

The supplies had to be kept coming.

That evening, the Japanese "Home and Empire" radio broadcast to its people showed real irritation with Kelly Turner.

This man Turner [said the Japanese announcer] is called and known as the "Alligator" in the American Navy. He is associated with this name because his work is very similar to that of an alligator, which lives both on land and in the water. Also, the true nature of an alligator is that once he bites into something he will not let go. Turner's nature is also like this. . . .

This man Turner, who has been responsible for the death of so many of our precious men, shall not return home alive—he must not, and will not. This is one of the many things we can do to rest at ease the many souls of those who have paid the supreme sacrifice.

One need scarcely add that Kelly Turner was never known as "Alligator" in the American Navy. The Japanese must have got the idea from the shoulder patch of Fifth Phib Corps.

On the afternoon of February 21, the Kamikazes came back.

Their first victim was the veteran carrier *Saratoga*, which was hit two glancing blows and three direct smashes and a bomb in the space of three minutes. Although her power plant was still in good condition, she could not recover planes, and the "chickens" she had in the air had to go to other carriers. Her crew was making good progress in controlling the damage, when another plane came over and dropped a bomb and then crashed off the flight deck and on overboard. Even then, she was in reasonable condition, and a confused CVE pilot set his plane on her flight deck while they still fought fires forward. As he climbed from his cockpit he remarked, "Gee, I'm glad I'm not on that old Sara. All Hell's broken out there!"

Replied a plane pusher: "Take a good look around, brother. This *is* Hell!"

In spite of everything, *Saratoga* was out of the fight. She left for Eniwetok and then went on to the west coast of the United States for repairs. She was lost for three months.

Two other carriers caught it that night, both CVEs. *Bismarck Sea* exploded when gasoline fires got out of hand, and she had to be adandoned with the loss of 218 officers and men. *Lunga Point* was damaged by a Kamikaze which dived into her after dropping a torpedo. Only slight damage resulted, and the torpedo missed. New cargo ship *Keokuk* and *LST-477* were both victims of Kamikaze attacks, but both remained afloat and continued to carry out their duties.

During the night, the ships of Task Force 58 were heckled by Japanese planes, but no more serious attacks developed until TF 58 departed on the 23rd for another raid on Tokyo.

Colonel Liversedge by this time had completely isolated Mount Suribachi and was blasting and burning Japanese out of the caves that defended the base and the slopes. Looking up, he could see Japanese leaping from cliffs to their deaths on the rocks below. Colonel Kanehiko Atsuji, commanding the Japanese on Suribachi, had requested permission from Kuribayashi to lead his men in a Banzai charge. Kuribayashi curtly refused. He did not intend to waste his men in futile charges. Let the Americans come to the Japanese in their well-placed defenses. Let the Americans be exposed to withering fire while the Japanese were protected.

The suicides were Atsuji's response to Kuribayashi.

An American patrol reached the top. It spread out and found nothing.

Suribachi had been taken.

Lieutenant Harold Schrier had brought an American flag with him, and somewhere in the rubble a Marine found a length of pipe. They fastened the flag to it and jammed the base of the pipe in between rocks. Old Glory fluttered in the breeze.

From the base of Suribachi, Marines could scarcely see the 28-by-54-inch flag, so one of them went aboard an LST and borrowed a battle ensign measuring 56 by 96 inches and took it up to the top. It was this second flag-raising that resulted in one of the most dramatic photographs of the war.

Photographer Joseph Rosenthal saw the new flag going up the slopes and followed with his camera. He almost missed his opportunity, for he was trying to pile some rocks up to stand on for a better camera angle when the flag went up. Hurriedly and off balance, Rosenthal snapped the picture.

It was a terrible picture from a news point of view. It contained six figures, yet not one could be identified. But it won him a Pulitzer Prize. The composition is magnificent, and the six figures blend into a picture of common purpose symbolic of the Marine Corps and of Americans when aroused.

The picture was printed and reprinted. It has appeared in newspapers, magazines, and books, and it was used for a commemorative stamp, and was the model for the bronze monument to the Marine Corps made by Felix de Welden and installed near Arlington National Cemetery.

Secretary of the Navy James Forrestal, who observed the flag-raising, turned to Holland Smith and said, "Holland, the raising of that flag on Suribachi means a Marine Corps for the next five hundred years."

What of the men who raised the flag on Suribachi? They were Private First Class Ira Hayes, a Pima Indian from Arizona; Private First Class Franklin Sousley of Kentucky; Sergeant Michael Strank from Johnstown, Pennsylvania; Pharmacist's Mate Second Class John H. Bradley of Antigo, Wisconsin; Private First Class René A. Gagnon of Manchester, New

Hampshire; and Corporal Harlon H. Block of Weslaco, Texas.

Was it only by chance that they represented the north, the south, the east, the midwest, and the west as well as the Marine Corps and the Navy?

In a lighter vein, a sign soon appeared near the flag.

```
SURIBACHI HEIGHTS REALTY COMPANY
           OCEAN VIEW
          COOL BREEZES
      FREE FIREWORKS NIGHTLY!
```

Now it only remained to clean up the rest of the island. *Only* . . .

The fighting went on and on. The Third Marine Division was committed except for one reserve regiment, and the three divisions started to grind out the territory northward. The Fourth Division was on the right, the Third in the Center, and the Fifth on the west coast.

If any such distinctions can be made for Iwo Jima, it was on the Third that the toughest fighting fell, for they had to take the higher ground in order to protect the flanks of the others advancing along the coasts. It was a slow, bitter struggle, for the Japanese pillboxes and bunkers seemed unending. On March 1, No. 2 airfield and the village of Motoyama fell, but things got no easier.

The key to Kuribayashi's defense was a sector of the island known to the Marines as "the Meatgrinder." It ground meat, all right—theirs. It consisted of an amphitheater commanded on two sides by a hill known as Turkey Knob and another called simply Hill 382. From caves on the slopes of these hills the Japanese crisscrossed the Amphitheater with guns of many calibers. In the Amphitheater were tanks buried up to their turrets, whose guns could be trained to command all natural approaches to the area. Everything was mutually supporting, and everything was deadly.

378

The Marines made several tries to take Hill 382 and Turkey Knob, but when they got to the top, they were sorry for it, for they came under intense fire from all sides, even from the rear, for Japanese in concealed pillboxes would allow the Americans to pass them and then open fire just when the Marines thought success was theirs.

The fighting in this area went on for a full week, from February 25 to March 3. Then the Japanese began to weaken. Naval gunfire, bombs, napalm, and the rugged determination of the Marines won out. Caves were sealed with explosives or their occupants broiled to crisps with tank-mounted flame throwers. Bulldozers and tankdozers dug up pillboxes and piled rock and rubble over the wreckage.

The next major barrier was Hill 362, and this was taken by means of a night attack in the early morning hours of March 7. A tragic mistake enabled the Japanese to hold out longer than they should have been able to do, for in the confusion of darkness, the Marines captured the wrong hill. Before the mistake could be rectified, the Japanese had figured out the real direction of the attack and heavily reinforced Hill 362. It took a full day of hard fighting to win that important height.

Kuribayashi now made his second mistake. He sent his troops out in a counterattack. It began just before midnight on March 8. The Marines were glad to see it, for it made the Japanese easy to get at. The screaming Japanese hurled themselves against heavy artillery and rifle and machine-gun fire and were wiped out to a man.

The next day, the advance continued, and a patrol spearheading the Third Division punched its way through to the sea on the north coast. To the amazement of the Japanese in caves out of range of the patrol, the Marines proceeded to go swimming.

"We wanted to wash off the Jap dirt," explained one of them. They filled a canteen with sea water and sent it to Major General Graves Erskine, commanding the Third Division, as a sign of the breakthrough. It was labeled, "For inspection, not consumption."

Now the Japanese were split in two. One force was hemmed in by the Fourth Division on the east coast, and another was contained in the northwest in the region of Kitano Point.

The Marines did not make the mistake of relaxing the pressure. They smashed as hard as ever at the two enclaves, and these were gradually wiped out. At 1800, March 16, Holland Smith declared that Iwo Jima was secured, and ten days later pronounced "operation completed." The Army garrison forces had started to come ashore to relieve the battered Marines.

On the morning of March 27, General Kuribayashi emerged from the cave where he had taken his final refuge, faced the Imperial Palace 660 miles to the north, bowed three times, and then knelt and opened his abdomen with a knife slash. A staff officer beheaded him with a sword.

The battle for Iwo Jima was over.

It was the toughest fight in Marine Corps history. A full 30 percent of the landing force were casualties, including dead, wounded, and missing. Some regiments had casualty rates as high as 75 percent. In all 4,554 Marines and 363 Navy men lost their lives. Of the 21,000 Japanese, over 18,000 were killed, and the rest, except for a handful of prisoners, huddled in caves until the end of the war. After Japan's capitulation only a few score were rounded up.

"This," said Captain Robert C. Johnson, commander of the Seabees, "is the most expensive piece of real estate the United States has ever purchased. We paid 550 lives and 2,500 wounded for every square mile of this rock. Pretty expensive."

Was it worth it?

Ask the B-29 crews, adding up to 27,000 men, who landed on Iwo Jima during the rest of the war. Not all of them would have been lost had Iwo not been in American hands, but many would. One B-29, known as the "Oily Bird," came in so many times after being shot up over Tokyo that ground crews depended on her arrival.

Add to this total saved the imponderable number who might have been shot down over Japan had it not been for the protection of Iwo Jima based fighters.

There can be but one conclusion. Iwo Jima was worth the

cost to the winning of the war. Its possession hastened the Japanese surrender, and it saved many more lives than were paid to take it. And it added another proud tradition to Marine Corps history.

Last stops on the road to Japan for the Allies were in the chain of islands known variously as the Ryukyus or the Nansei Shoto. Largest and most important in the chain is Okinawa, located 360 miles from China, 340 from Formosa, and an equal distance from the nearest point of Kyushu, southernmost of the four main Japanese Home Islands.

In 1853, Commodore Matthew C. Perry raised the first American flag to fly over Okinawa when he forced the king to sign a treaty respecting the rights of American sailors in Okinawan ports. It would be ninety-two years before another American flag was raised near the same spot, following the bloodiest fighting in the Pacific war.

By the spring of 1945, it was clear by any objective standard that Japan had lost the war. Most of her navy was at the bottom of the sea. Her merchant shipping had been reduced by submarine and aircraft attacks from 10 million tons to 1 million tons, and her access to the Resources Area was barred by the Allied capture of the Philippines. She had plenty of men still under arms, but large numbers were in the by-passed areas where they were useless to the Empire and faced death from starvation or annihilation at the hands of merciless guerrillas who had many a score to settle for acts of brutality—murder, rape, and torture—the Japanese had committed when things were going their way.

Japan was defeated, but mere militarists would not admit it. In order to "save face" for the generals and admirals in Tokyo, the war dragged on nearly six months more, and thousands on both sides were to die. The elemental force of the universe would be released over Hiroshima and Nagasaki before the warlords would accept defeat.

Since Japan stubbornly continued the fight, Allied planners went on with preparations for her destruction. First on the schedule would be Okinawa and a few surrounding islands with

L-Day set for April 1, 1945. This would be followed, on November 1, by Operation Olympic, an invasion of Kyushu, followed by Operation Coronet in March 1946, a landing on Honshu in the Tokyo area. No one thought any of these operations would be easy. Japan had over a million men under arms in the Home Islands, and they would be fanatical in defending their own soil. Kamikazes, already a major threat in the Philippines, could be depended on to appear in ever larger numbers as hostile forces approached Nippon.

Grimly the Allies set about the business of beginning the campaign that need not have happened.

The team of Spruance, Turner, and Mitscher was set to work once again. Their job was to land the U.S. Tenth Army on Okinawa and keep it there. Commanding the ground forces was Lieutenant General Simon Bolivar Buckner, son and namesake of the hero of the Confederacy. Tenth Army comprised the III Amphibious Corps under Marine Major General Roy S. Geiger, which included the First, Second, and Sixth Marine Divisions, and the XXIV Army Corps under Major General John R. Hodge, with the Seventh, Twenty-Seventh, Seventy-Seventh, and Ninety-Sixth Divisions. A fifth infantry division, the Eighty-First, was in reserve at New Caledonia.

In preparation for the landing, Task Force 58 sortied from Ulithi on March 14 to knock out air strength on Kyushu. At the dawn strike on March 18, opposition was light because most of the Japanese planes were looking for the carriers, so the American pilots expended their bombs on hangars, barracks, and machine shops. The Japanese pilots had better luck and made bomb hits on *Enterprise* and *Yorktown* and damaged *Intrepid* when a Kamikaze near-missed.

The next day the Japanese were back just after sunrise, and a bomb hit on *Wasp* penetrated through the hangar deck into a galley, causing heavy loss of life.

Much more serious, though, was the attack at the same time on *Franklin*, flagship of Rear Admiral R. E. Davison's TG 58.2. At 0708, a plane came in low over the water, rose swiftly and dropped two bombs which exploded on and above the hangar deck just as the carrier was most vulnerable. She was launching planes above as she was refueling and rearming other aircraft on her hangar deck. Normally the fueling lines on a carrier are filled with carbon dioxide to reduce the danger of fire, but at the moment of the bomb hits, raw gasoline under pressure was in the pipes and hoses, and the results were disastrous. The after elevator was blown up and to one side, and the ship was swallowed up by flame and smoke.

As Captain Leslie H. Gehres swung his ship to port to bring the wind on the starboard beam, ready-service ammunition in the gun mounts began to go off, and shells began shooting in all directions. Tiny Tim rockets whooshed down the flight deck or climbed crazily up into the sky before tumbling into the sea.

No one at first thought *Franklin* could be saved. Admiral Davison ordered light cruiser *Santa Fe* to come alongside to assist fighting the flames. Destroyer *Miller* transferred the admiral and his staff to the *Hancock*, and as he left Davison advised Captain Gehres to order, "Prepare to Abandon Ship."

As soon as he could regain internal communication, Gehres ordered everyone except key damage-control personnel to abandon ship. Many jumped overboard and were picked up by destroyers.

In the engine spaces, the heat became so intense that they had to be evacuated, and the ship drifted to a stop about 1000. By this time, fire fighters were beginning to get the flames under control, and prospects improved that the ship might be saved.

The question now became, should she be saved? At that time TF 58 was less than a hundred miles from the coast of Japan, and if *Franklin* could not steam, she would have to be towed. That would reduce the speed of advance of the entire task force to 4 to 6 knots, the speed of the tow, for the entire air strength of all carriers would be needed to protect her. It was a hard decision, but the tradition of Lawrence was still strong in the United States Navy.

Heavy cruiser *Pittsburgh* passed a towline and gradually built up speed to 6 knots. *Franklin*'s engineers worked throughout the night and gradually got some semblance of order in the engine spaces. At 1100 the next day, she could make 15 knots and a little later cast off the tow. She survived and made her

383

way to Brooklyn Navy Yard for repair. No ship had ever taken such punishment and survived. *Lexington* at Coral Sea and *Yorktown* at Midway had been lost after far less damage. The difference was in the damage control and the Navy's fire-fighting schools which all hands on every fighting ship had attended.

As expected, the Japanese made every effort to finish *Franklin* off on March 20. They were unsuccessful, but destroyer *Owen* was near-missed by a Kamikaze and destroyer *Halsey Powell* was crashed by another after he had failed to hit carrier *Hancock*. *Enterprise* was slightly damaged by "friendly" antiaircraft fire.

The following day the Japanese brought out a new weapon, a flying bomb employing a rocket engine and a human pilot. It was carried to the scene by a twin-engine bomber (Betty), slung beneath the fuselage and connected with an umbilical cord for power and communications. Once released, its speed of 600 miles an hour made it practically impossible to shoot down with the antiaircraft weapons of the time. The Japanese poetically called this weapon *Oka* ("cherry blossom"). Americans, less poetically, called it *Baka* ("stupid").

*Baka*'s debut was a flop from the Japanese point of view. It so burdened the Bettys that they were all shot down before they could release any of their suicide rockets.

On this raid, Task Force 58 claimed to have destroyed 528 Japanese planes in the air and on the ground, and the Japanese admitted that their losses were "staggering." In any case, these strikes prevented heavy air interference with the invasion of Okinawa when it came off a few days later.

The cost to the United States was heavy. In addition to the 724 men killed on the *Franklin*, another 118 died as a result of the attacks on *Yorktown*, *Enterprise*, and *Halsey Powell*. Still that was not as bad as it might have been. The Japanese claimed that they had sunk 5 carriers, 2 battleships, and 3 cruisers. Once again they seem to have believed their own propaganda.

As March came to a close that spring, over 1,400 ships were approaching Okinawa. Among them was a group of ships of the

Royal Navy, which had not had units in the Pacific since the disasters to *Prince of Wales* and *Repulse* in December 1941.

Winston Churchill had been eager to have Royal Navy ships serve in the Pacific alongside American ones for a very long time, and in the summer of 1944, with the invasion of Europe successfully launched, and the German surface navy reduced to a negligible threat, he urged Roosevelt to accept a British carrier force. Admiral King, suspicious of the determination of the Royal Navy ever since the PQ-17 disaster,* wanted no part of Churchill's offer. His excuse was that their supply needs would put an intolerable strain on the American logistic system. When the Royal Navy agreed to provide its own logistic support, King grudgingly acceded to British ships entering *his* ocean.

Commander in Chief of the British fleet in the Pacific was Admiral Sir Bruce Fraser, with headquarters in Sydney. The carrier task force which would operate alongside Mitscher's Task Force 58 was under Vice Admiral Sir H. Bernard Rawlings, while the carriers *Indomitable*, *Victorious*, *Illustrious*, and *Indefatigable* were commanded by Rear Admiral Sir Philip Vian. These carriers, protected by battleships *King George V* and *Howe* and five cruisers and fifteen destroyers, made the equivalent of a fifth task group for Task Force 58, and they operated in cooperation with the Americans by taking over responsibility for the southern Ryukyus during much of the Okinawa operation. All in all, it was a very friendly and valuable arrangement once it got beyond the surly acceptance of "Ernie" King.

The first objective of the Okinawa operation was an anchorage known as Kerama Retto, which is formed by a group of irregular, mountainous islands about fifteen miles west of Naha on Okinawa. The islands could not support airstrips, but they sheltered a roadstead which could accommodate up to seventy-

---

* PQ-17, a North Russian convoy, lost 22 out of 34 ships in July, 1942, after the Admiralty ordered its escorting warships turned back because of a report that the *Tirpitz* was at sea. An American battleship and a heavy cruiser were in the covering force, and King strongly disagreed with the decision to turn back. See the author's *1942: The Year That Doomed the Axis* (New York: David McKay Company, Inc., 1967), pp. 254–58.

five large ships with good holding ground in 20- to 35-fathom depths. Operations for seizure began on Palm Sunday, March 25, with preliminary bombardments. The landings were to take place the next day. By March 28 the operation was completed, although some 300 Japanese holed up in the hills until the end of the war.

A grim taste of things to come was the unsuccessful attack of nine Kamikazes on the afternoon of March 26. The next morning the attacks continued, and destroyers *Gilmer* and *Kimberly* were both damaged. A suicide boat attack on March 28 was completely ineffective.

Now the stage was set for the last large amphibious assault of the war.

The assault took place along the Hagushi Beaches in the southern third of the island along the western shore. This was the obvious area, for the beach conditions were good and just inland were Yontan and Kadena Airfields, which Turner desired to exploit as soon as possible for air support. The Marine III Amphibious Corps landed two divisions abreast on the northern side of the Bishi River, and the Army's XXIV Corps also landed two divisions abreast on the south side.

For the men going ashore, it was a strange way to spend Easter, that April 1. Yet all seemed peaceful. Following the heavy and unnecessary bombardment, they went ashore with practically no opposition. It was technically the smoothest amphibious operation of the war.

There was practically no sign of enemy opposition. The men had been briefed that there were 60,000 fanatical Japanese on the island. Where had they all gone? Were the Japanese sucking them into a trap? By noon, Kadena and Yontan Airfields had fallen and they weren't supposed to be taken until L-plus-3 Day!

The Japanese were there, but they were waiting for the Americans to come to them. Entrenched in their pillboxes, dugouts, and bunkers, they waited. There were about 77,000 of them organized into the Thirty-Second Army under Lieutenant General Mitsuru Ushijima. Like his predecessors on Leyte, Luzon, and Iwo Jima, he had labored to prepare defenses intended to stop the invader cold. Although he had light forces in the north and on the Motobu Peninsula, Ushijima intended to make his main stand in a defense barrier extending across the island in the Shuri area where Commodore Perry had first raised the American flag.

North of the Bishi River, the Marines pivoted left and advanced rapidly until they hit the Motobu Peninsula. Then the going began to get rough. But it was not as rough as what the Army was encountering in the south. By April 5, XXIV Corps, meeting ever increasing enemy resistance, had reached the Shuri Line, and there they would stay for the next two weeks. It was just like Iwo Jima, and there were a lot more defenses and a lot more Japanese to overcome.

In order to give early warning of approaching Japanese aircraft, which were already beginning to come at ships either in conventional or Kamikaze attacks, Turner established radar picket stations all around the island of Okinawa at distances of 35 to 95 miles. Not all were covered at all times, but those that were usually had a destroyer and two LCSs, a new kind of landing craft which bristled with 20- and 40-mm. guns. These radar pickets proved to be a good idea in protecting ships at Okinawa, but they paid a terrible price.

A part of the defense of Okinawa rested on the cooperation of Japanese air power with the defenders at the Shuri Line. Although the Kamikaze attacks had not repulsed the Americans in the Philippines, they had exacted a ghastly cost, and more, better-coordinated attacks might just do the trick at Okinawa and turn the tide of war. This plan was quickly approved and given the name Ten-Go. It called for massed Kamikaze raids, escorted by fighters to make sure that they got through to their targets.

The first phase of Ten-Go took place on April 6 and 7. It included 355 Kamikazes protected by 344 other planes. The Japanese called these massed raids *Kikusui*, "floating chrysanthemums." The Americans had no words for them other than, "Geez! Look at them stupid bastards come!"

Never have small ships taken such a pounding as did the destroyers and LCSs at the radar picket stations. The first Kikusui attack heavily damaged destroyers *Leutze* and *Newcomb* for openers. Then they really got going.

Destroyer *Bush*, on radar picket station No. 1 north of Ie Shima, had a fairly quiet time of it until about 1500 on the afternoon of April 6. Then a large group of planes, estimated as between forty and fifty showed up and began orbiting overhead. As they attacked in groups of three or four, *Bush* shot down two and drove off another pair before a fifth crashed her between the stacks and exploded in the forward engine room. The ship went dead in the water and developed a 10° list, but prompt damage control improved the situation, and a CAP held the Japanese off for the time being.

Destroyer *Colhoun* on radar picket station No. 2 poured on

388

the knots to come to the aid of her sister. An augmented CAP arrived, and a lively mêlée developed in the skies above. *Colhoun* arrived on the scene of *Bush*'s agony, but before she could give assistance, another batch of Japanese planes showed up. With the aid of *LCS-64* nearby, *Colhoun* joined in the effort to shoot down the Hell Birds. As the first fell, *Colhoun*'s skipper remarked, "That's one down, eleven to go." Two more were quickly downed before a fourth slammed into *Colhoun*'s main deck. Its bomb exploded in the after fire room, but quick work by the engineers kept steam for 15 knots available.

*Bush* was by no means out of the fight. Although her guns had to be trained and fired in local control, she shot down a Val that was trying to crash into *Colhoun*. Unfortunately another plane hit *Colhoun* a few seconds later, breaking her keel and leaving her dead in the water.

There was no letup. Both *Colhoun* and *Bush* were hit again in the next few minutes, but they stayed afloat, even though *Colhoun* took a fourth Kamikaze about 1800. Other ships were standing by, and there was some hope of saving both destroyers.

*Bush* was holding together only by her keel, and the bow and stern sections twisted crazily in the swells. At about 1830 a "ninth wave" * caught her and the strain was too great for the tortured keel. *Bush* jackknifed and slipped under.

It soon became apparent that *Colhoun* could not be saved. Her pumps had given out and her portable fire-fighting equipment was exhausted. No ship nearby could help with the pumping, so she was abandoned and sunk by gunfire from destroyer *Cassin Young*.

The ordeals of these destroyers were typical of life and death off Okinawa on the radar picket stations. This first day of Operation Ten-Go had cost the Kamikazes 355 planes plus a large number of escorting aircraft shot down. But they still had plenty more.

The first Kikusui cost the Americans two destroyers, a

---

* An old superstition holds that every ninth wave is considerably larger than the others.

389

destroyer transport, an LST, and two ammunition ships sunk, eight destroyer types, a DE, and a minelayer badly damaged.

This was only the beginning. In addition to the organized Kikusui attacks encompassing large numbers of Kamikazes, individual efforts of one to twenty planes occurred daily. There were ten Kikusui attacks in all and hundreds of individual or small group ones. When it was all over 32 naval ships and craft had been sunk, almost all by Kamikaze attack, and 368 damaged, at a cost of more than 4,900 killed and 4,800 wounded.

But the fleet stayed.

The story of one ship must be told. It is worse than most, but in a way typical of the destroyers on radar picket stations.

On April 16, U.S.S. *Laffey* was manning radar picket station No. 1, where *Bush* had been on her last day. Overhead, the CAP was just being relieved when fifty Japanese planes appeared. The fighter director officer in *Laffey*'s Combat Information Center was busy vectoring the CAP aircraft, but the situation soon got out of hand. In an hour and seventeen minutes she was subjected to no fewer than twenty-two separate attacks, as the Japanese pilots ignored *LCS-51* on her port quarter to concentrate on the intrepid destroyer. A reconstructed log account can tell the story.

0830 Val splashed by gunfire on starboard bow, range 9,000 yards.

0830 Val splashed by gunfire on starboard bow, range 3,000 yards.

0830 Val splashed by gunfire astern, range 3,000 yards.

0830 Val splashed off port quarter by gunfire from *LCS-51*.

0835 Judy splashed by gunfire off starboard beam, close aboard.

0835 Judy splashed by gunfire off port beam, close aboard.

0839 Val glanced off stern hatch and splashed off starboard quarter.

0843 Unknown type splashed off starboard beam by gunfire.

0845 Judy crashed 20-mm. gunmount, port side, amidships.

0847 Val crashed No. 3 5-inch mount.
0847 Unknown type crashed No. 3 5-inch mount.
0847 Unknown type crashed No. 3 5-inch mount.
0848 Val made bomb hit aft, jamming rudder. Plane splashed on starboard beam.
0849 Unknown type on port beam crashed after deck house.
0850 Unknown type on port quarter crashed after deck house.
  ?  Oscar on port bow pursued by Corsair. Oscar clipped mast and splashed. Corsair pilot bailed out.
  ?  Judy approaching from port bow made bomb hit on No. 2 5-inch mount, splashed close aboard.
  ?  Judy splashed close aboard starboard quarter.
  ?  Oscar splashed by gunfire starboard beam, range 500 yards.
  ?  Val splashed by gunfire dead ahead, range 600 yards.
  ?  Val approaching from astern made bomb hit after deck house, clipped mast, and splashed ahead.
  ?  Val on starboard bow splashed after making bomb hit on 20-mm. mount forward.
0947 Judy splashed close aboard on port bow.

When this attack was over, all 5-inch and all 40-mm. guns had been knocked out, and only four 20-mm. guns could still operate. *Laffey* was settling by the stern, as survivors worked desperately to keep her afloat, to put out the raging fires, and to tend the wounded. Because of her jammed rudder, she could not keep a course. After three hours, help arrived, and pumps of the tugs, which took over on her in the afternoon, kept abreast of the flooding. At Hagushi anchorage she was patched up enough to make it to Guam. She was later repaired, but was out of the war.

The story of *Laffey* could be repeated many times off Okinawa, for the Japanese kept coming. Nor were destroyers the only victims. Carriers *Bunker Hill* and *Enterprise* were both hit so seriously that they had to return to the United States for major repairs and played no further part in the war. Battleships, cruisers, destroyers, destroyer escorts, LSTs, and every other class suffered, but the ships stayed to support the men who were fighting ashore.

There was little opportunity for fun during those dreadful weeks, but American humor will have its day.

One morning U.S.S. *Black*, a destroyer which had had more than her share of radar picket duty for one of the fast carrier task groups, drew alongside a large ship to refuel. Between her stacks was a large sign:

---

USS BLACK
WHY STOP HERE?
TASK FORCE 58 ONLY 40 MILES
⟶

---

The U.S. Navy was not always on the receiving end at Okinawa.

The mightiest battleship in the world was at anchor in the Inland Sea. Nearby were light cruiser *Yahagi* and eight destroyers. Aboard *Yamato* and *Yahagi* farewell parties were going on, for these ten ships were sailing the next afternoon on the largest suicide mission in the history of the world. They were to take on the ships of the United States and Great Britain off Okinawa, and then *Yamato* was to beach herself so that her 18.1-inch guns could serve as artillery for General Ushijima.

There could be no return. Each ship carried only enough fuel for the one-way journey.

The ships got under way at 1520, April 6, while the first Kikusui attack was in progress. They passed through Bungo Strait out into the Pacific and headed southerly at 20 knots. Although he had no way of knowing, Vice Admiral Seiichi Ito in *Yamato* had lost any chance of surprise. His force had been discovered by submarines *Threadfin* and *Hackleback*, both of which promptly reported the disposition's size, course, and speed.

Mitscher received the contact reports promptly and made every effort to prepare a warm reception for *Yamato* and her consorts. Spruance also warned Rear Admiral Morton L. Deyo, commanding the heavy bombardment ships off Okinawa, that the Japanese were fair game for him if they got that far. Mitscher did not intend to let them get that far.

At daybreak, April 7, Mitscher launched searches, holding his bombers and torpedo planes on the flight decks until the enemy was spotted. An *Essex* scout made contact in position 31°22′N, 129°14′E at 0823. After the contact had been verified, Mitscher launched a 16-plane tracking group at 0915, followed by a full strike of 280 planes beginning at 1000.

Aboard *Yahagi*, Rear Admiral Keizo Komura proved to be the best lookout, exclaiming, "Here they come!" to Captain Tameichi Hara. *Yamato* spotted the attack about the same time at 1232, and her commanding officer, Rear Admiral Kosaku Ariga ordered his ship to commence firing. The Japanese ships sent up a tremendous wall of flak, but the American pilots were not to be stopped. At 1241, *Yamato* received two bomb hits, and a few minutes later a torpedo. About the same time, a destroyer went down as torpedoes and bombs smashed her side open to the sea. *Yahagi* was hit by the same combination and went dead in the water.

There was no respite for the unfortunate Japanese. From 1300 to 1417 the planes kept coming, reducing the topside of the huge battleship to a shambles. Meanwhile torpedo hits were laying her open to the sea. She took on a heavy list. Things only got worse. By 1420, the *Yamato* was nearly on her beam ends, and the chief concern of Admiral Ariga was to save the Emperor's portrait. He learned that it was safe. The Gunnery Officer had locked himself in his cabin with the portrait and the battle ensign. There was no chance that the Americans would recover them from the wreckage.

Admiral Ito and Admiral Ariga refused to leave the ship. Ariga tried to bring her head around to the north, the traditional attitude of a dying man, but it was in vain. At 1423, *Yamato* went down with a mighty rumble of compartments bursting from pressure.

By this time *Yahagi* had already sunk as well as three other destroyers. The four remaining destroyers were so badly battered that it was doubtful that they would make it back to

Japan, but they did. After pulling survivors from the water, they
staggered into Sasebo, but they were finished.

Finished, too, was the Japanese Navy. For four years and
four months it had contested the Allied fleets for supremacy in
the Pacific. Now it was done, finally and irrevocably. Only the
Kamikazes and the Army stood between Japan and her
conquerors.

On Okinawa, the Shuri Line still stood, despite Tenth Army's
efforts to blast or dig the Japanese out of the defenses. It was
Iwo Jima all over again, but on a much larger scale. Three
divisions of XXIV Corps under General Hodge were getting
ready for a major attack, supported by naval gunfire and naval

air. The III Amphibious Corps had pretty well finished things in the north and were preparing to move against Ie Shima before coming to the assistance of XXIV Corps in the south.

It was Friday, the thirteenth, on Okinawa. Over the loudspeakers on the ships and by bullhorn and word of mouth ashore came the news, "President Roosevelt is dead." Not a few wept, and others were secretly glad but dared not share it amidst the general grieving. Colors were lowered to half staff afloat and ashore.

Then the war went on.

Ie Shima, a small island west of the Motobu Peninsula, was invaded by the Seventy-Seventh Division on April 16, against light opposition. As the G.I.s advanced inland, they came up against the all-too-familiar pattern of Japanese in caves and blockhouses, but there were too few Japanese to turn the island into another Iwo Jima. The island was secured by 1730, April 21, after bitter fighting that cost over 1000 casualties, killed and wounded.

One of those killed was the beloved correspondent, Ernie Pyle, who had told the story of the G.I. in North Africa and Italy in a way that made the people back home understand what their sons, brothers, and husbands were doing and thinking. He had come to the Pacific out of a sense of obligation to tell the story of the soldiers and in the war against Japan. Ernie was more comfortable with the G.I.s he knew so well than he was with the sailors, and he went ashore at the first opportunity. He was riding in a jeep when a machine gun opened up on the road. He dove into a ditch and then raised his head to have a look around. A bullet drilled him through the temple and he died instantly.

"It seems a shame that such a big guy had to get it on such a lousy little island," said one man later. Later a monument was raised over the spot where he died: "At this spot the Seventy-Seventh Infantry Division lost a buddy, Ernie Pyle, 18 April 1945."

The day following Ernie Pyle's death, XXIV Corps attacked the Shuri Line in three-division strength. The jump-off was preceded by a massive bombardment by artillery and naval guns, including fire from six battleships, supplemented later that morning by that of three others on loan from Task Force 58. At the same time, some 650 Navy and Marine planes made their contributions of bombs, napalm, and machine-gun strafing. It was almost reminiscent of the barrages of the trench fighting in World War I. And it had much the same result. The Japanese crawled out of their caves and manned their guns to stop the advance in its tracks. Only on the extreme west side, where the Twenty-Seventh Division redeemed itself after Makin and Saipan, was any advance made, and this was against the weakest part of the Japanese defenses.

Five bitter days of fighting ensued, where progress was measured in feet and yards. At length the superior American force began to tell, and on the evening of April 23, General Ushijima ordered a withdrawal to his next defense line, closer to Shuri Castle.

The pattern kept repeating itself. The stubborn Japanese held each line until it was penetrated in several spots. Then Ushijima would withdraw to the next. And the next.

April moved on into May, and there was no end in sight. On May 1, the Marine's III Amphibious Corps, having finished up their jobs on the Motobu Peninsula, moved south to take up positions on the right of the XXIV Corps. The battered Twenty-Seventh and Ninety-Sixth Infantry Divisions were relieved in the process.

The break came, not from the addition of the Marines to the fighting front, but from the Japanese themselves. Ushijima's Chief of Staff, Lieutenant General Isamu Cho, a robust, active, arrogant man, had no stomach for Ushijima's defensive tactics. He demanded an all-out counterattack, supported by a maximum Kikusui effort. This was the way of the Japanese warrior, he declared. The Americans had thrown in their full strength, and the time to counter it was before it could be well organized, while the III Amphibious Corps was taking up its position. There would be no Banzai charge; this would be a well-organized counterattack designed to drive a hole in the middle of the

American lines, so that the Japanese could spread out behind, causing confusion and destruction everywhere.

Ushijima listened in silence. The Operations Officer, Colonel Hiromichi Yahara, agreed that Cho's tactics were sound, if the Japanese had the strength to follow up. But they did not.

"To take the offensive with inferior forces against absolutely superior enemy forces is reckless and will lead to certain defeat. . . . We must continue the current operation. . . . If we should fail, the period of maintaining a strategic holding action, as well as the holding action for the decisive battle for the homeland, will be shortened. Moreover, our forces will inflict but small losses on the enemy, while on the other hand, scores of thousands of our troops will have been sacrificed in vain as victims of the offensive."

He sat down. General Ushijima considered his words for a moment and then nodded to General Cho. The Japanese would attack.

It was set for May 4, with Kamikazes preceding the main event.

At 1800, May 3, the Kamikaze attacks began and in two days sank destroyers *Little*, *Luce*, and *Morrison* and three LSM(R)s. They damaged escort carrier *Sangamon*, cruiser *Birmingham*, and destroyer types *Aaron Ward*, *Macomb*, *Ingraham*, and *Shea*. But the rest stayed.

On the night of May 3, Japanese barges attempted to creep up along both coasts to land troops in the rear of American lines. The results were disastrous for the Japanese, for they were annihilated to a man.

At dawn on May 4, Cho's offensive began. Its weight fell on XXIV Corps as the Japanese emerged from their defensive positions to be killed. Naval guns and artillery cut swaths through their living flesh. The weight of American metal was too much for the Japanese, however heroic they were individually. By May 5, the attack was completely broken at a cost to the Japanese of 6,227 dead. Meanwhile, the Marines had taken advantage of the Japanese preoccupation with their offensive to mount one of their own and gain 700 yards in the same two days.

A lot still lay ahead before the end came on Okinawa. Thousands more would die on the island and on the ships offshore. There would be no more Japanese counterattacks. Ushijima was going to stick to his prepared defenses and force the Americans to come to him. He told Yahara that he would listen to no one but him from now on. General Cho sulked and then became stoic. He could die on Okinawa as well as anywhere else.

News of V-E Day on May 8 was received with indifference by the Americans fighting on Okinawa. It was all so far away—it was another war. The guys on the other side of the world had lucked out. Here on Okinawa there was another job to do.

Nature contributed a new worry to the Americans fighting on Okinawa, for the heavens opened on May 8, and torrential rains combined with Okinawan soil to create the gooiest mud in the experience of anyone. Wheeled vehicles were simply no good at all, and even tanks and bulldozers sometimes got stuck. Water soaked the uniforms of the men fighting and the mud permeated everything. It crept into a man's eyes and ears, his nose and mouth. He could taste it in his food and in his cigarettes, if he could keep them lighted. It plugged the muzzle and breech of his rifle. Men threw their boots away because it was easier to walk in bare feet than to lift ten or fifteen pounds of mud with each step.

In spite of everything, the attack went on. A principal barrier on the right side of the island, in III Corps area, was a hill known as Sugar Loaf. Like the terrible Meatgrinder on Iwo Jima, Sugar Loaf was protected by two other hills, and it in turn protected them. On May 14, in face of driving rain, the attack began and the Marines, a pitiful few of them, made it to the top of Sugar Loaf. But they couldn't stay. The small number of survivors was driven off and the Japanese held out for another two days until a tiny depression was discovered which offered a route with some cover. On May 18 a message came in to headquarters, "Send up the PX supplies. Sugar Loaf is ours."

The anchor of Ushijima's defenses fell when the Marines

took Shuri Castle on May 29. They weren't supposed to take it, for that was the job of the Seventy-Seventh Division. As it happened, Major General Pedro del Valle, commanding the First Marine Division, spotted a gap in the Japanese defenses and drove through it. Suddenly the Marines found themselves in the courtyard of the castle, and shortly the American flag was hoisted and beside it the standard of the First Marine Division, the same standard that had flown over Guadalcanal, New Britain, and Peleliu.

Ushijima made his last stand in the south of the island, in caves often half flooded by the same rains that were making life a misery for the Americans. It was even more miserable for the Japanese, for they had little food and few medical supplies. The weakened men were easy prey to pneumonia, and wounds that should have been minor were often fatal as infection and physical weakness combined in deadly work.

But the Japanese still fought on. Every man was sure he would die, and each one intended to fight to the last.

On June 18 the final push began. General Simon Bolivar Buckner was at a forward observation post of the First Marine Division to observe progress. Suddenly five Japanese shells dropped nearby, and a large chunk of coral flew through the air. It struck General Buckner in the chest, leaving a gaping hole. In ten minutes he was dead, but he knew that his Tenth Army had won the fight.

Lieutenant General Roy Geiger, who had taken over from Vandegrift on Guadalcanal, the first Marine campaign of the war, now took over the last, by becoming acting commander of the Tenth Army, the only time a Marine general has commanded a United States Army in the field. Three days later, he was able to declare Okinawa secured.

General Ushijima agreed with General Geiger, although he knew nothing of his declaration. On June 22, he and General Cho consumed the last can of sliced pineapple and took their own lives in the most ceremonial manner they could devise. Colonel Yahara was ordered not to commit suicide. "If you die," Ushijima told him, "there will be no one left who knows the truth about the battle of Okinawa. Bear the temporary shame but endure it. This is an order from your Army commander."

Curiously enough, even with the fanaticism of the Okinawa campaign—the Kamikazes and the last-ditch fighting in the Shuri Line—more Japanese soldiers surrendered than in any other campaign of the Pacific war. Indoctrinated as they were with the code that a prisoner was eternally disgraced and with the propaganda that the Americans tortured their prisoners, the Japanese rarely surrendered. But on Okinawa it was different. Those who surrendered early were able to convince their fellows that they really did get good treatment. Over 3,000 surrendered themselves, while other diehards held out until the end of the war and after.

The cost of taking Okinawa was grim. In addition to the naval casualties mentioned earlier, the Tenth Army lost 7,613 killed or missing in action and 31,807 wounded. The Japanese lost 110,000 troops, and the civilians on Okinawa, caught between the huge forces, suffered dreadfully. At least 75,000 men, women, and children died, and thousands of others were injured.

All of this was for the campaign that need not have taken place. The Japanese were already beaten, but they would not admit it.

Already planning was well advanced for the next step in the Pacific war, the landing on Kyushu, scheduled for November 1, 1945.

On July 16, 1945, a light such as had never been seen before blazed in the desert near Alamogordo, New Mexico. The Atomic Age had arrived.

CHAPTER TEN

# To Bear the Unbearable

*We have decided to effect a settlement*
*of the present situation by resorting*
*to an extraordinary measure.*

Hirohito

MAJOR General Curtis LeMay was dissatisfied. He was glad to be quit of China with all the problems of logistics and intrigue that he had known there, and he was glad to be heading up XXI Bomber Command in the Marianas. But the results of the bomb attacks by B-29s on Japan had been a lot less than he hoped they would be. "This outfit has been getting a lot of publicity," he grumbled to his public relations officer, Lieutenant Colonel St. Clair McKelway, "without having really accomplished a hell of a lot in bombing results."

The high explosive bombs, which had been so effective against Germany's concentrated industrial complex, had been disappointing against Japan, where much of the production was still piecework, done in homes and small factories.

LeMay hit upon a scheme and decided to try it out without bothering to refer it to Washington.

Gathering in their briefing rooms on the morning of March 9, 1945, B-29 crews protested aloud at their orders. They would go in low, at altitudes of 5,000 to 8,000 feet, at night, with all armament except tail guns stripped from their planes to increase the bomb loads. Instead of blockbuster bombs, they would carry packages of napalm-filled M47 incendiary pieces, slim, two-foot-long bombs which would flame on impact, spreading their jellied fires into the tinder-box houses of sprawling central Tokyo.

That afternoon, at 1736, the first B-29 rolled down the long runway of North Field, Guam, and painfully lifted itself into the air, the whole structure groaning at the heavy bomb and fuel load. At fifty-second intervals others followed. One didn't make it. Its brakes locked, and it careened off the runway in a fearsome explosion amidst the coral.

The disaster did not stop the others, and they were joined by more B-29s from Tinian and Saipan until 333 were throbbing their way northward on the seven-hour flight to Tokyo.

Passing Iwo Jima, the airmen could see flashes of explosions resulting from General Senda's final, futile suicide charge. They paid little heed, for their time was to come.

It was a clear night over Tokyo, and bombardiers in the pathfinder planes could see the stars shining brightly above and the three-by-four-mile-square section of downtown Tokyo that was their target. Fires in this section were commonplace, even in the best of times, for the varnished wooden buildings, jammed together like kernels of corn on a cob, were ready invitations to carelessness or spontaneous combustion. So had it been when the city was known as Edo, and so was it just after midnight in the early morning hours of March 10, 1945. These recurrent fires were known poetically as "the flowers of Edo," and the Japanese were about to see the largest blossom they had ever known.

The first two pathfinders flew a crossing pattern low over the center of the target area, and at a hundred feet the packaged M47 incendiaries split apart, falling along the bomb lines to form a flaming X in the center of downtown Tokyo. The jellied gasoline of the napalm began to spread, and the aiming point was clearly marked for the remaining bombers.

Over they came in three wings, dropping more of the deadly M47s. Laggard planes were buffeted by the overwhelming heat, some of them tossed 1,000 feet or more up into the air.

The intense fires quickly exhausted the oxygen nearby, but it was replaced as the hellish heat created a massive updraft, and air rushed into the center of the fires in winds of hurricane force. The temperature at the heart of the flames rose to over 1,800° Fahrenheit. No living thing could survive in the center of the flaming area.

Around the fringes frantic Japanese civilians tried desperately to save themselves. The only safety lay in the river. Some rushing to reach it were overtaken by the onrushing flames and died horrible, screaming deaths. Some took refuge in buildings such as the huge Buddhist temple in Asakusa where they were either roasted alive or died of suffocation as the flames devoured the oxygen needed for life. They were the lucky ones, for the end was comparatively painless.

The stench of burning flesh spread, reaching even to the bombers above. Some American crewmen vomited, and others looked in awe and not a little horror at what they had done. Yet to most, it was a job. The Japanese had brought it on themselves. Men in arms and the people back home were hardened to the terrors of bombing, burning cities, dead men, women, and children. The brutalization of the human spirit was an inevitable by-product of the war.

This single raid destroyed 16 square miles of the center of Tokyo, and the dead were estimated at 130,000, almost the same number as had died in the huge raid on Dresden on the night of February 13, less than a month earlier. The Dresden raid was the last massive attack on Germany, but the fire bomb attack on Tokyo was by no means the last on Japan. The very next night, 313 B-29s gave a repeat performance at Nagoya, the third largest city in the Empire, with the same kind of result. Incendiary attacks on Osaka and Kobe followed quickly, and at the end of the first week, 45 square miles of crucial industrial areas of Japan were ashes. There was no question Japan's capacity to wage war was being systematically destroyed. Yet she fought on.

The series of disasters, including the fire raids and the loss of Leyte and Iwo Jima brought the downfall of Prime Minister Kuniaki Koiso's regime. All reasonable men in the Japanese leadership recognized that the war was lost, but the military leaders were not reasonable, and without them no cabinet could be formed. The problem facing Emperor Hirohito was how to end the war in spite of the fanatics who would fight on to the point of national suicide.

A strange figure emerges at this juncture in time, Marquis Koichi Kido, Lord Keeper of the Privy Seal, perhaps the most trusted adviser of the Emperor. Kido it was who masterminded the selection of the next cabinet.

Everyone knew that the next cabinet must be the last wartime cabinet. It must be two-faced, for the Emperor intended that it seek peace while actively carrying on the war and encouraging the people to fight on in the useless struggle.

On April 5, Koiso formally tendered his resignation to the Emperor. Kido, meanwhile, had sounded out the military leaders to get their views ostensibly on who should fill the posts of the Army and Navy in the new cabinet but really to find out whether they thought the war could still be won. In the oblique Japanese way, most of the high command let him know that they saw no way to victory. But this was still a long way from surrender.

That afternoon at 5:00 P.M., the *Jushin* met to select the new cabinet. The *Jushin* was an advisory body composed of former Prime Ministers and other high officials, and its function was to advise the Lord Keeper of the Privy Seal whom to recommend to His Majesty as the next Prime Minister.

By this time, Kido had already found his man. During the meeting of the *Jushin* he would have to guide the others into recommending this man to him, Admiral Baron Kantaro Suzuki.

It was difficult sledding during the meeting of the *Jushin*, for the fallen former Prime Minister Tojo tried to dominate the proceedings, hoping that he would either regain the post himself or that it would go to a fanatic who would fight on regardless of death, fire, pestilence, and famine.

Eventually Suzuki suggested that one of the *Jushin* ought to have the job. All but one had been Prime Minister. For this post, Suzuki had a nominee: "Since the physical strain is so great, I should like to ask Prince Konoye, the youngest in the group, to come forward."

But Konoye would not agree. He was too compromised by

past mistakes in three administrations. He had failed to prevent the war that had brought Japan to her present plight. In fact, the only man in the room who was not compromised by past errors was Baron Suzuki.

Recognizing this fact, Baron Hiranuma nominated Suzuki as Prime Minister, to the dismay of that elderly admiral. The response was enthusiastic for the most part, but Suzuki begged to be excused. He had promised his family he would not take the post, and he felt strongly that the military leaders should stay out of politics. "I think I told Admiral Okada once," he expostulated, "that if a military man goes into politics, he would only lead the nation to defeat. This is proved by the fall of Rome, the eclipse of the Kaiser and the fate of the Romanovs. Because of this principle, I cannot accept the honor. Besides, I am hard of hearing."

Despite Suzuki's protests, the appointment met the favor of everyone in the room except for Suzuki himself and diehard General Tojo. He could not object to Suzuki himself, for his reputation was impeccable, but Tojo wanted an Army man on the active list. He threatened that unless he got his way, the Army would *soppo o muku* [turn its head away] from any nominee. Without Army approval, no cabinet could be formed. Kido was infuriated. "Perhaps the people will turn their heads away from the Army!" he retorted.

Tojo backed down. "I take back what I just said. I meant to say that the Army will find such a choice disagreeable."

With that the *Jushin* adjourned for dinner, and before it was over, Kido took Suzuki aside and urged him to accept. Suzuki lacked confidence in his ability to do the job, but Kido persisted. "It is beyond that, Admiral," he stressed. "We must recommend someone to the Emperor whom he trusts implicitly."

This was too much for Suzuki. "If the Emperor orders me to form a new cabinet," he said falteringly, "I will do it."

Within the next hour, before he could be taken into the presence of His Majesty, he had changed his mind twice. When he entered the Emperor's study and was bidden to form a new government, he demurred. "I am very pleased to be so honored

405

by His Majesty's offer but I beg to decline as I did at the *Jushin* meeting held late this afternoon. I am merely His Majesty's humble naval officer and have had no experience in political affairs. Further I have no political opinions. My motto has been to abide by the adage of Emperor Meiji to the effect that military men should never interfere in politics. Therefore, begging His Majesty's pardon, I must refrain from accepting His Majesty's offer."

Hirohito smiled but persisted. "At this critical moment," he said, "there is no one but you for the task. That is why I have asked you."

Suzuki capitulated. Although he asked time to think it over, he had made his decision. He later stated that he understood fully what the Emperor was saying to him. In unspoken words, the Emperor was telling him to end the conflict as soon as possible.

At this moment in time, Japan's fate was entrusted to a seventy-eight-year-old retired admiral who had spent seven years as Grand Chamberlain. He was something of a national hero, having fought with distinction in the Sino-Japanese War of 1894–95 and the Russo-Japanese War a decade later. As Grand Chamberlain he had nearly been assassinated by hotheads who opposed the Emperor's acquiescence in the London Naval Conference which seemed to condemn Japan to naval inferiority. As he stood face to face with the fanatics, one of them pumped four bullets into his body, yet he lived. He knew full well that he faced the same danger again if he was to carry out the will of the Emperor to end the war.

Truly an innocent in the jungle of Japanese politics, Suzuki set about forming his cabinet. The first man he asked was Admiral Keisuke Okada, a known advocate of peace, to be munitions minister. Okada was appalled at the idea. He had been retired for seven years and was, he knew, unacceptable to both the Army and Navy leaders.

He hastened to Suzuki's house and found a scene of wild confusion. The new Prime Minister was surrounded by well-meaning amateurs who could hardly use a telephone, let alone give sound advice on forming a cabinet. Something needed to be done—and fast—before Suzuki made any irreparable mistakes.

Seizing the telephone, Okada summoned his son-in-law, Hisatsune Sakomizu, an official at the Finance Ministry, and urged him to come at once. Sakomizu had a shrewd understanding of both Japanese politics and the Japanese military and would be able to keep the new Prime Minister from many a pitfall. With no urging he took over the post of Cabinet Secretary. After that, things gradually began to shape up.

The first and key appointment was that of War Minister. If the Army would not nominate a man, no cabinet could be formed. Suzuki wanted for the post General Korechika Anami, whom he had known for fifteen years or more and trusted and respected. But it was customary for the Army to nominate a man of its own choosing.

First Suzuki called on the outgoing War Minister, Marshal Gen Sugiyama, who let it be known that the Army had its price for that nomination: (1) prosecution of the war to the bitter end; (2) proper settlement of the Army-Navy unification problem; and (3) organization of the nation to carry out the decisive battle in the Homeland.

The second point is of minor importance in the story, but it was a burning issue among the services as Japan's resources became scarcer and scarcer. The other two were in direct opposition to Suzuki's role as he understood it, the man who would end the war. Yet he immediately agreed to all of the items, and General Anami became War Minister.

If anything, Suzuki sounded more belligerent than the man he had replaced, former Prime Minister Koiso. To the Diet he said:

If our Homeland becomes a battleground, we will have the advantages of position and of personnel working in harmony against the enemy. We will have no difficulty in concentrating huge numbers of troops at any desired position and providing them with materiel. The situation then will be different from the battles fought on isolated islands in the Pacific. We will then be able to annihilate the enemy forces. At this stage of the intensified war, we are not

407

assured of abundant food supplies. Nor is transportation unhindered. Moreover, munitions production will become increasingly difficult. . . . Frankly speaking, we need stepped-up efforts in the future. Judging not only from the trend of the domestic situations in enemy countries and the current delicate international situation, I cannot help feeling that the shortest cut to our victory is to fight this war through.

He was able to explain away defeats in the Philippines and the outlying islands with amazing sophistry. On the fall of Iwo Jima, he had this to say:

> We can never tell what a fatal blow the unyielding fighting spirit of Japanese soldiers on Iwo Jima and Okinawa has given the enemy mentally. When we compare the magnitude of this shock to the enemy with what we have lost on these islands, we can conclude that we are not losing the war.

This was the man whom the Emperor had chosen to end the war? How can the oppositions be reconciled?

Suzuki was indulging in what the Japanese call *haragei*, "stomach talk." *Haragei* is an old tradition in Japan, of saying one thing while meaning another. It developed from the crowded conditions in Japanese households, where no privacy was ever possible, so that the person addressed learned to read the unspoken message while those who overheard the conversation remained in the dark, or pretended to do so at least.

*Haragei* nearly deprived Suzuki of the services of the man who was to be his staunchest ally in the cabinet, Shigenori Togo, who was to become Foreign Minister. He had served in that post under Tojo until September 1942, when he resigned in protest against Tojo's "dictatorial and high-handed policies." Out of office, Togo was "rusticating" in the resort town of Karuizawa in the Japanese Alps when he received a telephone call from a go-between—nothing could be done directly in these delicate negotiations. Togo was abrupt. He would not accept until he had talked face to face with Suzuki and "reached an agreement of views."

Taking the next train to Tokyo, he met with Suzuki during

the evening of April 7 in private. Since Suzuki was not well acquainted with Togo, he was unwilling to abandon *haragei* even in a confidential conversation with someone who shared his aims. Togo was more direct:

"I assume you took office with some definite things in mind," he challenged, "since it will be anything but easy to manage the affairs of state now, with the war effort in its last throes."

It was *haragei* speaking in the old admiral's reply. "I think we can carry on the war for another two or three years."

There was no point in continuing the discussion as Togo saw it. "Modern war," he replied, "depends mainly on materials and production. Because of this Japan cannot continue even one more year. Even if I felt able to accept the grave responsibility of our diplomacy, the Prime Minister and I would be unable to cooperate effectively so long as we held divergent views on the prospects for the war."

Togo thanked Suzuki, declined the offer, and took his departure.

He was not to get off so easily.

The next day, several members of the *Jushin*, as well as Admiral Okada, begged Togo to reconsider. He was the one man with experience in foreign affairs who clearly recognized what must be done. Privy Seal Kido added his efforts, explaining that the Emperor himself wanted the war to end. All these men explained the Ancient Mariner's *haragei*, pointing out that it would have been too dangerous for Suzuki to have revealed his true feelings at their first meeting. Another was soon arranged. Suzuki now realized his error and said, "So far as the prospect of this war is concerned, your opinion is quite satisfactory to me; and as to diplomacy, you shall have a free hand."

Under the circumstances, Togo accepted the position. It was still a long way off, but with Togo's appointment, peace came a little nearer.

Meanwhile Japan's situation grew steadily worse. The fire raids did not end. They increased. Systematically Japan's cities were being reduced to ruins and ashes. Tokyo had been raided three more times by mid-May, and the greeting between friends was now, "Not bombed out yet?" On May 23, the B-29s came back and added another five square miles to the devastation of Tokyo. Thirty-six hours later came another raid which dropped 3,262 tons of incendiaries, destroying the heart of the financial, commercial, and government districts. One of the places wiped out was the detention house of the Tokyo Army Prison, where among thousands of Japanese, 62 American prisoners of war were cremated. A large portion of the Emperor's Palace was burned out, although no bomb had fallen on it. From the first, the Palace was off limits to American airmen, but the sweep of the flames could not be confined. Leaping across the moat, the fires destroyed several wings of the sprawling Palace and killed twenty-eight members of the imperial staff before the blazes were under control. The Emperor and his family remained safe in their underground shelter, an underground annex to the *obunko,* the imperial library.

It was only five nights later that LeMay's bombers returned, this time laying waste to Yokohama, leaving 85 percent of the city in ruins. With Tokyo, Yokohama, and Nagoya no longer worthwhile targets, LeMay's B-29s concentrated on Osaka and Kobe, eliminating both as targets in the space of two weeks. LeMay's "Urban Area Project" by early June had destroyed 2 million buildings and left 13 million people homeless. And more was to come.

Things were going no better for the Japanese in other parts of the world. Although huge numbers of troops were still tied down in the inconclusive war in China, neither the Japanese nor the troops of Chiang Kai-shek were able to reach significant objectives. Thus the largest number of forces on each side in the Pacific war tended to cancel each other in a strategic stand-off.

Starting in February 1945, MacArthur, sidelined temporarily from the Iwo Jima and Okinawa shows, began to plan further operations in his bailiwick in the Southwest Pacific. The obvious target was Borneo, and the first operation in this area took place at Tarakan Island, a small bit of land in the Sesajap River Delta off the east coast of Borneo. D-Day was May 1, 1945, and the assault troops were largely Australian, members of the Twenty-Sixth Brigade of the Ninth Australian Division. There was tough fighting for the first week, followed by the customary process of digging and burning out isolated pockets of diehard Japanese fanatics. Fighting did not end until the general surrender in August.

The spacious harbor of Brunei Bay on the northwest coast of Borneo was MacArthur's next target, and again the troops were Australian. Opposition was even lighter than at Tarakan, and from D-Day, June 10, until July 1 the Aussies lost only 114 men killed and had taken over the entire area of North Borneo.

Balikpapan on the southeast coast was the final objective of the Borneo campaign. Because of heavy defenses, preliminary bombardment and air attacks extended for sixteen days before the landing on July 1, which was made by the Seventh Australian Division, reinforced by R.A.A.F. units to a strength of 35,000 men. As had become their habit, the Japanese made only a token resistance at the beachhead and had to be dug out of prepared defenses inland. The area was secured by July 22, at a cost of 229 Aussies killed in action.

The Balikpapan operation proved to be the finale for MacArthur's Southwest Pacific Forces, although no one expected it at the time. He had recommended that he be allowed to move against Java, where the Japanese were firmly entrenched and were combining with Indonesian communists and nationalists to oppress the Dutch colonists. The Joint Chiefs of Staff, however, had their eyes riveted northward and refused to make the necessary shipping available for any operations in the Netherlands East Indies.

Nor is MacArthur's staff free from all blame in the strategic errors made in that part of the world. If Southwest Pacific Forces had bypassed the Visayan Islands in the Central Philippines and Mindanao, they could have taken Java and Sumatra with little difficulty, and the history of that area might have been different. But the Philippines were a symbol to MacArthur, and the Joint Chiefs of Staff had eyes only for the road to Tokyo. The opportunity was lost as postwar political objectives took second place to the direct, simple strategy leading to an early end to the war. The situation resembles

Eisenhower's decision not to capture Berlin before he had cleaned out the "strongpoint" in central Germany.

The result in the Netherlands East Indies was that when the Japanese surrender came, the Allies had no troops immediately available to move into the islands, and the Japanese troops remained in power, ostensibly servants to a puppet government under Sukarno. Netherlands authority was flouted, and Europeans, the Dutch most of all, remained shut up in internment camps. Their sufferings did not end until September 15, 1945, when a Dutch and a British cruiser put in at Batavia.

Although the Europeans were released, Sukarno was too strongly established to leave the scene. The state of Indonesia came into being, and the Netherlands East Indies were a casualty of the war.

An almost forgotten part of the war against Japan was the brilliant campaign waged by Lieutenant General Sir William Slim in Burma. After holding against overwhelming Japanese strength during 1943 and the first part of 1944, Slim opened an offensive in Northern Burma. By mid-November, he had established a bridgehead over the Chindwin River and was hoping to trap the Japanese in the open spaces with his superior armor. It became clear, however, that the Japanese were falling back to positions on the Irrawaddy near Mandalay. Slim, therefore, recast his plan. While four divisions of Lieutenant General Montagu Stopford's XXXIII Corps drove on Mandalay from the north, Major General F. W. Messervy's IV Corps circled stealthily to the south and cut off the Japanese in Mandalay from their source of supply in Rangoon. Although the Japanese position was hopeless, they fought on with customary fanaticism until March 20, 1945, when Mandalay fell. The Japanese then retreated southward, and North and Central Burma were in British hands, and the way to Rangoon lay open.

Since the monsoon season was coming, the British had to move fast. In case Slim's forces did not reach Rangoon in time, Admiral Mountbatten scheduled an amphibious assault and parachute troop attack in the Rangoon area. On May 1 the attack took place at the mouth of the Rangoon River, just in time to meet a spearhead of Messervy's IV Corps driving southward. There was nothing left to do but mop up the 60,000 Japanese troops still holding out in the Burmese jungles. This task took until the end of the war.

The end of the war in another section of the world, the unconditional surrender of Germany, took place only two days after the recapture of Rangoon, and it seems to have had little effect on the Japanese psychology. Americans in the Pacific had strangely mixed reactions. Amidst the rejoicing that one part of the war was over, there was a fear that they would be forgotten while the folks back home turned to a peacetime mentality. Was the main show over and would the guys left in the Pacific have to do a dirty job that no one cared about?

Fortunately these fears were groundless. In spite of the horrors of Buchenwald and Dachau, which were just being revealed to a shocked world, the Americans had never really hated the Germans the way they had hated the Japanese. The Germans had not struck at Pearl Harbor. They had not beheaded some of Doolittle's fliers. The American people were determined to have a full measure of revenge.

It was with a complete knowledge of this attitude that President Harry S Truman, still somewhat in a state of shock from his sudden accession to the awesome power and responsibility that goes with the office of President of the United States, boarded the cruiser *Augusta* at 0600, July 7, 1945, at Newport News, to participate in the last Big Three conference of the war, aptly code-named "Terminal," to be held in the old Hohenzollern Palace at Potsdam. It was a striking symbol of the utter defeat of Germany to have her conquerors gather there.

As the *Augusta* made her way across the Atlantic, President Truman established a routine which he followed for the next week.

It was a wonderful crossing. The *Augusta* had a fine band which played during the dinner hour each evening. There were movies every night in Secretary Byrnes' cabin. I was up early every morning to take some exercise on the deck and spent a good deal of

413

time talking with the members of the crew. I also ate a meal in every mess aboard the ship, taking my place in the "chow lines" with my aluminum tray along with the men.

During this time, his mind must have cast back to the turbulent events of his Presidency, less than three months old.

The very first decision Truman had made as President was that the San Francisco Conference to write the Charter of the United Nations would go on as scheduled less than two weeks after the death of President Roosevelt. Something had been retrieved in the mourning for the former President, for Stalin had relented and agreed to permit Molotov, the Russian Foreign Minister, to attend the conference after all. Earlier Stalin had deliberately snubbed the conference as a result of arguments over the Polish question and blandly announced that Gromyko would be there instead.

All, however, was not sweetness and light when the San Francisco Conference of the United Nations opened on April 25. Truman, a much less complex man than Roosevelt, had made some mistakes during his first few weeks in office, most of them as a result of his having been excluded from the inner circle of government during his time as Vice President. Perhaps the most damaging was the decision to terminate, or at least drastically reduce, Lend Lease shipments to European countries now that the war against Germany was a thing of the past. This measure was urged on Truman by Foreign Economic Administrator Leo T. Crowley, and Acting Secretary of State Joseph C. Grew, former Ambassador to Japan, and minding the store while Secretary of State Edward R. Stettinius, Jr., was in San Francisco attending to American interests in the formation of the United Nations.

Crowley and Grew, presenting the proposal to Truman, said that Roosevelt had "approved" the statement and had only been prevented from signing it by his untimely death. Taking their word for it, Truman reached for his pen and signed the document, only to regret it immediately. It was obviously inspired by a desire not to provide the Soviet Union with the materials to extend further its sphere of influence in Eastern

Europe. Since the Soviets were going to do just that in any event, the order served no purpose other than to alienate the Soviet Government and to cause a good deal of worry among other allies whose economies were not yet self-supporting. Three days later the order was rescinded, but the damage had been done. Stalin threatened to boycott further proceedings at San Francisco.

By the second week in May the San Francisco Conference seemed to be on the rocks. Several petty issues kept the delegates upset, but the most serious were the admission of Argentina in the interests of "inter-American solidarity," and the issue of the veto for the five permanent members of the Security Council. At Yalta it had been agreed that the initial members of the United Nations would be those who were at war with Germany as of March 1, 1945. Argentina, whose Nazi sympathies were widely suspect during the war, had not so declared war, but was to be admitted in spite of everything. The decision so annoyed Molotov that he promptly left for home, Gromyko remaining in San Francisco, but with no authority to agree to anything. It took days for him to get any answers out of Moscow.

The principal bone of contention was over the veto. The so-called "middle powers," those of substantial influence such as Canada, New Zealand, Australia, and others opposed the veto, but it was obvious that none of the Big Five would sign without it. As Truman himself had put it, "our experts, civil and military, favored it, and without such a veto no arrangement would have passed the Senate." Since the League of Nations had foundered in the American Senate, Truman did not propose to permit the United Nations Organization to suffer the same fate.

The actual sticking point was whether the veto applied to "procedural matters" as well as to matters of substantial importance. If it did, then any one of the Big Five, the United States, the Soviet Union, the United Kingdom, China, or France, could prevent any item from even getting on the agenda for discussion. The United States and, reluctantly, Britain agreed that the veto would not apply on procedural matters but only to matters of substance. The Soviet Union, however, insisted in sticking to the original proposal which had been turned down at Yalta, that the veto would apply to all issues. Gromyko, speaking for Molotov, would not yield an inch. It looked as though the San Francisco Conference had failed.

At this juncture the emaciated figure of a familiar friend emerges from the wings. Harry Hopkins had left the hospital at Rochester, Minnesota, against his doctors' orders, in order to attend the funeral of his closest friend, Franklin D. Roosevelt. He had remained in Washington in order to brief Truman with all of the intimate knowledge he possessed of Roosevelt's opinions, decisions, ideas, plans, prejudices, attitudes, and impressions. No other man had such a knowledge, and no other man could have so risen to the occasion in spite of an illness which gave him only a few more months to live. "He looked," wrote Robert Sherwood, "like death, the skin of his face a dreadful cold white with apparently no flesh left under it." But the spirit was still there, and the "fire was shooting out of his sharp eyes in their sunken sockets." He was ready to do what had to be done in his country's service.

Despite his physical condition, Hopkins was to undertake one more mission. Could he, Truman asked, go to Moscow, to try to reestablish the cordial relations which were fast fading in face of apparent Soviet intransigence in Europe and at San Francisco. Hopkins knew Stalin, and the Marshal trusted him as he did perhaps no other American. Hopkins's only worry was that Ambassador Averell Harriman would resent his appearance in Moscow as undercutting to his own position. But Harriman enthusiastically supported the idea that Hopkins make the trip. No one else in the world could have performed the service Hopkins did on the trip, for no one had the trust of Stalin and the intimate knowledge of American policies for the previous five years.

Since there was now peace in Europe, Hopkins was accompanied by his wife and by Ambassador Harriman, who had attended the San Francisco Conference, and by Charles E. Bohlen, a career State Department man, who was later to serve as Ambassador to Russia in his own right. Departing from Washington on May 23, Hopkins and his party flew to Paris, then straight across Germany. Looking down on the ruins of Berlin, Hopkins exclaimed, "It's another Carthage!"

Arriving in Moscow on the evening of May 25, Hopkins enjoyed a day of rest before beginning conversations in the Kremlin with Stalin and Molotov at 8:00 P.M., May 26. Six meetings in all took place, and while little of substance was decided, the sessions were useful in clearing the air of suspicions. The Soviets had interpreted the admission of Argentina as a slap in the face; Hopkins was able to convince Stalin that it was a matter of inter-American politics. Stalin agreed to meet with Churchill and Truman at Potsdam in mid-July, and it was to that meeting that Truman was even then bound as he remembered more about Hopkins's mission.

The most difficult problem had been Poland. Stalin was determined that Poland would have a "friendly" government and to this end had unilaterally recognized the Lublin Poles, a communist group. Shrieks of anguish from Britain, where the Polish government-in-exile had maintained its headquarters, had been echoed by the British Government, and as we have seen, had occasioned much talk at Yalta. Although nothing specific was settled, Stalin did agree that other Poles could have a voice in their own government. It just had to be "friendly." As Winston Churchill wryly pointed out, it depended on what word one used to translate "friendly."

The most important achievement of the Moscow talks was Russian agreement that "procedural matters" in the United Nations should not be subject to the big power veto. Apparently Molotov and Gromyko had not kept Stalin fully informed on this issue, for when Hopkins brought it up at the last meeting, Stalin seemed surprised at all the furor, remarked that it was an insignificant matter, and that they would accept the American position.

Hopkins returned home from his last mission in public life with a sense of real accomplishment.* He had done what could

* President Truman invited him to accompany him as a member of the delegation to Potsdam, but Hopkins refused on the ground that his presence would undercut the

417

be done to ease Soviet-American relations and had paved the way for the success of the Potsdam Conference. Also he had saved the United Nations Organization.

Once the procedural matter of the veto was out of the way, the Charter of the United Nations was unanimously adopted on June 25. President Truman addressed the closing session:

> The Charter of the United Nations which you have just signed is a solid structure upon which we can build a better world. History will honor you for it. Between the victory in Europe and the final victory in Japan, in this most destructive of all wars, you have won a victory against war itself. . . .
>
> Out of all the arguments and disputes, and different points of view, a way was found to agree. Here in the spotlight of full publicity, in the tradition of liberty-loving people, opinions were expressed openly and freely. The faith and the hope of fifty peaceful nations were laid before this world forum. Differences were overcome. This Charter was not the work of any single nation or group of nations, large or small. It was the result of a spirit of give-and-take, of tolerance for the views and interests of others. . . .
>
> This new structure of peace is rising upon strong foundations.
>
> Let us not fail to grasp this supreme chance to establish a worldwide rule of reason—to create an enduring peace under the guidance of God.

As the *Augusta*'s bow rose and fell gently in the Atlantic summer swell, Truman knew that the United Nations had to work. For he knew another fearsome secret. In Alamogordo, New Mexico, an important test was to be held in a few days.

The very evening that Truman had been sworn in as President, Secretary of War Stimson had taken him aside and said he would like to speak to him about "a most urgent matter." Truman later wrote, "Stimson told me that he wanted me to know about an immense project that was underway—a

<hr>

authority of the newly appointed Secretary of State James F. Byrnes. He felt that Stalin and Molotov, knowing him so well, would ignore Byrnes and address their remarks to him. Hopkins resigned his many government posts as fast as he could remember what they were and died in New York on January 29, 1946, a truly unique figure in American history.

project looking to the development of a new explosive of almost unbelievable destructive power. That was all he felt free to say and his statement left me puzzled. It was the first bit of information that had come to me about the atomic bomb but he gave me no details. It was not until the next day that I was told enough to give me some understanding of the almost incredible development that was underway and the awful power that might soon be placed in our hands."

Matters had gone a long way since the first test in Chicago that had proved the atomic bomb was a practical as well as a theoretical device. Truman, as chairman of the "Watchdog Committee of the Senate," had come close to the bomb once when his investigators were stopped at the gate of the Oak Ridge Plant where scientists were producing uranium 235. After conferring with Stimson, Truman accepted his word that the work was of crucial importance to the nation and agreed to skip that part of his investigation.

Since the Chicago test, mystery cities had sprung up at Oak Ridge, where the isotope U-235 was extracted by the gaseous diffusion process from the natural uranium 238; at Hanford, in the desert of eastern Washington, where the artificial element plutonium was created from U-238; and at Los Alamos, in the deserts of New Mexico where the actual bombs were designed and manufactured. Each of these cities lived a life of its own. Security was strict to the point that each seemed a prison camp, but the strict security was not enough to prevent leaks by such men as Klaus Fuchs who were willing partners with Russian spies.

In charge of the whole Manhattan Project, as the atomic bomb program was called, was Dr. Vannevar Bush, Chief of the Office of Scientific Research and Development. A policy committee was established early by President Roosevelt consisting of then Vice President Henry A. Wallace, Secretary of War Henry L. Stimson, Chief of Staff General George C. Marshall, and Dr. James B. Conant, President of Harvard University. In turn a committee of scientists was headed by Dr. Arthur Holly Compton of the University of Chicago. In 1942 actual charge of the project was given to Major General Leslie

Groves who coordinated the work of the three secret installations and supplied for their physical needs.

In charge at Los Alamos was the brilliantly controversial theoretical physicist Dr. J. Robert Oppenheimer. A latter-day Renaissance man, he wrote poetry, collected stamps and butterflies, was elected to membership in the New York Mineralogical Society at the age of twelve, developed while still in his teens a keen interest in chemistry, and learned several languages, including Sanskrit. After completing the Harvard course in three years, he decided to become a theoretical physicist and studied abroad in England, Germany, Switzerland, and the Netherlands before returning to the United States in 1927 to accept professorships simultaneously at the University of California and the California Institute of Technology.

Through his wife, a political activist of the far left, Oppenheimer attended meetings of many "Communist-front" organizations. His mind was too subtle and sophisticated to be taken in by dialectical materialism, and he was never a communist, but in later days these associations would rise to haunt him.

His chief contribution in the world of science was to act as catalyst to other men, to see where their work could be improved upon and to lead them to do it. After he had criticized the work of P. A. M. Dirac on the positron, Dirac revised his work and it led him to a Nobel Prize. After Oppenheimer had done the same service for Carl D. Anderson's work on the meson, Anderson also won the Nobel Prize.

This kind of mind was ideal for the director at Los Alamos. Working with Oppenheimer were such men as Leo Szilard, James Franck, Harold C. Urey, Enrico Fermi, and many other men of like distinction. The British, recognizing that the greater resources of the United States could best bring the project to fruition, contributed their scientists and the results of their "Tube Alloy" experiments, their own code name for the Manhattan Project.

Two types of bomb were under development at Los Alamos. The first was the "Lean Boy," using two subcritical masses of U-235 at opposite ends of a gun barrel. When the "gun" was fired, one mass was hurled into the other so that the explosion would occur instantaneously. This bomb was comparatively simple and needed no testing. The other type, employing plutonium, was an implosion type, with several subcritical masses arranged around a sphere and simultaneously fired into a common center. The size of the sphere gave this type its nickname of "Fat Boy." Since the machinery was very complicated, scientists concluded a test must be held. It would not do to have a dud fall on Japan.

Since all scientists were agreed that the bomb *would* work, the question began to rise as to whether it *should* be used. A group of physicists formed a Committee on Social and Political Implications, led by Franck and supported by Szilard, who did much of the writing of a report to Secretary Stimson.

"All of us, familiar with the present state of nucleonics," began the report, "live with the vision before our eyes of sudden destruction visited on our own country, of a Pearl Harbor disaster repeated in thousand-fold magnification in every one of our major cities." There was no chance of keeping the bomb an exclusive possession of the United States, the report went on. "The experience of Russian scientists in nuclear research is entirely sufficient to enable them to retrace our steps within a few years, even if we should make every effort to conceal them." Also, the United States was more vulnerable to nuclear destruction than a country "whose industry and population are dispersed over a large territory."

Szilard, independently, made an effort to restrain the use of the bomb. He persuaded Einstein to write Roosevelt asking him to listen to Szilard, but the letter was unanswered by Roosevelt before his death. It was forgotten for some weeks before Truman came upon it and turned it over to an "Interim Committee" charged with "advising the President on the various questions raised by our apparently imminent success in developing an atomic weapon." James F. Byrnes, marking time until he should become Secretary of State, served as Truman's representative on this committee. He agreed to listen to Szilard, and the meeting was a total failure from Szilard's point of view.

No meeting of minds was possible between the Hungarian-born liberal physicist and the conservative Southern gentleman politician from South Carolina.

Franck's report fared little better with Stimson when Compton sent a note basically disagreeing with Franck's conclusions and stressing the number of American lives that could be saved if the bomb was employed. Many of the scientists felt that Compton had betrayed their cause, but in retrospect it seems inevitable that the bomb would be used, even if all scientists had been unanimous in their opposition. The men charged with the actual decision had no real understanding of what it could do, and their responsibility was winning the war.

The Interim Committee met in a crucial session on May 31, 1945, in Secretary Stimson's office to consider three basic questions: *First,* was it necessary to use the bomb to force Japan's surrender? There were conflicting opinions on this question, for the Air Force felt that the fire bomb raids were reducing Japan's ability to conduct war to nearly nothing. There was evidence from the Navy, if it had been heeded, that the blockade was so complete that Japan would be literally starved out in a matter of months. Of the ten million tons of merchant shipping with which Japan had started the war, barely a million remained, and most of those ships dared not stir out of port.

These views were overcome by those of others who maintained that the fanatical Japanese would never yield unless the bomb were used. No conventional weapons could force surrender—witness the Philippines, Iwo Jima, and Okinawa. The Kamikazes had been at their worst after Japan had lost her Navy, and there were thousands of them waiting for the American ships which would approach Kyushu for the invasion in November. In addition a million or more men would die where they stood in defense of their Homeland. And they would take, it was estimated, half a million Americans with them in death.

*Second,* would a demonstration serve to convince the Japanese to surrender without using the bomb on a "live" target? After considerable debate the members agreed that such a demonstration was impracticable. If the Americans warned the Japanese to evacuate a certain area because a super bomb would fall there at a certain time, the chances were that the Japanese would concentrate what was left of their air power to shoot down the plane carrying the super bomb. Another possibility was that they might fill the target area with American prisoners of war. If on the other hand they invited the Japanese to send representatives to a demonstration on an island or in the desert area, the results would not be so apparent. To men of little imagination, the creation of a crater in sand would not be impressive. Most men see what they want to see, and to only a few gifted persons would the mushroom cloud over the desert near Alamogordo reveal the four-square-mile area of utter devastation at Hiroshima.

*Third,* was the use of the atomic bomb any worse morally than attacks by conventional weapons? LeMay's fire bomb raids had already caused far more damage and loss of life than would the two atomic bombs that were dropped later. By the time the war was over, LeMay's bombers had laid waste 178 square miles in 69 Japanese cities, and the losses to civilians were double those of all the Japanese armed forces in the entire war. There was little debate on this point. All weapons are evil in the great evil of war, but those that bring victory must be used by men who consider their cause is just. What was never considered by these men was that the entirely new kind of bomb would capture the imagination of the world. Everyone knows the meaning of Hiroshima and Nagasaki, but few remember the fire bomb raid on Tokyo of March 9–10 which caused more damage and killed more people than either atomic bomb.

The lone voice in opposition seems to have come from bluff old Admiral Leahy, Chairman of the Joint Chiefs of Staff. He later wrote, "My own feeling was that in being the first to use it [the atomic bomb] we had adopted an ethical standard common to the barbarians of the Dark Ages. I was not taught to make war in that fashion, and wars cannot be won by destroying women and children. We were the first to have this weapon in our possession, and the first to use it. There is a

423

practical certainty that potential enemies will have it in the future and that atomic bombs will sometime be used against us."

Whatever thoughts of these and other matters were on Truman's mind as the *Augusta* crossed the Atlantic those July days, he had to think ahead to the coming meeting with Churchill and Stalin at the Cecilienhof Palace in Potsdam. The war in Europe was over and the victors had to see to it that the fruits of victory were not thrown away by divisions among themselves. There was the unfinished war against Japan, and, while Russia was not a belligerent, one of the American objectives was to see to it that she kept her promise made at Yalta to enter the war three months after the defeat of Germany.

The *Augusta* arrived at Antwerp on the morning of July 15, having been escorted through the English Channel by a naval honor guard consisting of H.M. cruiser *Birmingham* and six destroyers. Here the President was met by General Eisenhower as well as many other military and political leaders. Going by car from Antwerp to Brussels, the Presidential party arrived at the airfield about noon and embarked in the *Sacred Cow*, Truman's personal plane. With two other C-54s, the party left for Berlin.

The opening of the conference was delayed a day because of a minor heart attack suffered by Stalin, and it was not until July 17 that the conference got under way.

But before the conference had begun, Truman had been given an ace in the hole which changed the American approach to the Russians. On the evening of July 16, Stimson received the following cablegram:

OPERATED ON THIS MORNING. DIAGNOSIS NOT YET COMPLETE BUT RESULTS SEEM SATISFACTORY AND ALREADY EXCEED EXPECTATIONS. LOCAL PRESS RELEASE NECESSARY AS INTEREST EXTENDS GREAT DISTANCE. DR. GROVES PLEASED. HE RETURNS TOMORROW. I WILL KEEP YOU POSTED.

The operation referred to in this cablegram as performed by "Dr. Groves" took place in New Mexico that morning at 0530. It was the first explosion of an atomic bomb in the history of the world.

The bomb, a plutonium "Fat Boy," was placed on the top of a 100-foot-high steel tower. As he waited for the rain to stop so that the test could be made, Oppenheimer nervously paced about near the control tower, 10,000 yards from the bomb. Steadying him was General Groves, and he needed steadying, for his vision could see what Groves could not, the full effect of the explosion and its meaning to humanity. Oppenheimer later told William L. Laurence that when the bomb went off two passages from the Hindu sacred epic, the *Bhagavad-Gita*, flashed through his mind. "If the radiance of a thousand suns were to burst into the sky, that would be the splendor of the Mighty One." The other said, "I am become Death, the shatterer of worlds."

The steel tower was instantly vaporized, and the intensity of light was almost blinding, even through nearly opaque goggles. The eerie light was seen as far away as Albuquerque, Santa Fe, Silver City, El Paso, and other cities up to a radius of 180 miles. A massive cloud formed, rising swiftly to 41,000 feet, topped by the mushroom shape, a symbol of the poison within.

Truman and Churchill were elated. Now it would not be necessary for them to pay the price for Russian entrance into the war against Japan. The immediate question was how to use this new power to bring about a quick end.

For weeks before the conference, men in the State Department and in the Cabinet had worked on the wording of a document calling for the Japanese to surrender. Their labor was to emerge in a document known as the Potsdam Declaration, but it had undergone substantial change since it was first drafted. On the advice of former Ambassador Joseph C. Grew, who knew the Japanese people better than most Americans, the original draft had permitted the Japanese people to retain the Emperor, although as a figurehead. Since, however, unconditional surrender was the official Allied policy, Byrnes and the

Joint Chiefs of Staff were opposed to suggesting any conditions, which might lead to other conditions and concessions. After considerable debate, the offending reference to the Emperor was removed, and the unconditional surrender proponents carried the day.

Since Russia was not at war with Japan, the declaration was released to the press and radio without her approval, although a copy was given Molotov with the release. He tried to hold it back, but was blandly informed that it was none of their affair.

After a preamble describing the devastation that had happened to Germany, the declaration went on:

> The time has come for Japan to decide whether she will continue to be controlled by those self-willed militaristic advisers whose unintelligent calculations have brought the Empire of Japan to the threshold of annihilation, or whether she will follow the path of reason.
>
> Following are our terms. We will not deviate from them. There are no alternatives. We shall brook no delay.
>
> There must be eliminated for all time the authority and influence of those who have deceived and misled the people of Japan into embarking on world conquest, for we insist that a new order of peace, security, and justice will be impossible until irresponsible militarism is driven from the world.
>
> Until such a new order is established *and* until there is convincing proof that Japan's war-making power is destroyed, points in Japanese territory to be designated by the Allies shall be occupied to secure the achievement of the basic objectives we are here setting forth.
>
> The terms of the Cairo Declaration shall be carried out and Japanese sovereignty shall be limited to the islands of Honshu, Hokkaido, Kyushu, Shikoku and such minor islands as we determine.
>
> The Japanese military forces, after being completely disarmed, shall be permitted to return to their homes with the opportunity to lead peaceful and productive lives.
>
> We do not intend that the Japanese shall be enslaved as a race or destroyed as a nation, but stern justice shall be meted out to all war criminals, including those who have visited cruelties upon our prisoners. The Japanese Government shall remove all obstacles to the revival and strengthening of democratic tendencies among the

Japanese people. Freedom of speech, of religion, and of thought, as well as respect for the fundamental human rights shall be established.

Japan shall be permitted to maintain such industries as will sustain her economy and permit the exaction of just reparations in kind, but not those which would enable her to re-arm for war. To this end, access to, as distinguished from control of, raw materials shall be permitted. Eventual Japanese participation in world trade relations shall be permitted.

The occupying forces of the Allies shall be withdrawn from Japan as soon as these objectives have been accomplished and there has been established in accordance with the freely expressed will of the Japanese people a peacefully inclined and responsible government.

We call upon the government of Japan to proclaim now the unconditional surrender of all Japanese armed forces, and to provide proper and adequate assurances of their good faith in such action. The alternative for Japan is prompt and utter destruction.

Released at 9:20 P.M., July 26, from Berlin, the Potsdam Declaration was beamed toward Japan by American radio stations on the west coast. Now there would come the time of waiting.

Little else was accomplished at Potsdam up to that time. The presence of Truman as the newest member of the most exclusive club in the world, the Big Three, was inhibiting to the free discussion that had gone on earlier. Also relations between Churchill and Stalin were less cordial than they had been as Russian and British postwar aims diverged. Although Churchill came to respect Truman as a tough, no-nonsense man, he scarcely knew him. Missing was the close personal friendship of the years, the intimate understanding of each other's minds that had marked his relationships with Franklin Roosevelt. And then there was the skeleton at the feast.

Sitting quietly as a part of the British delegation was the Deputy Prime Minister, Clement Attlee, a balding, colorless man, who had just concluded an election campaign against his leader. Churchill once described him as "a sheep in sheep's clothing." The voting had been conducted in Britain's first wartime general election on July 5, but the results would not be known for three weeks in order to count the absentee ballots from servicemen.

It had been a rough campaign. The end of the war in Germany brought domestic issues into the minds of everyone, and the people were weary of wartime restrictions. Yet they did not ease. In fact they got worse. In early June there was an acute shortage of bread, and the weekly ration of cooking fat was cut in half to 1 ounce per person, while bacon was reduced from 4 ounces to 3. These were but symptomatic of the dislocations caused by the conversion from war to peace. It would not be fair to say that most Britons cared little for the war still going on against Japan, but it was so far away, and the Japanese had never threatened their very lives and homes as the Germans had. Germany had been the enemy, and now they were beaten. Let us begin to live again.

Winston Churchill had promised a general election soon after the defeat of Germany, and now it was a case of keeping that promise. The National Coalition Government had been in office five years and Members of Parliament had held their seats for ten. Despite Churchill's plea that the Government remain intact until Japan was beaten, Attlee and the Labour leaders refused, suggesting that the election be held in October. Ironically, this would have accomplished Churchill's purpose of keeping the Coalition intact until the end of the Japanese war, but he did not see it that way at the time. Everyone expected that spring that it would take at least a year to defeat Japan, and the Conservative Party leaders predicted that Labour would be stronger in October than in July.

As it happened, most of the Conservative local party leaders were serving in the armed forces, so the party machinery was neglected. By contrast, Labour local leaders, while willing to serve, had been needed for production in the factories, so their political organizations were thriving.

Churchill, his mind on world affairs, made a bad campaign. He allowed Lord Beaverbrook and Brendan Bracken to plan the strategy, and it was disastrous from the Conservative point of view. Beaverbrook was better at bringing down governments

428

than electing them, and so it was this time. Churchill himself made a grave error in attacking Labour candidates in terms that he had previously applied to the Nazis.

When the votes were counted, it was a decisive landslide for Labour. Churchill won his own battle for the Woodford constituency and so was returned to Parliament, but he would no longer be Prime Minister.

"It may well be a blessing in disguise," said his wife, thinking of his health and the tremendous demands of the office.

"At the moment," he replied bitterly, "it seems quite effectively disguised."

Thus the British voters cast aside the one man who had been able to save Britain from disaster in 1940, who had guided her through the turmoils of five years of global war and whose well-known voice had given tongue to their courage and steadfastness in adversity. "May God forgive England for it," wrote Brooke in his diary.

The hurt went deep into Churchill's soul, but there was no hint of it in the statement issued from 10 Downing Street after he had tendered his resignation to the King. "The decision of the British people has been recorded in the votes counted today," he said. "I have therefore laid down the charge which was placed upon me in darker times. I regret that I have not been permitted to finish the work against Japan. For this, however, all plans and preparations have been made, and the results may come much quicker than we have hitherto been entitled to expect. Immense responsibilities abroad and at home fall upon the new government, and we must all hope that they will be successful in bearing them. It only remains for me to express to the British people, for whom I have acted in these perilous years, my profound gratitude for the unflinching, unswerving support which they have given me during my task, and for the many expressions of kindness which they have shown towards their servant."

Clement Attlee, now Prime Minister, went back to Potsdam, and the conference dragged on to its dreary conclusion. None of the decisions made there really mattered. Strategic plans became meaningless as the war ended before they could be implemented. Political settlements involving eastern Europe were generally in Russia's favor, owing partly to the inexperience of Truman and Attlee, and where they were not, it made no difference. In Churchill's words, an Iron Curtain descended, and behind it Russian will was unimpeded.

The Potsdam Declaration was the most substantial accomplishment of the conference. Since it called upon the Japanese to surrender, the answer would have to come from Tokyo. Meanwhile, there was to be no letup in the war against the Land of the Rising Sun.

The end of the Okinawa campaign released the Pacific Fleet to intensify the pressure on Japan. Admiral Halsey relieved Spruance on May 27, and the Fifth Fleet once more became the Third Fleet. Just over a week later, Halsey managed to run his fleet into another typhoon.

Like the typhoon of December 18, the one that hit the Third Fleet on June 5 was small but packed a mighty wallop. It was first spotted by a search plane on the early morning of June 3 and was not seen again for thirty-six hours. Everyone guessed where it was and where it was going, but no one knew for sure. It turned out that the guesses of Halsey's meteorologists were among the worst. Fortunately, Halsey was able to refuel his ships on June 4, so there was no repetition of disasters through capsizing of destroyers, but ships suffered punishment enough.

So small was this typhoon that not all groups felt its full impact, but Jocko Clark's TG 38.1, in maneuvering to avoid the storm and find a comfortable course,* managed to run right through the eye of the storm. Here the waves were mountainous, up to sixty feet from trough to crest, and the wind force well over 100 knots. Once through, however, the ships of TG 38.1 found the winds and seas moderating, and in a few hours were in westerly winds of 15 knots.

While they were in the dangerous semicircle and in the eye, nearly every ship was damaged, including all four carriers.

---

* Comfortable course here means not the course that is easiest on the men but that in which the ship rides best so as to suffer least structural strain.

*Hornet* and *Bennington* had the forward twenty-five feet of their flight decks collapsed and the next twenty-five feet so weakened that they were unable to support aircraft. A tractor broke loose on the hangar deck of *Belleau Wood* and damaged a number of aircraft before the men could get lines around it and lash it securely in place.

The worst damage of all was to the heavy cruiser *Pittsburgh.* Laboring heavily, she practically lay to on course 160 at a speed of 3 knots and seemed to ride better. Her skipper, Captain John E. Gingrich, as a precaution ordered Condition Zebra set, which meant that all watertight doors were tightly dogged, at the same time sending the crew to General Quarters. This meant that everyone was pulled out of the berthing spaces in the forward part of the ship, an act which undoubtedly saved their lives.

Just fifteen minutes later, at 0630, June 5, *Pittsburgh* encountered two tremendous seas which ripped off 104 feet of her bow at frame 26. The bow section floated clear and remained afloat, while by stupendous efforts, damage control personnel were able to shore up the transverse bulkheads and keep the ship afloat. This involved working five hours in partially flooded compartments, the ship rolling and pitching heavily, and debris sloshing about in the water, inflicting painful bruises on the men as they worked.

*Pittsburgh* made it safely into Guam on June 10. The next day her bow arrived, brought in by tugs *Munsee* and *Pakana.* *Munsee* made the first contact and sent the following message: HAVE SIGHTED SUBURB OF PITTSBURGH AND TAKEN IT IN TOW.

Following the typhoon, Third Fleet ships supported the Okinawa campaign until it ended and then carried the naval war to the shores of the Japanese Home Islands. Carrier strikes began in early July and continued right up to the surrender. In addition, on July 15, a bombardment unit consisting of battleships *South Dakota*, *Indiana*, and *Massachusetts*, heavy cruisers *Quincy* and *Chicago*, and nine destroyers dropped the first naval shells on the Home Islands with a bombardment of the iron works at Kamaishi in northern Honshu. The plant was completely wrecked.

From then to the end of the war, Third Fleet ships struck practically every day, and practically every day something was wrecked, either by guns or bombs. It was an arrogant display of American sea power, and the humiliated Japanese Navy could do nothing about it. Only their submarines were still active, and one of them had an important rendezvous.

On July 16, East Longitude Date, Lieutenant Commander Mochitsura Hashimoto, IJN, took submarine *I-58* out of Kure on what would be her last war patrol. On July 16, West Longitude Date, Captain Charles Butler McVay III, USN, took heavy cruiser *Indianapolis* out of San Francisco on what would be her last voyage. If a person on the bridge of the *Indianapolis* had been looking eastward that morning, he might have seen a brief flash in the sky. If he had seen it and known what it was, he might have wondered about the special secret cargo that had been brought aboard early that morning. The *Indianapolis* was carrying the key elements for the two atomic bombs which were to be dropped on Japan as soon as weather permitted. The flash in the sky had, of course, been the explosion of the test bomb at Alamogordo.

Clearing the Golden Gate at 0836, *Indianapolis* set out alone and unescorted on a high speed run for Tinian. After a brief stop at Pearl Harbor to drop off passengers and refuel, she arrived at Tinian on July 26, where the still-secret cargo was offloaded.

Captain McVay did not know what his cargo had been, but he was relieved to have done with it and looked forward to a training period to tune his ship up once again to serve as Admiral Spruance's flagship. *Indianapolis* sailed from Tinian as soon as the atomic bomb parts were unloaded and moved on to Guam for a briefing and routing orders from Port Director Guam. She was to go on to Leyte to report to Rear Admiral Lynde D. McCormick, who commanded a training unit in Leyte Gulf. After two weeks of Admiral McCormick's attention, *Indianapolis* would report for duty to Oldendorf's Task Force 95 off Okinawa. Captain McVay asked if an escort was

432

available and when told that none was, dismissed the matter and prepared to sail alone. After all, he had crossed the 5,000 miles of water between San Francisco and Tinian with no escort. It was a routine matter this late in the war.

It was also routine that Port Director Guam sent a movement report "action" to the Shipping Control Officer, Marianas Area, to the Port Director at Leyte, and to Admiral McCormick advising that *Indianapolis* would leave Guam at 0900, July 28 and arrive off Leyte Gulf at 0800, July 31, traveling at a speed of advance of 15.7 knots. This message was routinely sent and routinely handled, except that the most important addressee, Admiral McCormick, never got it. It was received in his flagship *Idaho* in such badly garbled form that it could not be decrypted, and the communications watch officer failed to ask for a repeat.

In his routine instructions, Captain McVay was told to zigzag "at discretion," and he did so by day but not at night. Reported submarine sightings did not disturb him unduly, for at that time, as throughout the war, they were a dime a dozen, and any commanding officer who responded to them all would find himself unable to do much else.

On Sunday, the second day out, the weather was foul during the afternoon, but began to clear about the time the moon came up at 2000, shining through a thin overcast. About 2300, Captain McVay looked over the night orders written for him by the navigator and went to his bunk in his sea cabin. There was nothing in the night orders about resuming zigzagging if the weather cleared. It was not mentioned one way or the other.

Commander Hashimoto saw the moon when he surfaced about 2305, and he saw something else, silhouetted by a moonbeam shining through a rift in the clouds. It was the *Indianapolis*, advancing toward him. Hashimoto had the dream of a submariner's set-up.

The cruise of *I-58* had been unfruitful up to that point. One of the four remaining large Japanese submarines, she was equipped with *Kaitens,* manned suicide torpedoes, as well as conventional Long Lance torpedoes. He had expended two *Kaitens* against a tanker a few days earlier and had heard them

433

explode, but they hit nothing as far as can be learned. Hashimoto, considerably discouraged, had only a few hours earlier gone to the shrine to pray. The sighting of the *Indianapolis* was as if in answer to that prayer.

The fire-control solution was no problem. Hashimoto had nothing to do but wait for the cruiser to come by. He submerged to periscope depth and fired a spread of six torpedoes at 2332, from a range of 1,500 meters to track. Two of them hit on the starboard side forward, knocking out all internal communications and rupturing fire mains. Tons of water poured in as the officer of the deck could not get word to the engine room to stop, and the holes in the ship acted as a giant scoop to make the problem of flooding worse. She developed a heavy list to starboard, and it quickly became evident that she could not be saved. Rushing to the bridge, Captain McVay ordered a distress signal sent out, but apparently the loss of power extended to the radio shack, for no shore station picked up the SOS call.

In a few minutes, Captain McVay ordered Abandon Ship, but the word had to be passed from one man to another and some were slow in getting off. In less than fifteen minutes, shortly before midnight, the *Indianapolis* went down in 1,200 fathoms in position 12°02′ N, 134°48′ E.* It is estimated by survivors that 800 to 850 men were alive in the water when the ship sank and that about 300 to 350 were killed in the explosions or were unable to get free when she went down.

Now came the most incredible part of the story. The ship was not even missed when she failed to arrive at Leyte on the morning of July 31 as scheduled. Routine demanded the meticulous reporting of the arrival and departure of merchant and naval auxiliary ships, but it did not demand reporting of the arrival or nonarrival of combatant ships. Although the message to Admiral McCormick had not reached him because of the garble, he had been told that she was coming to his command about that time, but he "assumed" that she had been

---

* Commander Hashimoto reported the position as 12°31′ N, 134°16′ E, approximately 50 miles northwest of that accepted by the U.S. Navy, which is about 265 miles north of Palau.

diverted to another command or other duties. But as Captain Queeg put it so well, "You can't assume a goddamn thing in the Navy!"

It was eighty-four hours before the survivors were sighted in the water and by that time there were only 316 of them left alive. Several planes had passed over without spotting them, even though Captain McVay fired flares and the men contributed their best efforts by firing pistols and flashing reflector mirrors.

Oddly enough, at about 0200, Tuesday, July 31, an Army Air Force plane did spot flares, but the pilot thought he was witnessing a small naval engagement, and when he arrived at Guam and reported, he was "dismissed with the statement that if it was a naval action the Navy knew about it."

It was no business of the Army Air Force what the Navy was about. That was the routine. So far routine had conspired against the men of the *Indianapolis*.

It was routine that saved them—those who were saved. A Navy Ventura flying a routine search out of Peleliu spotted an oil slick in the water at about 1000 on the morning of Thursday, August 2, and the pilot, Lieutenant (jg) Wilbur C. Gwinn, went down low to investigate. Spotting men's heads in the water, he sent an urgent message to both Peleliu and Guam reporting 30 men. After that, things moved swiftly. As his radioman was transmitting, Gwinn revised his estimate to 150 and dropped all his life rafts, but since his plane was land-based could do no more to effect a rescue.

Some six hours later the first rescue plane arrived on the scene, a Navy Catalina, piloted by Lieutenant R. Adrian Marks, who dropped life rafts and rescue equipment and then landed in the twelve-foot swells to pick up survivors who appeared to him in the greatest need. He quickly saw that the job was beyond what he could do and sent out urgent messages for more help. Meanwhile he took 56 swimmers aboard, which so overloaded his plane that he could not take off.

As far as the survivors were concerned, being in the fragile Catalina was far better than being in the water, and they were content to remain until something better turned up. Later they transferred to a ship and Marks's battered plane was sunk by gunfire.

The ships began arriving on the scene about midnight, and it was then, for the first time, that naval authorities learned that the *Indianapolis* had gone down. The search for survivors lasted five days until it was certain that no more remained.

News of the sinking was not released to the public until August 15, perhaps in the hope that it would be lost in the general rejoicing following the surrender of Japan. If so, it was a vain hope, for the story became a front page affair, and the pressure grew that something be done. Accordingly, Secretary of the Navy James Forrestal, against the advice of most flag officers, decided to hush the clamor by bringing Captain McVay to trial by court-martial, despite the fact that a Court of Inquiry had already heard the evidence and given him an official reprimand, an action that meant the end of his career in any case.

He was tried on two charges, "Through negligence suffering a vessel of the Navy to be hazarded," and "Culpable inefficiency in the performance of duty." The "Specification" for the first was that he had not been zigzagging, and the second that he had not issued timely orders to abandon ship. Commander Hashimoto was flown over from Japan to testify, to the indignation of the press and many members of Congress. If anything, his testimony was more helpful than harmful to Captain McVay, but in the end he was acquitted on the second charge but convicted of the first.

The guilty verdict on the first charge resulted solely from the fact that the *Indianapolis* was not zigzagging, which constituted "negligence." There is no doubt that zigzagging was doctrine, but there was and still is considerable doubt as to its effectiveness. Any experienced submarine commander of World War II coped with a zigzag frequently and he was trained to do so. He simply waited for the target ship to zig and then fired, confident that it would probably not turn again before the torpedoes hit. Commander Hashimoto testified that it would have made no difference if the *Indianapolis* had been zigzagging. It is perhaps significant that no member of the court-martial had a submarine background.

No senior member of any command which sent or should have received the *Indianapolis* was brought to trial, although several subordinate officers received letters of reprimand. They were later withdrawn when one recipient pointed out that Seventh Fleet and Pacific Fleet orders both forbade him to take the action that he had been reprimanded for not taking. It was clear that the Navy couldn't have it both ways.

Captain McVay was sentenced to lose 100 numbers in seniority, but the sentence was remitted upon the unanimous recommendation of the court, and he was restored to duty.

The cargo that the *Indianapolis* had brought to Tinian had meanwhile been put to use.

The 509th Composite Bomb Group was something of a mystery and something of a joke to other groups of the Twentieth Air Force on Tinian. Its planes trained and flew secret missions but never seemed to be doing any bombing. It occupied a remote part of the field, surrounded by a barbed-wire fence, and no one could enter without a special pass.

The *Indianapolis*'s cargo was driven to this complex and there in an air-conditioned hut the first bomb was assembled. This was "Lean Boy," and would be dropped first.

Bad weather marked the first few days of August, but on the morning of the 5th the forecast was good for a takeoff after midnight. The bomb was loaded into the bay of a B-29 named *Enola Gay* after the mother of the pilot, Colonel Paul W. Tibbets, Jr. Navy Captain William Parsons, an ordnance expert, would go along to arm the bomb in flight so that a crash on takeoff would not destroy the northern end of the island.

Three weather planes preceded *Enola Gay*, taking off shortly after 0130. At 0245, August 6, *Enola Gay* lifted off the runway, using so much space with the heavy load that observers in the control tower feared she would never make it. "I never saw a plane use that much runway," said one.

Accompanying the atomic bomb carrier were two other

B-29s, loaded with observers and scientific instruments. They quickly vanished into the night. It would be a long haul to Japan and the crew settled down to routine duties, while Captain Parsons worked on "Lean Boy." Once the bomb was armed, Tibbets spoke to the crew over the intercom, warning them that everything they said would be recorded. "This is for history," he warned, "so watch your language."

Over Iwo Jima, Tibbets reported that everything was going well and that he was proceeding to target.

Target selection had occupied much time. Atomic scientists wanted a fairly open city so the blast would not be confined and its effects could be measured. It must be a target which had not suffered from one of LeMay's fire bomb raids. Any damage, then, would be a result of the atomic bomb. And it must have an important military establishment and a main industrial or other commercial installation.

Hiroshima, near the southern tip of Honshu, filled all these specifications. The terrain was ideal, and it had been out of bounds for LeMay's fire bombers, so had been spared. In fact, many residents of Hiroshima believed their city was so beautiful that, like Kyoto, it was being spared so that Americans could enjoy it after the war. It was even rumored that President Truman's mother lived nearby. Hiroshima was an important military target since it housed the headquarters of the Second General Army, and it was a seaport and a major military port of embarkation. All of these conditions moved Hiroshima to the head of the least desirable list in the history of the world—targets for the first atomic bomb. In order behind Hiroshima were Kokura and Nagasaki.

Hiroshima might well have been spared the ordeal that was about to come had the Japanese leaders been more careful of their language.

The text of the Potsdam Declaration was picked up by Japanese radio monitors on the morning of July 27, and Foreign Minister Togo's first reaction was one of relief that it was not simply a call for unconditional surrender. Perhaps the Allies had picked up some of the so-far ineffectual Japanese peace feelers. Hirohito, himself, had taken a hand and encouraged an approach through Russia to seek her good offices, but the approach had come 'to nothing. The Russians, speaking through Deputy Commissar Alexander Lozovsky (Molotov was in Potsdam), stalled. They had already made up their minds to enter the war in order to share the victors' feast in the Orient. They had no intention of seeing the war end before they could get into it.

Encouraged by the seeming moderation of unconditional surrender, Togo reported to the Emperor that negotiations should begin on the basis of the document and that it should be "treated with the utmost circumspection, both domestically and internationally."

He repeated these ideas in a Cabinet meeting and at a meeting of the Supreme Council for the Direction of the War—SCDW—generally known as the Big Six. This group made all the real decisions. Usually the Cabinet simply approved these decisions and they were presented to the Emperor for his approval, a mere formality, since custom did not allow the Emperor to do anything else. Hirohito was soon to change that custom.

The Big Six consisted of Prime Minister Suzuki; Foreign Minister Togo; the Minister of War, General Korechika Anami; the Army Chief of Staff, General Yoshijiro Umezu; the Navy Minister, Admiral Mitsumasa Yonai; and the Navy Chief of Staff, Admiral Soemu Toyoda. When it met to consider the Potsdam Declaration, opinions were divided, Suzuki and Togo urging careful consideration and the military men outright rejection. Anami urged that they issue a statement calling the document absurd.

Everyone agreed that some notice had to be taken of it, since the newspapers could pick it up by radio. Refusing to face the situation squarely lest it be damaging to morale, they censored the declaration before releasing it to the press. One of the excisions was the phrase about "utter destruction of the Japanese homeland." They might better have paid more attention to those words.

A statement would have to accompany the release, and

439

Suzuki said that the government "should simply *mokusatsu* the declaration." He meant, he said later, to use the word *mokusatsu* as the equivalent of the English phrase, "no comment," which has no Japanese equivalent. However, the word also means "kill with silence," "ignore," or "treat with silent contempt." It was these other meanings that were taken by both the Japanese press and by the American government. The newspaper *Asahi Shimbun* stated, "Since the joint declaration of America, Britain, and Chungking is a thing of no great value it will only serve to re-enhance the government's resolve to carry the war forward unfalteringly to a successful conclusion!" *Mainichi* headlined the declaration "LAUGHABLE MATTER."

Suzuki told reporters that afternoon, "The Potsdam Declaration is only a rehash of the Cairo Declaration, and our government will place no importance on it. In short, we will *mokusatsu* it."

By this statement, he meant to keep his options open. But the United States leaders did not see it that way. *The New York Times*, on July 30, ran the headline, "JAPAN OFFICIALLY TURNS DOWN ALLIED SURRENDER ULTIMATUM."

From Potsdam, President Truman gave the order that the bomb was to be used anytime after August 2, as soon as the weather permitted.

It was a fine, clear day at Hiroshima the morning of August 6. Major Claude Eatherly, flying one of the weather planes that had left Tinian before the *Enola Gay*, could clearly see the six finger-like islands in the Ota River Delta on which Hiroshima was built. His radioman tapped out, "LOW CLOUDS ONE TO THREE TENTHS X MIDDLE CLOUD AMOUNT ONE TO THREE TENTHS X ADVICE X BOMB PRIMARY."

At 0725, Eatherly turned his plane back toward Tinian. Hiroshima had fifty minutes to live.

*Enola Gay* started the bomb run at 0809, from an altitude of 32,000 feet. Bombardier Major Thomas Ferebee leaned over his Norden bomb sight, watching the landmarks crawl past. At

0813:30, Tibbets said, "It's yours." The hairlines crept on toward the aiming point, the center of the Aioi Bridge.

At 0815:17 the "Lean Boy" dropped away, and the *Enola Gay*, lighter by 9,000 pounds, surged upward. Tibbets turned sharply around 150° from the course he had been flying and dove sharply to build up speed to get away from the bomb blast.

The clocks of Hiroshima were frozen in time at 0815 as the fireball seared the sky and earth. It exploded in the air only 300 yards from its aiming point, and the 300,000° centigrade heat obliterated everything within 1,000 yards. One second people were standing talking; the next they no longer existed, not a trace of hair, flesh, or bone remaining. Others left a ghostly memorial as their bodies momentarily shielded the walls from the flash. Only their silhouettes remained, white on charred black.

The blast wave obliterated nearly everything within a radius of two miles, and the blast was followed by flames that became a roaring inferno in the tinder of wooden wreckage and in the houses that had escaped the wreckage of the blast. Survivors walked dazedly, some naked as their clothes had been blown off. No one paid any attention. Others had strips of skin and flesh hanging from their arms and legs and faces. No one noticed that either. It was too incredible to be accepted.

Fifteen minutes later an obscene black rain began to fall. Water vapor drawn up from the river had been carried up by the heat, had encountered radioactive dust, and had risen high enough to condense and fall back. Horrified survivors thought the black rain was another secret weapon, that the drops were poisoned. They were, but not in the way the Japanese believed. They carried the deadly venom of radioactivity and would add to the grisly list of those who would die in the coming days and weeks and months.

From the *Enola Gay* the crew looked down on the huge cloud as Colonel Tibbets fought to overcome the blast wave. "My God," said one, "what have we done?"

They had killed instantly some 80,000 people; another 10,000 would never be found; 37,000 more were seriously injured, and many of them would die from radioactive poison that ate their blood.

*Enola Gay* turned back. The job was done. There was the report to be made: RESULTS CLEAR CUT SUCCESSFUL IN ALL RESPECTS X VISIBLE EFFECTS GREATER THAN TRINITY [the Alamogordo test] X CONDITIONS NORMAL IN AIRPLANE FOLLOWING DELIVERY X PROCEEDING TO PAPACY [Tinian].

President Truman was eating lunch with crew members in the after mess hall of the *Augusta* when he was handed the news of the Hiroshima blast. "This is the greatest thing in history," he told the cheering men. "It's time for us to get home."


It was some time before fragmentary reports from Hiroshima began to reach Tokyo. All attempts to raise Second General Army Headquarters failed. All that the Japanese leaders could learn was that some unprecedented disaster had taken place. A few even suspected that it had been an atomic bomb, but most simply had no idea.

Marquis Kido rushed to tell the Emperor, who recognized the implications immediately. "Under the circumstances," he said heavily, "we must bow to the inevitable. No matter what happens to me, we must put an end to this war as soon as possible. This tragedy must not be repeated."

The question remained, how to carry out the imperial will. Under Japanese custom and under the constitution, the Emperor was revered by all, his person was sacred, but he had no power. He could only approve decisions made by others. Hirohito, however, had other ideas. He would use the power of the throne if he had to. But first, Kido would try to get the Big Six and the Cabinet to come up with the decisions His Majesty desired.

The Americans were leaving nothing to chance. Broadcasts in the Japanese language were beamed toward Tokyo stating that an atomic bomb had destroyed Hiroshima in a single blast and that more would follow unless the government of Japan sued for peace. Because most Japanese had no access to a radio and dared not listen to foreign broadcasts if they did, B-29s dropped 16 million leaflets over their cities.

### TO THE JAPANESE PEOPLE

America asks that you take immediate heed of what we say in this leaflet.

We are in possession of the most destructive explosive ever devised by man. A single one of our newly developed atomic bombs is actually the equivalent in explosive power to what 2,000 of our giant B-29s can carry on a single mission. This awful fact is one for you to ponder and we solemnly assure you that it is grimly accurate.

We have just begun to use this weapon against your homeland. If you still have any doubt, make inquiry as to what happened to Hiroshima when just one atomic bomb fell on that city.

Before using this bomb to destroy every resource of the military by which they are prolonging this useless war, we ask that you now petition the Emperor to end the war. Our President has outlined for you the thirteen consequences of an honorable surrender. We urge that you accept these consequences and begin work on building a new, better and peace-loving Japan.

You should take steps now to cease military resistance. Otherwise, we shall resolutely employ this bomb and all our other superior weapons to promptly and forcefully end the war.

Evacuate your cities now!

The Japanese wasted most of August 6 in trying to find out what had happened at Hiroshima. As the evidence of complete destruction poured in, the military leaders simply would not believe it. They sought ways to discredit the bomb, any tiny clue that would deny the awful reality.

"We do not yet know if the bomb was atomic," blustered General Anami at a Cabinet meeting the next afternoon. He proposed that Dr. Yoshio Nishina, Japan's leading physicist, be sent to find out. Home Minister Genki Abe, to whom the nation's police reported, gave what information he had. "An unknown type of bomb," he said simply, "completely different from known types, hit Hiroshima. It killed a tremendous number of citizens and destroyed almost all buildings. Hiroshima was completely devastated."

443

Anami and the other military leaders were not impressed. The Cabinet adjourned without taking any action.

Following an interview with the Emperor on August 8, during which Hirohito reiterated his desire for peace, Togo called an immediate meeting of the Big Six for that evening, only to learn that some of the military were unavailable and would not be able to meet until the next morning. Togo, accordingly, had to settle for a conference at 10:30 the following day.

Togo resolved to make one last try through Russia and telegraphed Ambassador Naotake Sato in Moscow:

THE SITUATION IS BECOMING SO ACUTE THAT WE MUST HAVE CLARIFICATION OF THE SOVIET ATTITUDE AS SOON AS POSSIBLE. PLEASE MAKE FURTHER EFFORTS TO OBTAIN A REPLY IMMEDIATELY.

Much to his surprise, when Sato telephoned for an immediate appointment with Molotov, he got it right away. The Russians had been stalling for weeks. Now, it appeared, they were ready to talk.

At the appointed time, Sato appeared in Molotov's office and began with small talk on the latter's trip to Berlin. Molotov interrupted and gestured to a chair. "I have here," he said, "in the name of the Soviet Union, a notification to the Japanese government which I wish to communicate to you."

It was a declaration of war, to begin six hours from that moment. The Russians had decided that they had better get into the war before it was too late. The atomic bomb might bring an end before they could act.

Gravely shaken, Sato asked permission to wire the Russian statement to Tokyo during the time before hostilities began. "Naturally," Molotov replied blandly, "you have liberty to do so. Not only that, but you can wire in code."

Sato's message, however, never reached Tokyo. The next message the Japanese received from the Russians was in the language of guns across the Siberian-Manchurian border, only two hours after Molotov had handed Sato the declaration of war. So much for a six-hour delay.

As the Big Six met the next morning in the underground bomb shelter of the Prime Minister's office building, its members were shaken by the Russian declaration of war, more so it seemed than by the atomic bombing of Hiroshima. Togo had been running around since eight o'clock, conferring with Suzuki and Yonai, the Navy Minister, both of whom agreed that Japan had no alternative but to accept the Potsdam Declaration, provided only that the position and person of the Emperor could be preserved.

As Togo was conferring with Suzuki, two B-29s were circling off the south coast of Kyushu, waiting for a third, a photographic plane, which never showed up. One of them was called *Bock's Car*, and it carried "Fat Boy," the second atomic bomb to be dropped on Japan, this one the plutonium type. The other plane, *The Great Artiste*, carried scientific observers.* At 0349, Major Charles Sweeney lifted *Bock's Car* off the final few feet of the runway at North Field, Tinian, and began to claw for altitude as he directed the plane toward Japan. Bad luck dogged the flight from the first, as Sweeney discovered that a defective fuel selector meant that 600 gallons in his bomb-bay tank had become so much useless weight. This fact raised grave doubts on whether *Bock's Car* could make it back to Tinian. Fortunately, Iwo Jima was available.

Arriving off Kyushu, the two B-29s circled for forty-five minutes waiting for the photographic plane. Finally Sweeney said to his co-pilot, "The hell with it. We can't wait any longer." Signalling the other plane, Sweeney headed for the primary target, Kokura, a port city on the north coast of Kyushu.

Bad luck continued as Kokura was obscured by smoke and haze. Bombardier Kermit Beahan could not see the aiming point. "No drop. Repeat. No drop," announced Sweeney to the crew. The plane went around for another try.

The second attempt was no more successful. By this time the

---

* Considerable confusion has existed as to which plane dropped the second bomb. The first reports stated that it was *The Great Artiste*, and that plane has been credited in many histories with doing the job. The error was discovered in 1946. Major Sweeney piloted *Bock's Car*, while its usual pilot, Captain Frederick Bock, Jr., flew Sweeney's regular plane, *The Great Artiste*.

fuel situation in *Bock's Car* was getting critical, and the flight engineer advised Sweeney that they had just enough on hand to reach Iwo Jima. "Roger," acknowledged Sweeney. He turned to Commander Frederick Ashworth, the Navy man in charge of the bomb. "We'll go on to secondary target, if you agree." Commander Ashworth nodded. Sweeney turned the plane on a southwest heading. "Proceeding to Nagasaki," he told the crew.

In the sixteenth century, Nagasaki had become Japan's chief port for foreign trade. Like San Francisco, it was built on steep hills, and was the most Europeanized of all Japanese cities, and one of the most beautiful.

Bad luck continued for *Bock's Car*, for the weather deteriorated as the plane neared Nagasaki. With the fuel remaining, Sweeney told Commander Ashworth, they would be able to make only one pass over the target. He suggested dropping the bomb by radar. Ashworth thought for a moment. His orders were to bomb visually, and if he could not, to drop the bomb into the sea. What a waste, he thought. He decided to disregard orders. "Go ahead and drop it by radar," he said, "if you can't do it visually."

At the last minute, the luck changed. An opening appeared in the clouds. "I've got it! I see the city," reported Bombardier Beahan. So Ashworth did not have to disregard his orders after all.

"Fat Boy" fell at 1101, August 9, and a few seconds later Nagasaki ceased to exist as a city. Because of the hills, the damage and the loss of life were not as extensive as at Hiroshima, but they were fearsome enough. The Americans estimated 35,000 dead; the Japanese put the figure at 74,800. Probably the differences will never be reconciled. It is a ghastly commentary on modern war that no one can tell whether 39,800 persons lived or died.

With less than 300 gallons of usable fuel aboard, *Bock's Car* shaped a course for Okinawa. Iwo Jima was out of the question. Sweeney tried to alert the air-sea rescue forces, but they had all gone home, assuming that the primary target had been bombed successfully and that *Bock's Car* and her consorts were returning to base. As he neared Yontan Field on Okinawa,

446

Sweeney tried to contact the tower, but got no response. Probably there was some mix-up over frequencies. Sweeney was getting desperate. There was no chance to circle the field to attract attention. He had only enough fuel for one pass. He fired flares with no success, and the situation was grim, because the field was busy with takeoffs and landings of P-38s and B-25s. Sweeney tried again. "Mayday! Mayday! I want any goddamn tower on Okinawa."

Still no answer.

"Shoot every flare you've got," he ordered. Those fireworks finally worked, and Sweeney was cleared to land. He set the big plane down hard, the small fry scattering like geese before him. Two engines quit cold just after he touched down, and there were only a few cupfuls of gasoline left to use to reverse the props and bring the B-29 to a stop before it ran off the runway.

*The Great Artiste* landed a few minutes later, and then the missing photographic plane turned up and received an unmerciful ribbing from the men of the other planes.

But engraved in the minds of the crews of *The Great Artiste* and *Bock's Car* was what they had seen at Nagasaki. Correspondent William Laurence in *The Great Artiste* described it as a "living thing, a new species of being, born right before incredulous eyes."

An officer brought news of the Nagasaki bomb into the room where the Big Six were debating. The men sat silent.

"I believe," said Suzuki finally, "that we have no alternative but to accept the Potsdam Declaration, and I would now like to hear your opinions."

No one seemed disposed to speak, but finally Admiral Yonai broke the silence. "We're not going to accomplish anything," he said, "unless we speak out. Do we accept the enemy ultimatum unconditionally? Do we propose conditions? If so, we had better discuss them here and now."

It quickly became evident that there was only one thing that they could all agree on, that the national polity—that is, the Emperor system—must be preserved. Otherwise they were split right down the middle, Suzuki, Togo, and Yonai urging acceptance of the Potsdam Declaration as the only means of saving Japan from destruction, and Anami, Umezu, and Toyoda stubbornly insisting on fighting on to the end, even if it meant leaving Japan a group of depopulated desert islands.

At one o'clock the Big Six adjourned, still as divided as ever, to get lunch before the Cabinet meeting later that afternoon.

The Cabinet was no more able to reach agreement than the Big Six had been. After Togo had summed up the events leading to the meeting, Yonai spoke for the peace faction. He took strong issue with Anami's position that the Japanese could inflict such heavy losses on an invading force that the Americans would be discouraged.

"We might," said Yonai, "win the first battle for Japan, but we won't win the second. The war is lost to us. Therefore we must forget about 'face,' we must surrender as quickly as we can, and we must begin to consider at once how best we can preserve our country."

General Anami summed up for the other side.

"We cannot pretend," he said, "to claim that victory is certain, but it is far too early to say that the war is lost. That we will inflict severe losses on the enemy when he invades Japan is certain, and it is by no means impossible that we may be able to reverse the situation in our favor, pulling victory from defeat.

"Furthermore," he went on, "our Army will not submit to demobilization. Our men simply will not lay down their arms. And since they know they are not permitted to surrender, since they know that a fighting man who surrenders is liable to extremely heavy punishment, there is really no alternative for us but to continue the war."

Persons concerned with life at home, such as the Ministers of Agriculture, Commerce, Transportation, and Munitions, tried to bring a voice of sanity to oppose Anami's fancies. They pointed out that the Americans were already on Okinawa, that the rice crop was the poorest in years, that production was near a standstill, and that American ships roamed at will the seas around Japan and American planes made themselves at home in the skies above.

"Yes, yes!" interrupted Anami impatiently. "Everyone understands the situation, but we must fight the war through to the end, no matter how great the odds against us!"

Anami at heart knew that Japan was beaten, but he, like Weygand of France in June of 1940, was more concerned with the honor of the Army than in the preservation of the country. To save the face of the military, he and Umezu and Toyoda insisted that in addition to the preservation of the Emperor, three other conditions be added as the price of Japanese surrender. These conditions were: limited occupation of Japan, that the Japanese try war criminals themselves, and that Japanese troops be disarmed by their own officers. In other words, Anami wanted it to appear that the Japanese Army had not been defeated.

The Cabinet broke for dinner at 5:30 and resumed debate an hour later. After three and a half hours of futile argument, no consensus could be reached and the Cabinet adjourned, no decision taken.

Suzuki and Togo knew what had to be done. Normally if a Cabinet could not reach unanimous agreement on a matter of major policy, it resigned and a new government tried again. But Suzuki believed he had been given a mandate by the Emperor to bring about peace, and he had no intention of resigning. He intended to end the war.

Since no agreement could be reached, His Majesty must break all tradition and tell his leaders what he wanted done. It was extraordinary and unprecedented, but it must be done.

Suzuki and Togo hustled to the Palace and were immediately granted an audience with Hirohito. After listening to their tale of dissension and disunity in the Big Six and in the Cabinet, the Emperor agreed to call the Supreme Council for the Direction of the War (the Big Six) in for a meeting that very night.

Shortly before midnight eleven men gathered in a conference chamber in the underground Palace complex known as the *obunko*. It was a poorly ventilated room, and the men in dress uniforms or in cutaways (the civilians) were sweltering. It was a gloomy room, paneled in dark wood, and the ceiling supported by steel beams. Two long parallel tables were covered with striped green, red, white, and black cloths. At the end opposite

449

from where they had entered, a door was partially concealed by a six-panel gilt screen. Before the screen was placed a chair and a small table covered with gold brocade cloth. That was the Emperor's place.

At 11:50 the door at the far end opened and Hirohito, Emperor of Japan, entered and took his seat. He was dressed in a military uniform and looked tired and careworn. The other men bowed respectfully and took their seats.

Suzuki began the proceedings by asking the Chief Cabinet Secretary, Hisatsune Sakomizu, to read the Potsdam Declaration. Each member of the Big Six stated his position, which was precisely as it had been. When all had had their say, Suzuki turned to the Emperor.

"Your Imperial Majesty's decision is requested as to which proposal should be adopted, the Foreign Minister's or the one with the four conditions."

There were gasps of amazement. The only ones in the room who knew that the question would be asked were Suzuki and Togo. None of the others could believe his ears. Anami seemed about to speak, to voice violent objections, when the Emperor took a hand. Gesturing Suzuki to sit down, Hirohito rose to his feet. An absolute silence fell over the room.

At last he spoke.

"I agree with the Foreign Minister's plan," he said slowly. "I have given serious thought to the situation prevailing at home and abroad and have concluded that continuing the war can only mean destruction for the nation and a prolongation of bloodshed and cruelty in the world. Those who argue for continuing the war once assured me that new battalions and supplies would be ready at Kujukurihama by June. I realize now that this cannot be fulfilled even by September. As for those who wish for one last battle here on our own soil, let me remind them of the disparity between their previous plans and what has actually taken place. I cannot bear to see my innocent people struggle any longer. Ending the war is the only way to restore world peace and to relieve the nation from the terrible distress with which it is burdened."

Those were strong words for the diehards, and it is possible that at that moment Anami made up his mind to commit suicide as soon as his duty was done.

"I cannot help," Hirohito went on, "feeling sad when I think of the people who have served me so faithfully, the soldiers and sailors who have been killed or wounded in far-off battles, the families who have lost all their worldly goods, and often their lives as well, in the air raids at home. It goes without saying that it is unbearable for me to see the brave and loyal fighting men of Japan disarmed. It is equally unbearable that others who have rendered me devoted service should now be punished as instigators of war. Nevertheless, the time has come when we must bear the unbearable."

The Emperor paused and there was absolute silence in the room.

"When I think," he concluded, "of the feelings of my Imperial Grandfather, Emperor Meiji, at the time of the Triple Intervention, I cannot but swallow my tears and sanction the proposal to accept the Allied Proclamation on the basis outlined by the Foreign Minister."

Without saying another word, Hirohito wiped the tears from his eyes and walked slowly out of the room.

After a few moments Suzuki rose to his feet. "His Majesty's decision," he said, "should be made the decision of this conference as well."

There was no argument. The Big Six adjourned to attend a full Cabinet meeting a few minutes later.

Cabinet members wrangled over the wording of the message accepting surrender. The statement about the Emperor was of paramount importance. It had to satisfy Japanese self-respect, but it could not be so strong that the Allies would reject it out of hand. Finally the document was ready. It was a simple acceptance of the Potsdam Declaration "with an understanding that the said declaration does not compromise any demand which prejudices the prerogatives of His Majesty as a sovereign ruler."

At 7:00 A.M., the message was sent in code to the Japanese

451

ministers in Switzerland and Sweden for delivery to appropriate Allied officials. Now Japan could only wait to see how the proviso would be received in the capitals of her enemies.

Later that day, Japanese radio transmitters beamed the Japanese acceptance directly toward the United States, so that the official and unofficial replies were both received about the same time in Washington. Because of the thirteen-hour time difference, they arrived in the early morning hours of August 10. As far as the Americans were concerned, the problem of the Emperor was quickly settled. "Even if the question hadn't been raised by the Japanese," Stimson told President Truman, "we would have to continue the Emperor ourselves under our command and supervision in order to get into surrender the many scattered armies of the Japanese. . . . Something like this use of the Emperor must be made in order to save us from a score of bloody Iwo Jimas and Okinawas all over China and the New Netherlands."

Britain and China quickly wired their concurrence, but the Russians proved difficult. Instead of a single Supreme Commander for the occupation of Japan, Molotov told Harriman in the Kremlin that night, the Russians would like to see several, including, of course, a Russian to be on the same level as the others. Harriman took it on himself to reject this demand without referring it to Washington. The United States, he said bluntly, had carried on the war and borne the major share of the fighting for nearly four years, and the Russians had been in it for less than a week. The Supreme Commander would be an American.

Molotov became angry and insisted that the Russian proposal be sent as he had delivered it. Harriman went back to the Embassy to prepare the text for transmission. While he was working on the job, the phone rang. It was Molotov's interpreter, saying that there had been a misunderstanding. Molotov had consulted Stalin, and the Russians simply wanted to be consulted about the Supreme Commander. They did not demand several.

With the major powers agreed, it only remained to reply to the Japanese message. It took quite a while to settle the details.

In one draft, the Emperor would have had to sign the surrender document himself; this was deleted on Grew's advice. It would humiliate the Emperor and might cause the Japanese people to resist the occupation.

The Allied reply was transmitted through Switzerland on August 11 and was also later broadcast worldwide by powerful radios. Japanese monitors picked up the broadcast a little after midnight on August 12, and it was immediately scrutinized by the Japanese leaders as they waited for the official text through Switzerland.

Events had not stood still while the Allies had pondered their answer. General Anami and Admiral Yonai realized that they would have to persuade the officers of the Army and Navy to accept the fact of surrender. They would have their work cut out for them.

Anami faced a meeting of senior Army officers in the Ichigaya Heights War Ministry building. "I do not know what excuse to make to you," he said, "but since it is the Emperor's decision, it cannot be helped. The important thing is that the Army shall act in an organized manner. Individual feelings must be disregarded. Those among you who are dissatisfied and wish to stave it off will have to do it over Anami's body."

The message was clear, but several hotheads chose not to believe it. A conspiracy began as the fanatics persuaded themselves that the Emperor had been misguided by disloyal advisers. They would defy the Emperor's words while they acted, as they believed, in accordance with his true wishes.

The disunity became obvious when conflicting statements went to the press from the War Ministry and the Information Board. The latter was a delicately phrased affair intended to prepare the Japanese people for the fact of surrender. "In truth," it began, "we cannot but recognize that we are now beset with the worst possible situation."

The military statement had originally been drafted to warn the Army to be prepared to continue the fight until surrender was actually arranged. Anami approved the text and left his office, but the hotheads decided the statement was not powerful enough and proceeded to strengthen the words. Since they could not locate Anami to get his approval of the revisions, they released the doctored text.

It read like Churchill's speeches in the summer of 1940. "Even though we may have to eat grass, swallow dirt and lie in the fields, we shall fight on to the bitter end . . . surge forward to destroy the arrogant enemy."

Who could have guessed from that rhetoric that Japan was on the verge of surrender? A military coup was not only possible but probable.

When the Cabinet met on the afternoon of August 12, Anami had already been approached by conspirators asking him to lead a revolt to stave off the surrender. He stalled, knowing that if he refused, they would simply cut him down and that would mean the collapse of the Suzuki Cabinet and chaos at the moment of Japan's worst ordeal in her history.

Togo cautioned the Cabinet as he opened the proceedings that the text of the message from the Allies was unofficial, having been picked up from a San Francisco station, and that mistakes might have been made in translation. He urged that it be accepted, subject to correction when the official text arrived. A wrangle broke out.

After a preamble, the Allied conditions were:

> From the moment of surrender the authority of the Emperor and the Japanese Government to rule the state shall be subject to the Supreme Commander of the Allied Powers, who will take such steps as he deems proper to effectuate the surrender terms.
>
> The Emperor will be required to authorize and ensure the signature by the Government of Japan and the Japanese Imperial General Headquarters of the surrender terms necessary to carry out the provisions of the Potsdam Declaration, and shall issue his commands to all the Japanese military, naval and air authorities and to all the forces under their control wherever located, to cease active operations and to surrender their arms, and to issue such other orders as the Supreme Commander may require to give effect to the surrender terms.
>
> Immediately upon the surrender the Japanese Government shall transport prisoners of war and civilian internees to places of safety, as directed, where they can quickly be placed aboard Allied transports.

The ultimate form of government of Japan shall, in accordance with the Potsdam Declaration, be established by the freely expressed will of the Japanese people.

The armed forces of the Allied Powers will remain in Japan until the purposes set forth in the Potsdam Declaration are achieved.

All morning long, the Japanese Government had been in a ferment as copies of the document were received in the Foreign Office, in the War and Navy Ministries, in the Palace, and elsewhere. Most of the reaction was negative, and objections burst forth in the Cabinet meeting. Meanwhile plots and more plots were being formed as military men planned to force their wills on the government.

The chief objections were to the statement that "the authority of the Emperor . . . shall be subject to the Supreme Commander . . . ," and the proviso, "The ultimate form of government of Japan shall . . . be established by the freely expressed will of the Japanese people."

The first of these would destroy the authority of the Emperor, argued the dissidents, and the second would destroy the Emperor system and the Emperor himself.

Even Suzuki defected from the peace ranks and declared, "If disarmament is to be forced on Japan, there is no alternative to continuing the war! To be disarmed by the enemy would be unbearable for a Japanese soldier and under such circumstances the Allied reply is unacceptable."

Stunned, Togo called for an adjournment on the ground that the official Allied message had not been received. He had to avoid a vote, for that would bring down the Cabinet and everything would be lost.

As soon as the Cabinet had adjourned, Togo took Suzuki into his office and behind closed doors berated the old man, threatening to resign as Foreign Minister if Suzuki and the others continued their opposition. Suzuki came back into the fold.

To avoid a premature showdown, Togo had his vice minister call the telegraph section of the Foreign Ministry and tell them to hold the official reply and to stamp the time of receipt as of

455

the next morning. Although the message was even then arriving, officially it was received at 7:40 A.M., August 13.

When Togo woke up on August 13, he knew that some answer had to be given and given speedily. Already the American press was accusing the Japanese of delay and stalling. American broadcasts threatened a rain of atomic bombs unless Japan surrendered promptly.

Yet nothing was accomplished that day. Neither in the Big Six meeting that morning nor in the full Cabinet meeting that afternoon was any agreement reached. The Big Six divided three to three, Suzuki having rejoined the peace faction. The Cabinet split was ten for peace, three for further negotiations, one who gave his proxy to Suzuki, and one who couldn't make up his mind. Anami, Umezu, and Toyoda wanted the Japanese to insist that the Emperor could not be ordered about by the Supreme Commander, that the Emperor system not be a matter for popular vote, that there would be no occupation of the Home Islands, and that the Japanese forces would be allowed to disarm themselves.

The arguments ranged like a debate of a meeting of semanticists, not one of government leaders. While it was going on, the plots grew more widespread and more menacing.

Suddenly Chief Cabinet Secretary Sakomizu was called out of the meeting. A reporter from *Asahi Shimbun* handed him a bit of paper and asked, "Do you know about this?"

It was a communiqué from Imperial General Headquarters and was to be released by the press and radio at 4:00 P.M., fifteen minutes from that moment, and read:

> The Imperial Army and Navy having hereby received the gracious Imperial Command to protect the national polity and to defend the Imperial Land, the entire armed forces will single-heartedly commence a general offensive against the Allied enemy forces.

It was impossible! If this were broadcast, it would be national suicide. The Allies would carry out their promise and utterly destroy Japan as a nation.

456

Hastening back into the Cabinet room, Sakomizu challenged Anami with the release. He knew nothing about it. Nor did General Umezu, when he was reached. Frantic telephone calls took place, and the release was killed just seconds before it was to go on the air.

Later it was discovered that the release was the work of subordinate officers in the press section of Imperial GHQ, and had been approved by the Vice Minister of War and the Vice Chief of Staff. No one thought it improper that such falsehoods should be released, even the falsehood of attributing the command to the Emperor. The incident revealed the utter breakdown of discipline in the Army. It also emphasized that peace, if it was to come, had to be made quickly before the fanatics made it impossible.

That evening, the Cabinet still unable to agree, Suzuki adjourned the meeting with the statement that he would once again ask His Majesty to give his gracious decision.

Another precious day had been wasted.

Meanwhile, the plots went on.

The next morning, August 14, there was scheduled to be a resumption of the debate, with little prospect of any agreement. As Suzuki wearily climbed out of bed that morning, B-29s were dropping the most explosive cargoes they had ever carried. There were no bombs; instead five million leaflets fluttered down upon all major Japanese cities and over the countryside. They told of the Japanese acceptance of the surrender and of the Allied reply, two items the Japanese leaders were desperately keeping from the Japanese people.

One of the leaflets was carried into the Palace, and Hirohito read it. There must be no more time lost. He summoned Suzuki, who said the time had come for the Emperor to summon an Imperial Conference. This was unprecedented, for an Imperial Conference was called at the request of the Big Six. The Emperor agreed and issued instructions to Kido.

Although instructions specified informal dress, all over town important officials were borrowing ties and jackets from subordinates. The tables had been removed from the conference room in the *obunko* annex in order to accommodate a larger number of persons. The room was steaming with humidity as the Emperor entered at 10:50, dressed in Army uniform and wearing white gloves.

The hold-outs had their say, urging continuation of the war until the terms could be eased. Hirohito listened carefully. There were no more opinions. Then he rose and spoke.

He reviewed at some length his reasons for accepting the Allied note. As he spoke, he often paused to brush the tears from his eyes. Many of his listeners were sobbing aloud. There was no mistaking his meaning.

"It is my desire," he concluded, "that all of you, my ministers of state, bow to my wishes and accept the Allied reply forthwith. The people know nothing about this situation and will be surprised to hear of my sudden decision. I am willing to do anything. If it is for the good of the people I am willing to make a broadcast. I will go anywhere to persuade the officers and men of the Army and Navy to lay down their arms. It is my desire that the Cabinet at once draw up an imperial rescript to end the war."

After that, there was nothing to do but have the cabinet formally ratify His Majesty's orders. The acceptance was drawn up that afternoon and evening, and at 8:30 P.M. it was ready. It took until eleven o'clock to round up all the Cabinet members and get their signatures, but at last the work was done.

Meanwhile the rescript had to be written, and this was time-consuming. It had to be in formal court language, much as one would write in the language of Shakespeare today. Endless disputes arose over the wording, with face-saving compromises. At one point the draft read, "the war situation is getting worse day by day." Anami insisted that it was an insult to Japan's fighting men, and it was changed to "the war situation has developed not necessarily to Japan's advantage." Those words appeared in the final rescript and were broadcast to the nation by the Emperor the next day.

When the rescript was done, Hirohito read it and requested a few minor changes. Then it had to be transcribed in a fair copy for history. The Emperor then read it twice into microphones to make a record for broadcasting at noon the following day.

Everything was done. The Emperor had affixed his seal to the surrender document, the rescript had been made ready, and the recordings had been made. It was all over.

It was by no means over. Other men had other ideas, and they were prepared to bring them about, whether it meant the deaths of millions of their own people, even if it meant defying the will of the Emperor.

As always, these fanatics convinced themselves that they were carrying out the real will of the Emperor, that he had listened to false councillors.

First they tried to steal the recordings that the Emperor had made so that they could not be broadcast to the people. They knew only that these recordings were in the custody of one of the chamberlains for safekeeping. Fortunately, there were too many chamberlains, and the conspirators never found the right one. In any case, the recordings were in a safe and would be delivered to the broadcasting station the next day.

A more serious plot was to take over the Palace and isolate the Emperor from his "disloyal" ministers. Among the most active leaders of the Palace revolt were Major Kenji Hatanaka and Lieutenant Colonel Masataka Ida, both attached to the Ministry of War. They tried to get Anami to lead the conspiracy, but he refused. He had other ideas. He was preparing to expiate his failure to win the war by committing hara-kiri that very night.

Failing with Anami, Hatanaka and Ida rushed into the office of Lieutenant General Takeshi Mori, Commander of the First Imperial Guards Division, who was responsible for the safety of the Emperor and the Palace. Mori patiently listened to an impassioned plea from the young fanatics and sparred for time. He said he would go to the Meiji Shrine to pray for guidance.

"This is all a waste of time!" shouted Hatanaka.

Mori was adamant, and the argument grew. Another conspirator, Captain Uehara drew his sword and cut down the General, whereupon Hatanaka administered the *coup de grâce* with his pistol.

The conspirators then proceeded to issue orders in Mori's name, instructing the Guards to take over the Palace.

459

The next morning, the Emperor and members of the court were literally prisoners. The guard force had been doubled, and they permitted no one to enter or leave the Palace.

In his home, General Anami lay dying, his abdomen slashed twice in the most painful form of hara-kiri. He refused the *coup de grâce* and all medical aid. He would not die for hours.

General Shizuichi Tanaka, Commander of the Eastern District Army, soon heard of the seizure of the Palace. Risking the fate of Mori, he went himself and assumed command. The troops marched off, and normal activities resumed. The revolt was over, although scattered efforts went on for days.

Promptly at noon, everyone in Japan stopped what he was doing to hear their Emperor speak. The acceptance of the Allied terms had already been sent to Washington, but the Japanese people knew it not. They had no idea what to expect in this unprecedented broadcast.

At noon, an announcer spoke. His words went to all the islands of Japan and to the Japanese overseas. Then, following the strains of "Kimigayo," the national anthem, the voice that most of the Japanese people had never heard began to speak.

"To our good and loyal subjects: after pondering deeply the general trends of the world and the actual conditions obtaining in Our Empire today, We have decided to effect a settlement of the present situation by resorting to an extraordinary measure. . . ."

People began to weep and sob uncontrollably. Most knelt as the Imperial words went on.

"We have resolved to pave the way for a grand peace for all the generations to come by enduring the unendurable and suffering what is insufferable. . . .

"Cultivate the ways of rectitude; foster nobility of spirit; and work with resolution so ye may enhance the innate glory of the Imperial state and keep pace with the progress of the world."

The voice ceased, and people began reacting according to their natures. Some wept and then went on to pick up the tasks of life once again. Not a few committed hara-kiri. Admiral Matome Ugaki, who had fought at Midway, led a group of suicide planes in a last sortie against the American fleet. The last report was from a pilot saying that they were diving on a ship. Strangely enough, there is no record of any attack made on American ships that day. On Kyushu a group of B-29 crewmen were taken from their prison camp and beheaded, one after another.

Most, however, turned to thoughts of peace. His Majesty had spoken, and there was no more to be said.

Off Japan, American Navy units received orders to cease fire before midnight. Admiral Halsey responded in a characteristic fashion by ordering his planes, "Investigate and shoot down all snoopers—not vindictively, but in a friendly sort of way."

Friendly or not, there was no need. The guns fell silent, the warplanes landed, the troops put down their arms. The most destructive war in the history of the world was over. The war was won.

It remained only to ensure that the peace would be won as well.

# Epilogue:
# These Proceedings Are Now Closed

*We have had our last chance. If we do not devise some greater and more equitable system, Armageddon will be at our door.*

Douglas MacArthur, September 2, 1945.

A great crowd assembled on Pennsylvania Avenue outside the White House on the evening of August 14, 1945. Rumors had flown all day that the Japanese had quit, and the milling thousands wanted to be at the center of history when the official word came.

Inside, President Truman called reporters into the Oval Study at 7:00 P.M. to read them a brief statement. Most of the Cabinet members stood behind the desk; on Mr. Truman's left sat former Secretary of State Cordell Hull who had given the whiplash of his tongue to the Japanese ambassadors on the opening day of the war minutes after the Pearl Harbor attack. On the President's right sat Secretary of State Byrnes and Admiral Leahy, representing the Joint Chiefs of Staff.

Gone was the clutter that had been there when Franklin D. Roosevelt sat behind that desk. A telephone, a microphone, and a small pile of papers were all that was there. In his right hand, the President held a single sheet which he read to the reporters.

"I have received this afternoon," said Mr. Truman, "a message from the Japanese Government in reply to the message forwarded to that Government by the Secretary of State on August eleventh. I deem this reply a full acceptance of the Potsdam Declaration which specifies the unconditional surrender of Japan. In the reply there is no qualification. . . . General

462

Douglas MacArthur has been appointed the Supreme Allied Commander to receive the Japanese surrender. . . ."

Newsmen bolted from the room to grab telephones and flash the word to the waiting pressrooms and to the world. Truman went out on the North Portico and spoke to the ever growing crowd briefly, flashing the famous V for victory sign in the manner of Churchill. Then he went back inside and called his mother in Missouri.

Although false news flashes had come in all day, most people waited for the official word before celebrating. President Truman's words set off scenes of wild celebration from coast to coast. In every major city there was dancing in the streets which often went on all night. Pretty girls kissed strange servicemen, and were eagerly kissed back. In San Francisco a girl climbed up on a fountain and took her clothes off and splashed around in the fountain before delighted eyes of men in khaki and blue.

Car horns honked, whistles sounded in factories, sirens screamed, and people yelled and cheered as the sounds of victory grew. As the hours passed, the celebrations showed no sign of abating; indeed they grew noisier. Bars and taverns did a rushing business, and drunken men and women added their bits to the confusion. In some places, the celebrations began to turn ugly. Street cars and buses were stripped and wrecked, liquor stores looted, and senseless fires set. Some stores had their window displays looted. It was worst of all in San Francisco. Nearly every window along Market Street was broken, and five people had been killed in the celebration that was approaching a riot. Another 300 were injured. Most of the damage was done by "boots" from receiving stations of all the armed forces nearby. These men, who had never known combat, went wild when they learned they would not have to face enemy fire overseas. Eventually military authorities declared San Francisco off limits for servicemen unless they were stationed there.

Similar scenes of celebration took place in London, Wellington, Sydney, Melbourne, in all the Allied capitals, and in cities great and small across the world.

But the dying was not yet over, and the guns occasionally spoke in a few sharp, deadly voices.

In China, teams of OSS men were dropped to release prisoners of war in remote camps. Some were shot by suspicious Japanese. Others met a similar fate at the hands of Chinese communists, who were moving into the vacuum left by the collapse of Japanese power and the absence of Chiang Kai-shek's troops. The Russians were still grinding out advances across Manchuria, determined to get the last foot of Japanese territory before peace-time adjustments had to be made.

Some OSS teams met with success. They were properly received by Japanese who had heard of the surrender, and they released prisoners. Among them were Major General Jonathan Wainwright, who had been left behind on Corregidor when MacArthur had been ordered to leave, and who had shared the rigors of brutal captivity with his men. Another was Lieutenant General Arthur E. Percival, RA, who had surrendered Singapore to the Tiger of Malaya, Lieutenant General Tomoyuki Yamashita, in the dark days of early 1942.

General MacArthur lost no time in asserting his authority as Supreme Commander. Almost before the echoes of Hirohito's voice had died away, a message was beamed to Japan from MacArthur's headquarters at Manila. It established his authority and set up communication procedures. The next ordered the Japanese to send a delegation to Manila to work out surrender arrangements and to receive orders for the occupation of Japan.

The Japanese had great difficulty assembling a suitable group for the journey. In the first place, the Suzuki government resigned immediately after the Emperor's broadcast. No Cabinet existed when MacArthur's order arrived. His Majesty's personal choice for the new Prime Minister was Prince Toshihiko Higashikuni, who conveniently held the rank of general in the Japanese Army. Thus he would be able to control Army hotheads. On August 17, Prince Higashikuni presented his Cabinet to the Emperor. Yonai was the sole holdover from the previous administration. Togo refused to continue as Foreign

Minister, and the job went to his predecessor in that office, Mamoru Shigemitsu.

The obvious choice to head the delegation to Manila was General Umezu, the Army Chief of Staff, but he refused point blank. The choice then fell on his deputy, Lieutenant General Torashiro Kawabe, who hated the mission but agreed to serve. A total of fifteen others was picked by Kawabe to go along, but not until several of the first choices had taken to the hills rather than go on such a disgraceful mission. They would have to reveal all of their country's secrets to the men who had been their enemies and were now their conquerors.

No one knew whether the delegation would ever reach Manila.

In addition to the possibility of being shot down by trigger-happy American pilots, they might be killed by diehard Kamikaze pilots who still would not accept the fact of their country's surrender. There was a question whether they would get off at all.

They were to leave from Henada Airport outside Tokyo on the morning of August 19. On the 18th, nearby Naval Air Station at Atsugi was commanded by a madman, who was whipping up his excitable pilots to fight on by any means and to destroy the "traitors" who had misguided the Emperor. If he learned any hint of the Kawabe mission, the planes were certain to be destroyed before they had gone a hundred miles.

It was not until the evening of August 18 that authorities regained control at Atsugi and took the raving Navy Captain Ammyo Kosono off in a straitjacket. Even then the situation was touch-and-go. There were still fanatics at Atsugi and at other airfields.

The two battered planes bearing the delegation got off without incident, however, and flew a dog-leg course to Ie Shima, where Ernie Pyle had died. There they were transferred to an American C-54 for the four-and-a-half-hour flight to Manila. On the way, the Japanese were served box lunches, which they ate with relish. Even the reluctant Kawabe managed to get his down.

465

About dusk the Japanese arrived at Manila, touching down at Nichols Field, where they were greeted by Colonel Sidney Mashbir, Chief of MacArthur's translation section, and by Major General Charles Willoughby, MacArthur's G-2 officer. While Mashbir's fluent Japanese dealt with the others, Kawabe and Willoughby were able to converse easily in German, which happened to be the latter's native language. He had lived the first twelve years of his life in Germany.

Although the American soldiers lining the streets leading from Nichols Field to Manila were good-natured and curious, the Filipinos were hostile. No matter that these particular men had had nothing to do with the wanton, useless destruction of their beautiful capital. They were Japanese and they were hated. Rocks were thrown at the cars, and insults were yelled. The Japanese looked straight ahead.

At length the Japanese arrived safely at the Rosario Apartments near the Manila Hotel and the harbor. They were shown comfortable rooms and given a turkey dinner. The Americans sat apart and ignored their unwilling guests. Then it was time to go to the City Hall, where the first session would be held.

MacArthur had no intention of participating in the discussions. Already he was putting into effect the careful, studied aloofness that would characterize his rule of Japan. While he had fearlessly exposed himself in the battle areas to be with his men during the fighting, he would become almost invisible to the Japanese. Only a few would ever see him, and those in the most formal of occasions. But he meant to have his presence known and felt.

His Chief of Staff, Major General Richard K. Sutherland, conducted the conferences. Everything was stiffly formal, military protocol being the order of the day. Instructions were given for the surrender of Japanese units in all areas of the Pacific and of Asia, just which ones would surrender to the Australians, the New Zealanders, the Russians, the Chinese, and the Americans.

A disagreement quickly developed. The Japanese were horrified that the advance party of Americans was scheduled to arrive at Atsugi Airbase on August 23, just four short days from

466

then. The Japanese protested. They needed at least ten days to get ready. The government was not yet in full control of the people. Hotheads might destroy the American party as it landed.

Sutherland made no comment.

"Maybe you should know," Kawabe said urgently, "that we are having trouble at home with some of the Kamikaze units. They delayed our trip, in fact."

Sutherland went on to other things, but as the conference was breaking up, he announced that the advance party would not arrive until August 28. He had conceded five days grace for the Japanese.

The implication was that they had better use them well.

As they departed, the Japanese glumly realized that they had given all their country's vital secrets to their conquerors, the location of every military unit, every submarine, every surviving ship, every air station, every troop concentration, every ammunition dump, every storage facility. Never before in Japanese history had such a thing been done.

The Japanese had retrieved something from the conferences. They had been handed a draft of an Imperial Rescript, the "Instrument of Surrender." It had been badly drafted by the Americans, and the Japanese regarded it as offensive and insulting. The very first word was wrong: *watakushi*. In official usage the Emperor never employed that word for "I." To him alone belonged the pronoun *Chin*, the Royal We. Mashbir reassured them, and MacArthur agreed. "Mashbir, you handled that exactly right," he said later. "I have no desire whatever to debase him [the Emperor] in the eyes of his own people." Willoughby wondered what the fuss was all about.

The journey home was not uneventful for the Japanese delegates. When they landed on Ie Shima, they discovered that one of the two Bettys was laid up with mechanical difficulties, so only the higher ranking delegates were able to proceed that night. Then a fuel leak developed in the one plane that did get off, and it had to land in the water a few yards from the coast of Japan. Incredibly they were able to wade ashore, and looking up could see the crest of Mount Fujiyama.

467

As August 28 approached, the Japanese nervously prepared for the arrival of the first of their new rulers. Mindful of propaganda which had depicted Americans as ravening beasts, families prepared to hide their women and girls. Wild rumors flew around that the Americans had already landed at Yokohama and were looting, raping, and murdering, in short, acting as Japanese troops had acted wherever they had been the victors. Women were told to wear loose-fitting clothes to disguise their figures and not to smile, as such courtesy would be taken as invitation by the American barbarians. In case of rape, women were told to "maintain their dignity while crying loudly for help," a very neat trick indeed.

In some factories women were issued cyanide capsules to help them preserve "their honor as Japanese ladies."

Groups of fanatics continued to assemble in key spots, but were either persuaded to go home by the police and Army leaders or they killed themselves where they were in protest against the fate that had overtaken their country.

Atsugi Airbase had been the scene of bitter fighting between fanatical diehard naval pilots and Army units sent in to bring them under control. When Lieutenant General Seizo Arisue arrived there to take over the field and prepare to receive the Americans, he found a shambles. Not a plane was fit to fly. Hangars had been destroyed by American bombing and by the recent battle between the Japanese themselves. Runways were pitted with bomb holes which would need to be repaired before the Americans arrived.

Colonel Charles Tench did not expect to live much longer. He had been selected to command the advance party which would land at Atsugi. It was a great honor to be the first American to set foot on Japanese soil as a conqueror, but he fully expected that the small group he would lead would be cut down by fanatics. Nevertheless, he did not shrink from the assignment. He wondered how they would be avenged.

After a stop at Okinawa, Colonel Tench, in the lead plane of forty-five C-47s, approached Atsugi early in the morning on August 28. The pilot mistook the wind indicator and landed down wind, so that the plane came to a stop at the opposite end of the field from where the reception party of General Arisue and his staff was waiting. The bewildered Japanese set out at a run across the field to reach the plane, and Colonel Tench believed his worst fears had come true. To him it seemed a mob of fanatics was rushing to kill him.

Nothing happened, however, and the planes continued to land. General Arisue led the colonel across the field to a tent and offered him a glass of orange juice. Colonel Tench hesitated, and Arisue, guessing the reason for his reluctance, drank it himself to show that it was not poisoned. Tench drank another glass, relaxed, lighted a cigarette, and set about doing what had to be done.

Two days later, the Atsugi Airbase was occupied in force by the Eleventh Airborne Division, arriving in planes that landed every two minutes, hour after hour. At 1419, August 30, the C-54 *Bataan* touched down and rolled to a stop. MacArthur emerged, paused at the top of the ladder to light his famous corncob pipe, and was heard to remark, "This is it." General Robert Eichelberger, who had arrived earlier, came up to salute and shake hands. MacArthur grinned. "Bob," he said, "from Melbourne to Tokyo is a long way, but this seems to be the end of the road."

A little fleet of dilapidated cars was waiting to take MacArthur and his party to the New Grand Hotel in Yokohama, where he set up temporary headquarters. After a good dinner and a quiet night surrounded by millions of Japanese unaccustomed to surrender, MacArthur set to work.

During dinner that evening, General Wainwright arrived and MacArthur sent for him immediately.

"Well, Skinny," he said to the emaciated figure who hesitantly entered the room.

"General," was all that Wainwright was able to reply.

He believed he was in disgrace for having surrendered to the Japanese.

"Why, Jim," replied MacArthur, "your old corps is yours when you want it."

The Navy had not been idle while MacArthur was moving in.

American prisoners of war at Camp Omori near Tokyo watched incredulously as landing craft bearing the Fourth Marine Regiment landed near them. In one of them was Commander Harold Stassen, sometime Governor of Minnesota, and now a member of Halsey's staff. He walked up to the gate of the camp. The Japanese commandant stopped him. "I have no authority to turn these men over to you."

Stassen brushed him aside. "You have no authority, period." The prisoners were released.

By this time ships were entering Tokyo Bay, carriers, cruisers, destroyers, auxiliaries, LSTs, ships of all kinds and types which had destroyed the Japanese Navy and isolated her homeland from the outside world. Then there were the battleships, among them U.S.S. *Missouri* flying the four-star blue flag of Admiral William F. Halsey, Jr. For a few hours this ship would be the center of the world's attention. On its deck would be gathered the victorious military leaders to receive the formal surrender of Japan.

The selection of the *Missouri* as surrender site was the result of political horse-trading in Washington. Secretary of the Navy Forrestal argued that since MacArthur had been selected as Supreme Commander, Nimitz should have the honor of conducting the ceremony. He was overruled and MacArthur was given that job. To recognize the role of the Navy in the war, Forrestal insisted that the signing take place aboard a naval vessel, and suggested the *Missouri*. Since this also honored President Truman's home state, the suggestion carried the day.

There was immense activity aboard the *Missouri* when her assignment became known. An intense field day was held, for the *Missouri* had to be shipshape and Bristol fashion when the great day arrived. The table on which the surrender documents would be laid came from the ship's mess hall and the green cover from the wardroom so that both enlisted and officers were symbolically represented. A difficulty arose over the green cloth, for none could be found that did not have a cigarette hole. A comparatively new one had only one such hole, and one of the documents was laid on top of it.

When Nimitz came aboard, Halsey temporarily shifted his

flag to the *Iowa,* and Nimitz's five-star flag was hoisted at the yardarm of the *Missouri.* Later MacArthur's would fly beside it, as would Halsey's on the day of surrender. The Stars and Stripes flew over nearby Yokosuka Naval Base. But two more historic flags were aboard the *Missouri.* At morning colors was hoisted the ensign that flew over the Capitol in Washington on the morning of December 7, 1941.* Mounted on a bulkhead, because it was too brittle to fly, was the thirty-one-starred ensign that Commodore Matthew Calbraith Perry had flown in Tokyo Bay ninety-two years earlier when he had opened Japan to the world. The ensign had been brought by special messenger from the U.S. Naval Academy Museum in Annapolis.

The dignitaries began to arrive that cold, gray morning of September 2, but it was bright and cheery in the hearts of those who gathered on the *Missouri* to await the Japanese.

At 0856, the Japanese delegation arrived aboard the American destroyer *Lansdowne.* They had to suffer the minor indignity of being brought to the scene of surrender in an American ship because there was not a single Japanese vessel fit to steam. All had fallen victim to the American battle might.

Foreign Minister Shigemitsu had great difficulty negotiating the ladder to the *Missouri*'s deck. Years ago an assassin's bomb had blown off a leg, and his wooden replacement had never fitted properly. It was rumored that the artificial leg had been given him by the Emperor and he had to wear it, even though it gave him excruciating pain. It would have been an insult to His Majesty if he had not used it or if he had had it altered.

Shigemitsu refused assistance as he came up and took his place beside the table. He was followed by General Umezu and nine others, three each from the Foreign Office, the Army and the Navy.

The Japanese were amazed at the informality of the bearing of the victors. All officers were in open-necked shirts, the Americans in khaki, the British in white shorts and knee stockings. Correspondents were everywhere, and enlisted crew

* It had flown over Casablanca, Rome, and Berlin, and would fly in a few days over the American Embassy in Tokyo when MacArthur moved there.

members were sitting or standing wherever they could find space clear of the ceremonial area. Some were even straddling the barrels of the 16-inch guns the *Missouri* had only a few weeks before been firing at Japan.

Precisely at 0900, MacArthur appeared, followed by Nimitz and Halsey. He stepped to the microphone. An absolute hush fell over the scene broken only by the screams of the sea gulls and the soft lapping of water against the ship's side.

"We are gathered here," said MacArthur, "representatives of the major warring powers, to conclude a solemn agreement whereby peace may be restored. The issues, involving divergent ideals and ideologies, have been determined on the battlefields of the world and hence are not for our discussion or debate. Nor is it for us here to meet, representing as we do a majority of the peoples of the earth, in a spirit of distrust, malice, or hatred. But rather it is for us, both victors and vanquished, to rise to that higher dignity which alone benefits the sacred purposes we are about to serve, committing all our people unreservedly to faithful compliance with the understanding they are here formally to assume . . ."

He paused, and the Japanese looked at him and at the array of officers who stood with him and behind him. Two were worthy of special note, for they had been captives of the Japanese only a few days before. Thin, emaciated, still showing the marks of their ill treatment, General Wainwright and General Percival stood among the victors.

MacArthur's deep voice went on.

"It is my earnest hope—indeed the hope of all mankind— that from this solemn occasion a better world shall emerge out of the blood and carnage of the past, a world founded upon faith and understanding, a world dedicated to the dignity of man and the fulfillment of his most cherished wish for freedom, tolerance, and justice."

At the moment he finished speaking, the clouds opened and the glittering peak of Mount Fuji could be seen. In a voice that cracked like a whip, MacArthur ordered, "The representatives of the Imperial Japanese Government and of the Imperial Japanese Staff will now come forward and sign!"

472

Shigemitsu hobbled forward and sat down in the chair placed before the surrender documents. One copy was in English and one in Japanese. Shigemitsu fumbled with his silk top hat, his gloves, his cane, giving the impression of stalling. Halsey wanted to shout, "Sign, damn you! Sign!" Of course he did no such thing. MacArthur realized that the Japanese Foreign Minister did not know what to do. "Sutherland, show him where to sign," he ordered. The Chief of Staff pointed to the correct line on each document. Shigemitsu marked the three Japanese characters of his name. Umezu was next. He did not stop to sit down as he scrawled his name.

Japan had formally surrendered. The time was 0904.

MacArthur was next. He used several pens, signing his name in fragments, so that several persons would have mementoes of the occasion.*

Now that the Supreme Commander had signed for the Allied Powers, representatives of the major warring nations signed for their individual countries. Nimitz signed for the United States. Then came General Hsu Yung-chang for China, Admiral Sir Bruce Fraser for the United Kingdom, Lieutenant General K. Derevyanko for the Soviet Union, General Sir Thomas Blamey for Australia, Colonel L. Moore-Gosgrove for Canada, General Jacques Leclerc for France, Admiral C. E. L. Helfrich for the Netherlands, and Air Vice Marshal Sir L. M. Isitt for New Zealand.

When everyone had signed, MacArthur spoke again.

"Let us pray that peace be now restored to the world and that God will preserve it always. These proceedings are now closed."

He walked over to Halsey and put his arm around his shoulder. "Bill," he asked, "where the hell are those airplanes?"

At that moment a roar was heard growing in the distance. It became louder and louder as 450 carrier planes from Task Force 38 swept over the ship mast-high, followed by B-29s. It

---

* There is considerable disagreement as to what happened to the pens. Wainwright and Percival each got one. Other recipients named are President Truman, the *Missouri*, the Archives, West Point, his aide, General Courtney Whitney, MacArthur's wife, and MacArthur himself. Since only five or six pens were used, the list is far too long. Somebody got left out.

was a tremendous display of strength of Allied air power, just as was the congregation of 258 warships anchored in Tokyo Bay that morning one of naval power.

MacArthur then made his way to another microphone to broadcast to the American people. It was a message of victory and of warning. His mind had already foreseen the troubles of the postwar world.

Today the guns are silent. A great tragedy has ended. . . . As I look back upon the long, tortuous trail from those grim days of Bataan and Corregidor . . . I thank a merciful God that He has given us the faith, the courage and the power from which to mold victory. . . .

A new era is upon us. Even the lesson of victory itself brings with it profound concern, both for our future security and the survival of civilization. The destructiveness of the war potential, through . . . scientific discovery, has . . . now reached a point which revises the traditional concept of war. Men since the beginning of time have sought peace. Various methods through the ages have been attempted to devise an international process to prevent or settle disputes between nations. . . . Military Alliances, Balances of Power, Leagues of Nations, all in turn failed, leaving the only path to be by way of the crucible of war. The utter destructiveness of war now blots out this alternative. We have had our last chance. If we do not devise some greater and more equitable system, Armageddon will be at our door.

It must be of the spirit if we are to save the flesh.

World War II had officially ended. It had lasted 2,192 days, 2 hours and 41 minutes. It was the most destructive war in the history of mankind, and mankind cannot afford another.

During the six years of the war, some 70 million men and women had borne arms, and at least 17 million had been killed on the battlefields, and in the air, and on the sea. Another 18 million civilians died as a result of bombing, plague, pestilence, and ruthless genocidal policies.

The war cost at least a trillion dollars in actual costs and losses, and it cost far more in lost production of goods than could be measured in money. How much more was lost in what might have been done by those who died can never be known. Were minds blotted out that, had they lived, would have cured cancer, erected great buildings, painted new masterpieces, composed great music, written great books, solved the problems of poverty, pain, and evil?

Victory was absolute for the Allies, in the military sense at least. All three enemy capitals were occupied; all three Axis nations were ruled by soldiers of the victors. There could be no denial of defeat as in the 1920s and 1930s when renascent Germany proclaimed that her troops had been betrayed by the politicians back home.

Defeat was absolute for the beaten. What could be rebuilt?

"It must be of the spirit if we are to save the flesh."

Mankind has shown no great wisdom in the years since World War II ended. A primitive instinct for survival has so far prevented the use in war of the weapons that were first revealed at Hiroshima and Nagasaki. Nations now have weapons that make those bombs look like fire crackers. Even with conventional weapons, the folly of politicians and demagogues has given scarce a day of peace in the quarter century and more since MacArthur's warning from the deck of the *Missouri*.

Yet all must not be left in the negative side of the balance. Even war brings something of good amidst the ruin and carnage. The Hitlers, the Mussolinis, the Himmlers, the Bormanns, the Tojos, the Yamashitas, the Quislings, the Lavals, the sadistic guards and murderers in Japanese prison camps and in Belsen, Auschwitz, Dachau, Buchenwald, and others revealed the depths of degradation of the human soul, but the supreme courage and dedication to the principle of freedom and to human decencies of the Churchills, the Roosevelts, the Trumans, the Kings, the Halseys, the Nimitzes, the Eisenhowers, the Marshalls, the Brookes, the Reynauds, yes, even the Rommels and the Rundstedts and the Mansteins, who carried on the war as professional soldiers in the service of their countries, offset the balance of evil to some extent.

Men who entered the armed forces were drawn together as never before. Fierce pride in units and in ships and in air groups developed, and the sense of never letting one's buddy

475

down was strong and grew stronger as the war went on. There were, of course, the rotters, the selfish, the no-goods, but there were more who gave and gave and gave until they had nothing left to give. They fought to preserve a way of life they saw as good—not perfect, but good. And they fought to get back home and make it better.

The war was begun by the men in highest office, it was planned by the high commanders, and the lesser commanders led their men in battle. But it was the little guy who won it—millions of him—and the folks back home who gave him the tools and kept him going with love and prayer.

And so he came home, mourning those who did not, but ready to live the life he had fought for.

# Bibliography

The bibliography that follows is a highly selective list based on two criteria: authority and general interest. Some books written during the war cannot pretend to authority, but they have sufficient topical interest to be read today. Some by participants have a natural bias, but their statements of feelings, ideas, reasons for decisions are valuable.

Extensive use has been made of magazine and newspaper files. *The London Times, The London Daily Mail, The Daily Telegraph, The Daily Express, The New York Times, The Washington Post, The San Francisco Chronicle, Time, Life, Newsweek, U.S. News, The Saturday Evening Post,* and *The New Yorker* have been especially valuable.

ADAMSON, HANS CHRISTIAN and GEORGE FRANCIS KOSCO, *Halsey's Typhoons.* New York: Crown Publishers, Inc. 1967.

AUPHAN, AMIRAL, *The French Navy in World War II,* trans. by Captain A. C. J. Sabalot. Annapolis: U.S. Naval Institute, 1959.

——, and JACQUES MORDAL, *La Marine Française pendant la Seconde Guerre Mondiale.* Paris: Hachette, 1958.

BARBEY, DANIEL E., *MacArthur's Amphibious Navy: Seventh Amphibious Force Operations 1943–1945.* Annapolis: U.S. Naval Institute, 1969.

BARUCH, BERNARD M., *The Public Years.* New York: Holt, Rinehart and Winston, 1960.

BAUMBACH, WERNER, *The Life and Death of the Luftwaffe,* trans. by Frederick Holt. New York: Coward-McCann, 1960.

BEKKER, CAJUS, *The Luftwaffe War Diaries,* trans. by Frank Ziegler. New York: Ballantine Books, 1969.

BRACHER, KARL DIETRICH, *The German Dictatorship: The Origins,*

*Structure, and Effects of National Socialism*, trans. by Jean Steinberg. New York: Praeger Publishers, 1970.

BRADLEY, OMAR N., *A Soldier's Story*. New York: Holt, Rinehart and Winston Inc., 1951

BRENNECKE, JOCHEN, *The Hunters and the Hunted*. London: Burke, 1958.

BROOKS, LESTER, *Behind Japan's Surrender: The Secret Struggle That Ended an Empire*. New York: McGraw-Hill Book Co., 1968.

BRYANT, ARTHUR, *The Alanbrooke Diaries*. 2 vols. New York: Doubleday and Co., 1957.

BRYANT, REAR ADMIRAL BEN, *Submarine Commander*. New York: Ballantine Books, 1958.

BUCHANAN, A. RUSSELL, *The United States and World War II*. 2 vols. New York: Harper and Row, 1964.

BULLOCK, ALAN, *Hitler: A Study in Tyranny*, revised ed. New York: Harper and Row, 1962.

BUTCHER, CAPTAIN HARRY C., USNR, *My Three Years with Eisenhower*. New York: Simon and Schuster, 1946.

CAIDIN, MARTIN, *Flying Forts*. New York: Ballantine Books, 1968.

CARELL, PAUL, *Invasion—They're Coming*, trans. by E. Osers. New York: E. P. Dutton and Co., 1963.

CHALMERS, REAR ADMIRAL W. S., *Full Cycle: The Biography of Admiral Sir Bertram Home Ramsey*. London: Hodder and Stoughton, 1959.

CHAMBLISS, WILLIAM C., *The Silent Service*. New York: New American Library, 1965.

CHANDLER, ALFRED D., JR., ed. *The Papers of Dwight David Eisenhower*. 5 vols. Baltimore: The Johns Hopkins Press, 1970.

CHURCHILL, WINSTON S., *History of the Second World War*. 6 vols. Boston: Houghton Mifflin Co., 1948–1953.

CLARK, ALAN, *Barbarossa: The Russian-German Conflict, 1941–45*. New York: William Morrow and Co., 1965.

CLARK, MARK, *Calculated Risk*. London: George C. Harris and Co., 1951.

COLLINS, LARRY, and DOMINIQUE LAPIERRE, *Is Paris Burning?* New York: Simon and Schuster, 1965.

CRAIG, WILLIAM, *The Fall of Japan*. New York: The Dial Press, Inc., 1967.

CUNNINGHAM, ADMIRAL OF THE FLEET VISCOUNT CUNNINGHAM OF HYNDHOPE, *A Sailor's Odyssey*. London: 1951.

DAVIDSON, EUGENE, *The Trial of the Germans*. New York: The Macmillan Company, 1966.

DAVIS, BURKE, *Marine: The Life of Chesty Puller.* Boston: Little, Brown and Co., 1962.

DAVIS, KENNETH SYDNEY, *Experience of War: The United States in World War II.* New York: Doubleday and Co., 1965.

DEAKIN, F. W., *The Brutal Friendship: Mussolini, Hitler, and the Fall of Italian Fascism.* New York: Harper and Row, 1962.

DE GAULLE, CHARLES, *Memoires de guerre.* 3 vols. Paris: 1954.

DE GUINGAND, MAJOR GENERAL SIR FRANCIS, *Operation Victory.* New York: Charles Scribner's Sons, 1947.

DE TASSIGNY, MARSHAL DE LATTRE, *The History of the French First Army,* trans. by Malcolm Barnes. London: George Allen and Unwin Ltd., 1952.

DOLLINGER, HANS, *The Decline and Fall of Nazi Germany and Imperial Japan.* New York: Bonanza Books, 1967.

EISENHOWER, DWIGHT D., *Crusade in Europe.* Garden City, N. Y.: Doubleday and Co., 1948.

EISENHOWER, JOHN S. D., *The Bitter Woods.* New York: G. P. Putnam's Sons, 1969.

ELLSBERG, REAR ADMIRAL EDWARD, *The Far Shore.* New York: Popular Library, 1960.

FALK, STANLEY L., *Decision at Leyte.* New York: W. W. Norton and Co., 1966.

FARAGO, LADISLAS, *The Broken Seal.* New York: Random House, 1967.

———, *The Tenth Fleet.* New York: Paperback Library, 1964.

———, *Patton: Ordeal and Triumph.* New York: Dell Publishing Co., 1963.

FEIS, HERBERT, *Japan Subdued: The Atomic Bomb and the End of the War in the Pacific.* Princeton: Princeton University Press, 1961.

FIELD, JAMES A., JR., *The Japanese at Leyte Gulf: The Shō Operation.* Princeton: Princeton University Press, 1947.

FLORENTIN, EDDY, *The Battle of the Falaise Gap,* trans. by Mervyn Savill. New York: Hawthorn Books, 1967.

FRANK, WOLFGANG, *The Sea Wolves.* New York: Rinehart and Co., 1955.

*Führer Conferences on Matters Pertaining to Naval Affairs.* In Brassey's *Naval Annual, 1948.* London: 1948.

FULLER, MAJOR GENERAL J. F. C., *The Second World War, 1939–1945.* New York: Duell, Sloan and Pearce, 1949.

GALLAND, ADOLF, *The First and the Last,* trans. by Mervyn Savill. New York: Ballantine Books, 1954.

479

GILBERT, G. M., *Nuremberg Diary*. New York: Farrar, Straus, and Cudahy, 1947.

GIOVANNITTI, LEN, and FRED FREED, *The Decision to Drop the Bomb*. New York: Coward-McCann, Inc., 1965.

GOODMAN, JACK, ed., *While You Were Gone*. New York: Simon and Schuster, 1946.

GREENFIELD, KENT ROBERTS, *American Strategy in World War II: A Reconsideration*. Baltimore: The Johns Hopkins Press, 1963.

———, ed., *Command Decisions*. Washington, D.C.: Office of the Chief of Military History, Department of the Army, 1960.

GROUEFF, STEPHANE, *Manhattan Project*. Boston: Little, Brown and Co., 1967.

GUDERIAN, HEINZ, *Panzer Leader*, trans. by Constantine Fitzgibbon. Foreword by Captain B. H. Liddell Hart. New York: Dutton and Co., 1957.

HALSEY, FLEET ADMIRAL WILLIAM F., USN, and LIEUTENANT COMMANDER J. BRYAN, III, USNR, *Admiral Halsey's Story*. New York: McGraw-Hill, 1947.

HARA, TAMEICHI, and F. SAITO, *Japanese Destroyer Captain*. New York: Ballantine Books, 1961.

HASHIMOTO, MOCHITSURA, *Sunk*, trans. by Commander E. H. M. Colegrave, RN. New York: Henry Holt and Co., 1954.

HASSETT, WILLIAM D., *Off the Record with F.D.R.* London: George Allen and Unwin Ltd., 1960.

HAVAS, LASLO, *Hitler's Plot to Kill the Big Three*, trans. by Kathleen Szasz. New York: Cowles Book Company Inc., 1967.

HIGGINS, TRUMBULL, *Soft Underbelly: The Anglo-American Controversy over the Italian Campaign, 1939–1945*. New York: The Macmillan Company, 1968.

HOLLIS, SIR LESLIE, *War at the Top*. London: Michael Joseph, 1959.

HOWARTH, DAVID, *D Day*. New York: McGraw-Hill Book Co., 1959.

HOYLE, MARTHA BYRD, *A World in Flames: A History of World War II*. New York: Atheneum, 1970.

HULL, CORDELL, *Memoirs*. 2 vols. New York: The Macmillan Co., 1948.

INOGUCHI, RIKIHEI, and TADASHI NAKAJIMA, with ROGER PINEAU, *The Divine Wind: Japan's Kamikaze Force in World War II*. Annapolis, Md.: U.S. Naval Institute, 1958.

ISMAY, HASTINGS, *The Memoirs of General Lord Hastings Ismay*. New York: The Viking Press, 1960.

ITO, MASANORI, with ROGER PINEAU, *The End of the Japanese Imperial*

*Navy*, trans. by Andrew Y. Kuroda and Rogert Pineau. New York: W. W. Norton and Co., 1962.

JACKSON, W. G. F., *The Battle for Italy*. New York: Harper and Row, 1967.

KARIG, WALTER, and WELBOURN KELLEY, *Battle Report*. 5 vols. New York: Farrar and Rinehart, 1944–1949.

KEITEL, WILHELM, *The Memoirs of Field-Marshal Keitel*, Walter Dörlitz, ed. New York: Stein and Day, 1966.

KEMP, PETER, *Victory at Sea*. London: Frederick Muller, 1957.

KENNEDY, MAJOR GENERAL SIR JOHN, *The Business of War*. London: Hutchinson, 1957.

KENNEY, WILLIAM, *The Crucial Years, 1940–1945*. New York: Macfadden Books, 1962.

KING, ERNEST J., and WALTER MUIR WHITEHALL, *Fleet Admiral King: A Naval Record*. New York: W. W. Norton and Co., 1952.

KIRKPATRICK, IVONE, *Mussolini, A Study in Power*. New York: Hawthorn Books, 1964.

LAWSON, DON, *The United States in World War II*. New York: Grosset and Dunlap, 1964.

LEASON, JAMES, *War at the Top: Based on the Experiences of General Sir Leslie Hollis*. London: Michael Joseph, 1959.

LECKIE, ROBERT, *Strong Men Armed: The United States Marines Against Japan*. New York: Random House, Inc., 1962.

LeMAY, GENERAL CURTIS E., with MACKINLAY KANTOR, *Mission with LeMay: My Story*. Garden City, N. Y.: Doubleday and Co., 1965.

LIDDELL HART, B. H., *History of the Second World War*. New York: G. P. Putnam's Sons, 1971.

———, ed., *The Other Side of the Hill*. London: Cassell and Co., 1948.

LINGEMAN, RICHARD R., *Don't You Know There's a War On?* New York: Paperback Library, 1971.

LOHMAN, W., and H. H. HILDEBRANDT, *Die deutsche Kriegsmarine*. 3 vols. Bad Neuheim: Verlag Hans-Henning Podzun, 1955–1964.

MACARTHUR, DOUGLAS, *Reminiscences*. New York: McGraw-Hill, 1964.

MACINTYRE, CAPTAIN DONALD, *Fighting Admiral: The Life of Admiral of the Fleet Sir James Somerville*. London: Evans Brothers Ltd., 1961.

———, *U-Boat Killer*. New York: W. W. Norton and Co., 1956.

MACMILLAN, HAROLD, *The Blast of War, 1939–1945*. New York: Harper and Row, 1968.

MAJDALANY, FRED, *The Fall of Fortress Europe.* New York: Modern Literary Editions Publishing Co., 1968.

MANSTEIN, FIELD MARSHAL ERICH VON, *Lost Victories.* Chicago: Henry Regnery Co., 1958.

MANVELL, ROGER, and HEINRICH FRAENKEL, *Himmler.* New York: Paperback Library, 1968.

————, *The Men Who Tried to Kill Hitler.* New York: Coward-McCann, 1964.

MARSHALL, S. L. A., *Night Drop: The American Airborne Invasion of Normandy.* Boston: Little, Brown and Co., 1962.

MARTIENSSEN, ANTHONY, *Hitler and His Admirals.* London: Secker and Warburg, 1948.

MARTIN, RALPH G., *The GI War, 1941–1945.* Boston: Little, Brown and Co., 1967.

MAULDIN, BILL, *Up Front.* New York: Henry Holt and Co., 1945.

MONTGOMERY, FIELD MARSHAL THE VISCOUNT, *Memoirs.* Cleveland and New York: World Publishing Co., 1958.

MOOREHEAD, ALAN, *Eclipse.* New York: Harper and Row, 1945.

MORAN, LORD, *Churchill: Taken from the Diaries of Lord Moran.* Boston: Houghton Mifflin Co., 1966.

MORISON, SAMUEL ELIOT, *History of United States Naval Operations in World War II.* 15 vols. Boston: Little, Brown and Co., 1950–1962.

MURPHY, ROBERT D., *Diplomat Among Warriors.* Garden City, N.Y.: Doubleday and Co., 1964.

NEWCOMB, RICHARD F., *Abandon Ship: Death of the U.S.S.* Indianapolis. New York: Henry Holt, 1958.

————, *Iwo Jima.* New York: Holt, Rinehart and Winston, Inc., 1965.

NICOLSON, HAROLD, *The War Years, 1939–1945,* Nigel Nicolson, ed. New York: Atheneum, 1967.

NOBÉCOURT, JACQUES, trans. by R. H. Barry, *Hitler's Last Gamble: The Battle of the Bulge.* New York: Schocken Books, 1967.

ORGILL, DOUGLAS, *The Gothic Line: The Italian Campaign, Autumn, 1944.* W. W. Norton and Co., 1967.

PATTON, GEORGE S., *War as I Knew It: Battle Memoirs of General George S. Patton.* Boston: Houghton Mifflin Co., 1947.

PERRAULT, GILLES, *The Secret of D-Day*, trans. by Len Ortzen. New York: Bantam Books, 1967.

POGUE, FORREST C., *George C. Marshall: Ordeal and Hope, 1939–1942.* New York: The Viking Press, 1966.

POLENBERG, RICHARD, ed., *America at War: The Home Front, 1941–1945.* Englewood Cliffs: Prentice-Hall, Inc., 1968.

POTTER, E. B., and FLEET ADMIRAL C. W. NIMITZ, USN, eds., *Sea Power.* Englewood Cliffs: Prentice-Hall, 1960.

RAEDER, ERICH, *Mein Leben.* 2 vols., Tübingen-Neckar: 1956.

————, *My Life.* Annapolis: U.S. Naval Institute, 1960.

RIDGWAY, MATTHEW B., *Soldier: The Memoirs of Matthew B. Ridgway*, as told to Harold H. Martin. New York: Harper and Bros., 1956.

RIESENBERG, FELIX, JR., *Sea War: The Story of the U.S. Merchant Marine in World War II.* New York: Rinehart and Co., 1956.

ROLLINS, ALFRED B. JR., ed., *Franklin D. Roosevelt and the Age of Action.* New York: Dell Publishing Co., 1960.

ROMMEL, ERWIN, *The Rommel Papers*, B. H. Liddell Hart, ed. New York: Harcourt, Brace and Co., 1953.

ROOSEVELT, FRANKLIN D., *Nothing to Fear*, Benjamin D. Zevin, ed. New York: World Publishing Co., 1946.

ROSKILL, S. W., *The War at Sea.* 3 vols. in 4. London: H.M.S.O., 1954–1961.

RUGE, VICE ADMIRAL FRIEDRICH, *Sea Warfare.* London: Cassell and Co., 1957.

RUSSELL, LORD RUSSELL OF LIVERPOOL, *The Knights of Bushido: The Shocking History of Japanese War Atrocities.* New York: Berkley Publishing Corp., 1958.

————, *The Scourge of the Swastika.* London: Cassell and Co., Ltd., 1954.

RYAN, CORNELIUS, *The Last Battle.* New York: Simon and Schuster, 1966.

————, *The Longest Day: June 6, 1944.* New York: Simon and Schuster, 1959.

SALISBURY, HARRISON E., *The 900 Days: The Siege of Leningrad.* New York: Harper and Row, 1969.

SCHRAMM, PERCY E., ed., *Kriegstagebuch des Oberkommandos der Wehrmacht, 1940–1945.* 4 vols. in 7. Frankfurt am Main: Bernard & Graefe Verlag für Wehrwesen, 1961–1965.

SEMMES, HARRY H., *Portrait of Patton.* New York: Paperback Library, 1964.

SHEPPERD, G. A., *The Italian Campaign, 1943–45: A Political and Military Reassessment.* New York: Frederick A. Praeger, 1968.

SHERWOOD, ROBERT E., *Roosevelt and Hopkins.* 2 vols. New York: Harper and Bros., 1948.

SHIRER, WILLIAM L., *The Rise and Fall of the Third Reich.* New York: Simon and Schuster, 1960.

SIMS, EDWARD H., *Greatest Fighter Missions*. New York: Ballantine Books, 1962.

SLESSOR, MARSHAL OF THE ROYAL AIR FORCE SIR JOHN, *The Central Blue*. London: 1961.

SLIM, FIELD MARSHAL THE VISCOUNT, *Defeat into Victory*. New York: David McKay Co., 1961.

SMITH, HOLLAND M., and PERCY FINCH, *Coral and Brass*. New York: Charles Scribner's Sons, 1948.

SNYDER, LOUIS L., *The War: A Concise History, 1939–1945*. New York: Dell Publishing Co., 1960.

SPEER, ALBERT, *Inside the Third Reich*, trans. by Richard and Clara Winston. New York: The Macmillan Company, 1970.

SPEIDEL, HANS, *Invasion 1944*, trans. by Theo R. Crevenna. New York: Paperback Library, 1968.

STAMPS, T. DODSON, and VINCENT J. ESPOSITO, *A Military History of World War II*. 4 vols. West Point, 1956.

Stars and Stripes *Story of World War II, The*, ed. by Robert Meyer, Jr. New York: David McKay Co., Inc., 1960.

TALBOTT, STROBE, ed. and trans. by, *Khrushchev Remembers*. Boston: Little, Brown and Co., 1970.

TEDDER, LORD, *With Prejudice: The War Memoirs of Marshal of the Royal Air Force Lord Tedder*. Boston: Little, Brown and Co., 1966.

*This Fabulous Century*, ed. by the Editors of Time-Life Books. New York: Time-Life Books, 1969.

THOMPSON, R. W., *Churchill and the Montgomery Myth*. New York: M. Evans and Company, Inc., 1967.

———, *The Battle for the Rhineland*. London: Hutchinson, 1958.

———, *The Eighty-Five Days: The Story of the Battle of the Scheldt*. New York: Ballantine Books, 1957.

THOMPSON, WALTER H., *Assignment: Churchill*. New York: Farrar, Straus and Cudahy, 1955.

THORPE, ELLIOTT R., *East Wind Rain: The Intimate Account of an Intelligence Officer in the Pacific, 1939–49*. Boston: Gambit, Inc., 1969.

THORWALD, JUERGEN, ed. and trans. by Fred Wieck, *Defeat in the East*. New York: Ballantine Books, 1959.

TOLAND, JOHN, *The Rising Sun: The Decline and Fall of the Japanese Empire, 1936–1945*. New York: Random House, 1970.

TREVOR-ROPER, H. R., ed., *Blitzkrieg to Defeat*. New York: Holt, Rinehart and Winston, 1964.

————, *The Last Days of Hitler.* New York: The Macmillan Company, 1947.

TRUMAN, HARRY S, *Memoirs.* 2 vols. Garden City, N.Y.: Doubleday and Co., 1956.

URQUHART, R. E., *Arnhem.* New York: W. W. Norton and Co., 1958.

VANDEGRIFT, A. A., and ROBERT B. ASPREY, *Once a Marine.* New York: W. W. Norton and Co., 1964.

VIAN, ADMIRAL OF THE FLEET SIR PHILIP, *Action This Day.* London: Frederick Muller, 1960.

WARLIMONT, WALTER, *Inside Hitler's Headquarters, 1939–1945.* New York: Praeger, 1964.

WERTH, ALEXANDER, *De Gaulle: A Political Biography.* New York: Simon and Schuster, 1965.

————, *Russia at War, 1941–1945.* New York: E. P. Dutton and Co., 1964.

WILLOUGHBY, MAJOR GENERAL CHARLES A., and JOHN CHAMBERLAIN, *MacArthur, 1941–1951.* New York: McGraw-Hill Book Co., 1954.

WILMOT, CHESTER, *The Struggle for Europe: World War II in Western Europe.* New York: Harper and Bros., 1952.

WOODWARD, C. VANN, *The Battle for Leyte Gulf.* New York: The Macmillan Company, 1947.

YOKOTA, YUTAKA, with JOSEPH D. HARRINGTON, *The Kaiten Weapon.* New York: Ballantine Books, 1962.

YOUNG, DESMOND, *Rommel: The Desert Fox.* New York: Harper and Brothers, 1951.

# Index

488

Brindupke, Commander Charles F., 64

British Broadcasting Corporation (BBC), 16, 17

Brittany, 44, 45

Brooke, General Sir Alan, 7, 48, 234, 237–38, 260, 429; on Eisenhower, 235; Montgomery and, 237, 254–55

*Brooks* (destroyer transport), 306

Broughton, J. Melville, 114

Brown, Commander Gaylord B., 100

Brown, Lieutenant George B., 104

Bruce, Major General A. D., 286, 289

Brunei Bay, 319, 411

Brussels, 53

Bryant, Sir Arthur, 260

Bryant, Rear Admiral Carleton F., 27

B-17 (bomber), 360

B-24 (bomber), 360, 362

B-29 (bomber), 60, 360–62, 380. *See also* Japan, fire attacks on

Bucharest, 127

Buchenwald, 335, 336, 338, 413, 475

Buckner, Lieutenant General Simon Bolivar, 382, 399

Budapest, 256, 258

Bulgaria, 127

Bulge, Battle of the, 233, 241–51, 320

*Bull* (destroyer escort), 223

Bull's Run, Battle of, 230–32

Buna-Gona campaign, 67

*Bunker Hill* (carrier), 65, 85, 99, 104, 391

Buracker, Captain William H., 187

Buri, 279, 285

Burke, Commodore Arleigh, 106, 192–93

Burma, 119, 412–13

*Burns* (destroyer), 305

Bush, Dr. Vannevar, 419

*Bush* (destroyer), 388–89, 390

*Butler, J. C.* (destroyer escort), 214

Byrd, Harry F., 112

Byrnes, James F., 113, 413, 418, 421–22, 425, 462

*Cabot* (carrier), 85, 187, 282

Caen, 9, 32, 36, 37, 43–44

Cairo Conference, 9

Cairo Declaration, 426, 440

Calais, 5, 13

*Caldwell* (destroyer), 288

Calhoun, Lieutenant Commander C. R., 300–1

*California* (battleship), 200, 307

*Callaway* (attack transport), 309

Camel Force, 50–51

Camp Omori, 470

Campbell, Commander E. G., 287

Camranh Bay, 313–14

Canada, U.N. and, 415

Canaris, Admiral Wilhelm, 16

*Canberra* (cruiser), 165, 166

*Carmick* (destroyer), 28

Carney, Mick, 229

Carney, Rear Admiral Robert M., 191

Caroline Islands, 71

Carpathian Mountains, 257

Carriers, escort, 206

Casablanca, 471

Cassidy, Hopalong, 295

*Cassin Young* (destroyer), 185, 389

Casualties, 474

Cates, Major General Clifton B., 143

*Catoctin* (ship), 272

*Cavalla* (submarine), 100

Cebu, 319

Cecilienhof Palace, Potsdam, 424

Center Force, Japanese, 177, 183, 184, 187, 191, 192

Chandler, Rear Admiral Theodore E., 307

*"Chanson d'Automne,"* as code, 16–17

Cherbourg, 9, 10, 11, 30, 32, 33–34

Chernyakhovsky, General, 256

Chiang Kai-shek, 271, 410, 464

*Chicago* (cruiser), 431

Chichi Jima, 360

Chickering, William, 306

*Chikuma* (cruiser), 217, 232

China, People's Republic of, 464

China, Republic of (Taiwan), 271–72

*Chitose* (carrier), 96, 225, 226

*Chiyoda* (carrier), 96, 105, 225, 226, 230

489

Cho, Lieutenant General Isamu, 396–98, 399
*Chokai* (cruiser), 218, 232
Chuikov, General, 356
Churchill, Winston, 385, 454; Eisenhower and, 237–38; election campaign (1945), 428–29; Normandy invasion, 7, 14, 47, 48; Potsdam Conference, 417, 424–27, 430; Roosevelt and, 273–74; Scobie and, 131–32; Stalin and, 427; Yalta Conference, 261–72
"Cicero" (German spy), 3
Cigarettes, 118–19
CIO Political Action Committee, 112, 260
Civitavecchia, 119
Claggett, Commander Bladen D., 181–83
Clark, Bennett, 114
Clark, Rear Admiral Joseph J. ("Jocko"), 87–88, 93, 215, 430
Clark, General Mark, 120, 121
Cleves, 321
Codes, radio, 228–29
*Colhoun* (destroyer), 388–89
Collins, Major General J. Lawton, 33
Colmar Pocket, 238, 248
*Colorado* (battleship), 144, 312
*Columbia* (cruiser), 168, 307, 310
Committee on National Liberation, Polish, 125, 131, 266–67, 276, 417
Committee on Social and Political Implications, 421
Commodity Credit Corporation, 330
Compton, Dr. Arthur Holly, 419, 422
Conant, Dr. James B., 419
Concentration camps, 335–40. *See also* Extermination camps
"Concertina," 23
Condition Zebra, 431
Coney, Captain Charles E., 197–98
Conolly, Rear Admiral Richard L., 81, 146, 148
Conservative Party (Great Britain), 428–29
Conspiracies, German, 40–42
Conway, Brigadier General Thomas, 237

Copeland, Lieutenant R. W., 214
"Corncobs," 11
Corregidor, 464
*Corry* (destroyer), 28
COSSAC, 8–11
Cotentin Peninsula, 8, 9, 19, 33
Coward, Captain Jesse B., 200–1
*Cowpens* (carrier), 85, 227
Cracow, 258
CripDiv, 165–67
Cronyn, Hume, 116
Crosby, Bing, 116–17
Crowley, Leo T., 414
Crutchley, Rear Admiral V. A. C., 77
Curzon, Lord, 264
Curzon Line, 265, 266, 276

*Dace* (submarine), 181–83
Dachau, 335, 413, 475
Dairen, 271
Damaskinos, Archbishop, 132
Danzig, 258
*Darter* (submarine), 181–83
Dauntlesses (planes), 65, 103
Davis, Commander George F., 306
Davis, Jeff, 110
Davis, Rear Admiral Ralph E., 184, 196, 229, 383, 384
D-Day (June 6, 1944), 1, 2, 14–16. *See also* Normandy invasion
de Gaulle, Charles, 131, 234, 248, 274
De Mille, Cecil B., 116
de Tassigny, General Jean de Lattre, 52
de Welden, Felix, 377
"Decisive Battle" concept, 62, 63
Del Valle, Major General Pedro, 399
Delano, Laura, 330
Democratic National Convention (1944), 111–16, 154
Dempsey, Lieutenant General Sir Miles C., 19, 29, 31
Denmark, 327, 343
*Dennis* (destroyer escort), 214
*Denver* (cruiser), 168
Derevyanko, Lieutenant General K., 473
*Desert Song* (movie), 116
DesRon 24, 202

490

494

179–232; Japanese forces in, 177–78; U.S. forces in, 178–79
Liberator (B-24), 360
*Liddle* (destroyer transport), 287
Liège, 244
*Lifeboat* (movie), 116
"Lili Marlene" (song), 5
Lingayen Gulf, 289, 291, 303, 305–6, 318
*Little* (destroyer), 397
Livadia Palace, 262
Liversedge, Colonel Harry B., 374, 376
Ljubljana Gap, 47–48
Lockwood, Vice Admiral Charles A., 97, 178, 364
*Lodger, The* (movie), 116
London, V-1 attacks on, 130–31
*Long* (destroyer), 306
"Lord Haw-Haw" (William Joyce), 5
Los Alamos, New Mexico, 419, 420–21
*Louisville* (cruiser), 305, 307
Lozovsky, Deputy Commissar Alexander, 439
Lübeck, 343, 348
Lublin, 125
Lublin Poles, 125, 131, 266–67, 276, 417
Lucas, Scott, 114, 115
*Luce* (destroyer), 397
Luciano, "Lucky," 110
Ludendorff railway bridge, 322–23
Luftwaffe, 130, 240
Lumsden, Lieutenant General Herbert, 306
*Lunga Point* (carrier), 376
Lüttwitz, General Heinrich Freiherr von, 249
Luxembourg, 247, 249, 250
Luzon, 156–57, 281, 288, 289, 302–13, 316–17, 318

Maastrict, strategy conference at, 236–37
MacArthur, General Douglas, 13, 111, 168, 270, 271; Borneo, 410–11; Leyte, 157, 159, 171–73, 279, 285, 289; Leyte Gulf, 197–98; Luzon, 308–9; Manila, 317–18;

Mindanao, 153; New Guinea, 66–80; Philippines, 153–54, 171–73, 318–19; strategy, 57–58, 59–61, 154–56, 411–12; as Supreme Allied Commander, 462–63, 464, 466, 469–75; surrender of Japan and, 472–74, 475
McAuliffe, Brigadier General Anthony C., 247, 249
McCain, Vice Admiral John Sidney: Leyte Gulf, 184, 192, 227–28, 231; Luzon, 281, 294, 303; South China Sea, 314, 315
McCampbell, Commander David, 185, 226
McCarthy, Major Edward, 139
McClintock, Commander David H., 181–83
*McCook* (destroyer), 27
McCormick, Rear Admiral Lynde D., 432–33, 434
McCreery, Lieutenant General R. L., 121
*McDermut* (destroyer), 201
*MacDonough* (destroyer), 87
*McGowan* (destroyer), 201
Machiavelli, 42
McIntyre, Marvin, 274
McIntyre, Admiral Ross T., 331
McKelway, Lieutenant Colonel St. Clair, 401
McKenna, Captain F. J., 222
McManes, Captain K. M., 202
McNutt, Paul V., 114, 115
*Macomb* (destroyer type), 397
McVay, Captain Charles Butler, III, 432–37
*Maddox* (destroyer), 296, 315
*Mahan* (destroyer), 286–87
*Mainichi* (newspaper), 440
Makino, Lieutenant General Shiro, 171
Malinovski, General Rodion, 257, 258
Malmedy Massacre, 244
Malo, Lieutenant Raymond, 359
Malta, 255, 260–61
Manchuria, 464
Mandalay, 412
Manhattan Project, 419–24

497

Manila, 270, 282, 316, 317; surrender of Japan, 464, 465–67
*Manila Bay* (escort carrier), 305
Manteuffel, General Hasso von, 239–40
Mao Tse-tung, 272
*March of Time,* 117
Marcus Island, 164
*Marcus Island* (escort carrier), 292
Mareth Line, 43
Margival, 34–36
Mariana Islands, 58–59, 78, 81–90
"Marianas Turkey Shoot," 100–1
Marks, Lieutenant R. Adrian, 435–36
Marquand, John P., 372
Marseilles, 51, 52–53
Marshall, General George C., 9, 48, 153, 168, 254, 255, 270; atomic bomb and, 419; Leyte, 159–60
*Marshall* (destroyer), 230
Marston mats, 373
"Martin, Major William," 12
Martin, Commander William I., 85–87
*Maru* (flagship), 370
*Maryland* (battleship), 200
Mashbir, Colonel Sidney, 466, 467
*Massachusetts* (battleship), 224–25, 431
*Maya* (cruiser), 105, 182–83
Meiji, Emperor, 406, 451
*Melvin* (destroyer), 201
Merkers, 334–35
Messervy, Major General F. W., 412, 413
Metz, 238, 248
Meuse River, 244, 250
Meyer, Lieutenant Colonel Hellmuth, 17
M47 incendiary bombs, 401–3
*Miami* (cruiser), 225, 230
Michael, King of Rumania, 276
*Michishio* (destroyer), 200, 201, 202
Middleton, Major General Troy H., 240–41, 244
*Midway* (escort carrier), 221–22
Midway, Battle of, 91, 100
Mikawa, Vice Admiral Gunichi, 178, 184–85

Mikolajczyk, Stanislaw, 266
*Miller* (destroyer), 230, 231, 383
Mindanao, 60, 153, 157, 159, 160, 319, 411
Mindoro, 286, 288, 289–93
*Mississippi* (battleship), 200, 310
*Missouri* (battleship), 470–74, 475
Mitchell, Richard, 114
Mitscher, Vice Admiral Marc A., 64, 170; Leyte Gulf, 179, 184, 192–93, 225, 230–31; Marianas, 81, 85; Okinawa, 382, 385, 392; Philippine Sea, 92–93, 95, 99, 101–7; Tokyo, 369–70
Mitsubishi Aircraft Engine Works, 366
Miwa, Vice Admiral Shigeyoshi, 177
*Mobile* (cruiser), 166, 225, 230
Mobile Force, Japanese, 177
Mobile warfare, Rommel on, 6–7
Model, Field Marshal Walther, 123–24, 241
*Mogami* (cruiser), 200–5
Molotov, Vyacheslav, 414–18, 426, 439, 444, 452
*Momi* (destroyer), 305
*Monaghan* (destroyer), 301
Money, German cache of, 334–35
Mongolia, Outer, 271
Monschau, 245
*Monssen* (destroyer), 201
*Montcalm* (cruiser), 22, 27
*Monterey* (carrier), 85, 227, 299–300
Montgomery, Rear Admiral Alfred E., 93, 99
Montgomery, Field Marshal Sir Bernard Law, 233–34, 245–46, 251; Ardennes, 245, 250; Eisenhower and, 234–37, 252-54; Normandy invasion, 1–2, 19, 30, 36, 37, 43–45, 53–55; Patton and, 324–25; Rhineland, 320, 321, 322
Moon, Admiral, 29
Moore-Gosgrove, Colonel L., 473
Moran, Charles Wilson, Lord, 261
Morell, Dr. Theodor, 325, 345
Morgan, Lieutenant General Frederick E., 8, 9, 10

Mori, Lieutenant General Takeshi, 459

Morotai, 157, 159, 160

*Morrison* (destroyer), 185, 397

Motobu Peninsula, 387, 396

*Mount Olympus* (amphibious command ship), 310

Mountbatten, Admiral Louis, 119, 412

Movies, 116–17, 295

Mudge, Major General V. D., 170

"Mulberries," 11, 32

*Munsel* (tug), 166, 431

Murphy, Frank, 114

Murray, Philip, 113

*Musashi* (battleship), 62, 65, 78, 92, 362; Leyte Gulf, 181, 187–88

Musashino, 361

Mussolini, Benito, 353–54

*Myoko* (cruiser), 78, 188

*Nachi* (cruiser), 204, 205, 280, 281

Nafutan Point, 133, 134, 136

Nagasaki, 438, 446–47, 475

*Nagato* (battleship), 181

Nagoya, 366, 403, 410

Nagumo, Vice Admiral Chuichi, 83, 91, 137–38

Nansei Shoto, 381. *See also* Okinawa

Naples, 10, 11

Narev River, 256

*Nashville* (cruiser), 68, 75, 159, 172, 197–98, 290–91

National Coalition Government (Great Britain), 428

National Redoubt, 326–28

Neely, Matt, 115

Negros, 319

Neisse River, 258, 320

Nelson, Lieutenant Robert S., 102–3

Netherlands East Indies (Indonesia), 319, 411, 412

*Nevada* (battleship), 370, 371

New Guinea, 63, 66–80

*New Jersey* (battleship), 157, 296, 299, 301; Leyte Gulf, 191, 224, 230, 231

*New Mexico* (battleship), 306

*New Orleans* (cruiser), 225, 230

*New York Times*, 440

New Zealand, U.N. and, 415

*Newcomb* (destroyer), 203, 307

Nichols Field, 466

Nimitz, Admiral Chester W., 13, 82, 85, 168, 270, 271; Iwo Jima, 319; Leyte, 159; Leyte Gulf, 179, 228–29; Palau, 153, 160, 161; strategy, 57–58, 59–61, 154–56, 360; surrender of Japan, 470–71, 472, 473

XIX Corps, U.S., 32–33

Ninety-sixth Army Division, 170, 382, 396

Ninth Armored Division, U.S., 322–23

Ninth Army, U.S., 237, 238, 252, 327; Ardennes, 245, 248, 250; Rhineland, 321–22

Ninth Division, Australian, 411

Nisei 442nd Regimental Combat Team, 121

Nishimura, Vice Admiral Shoji, 177, 179, 184, 196–205, 224, 228

Nishina, Dr. Yoshio, 443

Noemfoor Island, 79–80

*Norman Scott* (destroyer), 144

Normandy invasion, 1–3, 18–29, 32–33; Germany and, 3–7, 16–18, 29–32, 34–37; planning of, 8–17

*North Carolina* (battleship), 372

Northern Force, Japanese, 177, 185, 191–92

*Noshiro* (cruiser), 78, 280

Oak Ridge, 419

Obata, Lieutenant General Hideyoshi, 83

O'Brien, Lieutenant Colonel William J., 139

*O'Brien* (destroyer), 287, 307

Oder River, 258, 320

O'Donnell, Brigadier General Emmett, 261

Ogata, Colonel Kiuochi, 142, 143–44

Ohnishi, Vice Admiral Tonosuke, 178

Ohrdruf, 335

Oil shortages, Japanese, 62, 91, 176

*Oka* (suicide rocket), 384

Okada, Admiral Keisuke, 406–7, 409

499

502

Seventh Armored Division, U.S., 244, 245

Seventh Army, German, 5, 17, 20, 31, 45, 46; Ardennes, 243–44; Rhineland, 323

Seventh Army, U.S., 51; National Redoubt, 327

VII Corps, U.S., 33

Seventh Division, 170, 284, 286, 382

Seventh Division, Australian, 411

Seventh Fleet, 167–68, 281, 437; Leyte Gulf, 178, 227, 232; Luzon, 310, 313

Seventy-seventh Infantry Division: Guam, 146, 147, 149, 151; Okinawa, 382, 395, 399; Ormoc, 286, 289

Seventy-third Bombardment Wing, 361

Sextant Conference, 58

SHAEF, 9, 234–36, 243

*Shark* (submarine), 83

*Shea* (destroyer type), 397

Shepherd, Brigadier General Lemuel C., 149, 151

Sherman, Rear Admiral Forrest, 156–57

Sherman, Rear Admiral Frederick C., 184–85, 192, 229

Sherrod, Robert, 374

Sherwood, Robert, 416

"Schichesei Hokoku" (password), 136, 138

Shigemitsu, Foreign Minister, 471, 473

*Shigure* (destroyer), 196, 200, 203, 205

Shikoku, 426

Shima, Vice Admiral Kiyohide, 167, 280; Leyte Gulf, 178, 184, 197, 199, 204, 224, 228

*Shinano* (carrier), 362–66

"Shingle," 23

*Shiranuhi* (destroyer), 280

*Shiratsuyu* (destroyer), 77

Sho-Go, 59, 164, 168

*Shokaku* (carrier), 100

Sho-1, 168, 176, 179

Shoumatoff, Elizabeth, 330

Shuri Line, 387, 388, 394, 395, 400

Sibert, Major General F. C., 283

Siegfried Line, 252

Simpson, Lieutenant General W. H., 321–22

Sinatra, Frank, 116

*Since You Went Away* (movie), 117

Singapore, 464

Sixteenth Division, Japanese, 171

XVI Tank Corps, Russian, 126

Sixth Airborne Division, British, 19

Sixth Army, Germany, 35, 127

Sixth Army, U.S.: Leyte, 169, 173, 283; Luzon, 303, 310, 316–17, 318

Sixth Army Group, U.S., 235, 238, 248, 251, 320

Sixth Base Air Force, Japanese, 178

VI Corps, U.S., 53

Sixth Infantry Division, 303

Sixth Marine Division, 382

Sixth Panzer Army, 240, 243–44

Slezak, Walter, 116

Slim, Lieutenant General Sir William, 412

Smith, Lieutenant General Holland M., 81, 90; Guam, 146, 147, 151; Iwo Jima, 369, 373, 377, 380; Saipan, 133–36, 138, 140; Tinian, 141, 143

Smith, Major General Ralph, 81, 134–36

Smith, Major General Walter Bedell, 1, 9, 255, 358

Smoot, Captain R. N., 202

*Song of Bernadette, The* (movie), 116

*Soryu* (carrier), 100

Sousley, PFC Franklin, 377

South China Sea, 313–36

*South Dakota* (battleship), 97, 224–25, 431

*Southard* (minesweeper), 307

Southern Force, Japanese, 177, 184, 191, 196, 197, 203

Southern Force II, Japanese, 178, 199

Southwest Area Force, Japanese, 177–78

Speer, Albert, 325, 350

*Spence* (destroyer), 296, 301–2

Sprague, Rear Admiral Clifton A. F.

Victory Operation. *See* Sho-Go
Vienna, 258, 325
Vietinghoff, General S. von, 121, 257
*Vincennes* (cruiser), 225, 230
Visayan Islands, 411
Vistula River, 124, 126, 256, 257
Vorontsov Villa, 262

Wadke, 70, 71–73
Wagner, Walter, 352
Wainwright, Major General Jonathan, 464, 469, 472, 473
*Walke* (destroyer), 287, 306
Walker, Colonel Edwin A., 50
Wallace, Henry A., 112–15, 260, 419
*Ward, Aaron* (destroyer type), 397
Ward, Paul, 130
*Ward* (destroyer transport), 287
Warm Springs, Georgia, 329–31
Warsaw, 124, 125–27, 257, 258
*Wasatch* (U.S. ship), 198
Washington, George, 237
*Washington* (battleship), 224–25, 372
*Wasp* (carrier), 88, 99, 227, 382
Watson, Major General Edwin, 274, 275
Watson, Major General Thomas E., 143
Wenck, General, 352
Werfel, Franz, 116
Wesel, 321
*West Virginia* (battleship), 200
West Wall, 234, 236, 238, 322
*Westralia* (Australian ship), 309
Weygand, Maxime, 449
Weyler, Rear Admiral George L., 200, 203, 306
"Whales," 12
*White Plains* (escort carrier), 210, 211, 216, 218, 222
*Whitehurst* (destroyer escort), 223
Whitney, General Courtney, 473
*Wichita* (cruiser), 165, 166, 225, 230
Wildcats (fighters), 210, 216–17
Wilkes, Rear Admiral John, 34

Wilkinson, Vice Admiral T. S., 169
Williams, Radioman J. T., 85, 86
Willoughby, Major General Charles, 466, 467
Wilson, Sir Charles, 261
Wilson, General Sir Henry Maitland, 47
*Wilson* (destroyer), 312
*Wilson* (movie), 116
Winters, Commander T. H., 230
Wood, Commander Robert W., 107

*Yahagi* (cruiser), 215, 392–93
Yahara, Colonel Hiromichi, 397–98, 399–400
Yalta Conference, 259–73, 415–17, 424
*Yamagumo* (destroyer), 201
Yamamoto, Admiral Isoroku, 62
*Yamashiro* (battleship), 200, 201, 202, 203–4
Yamashita, Lieutenant General Tomoyuki, 171, 284, 289, 464
*Yamato* (battleship), 78, 92, 362; Leyte Gulf, 181, 183, 187, 213, 218; Okinawa, 392–93
Yap, 157, 159, 160
Yokohama, 410, 469
Yokosura Naval Base, 471
Yonai, Admiral Mitsumasa, 152, 278, 439, 445, 447–50, 453, 464
Yontan Airfield, 387, 446–47
*Yorktown* (carrier), 85, 382, 384
Yusupovski Palace, 262

Zamboanga, 319
*Zeilin* (attack transport), 312
Zeke (fighter), 96
Zero (fighter), 96
Z-Go, 62
Zhukov, Georgi, 257, 258
Zigzagging, 436
*Zuiho* (carrier), 96, 225, 226
*Zuikaku* (carrier), 100, 102, 104–5; Leyte Gulf, 189, 219, 225, 226